LISTEN TO OUR CHILDREN
Clinical Theory and Practice

Elaine S. LeVine
Alvin L. Sallee
New Mexico State University

Kendall/Hunt
Publishing Company
Dubuque, Iowa

10 9 8 7 6 5 4 3 2

LISTEN TO OUR CHILDREN

To our children

Marshall Thompson

Charles and Joan Sallee

From whom we learn so much when we listen.

PREFACE

Although most people would readily agree that children are a greatest treasure, a powerful natural resource, it is our contention that mental health and social services have fallen dramatically short of meeting the needs of our youth. Newspapers are replete with cases of children whose needs for basic protection have not been met. In 1983, an estimated 1,007,658 reports of child abuse and neglect were documented by child protective service agencies in the United States and participating jurisdictions (American Humane Association, 1985). Further, a 1981 study funded by the National Center for Child Abuse and Neglect (U. S. Department of Health and Human Services, 1981) reported that two-thirds of the cases identified by professional sources who are mandated by law to report child maltreatment were never reported to appropriate authorities. Compounding these distressing statistics, many emotionally and physically abused and neglected children are brought into some kind of social service care, only to be returned to nightmarish existence because our legal and mental health systems are not sufficiently refined and organized to protect them until the damaging circumstances are corrected.

However, it is not only in severe cases of abuse and neglect that the emotional needs of children are not heeded. Our review of mental health literature indicates that the education of mental health practitioners is limited in the area of psychosocial needs of children, and consequently, relatively few clinicians who are sensitive to these needs are found in either outpatient or inpatient settings. Few counseling, psychology, or social work schools offer specialized courses in clinical child practice. Few mental health centers have units and/or clinicians specializing in child and family care. Our survey of telephone books in a number of cities revealed as few as 10 % of the certified psychologists, social workers, and psychiatrists identifying themselves as child and family specialists. Thus, from training to practice, in both the private and public sectors, few professionals are ready and able to listen to the needs of our children.

Listen to our Children: Clinical Theory and Practice was written to assist present mental health and social service professionals and those in training to more effectively recognize and meet the psychological and social needs of children. The book is broadly based upon psychological, sociological, and developmental literature and is appropriate for clinicians in counseling, social work, psychology, psychiatric nursing, and related professions.

This book will first help alert the reader to the signals that a child is in need of intervention. Thus, Part One, "Children and Change," identifies the children with needs by reviewing present statistical indices of childhood disturbance and by highlighting historical and developmental research of expected and maladapted patterns in youth. The specific personal and social factors that catalyze emotional disturbance in children are detailed in Part Four, "Vulnerable Children."

Specialized theories and techniques required to be an effective advocate and clinician of children are presented in Part Two, "Theories of Child Therapy." In addition to major theoretical underpinnings of the most prominent and effective approaches to child therapy, the reader will find case studies which bridge theory and practice. Part Three of the text, "Developing Treatment Plans for the Child and Family," is a practical guide for establishing an individual treatment plan for a child. Means of child and family assessment, psychological testing, and how to work with a child in therapy sessions are discussed in depth.

We do believe that children are our nation's greatest treasure and a powerful resource that should be well preserved. The final and most important part of this text, Part Five, "Looking Forward," covers preventive and policy strategies. We hope each reader, upon completing this book, will feel more effective not only in recognizing and quelling desperate cries, but also in assuring the well being of children. . . because all children have a right to grow and to flourish to their maximum ability. Healthy children assure the future well being of our country.

The use of the editorial "we" in this text is appropriate as many persons contributed to its writing. The authors thank them for their support and encouragement. We would like to acknowledge the financial help we received through Dean Lowery Davis of the College of Human and Community Services, New Mexico State University.

A number of persons helped in the research, editing, and early typing: Jack Catlan, Cindy Dominguez, Roberta Sando, Doris Simpson, Alice Draving, Shirley Thorton, and Kathy Sallee. Patricia Thompson's and Barbara Myers' computer and editing skills were critical to this project.

We also thank William LeVine, University of Kansas Medical School, for his review of Chapter 11 and his comments; Elsa Iverson, Indiana University, for her comments on Chapters 7, 10, and 12; Katy McLane for the cover photo and art work; Rose H. Praisner, New Mexico State University, for art work; Christine Marlow, New Mexico State University, for editing and research for Chapter 5 and review of the total manuscript; Karen Brown, Southwest Texas State University, for her contributions on divorce in Chapter

14; Joyce Tinsley, for her editorial review of the total text; and Robert Ellison for his editing and research. The wisdom of Amado Padilla, University of California, Los Angeles, is a crucial essence of this text. For his efforts and consultation since the book's inception and especially for his research on Chapters 3, 5, and 15, our sincere gratitude.

A special word of thanks to our spouses Jim Thompson and Kathy Sallee for their continued encouragement, support, and love.

E. S. L.
A. L. S.

CONTENTS

PART I CHILDREN AND CHANGE

PART II THEORIES OF CHILD THERAPY

PART IV VULNERABLE CHILDREN

PART V LOOKING FORWARD

PART ONE
Children and Change

PART I

CHILDREN AND CHANGE

One of the greatest challenges to meeting the mental health needs of children is that this population is so dynamic, changing on so many dimensions. Our views of the psychological and social needs of children have changed dramatically through recent history. Studies of child development are redoubling in number and sophistication, and the effective child practitioner needs a broad understanding of those current findings in order to set appropriate goals for child clients and to know when and how to refer them for specialized services. Of course, the state of being-a-child is itself in constant flux, and the effective child practitioner must be exquisitely sensitive to the developmental issues and abilities of each client.

Part I will attempt to sensitize the reader to the dynamic issues of clinical treatment with children. Chapter 1 of this unit presents current data about the children in need of mental health services and those who are and are not receiving care. Historical attitudes about children by society at large and in varied mental health fields will be reviewed in Chapter 2. Special attention will be devoted to discussing the emergence of child social work, child counseling, and school counseling. Then, our present understanding of children's psychological needs and capacities will be identified in Chapter 3, which discusses developmental issues.

The major thesis of this book, that children have often not been listened to, is well exemplified in this Unit, in which you will learn of the historical maltreatment of children, of the many children whose needs are yet unmet, and, despite great gains, of the present limitations to our understanding of child mental health theories and practice.

CHAPTER 1

WHO ARE THE CHILDREN IN NEED?

It is often said that a great many children are in crisis and in need of mental health services. However, global estimates concerning childhood problems range greatly. Some epidemiologists base estimates of childhood emotional problems upon referral statistics (such as the number of children receiving in-patient care, out-patient community mental health services and private therapy) and report that between 1 to 5 % of children experience significant emotional problems.

However, when children's behavior is systematically observed and when broad questionnaire methodologies are employed to tap attitudes of teachers and parents, as high as 10 to 30 % of the childhood population may be considered emotionally disturbed (U.S. Department of Health and Human Services, 1980).

The American Humane Association's study of reports to the states revealed 23.6 children per 1,000 as abused in 1983. From 1976 to 1983, reporting levels have increased 142 % (A.H.A., 1985). Based upon interviews of representative families, Straus, Gelles, and Steimetz (1979) predicted more than 14 % of all children are physically abused at some point in time.

In one retrospective survey, 26 % of females had a sexual experience with an adult before age 13. Only 6 % of the incidents were reported to appropriate agencies (Gagnon, 1965). Some experts (O'Brien, 1983) state the average age of the sexually exploited child is 7 years with 75 % being females. Thus, the epidemiological and research design affects the estimate of children experiencing emotional problems.

In this chapter, we will review a range of descriptive data about children in the United States, with particular attention to the frequency, distribution, etiology, and longevity of childhood maladjustment. In order to interpret this data base, we will point out the research methodologies employed.

THE STATUS OF CHILDREN

Demographics

According to the latest census data, American children under age 14 total about 47.8 million. Figure 1.1 depicts the number of children under 14 years from 1950 and projects

Figure 1.1

Persons Under 14 Years of Age from 1950 to the Year 2 000

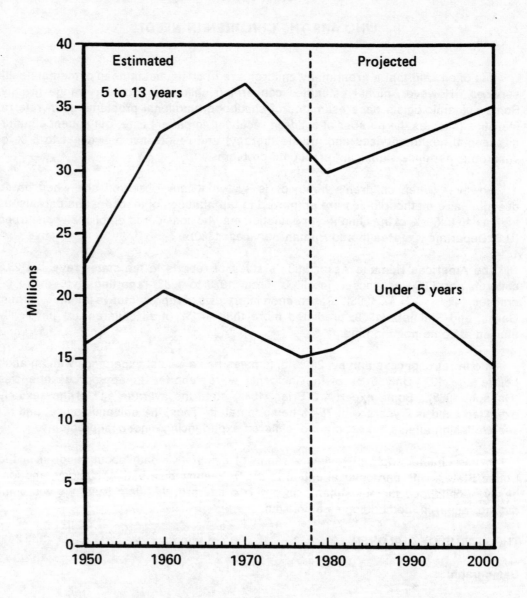

Source: Bureau of the Census. Population Profile of the
United States: 1978. Series P-20, No. 336. April
1979.

the number to the year, 2,000. Since the early 1960's, children under 14 years have become a steadily decreasing proportion of the American population (U. S. Bureau of Census, 1984). This decrease reflects the combined effect of several personal/social factors, which are: a growing preference for two-child families, an increasing proportion of women desiring to remain childless, women delaying childbearing in order to pursue education and careers and subsequently bearing fewer children, and parents feeling constrained to limit families because of the increasing cost of rearing a child while incomes are not keeping pace with inflation. Although the fertility rate (number of live births per 100,000 women) will probably continue to fall, the absolute number of children is likely to increase over the next ten years because the large number of post-World War II babies are now reaching child-bearing age. Even with a decrease in fertility rates, the child clinician can be assured that a significant proportion, approximately 18 %, of the U.S. population in the coming decade, will be children (U.S. Bureau of Census, 1979b).

Not only the number of children but also their demographic characteristics and the nature of families are changing in accord with the new values and demands of American life. The population of children in central cities and rural areas has decreased more dramatically than that in suburban areas and in small cities, as families continue to move to these semi-rural and semi-urban environments. Children of today are a relatively mobile population. In 1978, 53.4 % of children ages 3 and 4 and 41.4 % of children ages 5 to 9 moved during the previous 3-year period. Children growing up in small cities and semi-rural environments face some different dilemmas than those in large urban areas (U. S. Bureau of the Census, 1978).

At present, 83 % of children under 14 are white, 15 % are Black, 6 % are of Spanish origin, and 2 % are of other ethnicities and races (U.S. Bureau of the Census, 1979c). The majority of children of all ethnicities live in metropolitan areas, rather than rural areas or small cities. However, a larger percentage of Black and Hispanic children live in central cities than white children (U.S. Bureau of the Census, 1978). For these reasons, we may expect Black and Hispanic children to face some different problems from white children because of greater pressures associated with urban living, especially in central city areas.

Later in the text, we will present the position that child therapy procedures must be modified when working with children of ethnic minority families. We will outline approaches of pluralistic child therapy in which the child therapist orients goals and techniques towards helping the child adapt to her or his and the family's chosen ethnic milieu.

Figure 1.2 depicts the birth rate in the United States for the past 180 years. The birth rate of minority groups has tended to be higher than whites for the last 40 years

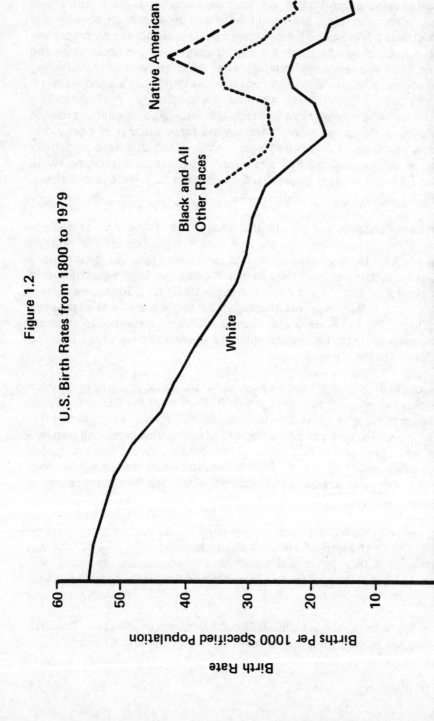

Figure 1.2

U.S. Birth Rates from 1800 to 1979

Native American

Black and All
Other Races

White

Birth Rate

Births Per 1000 Specified Population

Source: Snapper, Kurt J. "The American Legacy." In: Grotberg, Edith H., ed. 200 Years of Children. Washington: U.S. Department of Health, Education, and Welfare, Office of Child Development, 1976. (DHEW Publication No. (OHD) 77-30103) pp. 13-38.

WHO ARE THE CHILDREN IN NEED?

(Snapper, 1976). However, the birth rate of Blacks has decreased in the last two decades (U. S. Bureau of the Census, 1984). Similar data do not yet exist for Hispanics, and rate trends for Native Americans are unknown because of the lack of data until the past two decades. The child clinician should be familiar with demographic data such as these since they provide indirect information about the values that different ethnic/racial groups place on children and family life.

Family Status

Other important information for the child practitioner to consider is the changing form of family life. Concomitant with rising divorce, the percentage of children living with both natural parents has decreased since 1970. Over 13 million children under 18 are living with one parent and another 1.9 million are living with neither. As shown in Table 1.1, about 81 % of white children live with both parents in comparison to 42 % of Black children (U.S. Bureau of the Census, 1983).

Although many divorced individuals with children remarry within five or six years, accumulating research suggests that the psychological loss incurred through divorce and the subsequent child rearing by one parent can create significant stress for children. Moreover, children may experience further stress adjusting to step-parents. As will be discussed in Chapter 14, the psychological effects are complex. The divorced parents' adjustment, their availability to the child, economic factors, and the child's temperament make some children more prone to emotional problems following divorce than others. We consider children of divorce to be vulnerable children because they are more prone to problems than other children not experiencing these stress factors in their lives. The child practitioner needs to be aware of the increasing number of children facing this special vulnerability.

Poverty

Another group of special children are those raised in poverty. Although poverty rates have consistently decreased since 1950, about 13 million children live in families with income below the official poverty level, which was $6,697 per household of two persons in 1983 (U. S. Bureau of the Census, 1984). It is important to note that poverty rates vary significantly according to the gender and ethnicity or race of the head of household. As seen in Table 1.2, 50% of all children raised in households that are headed by a female live in poverty. Of these children 40.3 % are white, 65.7 % Black, and 68.6 % Spanish origin or Hispanic (U.S. Bureau of the Census, 1979a). As also shown in Table 1.2, a considerably smaller proportion of children living with a single male head of household live under poverty conditions. In Chapter 13, we discuss in detail the debilitating psychological effects of poverty upon children. Many of these children in poverty enter life with vulnerabilities beginning with low birth weight, illness,

Table 1.1

Living Arrangements of Children Under 18 Years, 1982 and 1970
(Excludes persons under 18 years who were maintaining households or family groups.)

Living arrangements of children under 18 and marital status of parent	1982					1970		Change 1970-82
	All races		White	Black	Spanish Origin[a]			
	Number in thousands	Percent			Number in thousands			Percent
Total	62,407	X	51,086	9,377	5,358		69,162	X
			Percent					
Total		100.0	100.0	100.0	100.0		100.0	X
Children living with—								
Two parents	46,797	75.0	80.8	42.4	69.1		58,939 / 85.2	-20.6
One parent	13,701	22.0	17.2	49.2	26.8		8,199 / 11.9	67.1
Mother only	12,512	20.0	15.3	47.2	25.3		7,451 / 10.8	67.9
Divorced	5,103	8.2	8.0	9.6	7.4		2,296 / 3.3	122.3
Married	3,518	5.6	4.3	13.6	10.1		3,234 / 4.7	8.8
Separated	3,099	5.0	3.6	12.7	8.6		2,332 / 3.4	32.9
Widowed	1,123	1.8	1.5	3.3	2.3		1,395 / 2.0	-19.5
Single (never married)	2,768	4.4	1.6	20.8	5.4		527 / 0.8	425.2

See footnotes at end of table.

Table 1.1 Part 2

Living Arrangements of Children Under 18 Years, 1982 and 1970—Concluded
(Excludes persons under 18 years who were maintaining households or family groups.)

Living arrangements of children under 18 and marital status of parent	1982				1970		Change 1970-82
	All races	White	Black	Spanish Origin [a]			
	Number in thousands	Percent	Percent	Percent	Number in thousands	Percent	Percent
Children living with - continued							
One parent-continued							
Father only	1,189	1.9	1.9	2.0	1.5	748	1.1	59.0
Divorced	658	1.1	1.1	0.9	0.7	177	0.3	271.8
Married	273	0.4	0.5	0.3	0.4	287	0.4	-4.9
Separated	255	0.4	0.4	0.3	0.3	152	0.2	67.8
Widowed	144	0.2	0.2	0.3	0.3	254	0.4	-43.3
Single (never married)	114	0.2	0.1	0.5	0.2	30	–	B
Other relatives only	1,556	2.5	1.5	7.6	3.4	1,547	2.2	0.6
Nonrelatives only	352	0.6	0.5	0.8	0.7	477	0.7	-26.2

– = zero. X = not applicable. B = base less than 75,000.

Source: Marital Status and Living Arrangements: March 1982, Current Population Reports, Series P - 20, No. 380, U.S. Bureau of the Census, 1983, Washington, DC: U.S. Government Printing Office.

[a] Persons of Spanish origin may be of any race.

Table 1.2

Children in Families below Poverty Level by Ethnicity and Head of Household in 1977

	Number of children under 18 years below poverty level (numbers in thousands)	Percent of children under 18 years below poverty level
All types of families		
All children	10,028	16.0%
White	5,943	11.4%
Black	3,850	41.6%
Spanish Origin	1,402	28.6%
Children in families with male head		
All children	4,371	8.5%
White	3,250	7.1%
Black	965	19.3%
Spanish Origin	716	17.9%
Children in families with female head		
All children	5,658	50.3%
White	2,693	40.3%
Black	2,885	65.7%
Spanish Origin	686	68.6%

Source: U.S. Bureau of the Census. Characteristics of the Population Below the Poverty Level: 1977. Series P-60, No. 119, March 1979.

and malnutrition. In turn, these physical vulnerabilities can lead to increased rates of mental retardation and problematic personality temperaments.

Substitute Care

Associated with the large number of single parent families and large number of poor families in which one or both parents must work, increasingly larger numbers of children are attending day care centers and preschools. In 1976-1977, approximately 900,000 children were enrolled in day care centers. Of course, the quality of these centers varies greatly. The child clinician will be called upon to deal with children with whom adults and peers at day care centers play significant roles in early life. In these cases, the child clinician needs knowledge of the child-rearing practices of the supervising adults at the day care center as well as the parents (U.S. Department of Health & Human Services, 1980). Table 1.3 presents the number of children receiving various kinds of social and psychological intervention (Young, Pappenfort, & Marlow, 1983). As can be seen in this 1981 survey of approximately 125,000 youth and children, the highest category for residential care was delinquency, followed by dependent and neglected and emotionally disturbed children.

The question of whether foster care is a source of damage was raised at an institute sponsored by the Child Welfare League of America and the National Association of Social Workers in 1963 (Fanshel & Shinn, 1978). The prediction that children removed from a permanent home were more vulnerable to cognitive and personality problems was not clearly supported by research. A longitudinal study by Fanshel & Shinn (1978) at Columbia University followed 624 children in foster care for five years on standardized IQ tests, projection tests, and behavioral ratings from teachers, social workers, and parents. At the end of five years, 36.4 % of the children were still in care.

Abnormal Versus Normal

It might seem a relatively easy task to extrapolate these statistics concerning the status of typical and vulnerable children to the frequency of problems. In fact, it is extremely difficult to define the parameters of abnormal child development because experts differ so greatly in their definition of childhood maladjustment. Some believe it is a distinct departure from normalcy. Others view it as an extension of typical range, distinctive only in degree. Still others view maladjustment as a combination of qualitative and quantitative factors differing from the typical (Anthony, 1970). The problem of defining maladjustment is especially difficult among children. Several studies lead to the conclusion that most children show disturbed behavior at some time.

In their now classic epidemiological studies, Lapouse & Monk (1959) and MacFarlane, Allen, & Honzik (1954) demonstrated many symptoms of pathology in the

Table 1.3

NUMBERS OF CHILDREN AND YOUTH, 1966 AND 1981, BY TYPE OF FACILITY

Type of Facility	Number of Children and Youth	
	1966	1981
Dependent and Neglected	60,459	24,533
Pregnant Adolescent	5,835	1,676
Temporary Shelter	1,832	3,893
Delinquent	55,000	40,335
Status Offenders	a	4,754
Detention	10,875	15,423
Substance Abuse	a	1,629
Emotionally Disturbed	13,876	20,397
Psychiatric	8,028	12,683
Total of Children	155,905	125,323

[a] Not recognized as a type of facility in 1966.

Source: National Survey of Residential Group Care Facilities, 1983, P. 53.

general population of children. Shepherd, Oppenheim, & Mitchell (1966) surveyed children brought to mental health clinics and compared their symptomatology to a control group of randomly selected children. They reported that the symptoms of the two groups of children were not significantly different, although the parents of the clinic children were easily upset, less able to cope with misbehavior, and more likely to consult others with their problems. Along the lines of these findings, Kanner (1962b) has said that child abnormality may be related more to the "annoyance threshold" of significant others than to any intrinsic quality of the child. McCoy (1976) requested doctoral clinical psychology students to assess children's pathology from filmed segments and parental reports. The judges based their treatment recommendations more upon parental reports than on observation of the child. Thus, it often seems unclear what symptoms the child therapist centers upon and whether the therapist treats primarily the child or the referring adult.

FREQUENCY OF CHILDHOOD PROBLEMS

Institutional Data

Given the lack of commonly accepted and valid means of classifying childhood disorders, it is not surprising that studies of the frequency of childhood maladjustment are very limited and do not always agree. Rather extensive data have been collected by the National Institute of Mental Health (Milazzo-Sayre, 1978a, 1978b, & 1978c; NIMH Survey & Reports Branch, 1979) concerning the frequency and type of childhood admissions to state and county hospitals, private hospitals, and to outpatient clinics. These data show that some trends in the frequency of childhood maladjustment are consistent across mental health settings, while in other cases important differences do emerge. In general, admissions to hospitals for psychiatric reasons have decreased dramatically within the last ten years. From 1962 to 1969, first admissions to state and county hospitals increased 26%. From 1969 to 1975, the trend was reversed and admissions decreased 26%. It is important to note, however, that from 1962 to 1975 admissions for children under age 15 has slowly, but rather steadily, increased (Milazzo-Sayre, 1978a). In general, it can also be stated that more male children are treated for maladjustment than females. From 1962 to 1975 the number of male children admitted to state, county, and private hospitals was much greater than the number of females. However, from 1972 to the present, the number of female admissions has increased so that in many settings the ratio of male to female admissions approaches equality (Milazzo-Sayre, 1978a, 1978c).

More specifically, considering admissions to state and county hospitals in 1975, approximately one-fourth of all admissions were youths under 25 years of age (2 % under 14 years, 4 % between 14 and 17, and 19 % between 18 and 24 years old). The rate of admissions for the general population was 182 admissions per every 100,000 individuals, which was higher than for children and adolescents. For children under 14 years of age, the admission rate was 171 per 100,000 and 99 per 100,000 for youths ages 14 to 17 (NIMH Survey & Reports, 1979). The NIMH research (1979) was collected from admissions to various treatment facilities.

In reviewing the frequency of specific diagnoses according to children's ages within the state and county hospital settings, for children under 14, 70 % were admitted for adjustment reactions and behavioral disorders. For the 14 to 17 age group, adjustment disorders decreased to 46.6 %, but schizophrenia (24.1 %) and personality disorders (14.5 %) showed marked increases. For the 18-24 age group, adjustment reactions dropped to 3.2 % of total admissions, while schizophrenia increased to 40 %, personality disorders to 13.1 %, and alcohol and drug disorders climb to 22.4 %. The sex and race distributions by diagnostic categories are clinically interesting. Males in the oldest age category hold the higher schizophrenia and alcohol or drug admission rates, while females are admitted at higher rates for depressive and personality disorders.

Comparable data from the Queen's Child Psychiatric Center collected between 1967 and 1971 suggest that males are admitted at a younger age than females and that a very large proportion of the children admitted were from large families (Chuda & Sankar, 1976).

The frequency of youth admissions to private hospitals is similar to that of state and county facilities. Again, approximately 25 % of the admissions are for youths under 25 years of age, 2 % under 14 years, 9.5 % in the 14-17 age range, and 15 % in the 18-24 age range (NIMH Survey & Reports, 1979). Adjustment reactions and behavioral disorders are the most common diagnoses for those younger than 14. Schizophrenia increases in frequency during the adolescent years, so that within the 14 to 17 age range, 18.6 % were diagnosed as schizophrenic. Marked increases are also shown for depressive disorders (21.5 %) as well as personality disorders (10.3 %). In the final age group, 18-24 years, schizophrenia has increased to 40 % and depressive disorders to 29.2 %. Note the higher rate again of depressive disorders for females, but schizophrenia for males.

Outpatient Data

Data collected from a representative sample of outpatient services (NIMH Survey and Reports, 1979) reveal some different trends. Over 40 % of the users were youths under 25 years of age in comparison to the 25 % admissions at public and private hospitals. Compared to the overall rate of use of outpatient facilities of 665 per 100,000, the rate of youths was as high or higher. From 55 % to 73 % of the youths 14 years of age or younger were diagnosed as adjustment reaction and behavior disorders. In comparison to the data of state and private hospitals, a large number of the adolescent referrals to outpatient psychiatric services are for adjustment reactions. Schizophrenia, depressive, and personality disorders are relatively infrequent, while many cases are classified as "other" unspecified conditions. The outpatient facilities show a lack of sex differences by diagnostic category.

Analysis of the Frequency Data on Childhood Problems

The statistics concerning childhood maladjustment are alarmingly high. Although admissions to state, county, and private hospitals are lower for children than adults, some 1 to 2 % of the childhood population is experiencing such significant disturbance as to require hospitalization. Moreover, the rate of hospitalization for youths has not decreased in the last ten years at the same rate as it has for adults.

The frequency data demonstrate that among young children, similar types and frequency of syndromes are reported at hospital and outpatient clinics. By adolescence, it seems that clients with more severe pathology are treated in hospital settings, while the outpatient facilities meet the needs of the less disturbed. We will see in a later chapter that hospitalization is rarely recommended as preferred treatment for children. Successful reentry into the family, school, and community is consistently stressed as necessary for effective childhood adjustment. The fact that more than 40 % of the users of outpatient facilities are youths is quite interesting but difficult to interpret since the primary childhood diagnosis, whether in an inpatient or outpatient facility, is adjustment reaction. Perhaps, encouragingly, most children receive outpatient care so that they can be kept in their homes Yet, one wonders under what conditions some children are hospitalized for adjustment reactions, while others receive outpatient care. Minority children are institutionalized in correctional facilities at a rate four times greater than nonminority children. Interestingly, minorities are institutionalized in medical and educational facilities at a rate only 20 % higher than white children (U.S. Department of Health & Human Services, 1980). Are there ethnic, social class, or sex biases such that some children receive outpatient assistance, while others, because of bias, are hospitalized? Or, perhaps the diagnosis of adjustment reaction is so broad that differences in symptoms of those hospitalized and those receiving outpatient care are masked.

The hospital and clinic data raise many questions that certainly alert us to the extent of maladjustment among children. Some researchers have attempted to determine what happens to the childhood population that has received treatment for maladjustment. Researchers have employed various classification schemes to evaluate the progression of childhood disorders.

LONG-TERM STUDIES OF CHILDHOOD PROBLEMS

Long-term studies of childhood maladjustment take several forms. One type is the follow-up study in which children treated for emotional problems are reexamined and retested some years later. Another type of long-term study is the longitudinal design. In the longitudinal study, the development of a group of children is investigated over a number of years with the goal of identifying factors contributing to health and maladjustment. A third type of long-term study is the retrospective design in which target adults are asked to think back and assess their own or another's childhood.

Follow-up Studies

In the follow-up studies, children with target problems are located and retested a number of years later. O'Neal and Robins (1959) followed up 526 adults who had been seen in psychiatric clinics for diagnosis with no treatment and matched controls some 30-40 years earlier. They reported that a large number of individuals who had been diagnosed as antisocial children turned out to be antisocial adults. Individuals with less severe diagnoses grew up with a range of symptoms of moderate severity. As a whole, the control group of children grew up to be well-adjusted adults. Thus, O'Neal and Robins demonstrate some relationship between child and adult disorders. The relationship seems to be one of intensity of pathology rather than of specific symptomatology. These findings are supported by the follow-up study of Pritchard and Graham (1966) who noted a significant relationship between antisocial children and adults and a significant correlation between childhood neurosis and later affective disorders.

Several researchers have attempted longitudinal studies of childhood maladjustment. These studies are exciting because they shed light on the relationship between childhood and adult disorders. However, they suffer from several limitations. It is difficult to continue to follow a group of children through to adulthood. Different evaluation instruments must be used at various developmental stages, and the relationship of the findings from testing to testing becomes unclear the older our subjects become.

Moreover, scientific advances tend to render some findings unfashionable or irrelevant before the study is actually completed (Anthony, 1970). Despite these limitations, several interesting findings have emerged. In the Berkeley Study, MacFarlane et al., (1954) evaluated 116 randomly selected children from ages 2 months through 14 years. They demonstrated that most disorders did not persist into adulthood. Douglas and Mulligan (1961) studied the development of 5,000 British children over 20 years and noted that few with significant behavioral disturbances were receiving therapy. Thomas, Birch, Chess, and Hertzig (1960) examined a broad cross section of children and identified normal differences in reaction time and temperament that antedated symptomatology.

Retrospective Studies

Some interesting findings have emerged from retrospective studies in which adults are asked to look back and evaluate their own or their children's childhoods. Clearly, recall studies are subject to much bias, and this limitation must be kept in mind in evaluating these findings. Lapouse and Monk (1958) pioneered this approach in child therapy research by interviewing a cross section of mothers with a 200-item questionnaire. They reported that over half the sample children considered normal had many fears, temper tantrums, and worries. About one-third experienced nightmares, wet their beds, and sucked their thumbs. Similarly, findings of equivalent symptoms among child clinic populations and controls have been reported in a number of retrospective studies (Renaud & Estess, 1961; Shepherd, Oppenheim, & Mitchell, 1966).

What can be concluded from these large-scale studies of childhood maladjustment? First, there is a sizeable number of children with rather severe personal and behavioral problems. The specific symptomatology varies with developmental level. With the exception of antisocial characteristics, most symptomatology expressed by children will not be evident when they mature. However, the tendency toward maladjustment does continue. Maladjusted children are likely to become maladjusted adults. Thus, early identification of childhood problems, removal of causative agents, and treatment are very important. We are "building our case" about the value of child theory when it is used to correct causes of maladjustment. With this point well-emphasized, we will turn to a discussion of the causative factors in childhood maladjustment.

ETIOLOGY OF CHILDHOOD MALADJUSTMENT

Genetics

Research is being conducted to ascertain the degree to which childhood maladjustment is genetically based. Evidence from concordance studies (in which emotional disturbance among twins and siblings reared together and separately is compared) suggests that some childhood emotional problems may be inherited. Chess and Hassibi (1978) summarize results of a number of concordance studies conducted about childhood schizophrenia. In sum, children with one schizophrenic parent have 8-10 times higher expectancies for becoming schizophrenic during their childhood. Siblings of schizophrenics have 6-7 times higher likelihood of becoming schizophrenic than siblings of nonschizophrenics. When children of schizophrenics are raised by nonschizophrenic guardians, their rate of acquiring schizophrenia remains similar to that as when raised by the schizophrenic parent. In contrast, children of nonschizophrenics adopted by schizophrenic parents do not show a higher rate of schizophrenia. Thus, development of schizophrenia seems more closely related to genetic disposition than to home environment.

Similarly convincing evidence has been collated about the development of manic-depressive psychosis. Concordance among identical child twins ranges from 50 % (Harvald & Hauge, 1965) to 100 % (Kallmann, 1953).

Researchers are attempting to understand what type of genetic messages are transmitted in cases of childhood schizophrenia and affective psychosis. An extensive field of research begun by Hill (1952) has suggested that brain wave patterns as evidenced in electroencephalograms are abnormal among some disturbed children. The irregular EEG pattern is particularly characteristic of about 50 % of the children diagnosed as hyperactive (Chess & Hassibi, 1978). Differences in blood serum and amino acids have been noted in some studies comparing adult schizophrenics and nonschizophrenics. Interestingly, these studies have not been successfully replicated with children, again suggesting that the adult and child syndromes, though showing similar symptoms, are dynamically different (Goldfarb, 1970). Other experts suggest that genetic predisposition toward maladjustment is expressed through the endocrine and/or nervous system. To some degree, the sympathetic, rather than the parasympathetic, nervous system predominates in children with tenseness and impulsivity (Anthony, 1970).

Prenatal and Postnatal Factors

Certain constitutional factors created by prenatal and postnatal experiences have been linked with a variety of childhood emotional problems. Most of the prenatal studies of childhood maladjustment are retrospective, correlational ones; that is, children with disturbance are identified, and their prenatal histories are investigated. The studies suggest that the pregnant mother's nutrition is correlated with infant intelligence (Harrell, Woodyard, & Gates, 1955). Severe malnutrition is associated with infant retardation. Commonly, we encounter infants who suffer from undernutrition and low birth weight and other more serious physiological problems because of maternal alcoholism or drug addiction. The fetal alcoholic syndrome is discussed in Chapter 3. The relevance here is that these children manifest a variety of prenatal and postnatal symptoms that are detrimental to their well-being. Further, it is now known that the social adjustment of these children can be affected during the school years.

Maternal illnesses, especially during the first three months of pregnancy, can also affect the embryo's well-being. Viral diseases that are relatively innocuous among adults, such as measles and colds, can cause blindness and deafness. Bacterial infections are also transmitted, although in most bacterial diseases, the infection is transmitted rather than the bacteria, spurring congenital malformation. The infant can be born with tuberculosis or syphilis or other bacterial illnesses transmitted through the infected mother's placenta.

Several perinatal factors also affect the neonate's well-being. Anoxia, lack of oxygen during birth, is associated with lower physiological reactivity scores and lower Stanford-Binet intelligence scores years later (Graham et al., 1961). Prolonged and complicated labor is associated with possible later retardation, behavioral disorders, and reading problems (Pasamanick & Knobloch, 1966). Prematurity also constitutes a factor that results in infants being grouped as high-risk for a variety of medical and psychological disturbances (Chess & Hassibi, 1978).

A number of postnatal factors such as infections of the central nervous system, brain trauma, and malnutrition affect the child's constitutional well-being.

We have described the physical effects of a number of prenatal and postnatal factors. Although the effect of these factors appears first to be physical, these toxic factors are easily and often transformed to temperament and personal disturbances. If the child's constitution is disturbed, her or his ability to develop effective social relationships may be disturbed.

Family Factors

A number of family factors may be causative in childhood maladjustment. Loss of a parent has been associated with childhood disturbance. When children under 2 are separated from a primary caretaker, they grieve. The degree of reversibility of the despair depends upon a number of factors: whether the separation is permanent or temporary, duration and frequency of separation, and the nature of substitute care (Freedman, Kaplan, & Sadock, 1976). As will be explored in Chapter 3, it is now well-documented that the infant needs a firm attachment to a primary caretaker. Bonding to the father and other significant adults is also important for the overall psychological well-being of the child. The intensity and quality of the bond is also critical (Bowlby, 1969) since these variables communicate to the child the extent to which the child is loved and wanted by parents and other adults.

As mentioned previously, separation or divorce has complex effects on the child. Children of poverty are at risk for maladjustment. In these cases, maladjustment may occur because of the family dysfunction and/or because of nonnurturing environmental conditions that are incurred following divorce or as a result of poverty. Also, parents' physical illnesses have been associated with childhood delinquency (Glueck and Glueck, 1952).

Clearly, pathology in the parent-child interaction can stimulate maladjustment. Much research has been conducted to ascertain the relationship between parents' emotional problems and those of their children, barring genetic influences. Several noncontrolled studies report that mothers with negative feelings towards themselves have children who are frequently ill, withdrawn, and passive (Anthony, 1959; Lewis,

1954). Wolking, Quast, and Lawton (1966) administered the Minnesota Multiphasic Personality Inventory (MMPI) to parents of children in six diagnostic groups. They reported elevations on several MMPI scales for parents of clinical children as compared to controls, but parental profiles and childhood disorders did not match on any dimension. We are becoming increasingly aware of how a child may be caught in her or his web of a pathological family system. The child's maladjustment may be the only way to cope within a disturbed world. Thus, too much, too little, or inconsistent child rearing have been linked to childhood maladjustment.

In general, it does seem that deviancy in the family is associated with higher rates of childhood maladjustment. Children with behavioral disorders have three to four times greater probability of becoming psychiatric patients as adults, although the pathognomic patterns are discontinuous (Goldfarb, 1970; Mellsop, 1972). Perhaps you know someone who was raised in a very pathological family environment, yet seems well-adjusted. Although the psychosocial stresses we have listed correlate strongly with childhood maladjustment, many children with great environmental liabilities do not become disturbed. Child specialists puzzle how that could happen. Do these children have more adaptive temperaments and constitutions? Are they receiving ameliorative support elsewhere? Clearly, the relationship between psychosocial stress and childhood maladjustment is not fully understood. The types of family deviancy and their effects are voluminous. There are many theories about the effects, but few documented, controlled studies which show how childhood rearing practices sculpture the behavior and temperament of a given child.

In reviewing the findings on etiology, we see that the child's biology and the physical and social environment can be menacing forces. In most cases, maladjustment is probably an interaction of self and environmental factors. Some say stress alone causes maladjustment (Axline, 1969). Others rely on biological explanations (Bender, 1947). Most believe that stress is a trigger that releases constitutional vulnerability (Selye, 1950). As our ability to diagnose childhood disorders is refined, and with more controlled, objective studies, perhaps we may move toward a resolution on this critical issue.

SUMMARY

Our review of the statistics concerning the status of children reveals some hopeful and some alarming findings. The decreasing birth rate allows for existing clinical services to reach more children than earlier, and we can expect this trend to continue. However, gains have not been uniform. A large number of female-headed, ethnic minority, and inner-city families are locked into poverty, and their children are particularly vulnerable to emotional problems. The data concerning childhood maladjustment create as many questions as answers. About 655,000 children under 18 years of age are admitted to organized mental health facilities (U.S. Department of Health & Human

Services, 1980); admission for children has not decreased in the last 20 years as it has for adult clients. Are children getting "more disturbed" or are more children being served? Long-term findings suggest that many children show pathological symptoms during some period of their growing up. We must ask: is it typical for children to show pathological symptoms during some period of their childhood? Or, are there a tremendous number of maladjusted children, many of whom are not receiving therapeutic assistance? Will the symptoms dissipate in time without intervention? Our review of epidemiological studies indicates that some symptoms carry on into adulthood. Yet, in other cases symptoms dissipate, but the tendency toward maladjustment remains. What exactly is the relationship between the maladjustment of childhood and adult symptomatology? What particular childhood symptoms has therapy been effective in ameliorating? A major issue is to determine which child therapy strategies are associated with long-term gains for particular problems. In order to assess these issues, we need a system of classification of childhood disorders. We have attempted to demonstrate that our assessments are improving but yet subject to many fallibilities.

It follows that since we are not yet completely clear on the nature and causes of childhood maladjustments, it is extremely difficult to assess the effectiveness of various treatment modalities. At times it appears that we are trying to evaluate the effectiveness of procedures upon phenomena that have not been well identified. A difficult task indeed! The reader is asked to keep these limitations in mind in later chapters of this text. We will present empirical support for our assertions when data exist and attempt to point out when the data are lacking. We will also summarize theoretical, descriptive, and expository writings that hold promise for treatment. It is important to carefully evaluate the validity of these untested premises in clinical work with maladjusted children.

CHAPTER 2

CHILDREN IN HISTORICAL PERSPECTIVE

Children of yestersday
Heirs of tomorrow,
What are you weaving?
Labor and sorrow?
Look to the looms again,
Faster and faster,
Fly the great shuttles,
Prepared by the Master.
Life's in the loom
Room for it - room!

Mary Artemisia Lathbury, "Sons of Hope,"
Stanza One, 1841-1913

CONCEPT OF CHILDREN AS MINIATURE ADULTS

The idea of childhood as a distinct developmental stage has not always existed. In ancient times, for example, children were regarded as chattel whose primary purpose in life was to be of help to their parents. To achieve this purpose, the children were required from early ages to assist their parents in the fields or wherever else their services were required. Instead of trying to understand the child and allowing the child to develop naturally, ancient people attempted to mold each child according to their standards of what a child should be and what the child should know as adolescence approached. Thus, children in Sparta were molded to become soldiers while in other cultures they were trained to become cultivators of the soil. The concept of childhood did not really exist--children were seen and treated as miniature adults (Kadushin, 1980). The little education provided was in preparation for the responsibilities that the child would assume at maturity.

In many societies, it was common practice for the father to have absolute authority in the decision of whether a newborn infant should live or die. Upon birth the newborn was inspected for physical deformities and for its sex. If the newborn was in any way deformed or, often, simply female, the father could decree that the infant should be put to death or abandoned to die from exposure to the elements. Continuing through medieval times, childhood was not conceived of as a distinct developmental phase. Children were seldom the subject matter of literature or art. As soon as children abandoned swaddling clothes, they were dressed like the adults of their class and treated as little adults. As youths, they were often forced to work at hard labor.

Often by age seven or eight, children were apprenticed to other families, perhaps never to live with their parents again. The family transmitted name and property; it was not a source of human sensitivity. The importance of the family as an institution is a recent social change. The family today is the primary if not sole social institution for children. This change is closely linked to the life expectancy of children.

In the few paintings depicting children in medieval times, the youngsters were often portrayed as emaciated or dead. Aries (1962) explains that children in the Middle Ages were cared for, but so many died that parents were hesitant to commit their attention and love to them. Infanticide and exposure were common practices for almost all cultures through history. Deformed, sickly, retarded children, or twins were exposed to the weather, thrown in freezing rivers, or strangled. The parents' right to kill their children existed until the 19th century in Europe (Radbill, 1980). The lack of public health and medical knowledge resulted in a very high infant mortality rate. For example, in the late 1600's, 59 % of the children born in London died before age five while 64 % died before age ten. Because of limited prenatal and perinatal care, many infants were born with significant deformities (Hewett & Forness, 1977), contracted infectious diseases, and fell victims to a wide variety of accidents that took their lives before age five. To think of children as full beings with a range of feelings and personality would make parents more alert to their children's fragileness and more fearful of their likely death. Thus, children were cherished by their parents at whim or according to economic dictates.

EMERGENCE OF THE CONCEPT OF CHILDHOOD AS UNIQUE

With the advent of the 17th Century, the idea of childhood as a special period, in which children were seen to have unique psychological, educational, and physical needs, came to hold influence. Children became the center of paintings and were dressed in special, more versatile clothing. At this time Johann Amos Comenius, a famous Slavic educational reformer, published *Orbis Pictus,* or the *World in Pictures,* which was the first children's reading material accompanied by pictures. The pictures enhanced the children's interest in and understanding of the book. Education was beginning to be related to children's abilities (Hurlock, 1942).

The emerging sensitivity for children's needs and abilities increased in vigor in the 18th Century. For example, Jean Jacques Rousseau of France, in his now classic *Emile,* published in 1762, described at length the application of his ideal of political freedom to the education of the child. Other notable individuals whose interests in children paved the way for a more humanistic understanding of childhood included the Swiss

Pestalozzi and the German physician Tiedemann. Pestalozzi in 1744 published the first scientific record of the development of a young child (Hurlock, 1942). The work based on observations of Pestalozzi's own child was followed by a similar study by Tiedemann in 1787. These two studies were the forerunners of the biographical studies of children which became so popular in the following century (Hurlock, 1942).

EMERGENCE OF CHILDREN'S SERVICES

Study of Children

The first half of the 19th Century was marked by little advance in the study of children, but during the latter part of the century, a succession of baby biographies increased our knowledge about childhood. For instance, Charles Darwin published his *Biographical Sketch of an Infant* in 1877, while Wilhelm Preyer wrote *The Mind of the Child* in 1882. Both of these books served as models for observational studies of children as well as for the experimental approach to the investigation of developmental processes in children. So influential was Preyer's book that he is often called the "father of child psychology." Preyer's diary was important because it replaced general observations and anecdotes found in other diaries with careful measurements of behavior--beginning with the development of reflexes from birth on.

Another important contributor in the last part of the 19th Century was G. Stanley Hall of the United States. Hall studied extensively the physical and mental capabilities of children, irrespective of educational issues. Hall aroused popular interest in the child and is often referred to as the "father of the child study movement" (Hurlock, 1942).

In 1893, at the time of the International Conference on Education held at the Chicago World's Fair, Hall organized the National Association for the Study of Children, the first child study society in the United States. In the following year, a Department of Child Study was formed as a part of the National Education Association. The child study society movement quickly spread across the nation as well as abroad with groups being formed in England in 1894, Poland in 1897, Germany in 1899, and France in 1901. So much interest was generated in this movement that in 1906 the First International Congress of Child Study was held in Berlin (Hurlock, 1942).

Child Welfare

During this time, the welfare of the child was emphasized as indicated through the formation of the Society for the Prevention of Cruelty to Children in 1875; the establishment of the first settlement house for children in 1887 in New York City; and the appearance of juvenile courts in Denver, Boston, Chicago, and New York between 1898 and 1900 (Hurlock, 1942).

In the 1850's, Charles Loring Bruce founded the Children's Aid Society to help the 10,000 homeless children wandering the streets of New York. The children were "farmed out" to rural families in New York state and the western frontier. This program was based on the theory that a change in environment and removal from a poorly functioning family would meet the child's needs (Zuckerman, 1983).

> Little orphan Annie's come to our house to stay,
> To wash the cups and saucers up, an' brush the crumbs away.
> An' shoo the chickens off the porch, an' dust the hearth,
>   an sweep, An' make the fire, and bake the bread,
> An' earn her board and keep.

> James Whitcomb Riley

Treatment of Children

Along with a commitment to the study of normal children, programs emerged for the study of maladjusted children. In 1896 Witmer established the Psychological Clinic at the University of Pennsylvania which was devoted to assisting children who were having problems at school or with their families. In the same year, the Psychiatric Institute was founded in New York City with the same purpose of counseling children who were having adjustment problems. The basic structure of these early clinics has continued until today so that presently there are child guidance clinics in almost every community in the United States (Kanner, 1962a).

The 20th Century has sometimes been called the "Century of the Child." More serious study about the child has been completed in this century than in the entire history of the world. Today, we have children's books, children's movies, children's television programs, and special games and toys for youth. Children usually have their own bedrooms, parks, zoos, schools, and organized activities. Clearly, children are considered unique in virtually every country of the world today. As proof of this, the International Year of the Child held in 1979 was observed in every country of the world through meetings devoted to special problems of children. Our interest in children has resulted in a marked improvement in how children are perceived by adults and in the love and attention they receive from parents.

A Complex World

Despite the concern for children that exists today, children still face a wide variety of problems in our technological society. Compared to the past, it looks as though children "never had it so good." Nonetheless, it appears that our concept of childhood is about to change again because of the effects of technology. The child of today plays few meaningful roles in society. The dependency of childhood and adolescence is often extended into the early twenties because youth are not skilled enough to work in a technological society that demands a high degree of educational sophistication. How are youth to acquire skills to compete in a society where scientific knowledge doubles in less than 10 years? What can the person hope to learn that will last? Thus, in a technological society, childhood and adolescence is extended, but meaningful values are not attached to this new concept of youth.

Feelings of the transciency and unsettledness in life are also characteristic of a technological society and are exacerbated by the media. "Fragmentation of the family and kinship group and alienation and anomie are the bitter fruits of a highly individualistic, mobile, and technically-oriented civilization" (Specht, 1981, p. 9). Through the slick sophistication and the violence and sex on television, children learn a superficial set of values without intellectual understanding and physical maturity to fully integrate what they emulate. Further, parents and teachers often feel lost to define future directions for children (Fullmer & Bernard, 1972). The solution exercised by many youths is to try to "get it now." The child "plays at being big because he is not given an opportunity to be a small partner in a big world" (Erikson, 1963, p.238).

Children have not had an easy time through most of history. Although time has brought increasing awareness about the state of childhood, growing up continues to be a difficult process. The child coming to the therapist today brings stress unique to her or his developmental stage and unique to our technological age. Some suggest that more children are disturbed today than in previous times because life in a technological age is so stressful and without meaningful roles for children. In order to explore this thesis, it is helpful to review how emotionally disturbed children have been viewed throughout history.

CONCEPTIONS OF CHILDHOOD PROBLEMS

Early Explanations of Maladjustment

Given the lack of interest in childhood and the fact that children over seven were considered adults, it is not surprising that there is a dearth of information concerning childhood maladjustment before the 18th Century. Shortly before the French and American Revolutions, new doctrines concerning the rights of individuals spurred humanitarian reforms. The mentally disturbed were considered physically ill and deserving of humane treatment. Even so, it was assumed that maladjustment represented underlying physical illness. Attention focused upon observable physical handicaps, and children's subjective feelings were little understood (Hewitt & Forness, 1977). It was believed that the best one could do was to teach the maladjusted child to control his physically-based maladjustment with moral integrity. Kanner (1962a, p. 97), using biographical material, describes the case of a seven-year-old child by the name of

Emerentia who in 1713 was taken to the local minister to cure her behavioral maladjustment. Let us read the case of Emerentia.

Case 2.1. The Case of Emerentia

This 7-year-old girl, the offspring of an aristocratic family, whose father remarried after an unhappy first matrimony, offended her "noble and godfearing" stepmother by her peculiar behavior. Worst of all, she would not join in the prayers and was panic-stricken when taken to the black-robed preacher in the dark and gloomy chapel. She avoided contact with people by hiding in closets or running away from home. The local physician had nothing to offer beyond declaring that she might be insane. She was placed in the custody of a minister known for his rigid orthodoxy. The minister, who saw in her ways the machinations of a "baneful and infernal" power, used a number of would-be therapeutic devices. He laid her on a bench and beat her with a cat-o'nine-tails. He locked her in a dark pantry. He subjected her to a period of starvation. He clothed her in a frock of burlap. Under these circumstances, the child did not last long. She died after a few months, and everybody felt relieved. The minister was amply rewarded for his efforts by Emerentia's parents.

Beyond Moral Interventions

Although the case of Emerentia may be extreme, it does show the callousness involved in caring for children who went against the wishes of their parents. With increasing interest in the 1800's in human rights and scientific rigour, methods for assisting maladjusted children besides religious and moral training were sought. A turning point was the treatment of the Wild Boy of Aveyron by one of Pinel's pupils, Jean Itard. Pinel (the great reformer of French mental institutions in the 1700's) found a totally unsocialized and nonverbal boy believed to have been raised by wolves. Pinel's student, Itard, greatly influenced by his teacher's humanitarian ideals, believed he could help the boy. Although it was later believed that the Wild Boy was severely retarded rather than raised by animals, Itard showed that with consistent attention over several years, the child could learn basic skills and rudimentary language (Alexander & Selesnick, 1966). Thus, Itard demonstrated that with patience, teaching, and persistence, one could systematically affect a child's behavior.

In the 1800's children's behavioral problems were considered to be caused by physical malfunctions, and rational ways of helping children modify their maladjusted behavior were not yet developed. As a whole, the primary form of treatment continued to be punitive. Kanner (1962b), for instance, summarizes an 1838 case study by Esquirol. To teach a 7 1/2 year-old to stop her temper tantrums and excessive masturbation and to punish her for saying she wanted her mother to die, the child was

Leo Kanner
(Photo by Leon Perskie, with permission)

told that a flour-water mixture was arsenic, and she was forced to swallow it. Eventually, she was sent to a convent and apprenticed to a jewelry cutter. The treatment was considered a success as the parents were pleased to find that their daughter became submissive and attended church regularly on Sunday.

By the mid-1800's, the punitive orientation to treatment was muted by a more humanitarian appreciation of the child. The relationship between child rearing and child development was given greater consideration. For example, in 1841 Descuret wrote of a boy who lived with a nurse during his first two years of life. Descuret puzzled that the boy became pale, refused to eat, and did not respond to adults when returned to his natural parents. Eventually, Descuret recommended that the nurse be brought to the home at which point the child seemed to recover immediately. Once recovered, the child was gradually separated from the nurse, first for a few hours, then for an entire day, followed by a week, until finally the child adjusted to the absence of the nurse (Kanner, 1962b). As Kanner (1962b) notes, this example marks the era when explanations for maladjusted behavior began to be sought on other than theologic or moralistic grounds.

By 1880, several texts on childhood insanity were authored in Germany, France, Ireland, and Great Britain. In each text, the disorders were described as irreversible, the product of heredity, degeneracy, parasites, masturbation, or overwork (Kanner, 1962b). Despite this general pessimism about the long-term outcome for maladjusted children, a psychodynamic orientation was emerging. The effects of separation, fear, and deprivation were noted, although systematic conceptualization about these factors would await another 20 years. Interest in the classification of childhood disorders also emerged in the mid-1800's. In the text, *Pathology of the Mind,* Maudsley (1880) devoted a chapter to classification of childhood psychosis, attempting to correlate symptomatology with developmental status. Efforts were made to distinguish emotional disturbance and mental retardation. Seguin, a student of Itard, proposed guidelines for systematically identifying and curing retardation through practical education. Seguin brought his ideas to the United States in the late 1800's and was responsible for establishing a number of centers to assist in the education of the mentally retarded (Hewitt & Forness, 1977).

The stage was set by the late 1800's for important developments in child care. Infant and child mortality rates decreased significantly. Adults were more committed to aiding children in their overall development. Scientists looked for logical explanations of human behavior. Understanding of childhood disorders would now mushroom in three main directions: (1) the development of systematic theories of child psychology, (2) the design of special treatment facilities for children, and (3) application of principles of child behavior to education.

Development of Techniques for Child Therapy

Psychoanalytic Approach

Some sophisticated writing on child psychology began to emerge in the late 1800's, as indicated earlier. In 1887, Frank Emminghaus published a systematic treatise on child psychiatry. The case histories of their children's development by Darwin and Preyer influenced later theorists, especially Sigmund Freud who published his systematic theory of infantile sexuality in 1905. Freud did not conduct therapy with children, but in 1908 he directed a father through letters to treat his son, little Hans, for horse phobia (Freud, 1928). As you are most certainly aware, voluminous publications from case reports to texts were stimulated by Freud's work. G. Stanley Hall stressed the importance of studying normal development in order to understand childhood maladjustment. He founded the *Pedagogical Seminary* in 1891, a journal devoted to the study of typical childhood behavior. Beginning his career under Hall, Gesell published the first comprehensive outline of normal child development in 1925 (Alexander & Selesnick, 1966).

By the second decade of this century, a number of theorists proposed methods of child treatment based upon psychodynamic suppositions about the causes of their emotional stress. Leo Kanner, generally viewed as the father of child psychiatry, was instrumental in identifying various syndromes of maladjustment and treatments for those disorders. He also closely studied the history of the treatment of emotionally disturbed children. Hug Hellmith, a Viennese psychoanalyst, published a systematic theory for treating children in 1919. In the 1920's, Melanie Klein greatly influenced the direction of child therapy by presenting a systematic play therapy approach. She pointed out that infants feel a range of emotions from anger to joy and that the mother becomes the primary object of support and hostility. She also emphasized that it was not the child's daily routine, but rather the child's subjective perception of reality that caused emotional disturbance. Klein maintained a strict analytic view advocating direct interpretation of the unconscious experiences of the child. In the 1930's, Anna Freud developed a theory of child therapy that veered from the strict analytic stance advanced by her father. In numerous writings, she specified ways in which child and adult analysis should differ. Shortly afterward, David Levy and Frederick Allen introduced "relationship therapy" with children. They recommended that the therapist become an ally of the child, assuming a permissive attitude. In structured play, the child was encouraged to reenact specific situations believed to be traumatic. Thus, much emphasis was placed upon appropporiate nurturing of the child. As we shall see, a tremendous number of theories for child therapy have been advanced since these early writings. Some of the theories are based upon principles very similar to those proposed by the early child therapists, while others are antithetical to the initial approaches to child therapy. We will note in later chapters how few of these approaches have been well-documented.

Behavioristic Approach

An approach to child therapy quite different from that proposed by Freud and other analytically-oriented child therapists was the behaviorally-oriented work of John B. Watson, who is sometimes called the "father of behaviorism." Beginning in 1917, Watson devised a series of new experimental techniques for studying children. One of these techniques was conditioning reflexive behavior, and Watson demonstrated that a fear response could be conditioned in a child. At the initiation of Watson's experiment a child, known as "Little Albert," was a normal, healthy child of nine months with no fear of animals. Watson allowed "Little Albert" to play with a white furry rat. Once it was established that the child demonstrated no fear of the rat, a loud gong was sounded when Albert approached the rat. The loud sound elicited a startled response in the child who began to cry. After a few pairings of the loud sound (Unconditioned Stimulus) and the rat (Conditioned Stimulus), the child would cry (Conditioned Response). This conditioned fear response generalized to other furry animals and objects. On the basis of this finding, Watson argued that all phobias are conditioned in the same fashion as Albert learned fear of the rat. Thus, Watson proposed that phobias and other maladjusted behaviors were due to conditioning, not to the presence of underlying internal conflicts and repression as put forth by Freud.

A student of Watson's by the name of Mary Cover Jones also developed a variety of methods for eliminating children's fears based upon conditioning principles (Jones, 1926). Later, Mowrer and Mowrer (1938) described the treatment of bedwetting by conditioning techniques. From this beginning, the behavioral modification techniques advanced by Skinner (1953) and Bandura (1969, 1977) became commonplace.

Today, a wide variety of behavioral therapies are available for the treatment of maladjustments in children (Fischer & Gochros, (1975). Behavioral modification techniques have been shown to be effective in eliminating childhood fears, school related behavioral problems, and a host of other problems shown by children. Possibly, the greatest use of behavioral approaches is with mentally retarded and autistic children. We will discuss the behavioral treatment approach in more detail in Chapter 5.

Medical Approach

A third approach to child treatment that evolved at the turn of the century was medically oriented. In the 1940's, Lauretta Bender emphasized the importance of the child's biological nature. She stressed the physiological basis of maladjustment and recommended minimal insight therapy. She relied heavily on drug treatment and electroshock therapy (Chess & Hassibi, 1978).

Child Guidance Clinics

Concomitant with the interest shown in therapeutic work with children in the early 1900's was the establishment of special treatment facilities for children with behavioral problems. In 1909, the National Committee for Mental Hygiene established by Clifford Beers, Adolph Meyers, and William James launched the "Child Guidance Movement." The purpose of the Child Guidance Movement was to establish special clinics for children in which psychiatrists, psychologists, and social service personnel worked as a team to help children and their parents (Kanner, 1962b). At the same time in Chicago, a philanthropist by the name of Mrs. W. F. Drummer commissioned Dr. William Healy, a gynecologist and general practitioner, to study the causes and treatment of delinquency. Healy published a text on the Individual Delinquent and with Drummer's continued financial support, established the first Institute for Juvenile Research (Freedman, Kaplan & Sadock, 1976). Delinquents were not considered "bad" by Healy but rather as wayward youths. Under Healy's guidance, the protective care for delinquents was to continue for several decades.

Special guidance centers for assisting normal children with everyday kinds of problems also emerged in the early 1900's. For instance, Frank Parsons began steering a vocational guidance movement to help match children with careers (Dimick & Huff, 1970). From the turn of the century to the mid-1940's, the child guidance clinics grew in number (Chess & Hassibi, 1978; Dimick & Huff, 1970). Some of the more important clinics and their theoretical thrusts are summarized below:

- The Yale Clinic of Child Development was established by Arnold Gesell in 1911 to study the stages of normal development.

- Vocational guidance clinics were established by Parsons in Boston in 1908 and shortly thereafter by Eli Weaver in New York public schools.

- The Judge Baker Guidance Center of Boston was established in 1917 under Healy's directorship to assist delinquent youths.

- The Phipps Clinic in Baltimore was founded in 1913 and was headed by Adolph Meyers to provide outpatient treatment for youngsters. At this clinic, Watson carried out his study of fear conditioning in Little Albert.

- In 1937, a special adolescent unit was established at Bellevue Hospital in New York, setting the standard for inpatient child care.

- After World War II, inpatient care for children was expanded to a number of hospitals. Establishment of these inpatient facilities was spurred by an outbreak of encephalitis lethargia which resulted in a number of behavioral disorders among infected children.

The growth of the Child Guidance Clinics seemed to terminate around mid-century. Kanner (1962a) reported that a minimum of 500 centers were functioning in 1930; a 1960 survey (Freedman, Kaplan, & Sadock, 1976) identified fewer than 300 clinics. Perhaps, the clinics attempted to do too much and failed in their own and others' expectations. Clearly, the Vocational Guidance Centers were negatively influenced by the Depression. Also, the clinics may have become places for dumping the unwanted and profoundly disturbed children of a community. The movement could also have been curbed by shocking exposees such as that of the President's Committee on Mental Health in 1960 which documented extremely dehumanizing conditions in a number of residential treatment institutions (Hewitt & Forness, 1977). Nevertheless, there is little doubt that history will credit the early Child Guidance Clinic Movement for providing leadership in the care and treatment of the whole child from a perspective that acknowledges that the child thinks and feels in ways different from adults.

Today, the Child Clinic Movement has been subsumed in some respects into larger enterprises such as the growth of Community Mental Health Centers which appeared after 1963 and which continue to the present day.

Individual Differences and Education

The relationship between cognitive and emotional functioning continued to perplex the child experts. Beginning in the 1890's, Alfred Binet, working in Paris, became concerned with ways of assessing the intellectual level of children thought to be retarded or slow learners. At the urging of the Minister of Public Instruction, Binet along with Simon, a French Psychiatrist, assembled a test consisting of 30 tasks ranging from the ability to follow a moving, lighted match to naming of simple objects, repeating sentences, arranging objects by weight, and using three words in a sentence. The test also required the child to complete simple arithmetic problems and to define abstract words such as "character" and "reputation." The first version of the Binet test appeared in 1905 and was subsequently revised in 1908. Using the test, Binet was able to differentiate between "bright" and "dull" children in about one hour per child. The Binet method proved to be more economical, efficient, and objective than previous methods used to assess intellectual development. The scale was introduced into the U.S. in 1910 by Goddard who was at that time administrating the Vineland Training School for the retarded in New Jersey. Soon thereafter, Louis Terman of Stanford University developed an Americanized version of Binet's scale. This test became available for widespread use in 1916 and is known as the Stanford-Binet Intelligence Test. The test was useful for children as young as 3 years and extended through adulthood. The publication of the Stanford-Binet and other tests of intelligence spurred much research on intelligence because the tests promised objectivity and the potential for studying facets of the child's intellectual growth and adaptation to the environment.

Out of the recognition of individual differences in intelligence, a movement for individualized instruction grew. John Dewey stressed that children learn through self-discovery and urged that educational curriculum be organized to allow children to learn through the method of self-discovery. Further, many states enacted legislation to promote the education of the retarded and other handicapped individuals. In Europe a movement known as Heidpadagojik arose, the intent of which was to make teachers aware of the problems and feelings of their pupils. The relationship between school and family was also recognized. In the 1920's, a Visiting Teacher Program was initiated in which 205 teachers in 34 states visited homes to secure school-family cooperation (Kanner, 1962a).

With the recognition that the proper education of a child requires an understanding of child psychology, the Child Guidance Movement, which was weakened in the Depression, was renewed within the schools. School counselors served largely an educational/vocational role in the 1930's and 1940's. Their function of guiding adolescents toward wise career choices was expanded after the 1950 launching of Sputnik. Mention of elementary school counselors began in the 1940's, but it was not until the 1960's that many counselors were trained and placed in the elementary schools. With rapid technological changes occurring in our society, school counselors have become less concerned with matching jobs and student personalities. Counselors' and school social workers' roles have now expanded to include consulting with teachers and parents, coordinating services, and counseling with students (Dimick & Huff, 1970). They increasingly find themselves needing to know about patterns of child maladjustment and methods of short-term treatment.

SUMMARY

We have seen that in earlier times, infanticide and cruel treatment of children were common. We have come to understand that childhood is a special state. Exploitation of children has diminished. Humane treatment and education have greatly expanded. Yet, we also know that the child in today's technological age has few meaningful roles to play and has the stress of rapid change to adapt to. How much has the child's lot improved?

The development of the concept of childhood, shifts in economic, political, and social institutions; and the evolution of protective services to children have all helped to place an emphasis on children in our society. The treatment of children is part of the larger human service system. Early concepts of treatment involved physical abuse and neglect. Only within the last hundred years have we developed scientific explanations of child maladjustment. By the 1950's, countless theories of child therapy evolved, but few are well-documented, and some are not based upon sound developmental principles. Yet, "in the midst of wrangling over what is or is not valued therapy or good therapy or properly trained and functioning therapists, the reforms of Dorothea Dix and

those who came before and after her seem at times to melt away in the face of continuing wasting away of countless mentally ill in poorly-equipped and badly-cared for
mental hospitals and other facilities" (Howells, 1975, p. 467). The need for sound
therapeutic techniques still exists despite our increased understanding of children.

In subsequent chapters, we will present evidence about etiological factors associated with specific syndromes, and you will learn of the complexity of these causative
agents. Some practitioners suggest a singular treatment approach for all kinds of
childhood disorders. It is important to ask whether these holistic approaches will hold
up to the test of time. When etiology is oversimplified, the suggested treatment that
follows may look sublimely logical but be harmful to children by not recognizing the
vicissitudes of forces impinging upon their lives.

In order to understand the complexity of forces acting upon children, we now look
at some of the findings from the field of developmental psychology that are of practical
relevance to the practitioner. Later we will address the means of treating and re-
searching childhood disorders.

CHAPTER 3

RELEVANT DEVELOPMENTAL ISSUES

At one time it was believed that children reacted passively to events around them. Today we know differently. The infant from birth brings with it a large variety of modes of functioning. These include reflexes and other motoric responses, sensory thresholds, perceptual abilities, and affective and cognitive response styles that enable the very young child to actively approach, avoid, select, and organize the stimulation around it. These same modes of functioning permit the child to act upon the environment. At birth the infant's responses are innately determined, but these are quickly altered through experience and learning.

This chapter overviews the developmental issues of relevance to child theory and practice from birth through adolescence. One chapter is not enough to communicate in detail all aspects of child development, so the processes deemed essential for the child therapist will be discussed. Other developmental processes will be discussed to clarify or facilitate insight into childhood maladjustment and treatment approaches.

Early in the 1900's, it became apparent it was necessary to understand normal development and process before one could identify and treat maladjustment patterns. Child specialists once thought that after we identified normal developmental sequences, we would clearly understand the abnormal sequence. This has proven to be not true. The literature on developmental therapy is, for the most part, separate from writings on child psychopathology and child clinical practice. This is an unfortunate circumstance. Children with behavioral problems can be better served by therapists who have expertise in developmental therapy and who can translate research literature about children to the practical problem of treating children with problems.

DEVELOPMENTAL THEORY

Developmental theorists study how individuals change across time. Like other theorists, their work is rooted in the scientific study of behavior and seeks to understand a wide variety of questions concerning how the person changes from conception to death. The developmental theorists should be concerned with every aspect of development.

For the sake of convenience, we can summarize the activities of developmental theorists into three broad categories. The first of these has to do with the study of physical processes which include body changes and motor development. At one time, this area constituted a very active focus of study, and as a consequence we know much about the milestones of motor development in infants and children. The second category is cognitive and language development. This is an extremely important area in the study of child behavior, and we will have much to say about this in a later section of this chapter. This category includes all the mental processes that are used to gain knowledge or to become aware of the environment, such as perception, imagination, memory, judgment, morals, thinking, and, of course, language. The final category is that of psychosocial development. This area focuses upon personality and social development. Of particular interest here is the impact on the child of the parents and family members. Also of interest is the role that other individuals such as peers and teachers have on the child.

Although the work of developmental theorists may seem fragmented because, for example, they focus on the acquisition of a particular speech form by children of a certain age or on father-child relationships, there is agreement that development is holistic and that the child cannot be understood just from the examination of any single perspective. This is an important concept to understand since it implies that childhood behavioral maladjustments can be understood only when the total child and her or his environment is considered.

At one time some developmental psychologists emphasized the inborn capacities and limitations of each person. This focus on "nature" or hereditary aspects contrasted with other psychologists who emphasized the importance of "nurture" or environmental factors, such as the influence of family, school, neighborhood, and culture on the child. This continuing debate over whether inherited or acquired traits are greater determinants of human behavior is called the nature-nurture controversy.

Most theorists today agree that both nature and nurture are essential to development and that the interaction between them is of crucial importance to the development of any individual. For example, most theorists believe that intelligence is determined by the interplay of heredity and such aspects of the social and physical environment as schooling and nutrition. Despite this usual acknowledgment of the interaction of nature and nurture on setting the limits of intelligence, some psychologists such as Arthur Jensen (1969) maintain that one's genes are more important in determining intelligence than is one's environment. We are all acquainted with the heated debate that Jensen has created since he initially espoused his ideas in 1969 in the context of whether head start programs could elevate the school performance of black children.

Another area where we have seen the appearance of the nature-nurture controversy is in whether mental illness is genetically or environmentally determined. It is generally conceded today that some people are born with a predisposition toward schizophrenia or manic-depression. Evidence of the genetic predisposition to mental illness comes from studies of monozygotic twins (Cohen, Allen, Pollin, & Hrubec, 1972; Gottesman & Shields, 1972). If one twin becomes schizophrenic or manic-depressive, chances are (estimates range from 20 to 80 %) that the other twin will have serious psychological problems too. On the other hand, the likelihood of dizygotic twins both becoming schizophrenic or manic-depressive is much lower than with monozygotic twins. In many cases, however, one idential twin is schizophrenic and the other is not mentally ill. Since monozygotic twins have identical genes and usually very similar environments, some specific, if hidden, environmental circumstances must have a large impact. The usual conclusion drawn from these studies is that genes make some people more vulnerable to mental illness than others, but personal experiences determine whether a person actually becomes mentally ill or not.

Another distinction that merits attention here is the one between maturation and learning. Maturation results from the aging process, while learning is produced by experience. Specifically, maturation is a series of autonomous internal processes that results from biochemical information transmitted via the individual's genes. The genetic mechanisms that control maturation determine the traits that typify a species and the sequence in which those traits emerge. Maturational effects are most clearly seen during childhood in the unfolding of motor abilities. Table 3.1 presents age norms for various motor skills. As can be seen from the Table, by about age 24 months, most children have mastered the essential motor skills that are required for effective functioning. The point that requires emphasizing is that maturation determines the sequence with which particular skills will appear, and this sequence usually is invariant. Thus, earlier skill development in a sequence is essential to the development of later skills (e.g., crawling usually precedes walking in infants).

Learning, in contrast, refers to changes within the individual that occur because of specific experiences. Some learning experiences are obvious, for example, observing a child acquire the skill of reading with the help of a teacher who promises a gold star for good performance. Other examples of learning are less obvious as in the efforts of an infant to walk by imitating others for the purpose of obtaining a bright shiny object that cannot be reached by crawling. The essential thing to remember here is that learning requires experience with a problem, a teacher or model, and some degree of practice. Further, learning and maturation interact to determine when a learned response will first be observed in a child. Assisting a child to walk, although important, will not facilitate walking until the child is maturationally "ready" to walk, which requires that the child possess the muscular strength and coordination to put together all of the movements required in walking.

At one time theorists argued over which was more important--maturation or learning. As with the nature vs. nurture controversy, it is now generally conceded that both maturation and learning interact in development. The critical thing to note is that for a

Table 3.1

Age Norms (In Months) for Motor Skills

Skill	When 50 % of all Babies Master the Skill (in Months)	When 90 % of all Babies Master the Skill (in Months)
Lifts head 90 Degrees when lying on stomach	2.4	4.9
Rolls over	2.8	4.7
Sits propped up (head steady)	2.9	4.2
Sits without support	5.5	7.8
Stands holding on	5.8	10.0
Walks holding on	9.2	12.7
Stands momentarily	9.8	13.0
Stands alone well	11.5	13.9
Walks well	12.1	14.3
Walks backward	14.3	21.5
Walks up steps	17.0	22.0
Kicks ball forward	20.0	24.0

Source: From the Denver Developmental Screening Test
(Frankenberg & Dodds, 1970)

therapist to be effective in understanding child behavior, he or she must have knowledge of both the genetic/maturational factors and the environmental/learning aspects of development. Both components interact to determine whether a child's behavior is appropriate for her or his age group. Further, the way in which treatment is oriented for children must take maturational/learning factors into consideration. This point will become clearer later when we discuss the topics of cognitive and language development.

IMPLICATIONS OF CHILD DEVELOPMENT FOR PRACTICE

Anyone who works with children is aware of the importance of a developmental framework. A child may express one set of symptoms at one stage of development and entirely different symptoms at another developmental level. For example, at age five, an anxious child may experience night terrors; if the source of anxiety is not removed, the same child at age thirteen may employ runaway behavior as a means of dealing with stress. Because of a child's biological disposition, personal stress may be greater at one developmental level than another. Thus, learning to walk may create significant stress for a frail child. Similarly, learning to keep a bed dry may create difficulties for other children with poor bladder control, especially if they sleep deeply and do not awaken easily. It is not clear if there are upper time bounds, that is "critical periods" for the development of skills so that if appropriate stimulus conditions are not provided within that time frame, the skill will never evolve. Perhaps there are critical periods for the acquisition of some skills (such as language) and not others (such as learning to swim). There do appear to be lower limits determined by central nervous system maturation for the age appearance of each skill. Thus, no amount of verbal stimulation leads to speech within the first half year of life. The early verbal stimulation plays a role in preparing the ground for later language acquisition, but the acquisition must await neurological development (Lenneberg, 1967).

Thus, syndromes of child maladjustment are shaped by the age and stage of the child and the equilibrium between the child's growing needs and the environmental potential for satisfaction of these needs. The effective child therapist must keep in mind an understanding of the major stages in language, cognitive, and social development. It is essential that the therapist keep note of the restrictions imposed by age on the child in each of these realms. Knowing these limitations the therapist can be more effective in intervening with children and families.

LANGUAGE DEVELOPMENT

During the early years following infancy, all normal children, and even many youngsters with below normal intelligence, master the language spoken around them. One might infer that language is a simple system, or pattern of elements, and one that is easily analyzed and explained. In fact, on examination, language proves highly complex, indeed so intricate that the area of language acquisition has begun to generate much interest among developmental theorists. Still, we know relatively little about the acquisition of language and how communication develops as accurately and as completely as it does in children.

Vocalization

Let us begin with the question of how language is learned by children. Children normally do not begin to speak meaningfully until after the first year of life, but such real speech is preceded by various forms of vocalization and reaction to vocalization in others. For example, Trevarthen (1977) found that a nine-week-old baby boy made small cooing sounds in response to his mother's repeated, rhythmic baby-talk questions. The baby responds to the sound of the human voice, and the adult treats the baby's cooings and babblings as meaningful responses. That hearing speech stimulates the baby is shown by the fact that deaf infants stop babbling at about six months of age; whereas, hearing infants continue to diversify their babbling experimentation (Lenneberg, 1967).

The content of children's vocalization changes rapidly during infancy. For the first two or three months of life, cries and grunts predominate. Then, at about three months, cooing begins. Whereas crying involves little more than the blowing of air along the vocal tract by the infant, cooing is sound produced by the articulatory organs, mainly the tongue. Infant cooing sometimes sounds "vowel-like" but differs from adult vowel production both functionally and acoustically. Social babbling develops after cooing and often sounds like an effort to communicate in a foreign language. Some observers have noted that babbling in infants appears to follow the intonation patterns of adult speech involving the use of questions and declarative statements (Miller & Ervin, 1970). Others have shown that infants in their babbling imitate the pitch, loudness, and intonation of adults (Weir, 1972). While babbling probably plays some role in later speech, the course of development between babbling and more sophisticated language does not appear to be direct. Baby's first words are usually made up of the sounds they babble most, and some children continue to babble for several months after they begin to produce real speech.

During the cooing and babbling stage, the infant makes many more sounds than he or she will actually use in the production of later language. Some sounds drop out as one's "native language" is acquired. At the same time, though, single sounds are transformed into groups called phonemes, which are the raw materials from which all later speech will be composed. In a general way, phonemes correspond to the usual vowel and consonant sounds of a language. The letter *b,* for example, is pronounced somewhat differently in *bat* than in *tab.* That the infant recognizes the sound *b* in both words is part of the competence of the child speaker as well as listener and is important in the acquisition in language.

Newborn babies can distinguish between sounds such as *ba* and *ga; r* and *l;* and *p, b, d,* and *t.* They can also discriminate among vowel sounds (Eimas, 1974, 1975; Trehub & Rabinovitch, 1972; Trehub, 1973). The first consonant-type sounds a baby makes are usually those that are produced in the back of the mouth, such as *k* or *g.* Conversely, the first vowel-type sounds, such as *o* or *u,* are produced in the front of the mouth (Kaplan & Kaplan, 1971). In their babblings, babies are able to produce the sounds of all languages.

In addition to the development of phonemes, the child must learn the relationship of language to meaning which is called semantics, as well as the rules to follow in producing permissable constructions which is called grammar. The study of grammar is divided into two parts—syntax and morphology. Syntax concerns itself with how words are combined into phrases and sentences, while morphology examines the formation of words themselves. A child who has mastered the semantics and the grammar of a particular language then reflects her or his linguistic competence in that language.

Communication

The ability to communicate, however, entails more than just linguistic competence. Appropriate communication entails knowing what to say as well as how and when to say it and thus demands that the speaker be sensitive to the person(s) to whom he or she is communicating as well as to the context in which the communication occurs. In recent years, the study of language acquisition has shown us that linguistic competence is achieved fairly early in the development of the child, whereas the broader ability to communicate effectively continues to develop well into adolescence.

Sentence Development

The first word that children almost everywhere produce sounds very much like *mama,* and it is believed that *mama* appears in so many diverse languages because it is derived from the natural nasal-like murmur that infants make when sucking (mmmh-ah). The single word *mama* is usually learned by infants by about the age of nine months. Shortly thereafter the infant begins to acquire a variety of other single words usually grouped into three categories. These categories include single words for animals, foods, and toys. So rapid is the acquisition of words by the child that by the age of 24 months, the vocabulary has multiplied 200 to 300 times so that by two years the child usually has a vocabulary of approximately 250 to 300 words.

By the age of 18 months or so, most children are producing dozens of words, usually spoken one by one. At various moments young speakers will be heard uttering such recognizable sounds as "doggie," "cookie," " come," "more," "no," etc. These brief utterances are called holophrases to indicate that the child's single word may be referring to something beyond the usual delimited meaning of the single word.   In saying "mama," a child might simply be naming the mother, or may be asking that the mother come closer, or that he or she wants milk given to her or him by the mother, or that he or she desires to be changed. In other words, holophrases can be interpreted in many ways, each of which can be meaningful both to the child and to the listener.

Within a few months after uttering her or his first meaningful one word sentence, the child will begin to produce pairs of words that make some type of statement. Careful observation has shown that the transition from two one-word sentences to a functional two-word sentence is a gradual one. After beginning to use a few single words, the child will string them together, pausing between each. Then, the location of the pause will gradually change so that the child will begin saying "baby" and "chair" together but will soon combine them to form a two-word sentence "baby chair" (Bloom, 1973).

Once children begin to produce two-word sentences, their use expands at a very rapid rate. It is as if children suddenly discover the power to express an almost un-limited set of ideas and cannot resist doing so. One case study has shown that more than 1,000 new and distinct two-word utterances per month appear during this phase of development (Braine, 1976). Brown (1973) has also pointed out that by the age of 36 months some children are so advanced in the construction process of their language that they are able to produce all the major varieties of English simple sentences up to a length of 10 or 11 words.

The Child's First Conversations

Although children communicate their assertions and requests from a very early age, there is an unmistakable one-sidedness to these communications. It is not until the age of two or so that real interchange, the beginnings of conversation, emerges. The child's first experience with language interactions comes through her or his association with parents. As soon as children begin to talk at all, parents seem to promote the idea of taking conversational turns and alternating the role of speaker and listener. Parents usually require the infant to produce words in communicating with them once the child has begun to acquire a vocabulary. Further, in teaching conversational skills, parents often model both sides of a dialogue so that their children can learn through observation how conversation should take place (Ervin-Tripp, 1973). For example, parents may model the child's role as well as their own in an effort to teach turntaking, creating such dialogues as:

Parent: What's the doggie doing?
Child: The doggie is eating.

By this means, the child begins to acquire turn-taking skills and learns that conversation proceeds in alternating between speaking and listening.

Child/Adult Communication

Anyone who has ever tried to talk to a young child conversationally knows very well that one cannot speak to a child as one does to an adult. One problem is simply getting the child's attention. Adults use a variety of devices for this purpose, such as using the child's name at the beginning of a sentence ("Johnny, look at the horse."), using exclamations (such as, "Hey, Johnny!"), repeating portions of what they have said in order to capture and hold the child's attention (for example, "Yes, horsey!"), or looking or pointing at the objects they are talking about (Snow, 1972).

Adults also simplify their speech in various ways when talking to young children (Snow, 1972). Articles and possessives are frequently omitted so that these words occur least frequently when adults talk to 2-year-olds, more frequently when they talk to 10-year-olds, and most frequently when talking to other adults. Adults also avoid pronouns when talking to young children, repeating the relevant noun instead. For example, an adult might not say, "See the boy. He is riding the horse." Instead, an adult might say to a young child, "See the boy. The boy is riding the horse." Presumably, these devices make it easier to understand what is being said.

By the time children reach the age of five or so, their conversational competence is impressive and is similar in many respects to communication among adults. Most major grammatical forms have appeared, and the child already possesses an adequate vocabulary. However, the child's language is rather egocentric and remarkably concrete.

In one of his early studies, Piaget (1926) asked children to teach other youngsters how to use mechanical devices, such as a syringe. Children under six years of age did very poorly at instructing others. They were unable to see the problem from the listener's point of view. The children used vague gestures and pronouns such as "this," "something," "here," or "there." This experimental arrangement has been repeated by Glucksberg, Krauss, and Higgins (1975). These researchers found that children between the ages of four and five years were unsuccessful in describing a series of squiggled lines to other children. Often these 4- and 5-year-olds would give idiosyncratic names to or neglect important details of the squiggled lines. It appears these 4- and 5-year-olds are egocentric; that is, they are locked into their own perspective, unable to assume the point of view of someone else, and unable to find out what the other already knows and needs to know. Accordingly, they communicate with difficulty. Not having the sense of what the other child knows, they oscillate between providing unnecessary information and failing to provide crucial information. It is as if they were always entering the conversation in the middle, not sure of what has been said or what needs to be said, or of what could not possibly be understood. On the other hand, 7- to 8-year-olds are capable of taking the position of another child, communicating with precision, acting flexibly to clarify a point, and recognizing the important features of both the speaker's and the listener's roles. These older children are able to suppress their own point of view and adopt instead the perspective of others for the purposes of effective communication.

Thought and Language

How are thought and language related? Does the child first get an idea and then try to find words to express it? Or does a child's language ability enable the child to think new thoughts? Are 6-year-olds more likely to know what they mean than how to say it? Do they talk to themselves in order to figure out what they think? Piaget believes that cognitive development precedes language. In other words, cognition makes language development possible. As support for his thesis, Piaget (1974) asked children to crawl and then to describe what they did. Even the 3-year-olds in his study could crawl without hesitation, but it is not until age five or six that the children could describe what they did when they crawled. Most of them mistakenly said they moved both hands together and then both knees, or the right hand with the right foot and then the left hand with the left foot. Even adults sometimes have difficulty with this task. Piaget argues that having the necessary motor skills and vocabulary does not mean a child has the necessary cognitive ability to understand and explain what he or she has done.

Piaget's position can be contrasted with that of Whorf (1956) and Sapir (1921). Both Whorf and Sapir argued that an individual's experience in language shaped one's thoughts. According to Whorf and Sapir, each culture has a unique world view that is transmitted from generation to generation through the medium of language. For example, Eskimos have a number of words describing various states of snow and ice that denote distinctions in quality that English-speaking individuals might not make. According to the Whorf-Sapir hypothesis, one's way of thinking reflects the structure and vocabulary of one's language. If this hypothesis is correct, children should begin to reason very differently once they have begun to talk. Moreover, since the world's languages differ markedly in many ways, children in one culture should begin to think differently from those in remote and linguistically distinct cultures Overall, little evidence to substantiates either this distinct form of thinking across cultures, or the Whorf-Sapir hypothesis.

Another contrasting position from that of Piaget is reflected in the work of Bruner (1964) who believes that by kindergarten, language ability affects almost every aspect of a child's thought and behavior to the extent that language becomes a means not only for representing experience but also for transforming it. In this view, Bruner is similar to the Russian psychologist Lev Vygotsky (1962). Vygotsky holds that the beginning of symbolic thinking which occurs at about age two is largely interrelated with language development so that they mutually influence each other in their development.

Both Bruner and Vygotsky argue that at some point during early childhood language helps form ideas. Although there is no definitive answer to which position is correct, it is clear that both language development and cognitive development are essential in our understanding of child development.

Implications of Language Development for Practice

Our review of language development has pointed out that the ability to speak is integrally related to the ability to understand. Therefore, the child practitioner must always be very cognizant of the child's linguistic abilities. The therapist, in working with young children, must obviously keep in mind the child's limitations in language development. Young children are able to comprehend more language than they are able to produce. Further, they have not mastered all of the adult conventions of social speech such as turntaking. They may have difficulty in describing sequences of events, how they feel, what they think, or in completely understanding what is being asked of them by adults, especially strangers. Given these limitations though, therapists can work effectively with young children if communicative demands are not excessive and if the therapists are oriented to the developmental level of the child.

COGNITIVE DEVELOPMENT

Due largely to the ground breaking work of the Swiss psychologist Jean Piaget (1976) and his colleagues, we now know much about the development of cognition in children. According to Piaget, adult intelligence is qualitatively different from that of a child, but all levels of intelligence are defined in terms of "adaptive thinking and action." Children arrive at the adult stage by passing through the four major stages of conceptualization. These are the sensorimotor, preoperational, concrete operational, and formal operational stages. Piaget holds that the ages at which individuals attain the various stages are somewhat variable and depend on environmental influences, but that the sequence of development is always the same. Thus, the formal operational stage can be attained only if a child has progressed first through the sensorimotor, the preoperational, and the concrete operational stages and only in this order. This process begins in infancy with the processing of sensorimotor information and progresses to the formal operational stage, typically attained by mid-adolescence.

A large and growing body of research tends to support the Piagetian view that the sequence of cognitive development is universal. Although not every person may attain the highest stage, individuals of every culture and background pass through the same stages. It is important to know a little about each of these stages since they do set limitations on therapeutic work with children. Accordingly, each stage will be described in more detail.

Jean Piaget
(Photo by C. Brulhart, with permission)

Sensorimotor Stage

In the early stages of infancy, behavior occurs as though the world were perceived as a continuous moving and changing series of objects and events. Young infants appear not to perceive permanence in objects. They behave as though they believe that objects disappearing from their sight no longer exist. The maxim "out of sight, out of mind" appears to be literally true for infants. They can be engrossed in playing with a toy or a person; then, when that object disappears from sight, they behave as though it no longer exists. This behavior begins to change during the closing months of the first year. At this point, infants cry when left by their mothers. One of the major cognitive achievements of the sensorimotor period is the establishment of object permanence which is the ability to be aware of the existence of objects even when they are not within sight or within a range where they can be touched, smelled, tasted, or heard. Another major cognitive achievement during the sensorimotor period is the acquisition of a notion of causality. During this period, infants begin to note the results of their actions and to anticipate certain results before they occur. For example, infants learn to play and to get attention by throwing their toys out of their crib. When they knock a toy out of the crib, they may look to the floor in anticipation that it will fall, and they may also anticipate an adult's reaction of picking up the toy and returning it. Spatial concepts are also established during this period as infants learn how to gain access to every part of their home.

During the first two years of life, infants make remarkable progress in their thinking about the world. Their concepts develop from perceiving the world only in terms of immediate sensorimotor experience to gaining a notion of object permanence, causality, and space. Although infants in their first years of life do not acquire the ability to clearly represent the world internally, Piaget feels that the sensorimotor stage is significant because infants construct all of the cognitive substructures that will serve as a point of departure for the development of perception and thinking. During this stage, there is a continuous progression from spontaneous movements and natural reflexes to acquired habits and to behavior clearly reflecting intelligence. Thus, adaptive thinking, which is the basis for adult intelligence, has its foundation in the earliest years.

Piaget (1976) presents evidence for two forms of cognitive adaptation during the early stages of infancy: accommodation and assimilation. By accommodation, Piaget means the infant's ability to adapt to external stimuli rather than to respond mechanically to these stimuli. By assimilation is meant the integration of stimuli into the infant's existing cognitive structures. In the case of an infant, accommodation is a motor activity involving a shaping of a new behavior; in the case of an 8-year-old, the accommodation is conceptual. Thus, children must accommodate their former concepts of, for example, sugar to include the concept of sugar in a dissolved state in order to understand, or assimilate, what actually occurs when sugar is dissolved in water. A younger child, who is not able to accommodate the concept of sugar in this manner, believes that the sugar disappears.

Other behaviors that emerge during the final months of the sensorimotor stage are deferred imitation and complete object permanence. Children can now imitate a behavior hours or days after they have observed it, and they have also formed a mental image of an object so they can follow it through a series of complex displacements even if they cannot see it. Thus, infants during the latter part of the sensorimotor stage are no longer fooled when objects are hidden from their sight. They no longer look for them in the place where they were last seen, but rather trace the movement of the objects and look in new locations where they believe them to be.

The Preoperational Stage

Between the ages of about two and six, children develop the ability to use symbols. Language development is a significant component of this stage, and there is also the emergence of symbolic play, dreaming, and deferred imitation. Mastery of symbolic function means that children are able, by themselves, to produce abstract representations. Symbolic function is evident when children are able to imagine that the kitchen table is a tent in the woods, when they have dreams and nightmares, and when they are able to imitate Superman several hours or days after they have seen their hero on television.

Once children become capable of symbolic thought, they learn to use thousands of words, as well as many objects and gestures, to represent ideas, actions, and things. It then becomes easier for them to remember the past, imagine the future, and deal with the present. During this period of cognitive development, creative play is a favorite activity of the child's. Children are now old enough to pretend but are not able to distinguish fantasy from reality very well. Imagination becomes more apparent with each passing year. Whereas the 1-year-old might play with a cup and saucer as two independent objects, the 2-year-old might place the cup on the saucer and pretend to drink, and the 3-year-old transforms the cup and saucer into almost anything. For this child, the cup and the saucer could just as easily become a race car, a space ship, or a house. By the end of the preoperational period, at approximately age six, the imaginary objects can be invisible, existing solely in the child's mind.

Another consequence of preoperational thinking is that children during this period have trouble understanding cause and effect, partly because they center on one aspect of an event rather than on the relationship between events. As a result, a child who falls down might blame the sidewalk, while another child might blame a child nearby but not close enough to have caused the fall. Because children during this period do not understand chance, they sometimes interpret the phrase, "It was an accident," to mean "Don't blame me." Thus, a child might very well hit her younger brother deliberately and then protest, "It was an accident." Parents who understand the cognitive characteristics of children during this period will realize that the child who deliberately hits a brother is not lying when saying that it was an accident.

Another interesting phenomenon to consider during this period is the child's thought processes that reflect egocentrism. By egocentrism, we mean that the child's ideas about the world are restricted by the her or his own narrow point of view. This means only that the child is naturally self-centered, not that the child is selfish. Egocentrism appears in different forms at various ages. During early childhood, for example, it is expressed in the child's difficulty imagining what it would be like to be someone else. Children assume that everyone reacts to the world as they themselves do. Children's descriptions of natural phenomena often show egocentric thought, as when preschool children declare that it has snowed so that they can make a snowman or that the grass grows so that they will not hurt themselves when they fall.

Children's egocentrism makes many young children think that everything in the world is alive, just as they are. This view is referred to by developmental psychologists as animism. Animistic children might bump into a table and then punish the table for hitting them, or when they drop a stuffed toy, they might begin to cry because they think they have hurt the toy. Similarly, the child during this period might ask questions such as, "Why does the radio talk so loud?" Other children might egocentrically reason that because they themselves make many things from blocks, sand, sticks, and the like, everything living, including themselves, is made in a similar fashion. Children whose thinking is influenced by this artificialism might try to manufacture a toy out of sticks, a puppy out of mud, or might imagine God creating the world by building a fire to make the sun. Both animism and artificialism seem amusing to older children and parents who prefer scientific explanations of natural phenomena. However, preschool ideas probably make sense if one does not know or believe in the rules and findings of science. Indeed, many have suggested that the preoperational child's concepts are very similar to those of folktales, myths, and some forms of religion and philosophy.

The limitations of preoperational thought often make it hard for children during this period to understand death, illness, or divorce. Children often blame themselves for these events. For example, a 4-year-old boy might think he killed grandma by disobeying her, or that God made his tonsils infected because he said a bad word, or that his father and mother are separating because he soiled on the carpet. Explanations to relieve the child's anxiety should be phrased in terms the preoperational child can understand. One little girl heard that her grandmother had died of old age, so she refused to eat any cake at her own birthday party crying, "I don't want to be five; I don't want to die like grandma." In such situations, parents face less difficulty in explaining death to children when they use religious ideas of afterlife since often children more readily can accept the idea that grandma died because she was ready for heaven than to understand the more scientific facts related to the gradual deterioration involved in the aging process. Similarly, preschool children who are told that their parents are divorcing because they no longer love each other may wonder if the parents will fall out of love with them as well. It is important to explain to children in these circumstances that love between parent and child is a bond that cannot be severed by divorce or weakened by time. By about the age of six, the child's social understanding grows and egocentrism declines. Similarly, children by this age can maintain and express internal representations of objects and events. When they have reached this age, children enter what Piaget calls the period of concrete operations.

Concrete Operations

It is during this stage that children begin to form notions of class, relations, and number. While preoperational children can use the language symbol *doggie* to stand for a specific dog, *Angel,* they also use the word *doggie* interchangeably with the dog's name to identify all other dogs and perhaps bears, foxes, and wolves. In other words, they cannot distinguish between using *doggie* for a single member of a class and for the class as a whole. Between the ages of 6 or 7 and 11 or 12, children emerge into "the age of reason" inasmuch as they develop the ability to internalize actions and to reason in an elementary fashion. They can deal with classes and can manipulate them in a manner analogous to elementary arithmetical operations. In this way, they understand that apples and oranges are part of the broader class of fruit and that boys and girls fit within the logical class children. Furthermore, they can reason that when boys are removed from the category of children what is left is girls. During this period, children become able to deal with the concept of time and can learn to read the clock and to understand historical time. Reasoning is internalized so that children can work out problems in their heads rather than attempting to solve them in the trial and error fashion that characterizes the preoperational stage. During the period of concrete operations, children become aware of constancies in their environment and recognize them as such, even in the face of seemingly contradictory perceptual evidence. One of the best examples of this phenomena is the conservation of quantity. Piaget believes that most children under 7 years old do not fully understand that when liquid from beaker B is poured into a narrower beaker, A, or a wider one, C, the amount of liquid remains the same. However, by the time children are seven or eight and have attained concrete operations, they know the amount of liquid is conserved. They will explain that even though the column of liquid is higher in beaker A than beaker C, this is made up for by the fact that it is also narrower. Moreover, the child will note that the amount remains the same, because the transformation of shape can be reversed by pouring the liquid back into the original beaker, B. Piaget holds that the ability of the child to conserve reflects the development of a new system of coordinated mental operations. With increasing age and experience, these operations are generalized to a wide variety of situations.

The development of concrete operations also affects the child's social relations and moral judgments. In studying children's understanding of games with rules, Piaget found that before the age of about seven, children tend to regard such rules as sacred, untouchable, and of "transcendent origin." Older children, on the contrary, regard rules as a result of agreement among contemporaries and accept the idea that rules can be changed by means of a democratically arrived at consensus. At this earlier age, children also have a touching faith in the potency of words. Many playground fights are justified with the assertion, "He called me a name." The fighting potential of particular insults depends more on local custom than literal meaning. For example, when a normally well-behaved boy suddenly attacked another boy in the classroom, and when the teacher told him he should know better, he explained, "He said my mother wears combat boots, and you know I couldn't let him get away with that." As children grow older, they realize that they can combat words with words. They are likely to answer an insult with another insult rather than with a blow. If a younger or less articulate child begins to get the worst of a verbal duel, he or she often resorts to physical fighting or responds with, "Sticks and stones may break my bones, but names can never hurt me." This is a defense that makes the victim feel better and exasperates the attacker, proving again the power of words.

Formal Operational Thought

Progression from concrete to formal operations occurs during early adolescence (between ages 11 or 12 and 15). Before adolescence, the child has an earthbound, concrete, practical-minded sort of problem solving approach. In the period of formal operations, the adolescent is able to reason with logical propositions as well as with concrete objects. Further, adolescents are able to speculate, hypothesize, and fantasize much more readily and on a much grander scale than children who are still tied to concrete operational thinking. By the end of adolescence, many young people can understand and create general principles or formal rules to explain many aspects of human experience. Consequently, Piaget calls the last stage of cognitive development, attained at about age 15, formal operational thought. This is the stage at which the adolescent begins to build systems or theories, in the largest sense of the term, about literature, philosophy, morality, love, and the world at work (Inhelder & Piaget, 1958).

Formal operations enable one to use "hypothetico-deductive," or formal, reasoning. Faced with a problem, one can now think through all of the logical combinations of factors that might account for a situation, deduce the consequences of each of these possible hypotheses, and then test to see which is correct. Acquiring formal operations also enables one to think at a new and higher level about such topics as social justice, beauty, or philosophy. Piaget believes that these new powers of reasoning often lead adolescents to engage in speculation about hypothetical, political, or social systems, or to develop strong emotional commitment to abstract ideals.

In addition to having the ability to be logical and imaginative and to see the hypothetical and the possible, most adolescents demonstrate another cognitive characteristic--adolescent egocentrism. Adolescents are long past the egocentrism of the preoperational thought typical of preschool children, who assume that everyone thinks the same way they themselves do, and that the world and all of its wonders are put on earth for them to enjoy. By adolescence, young people know quite well that others can have different opinions, and they also know that their personal existence is largely irrelevant to the forces of nature. They are fully aware, for instance, that it does not rain because they forgot their umbrella, even though they may curse the heavens instead of themselves. Nevertheless, the particular limits of adolescent judgment and logic make young people susceptible to egocentrism of another kind. Instead of believing the physical world centers on them, adolescents believe that the psychological universe revolves around them. That is, they believe that their unique thoughts are universally held and, at the same time, that they alone understand human experiences. It is not unusual for adolescents to inform their parents or other adults that they alone know what it is to be in love, to hate someone, or to be fearful of something.

Often, adolescents also create for themselves an imaginary audience as they fantasize how others will react to their appearance and behavior. Although adolescent boys and girls know that other people are not usually thinking the same things about them as they themselves are thinking, they sometimes have trouble realizing that they may not be the center of others' thoughts and concerns. For instance, adolescents often are so preoccupied with their physical appearance that they assume that everyone else judges the final result. Anticipation of a favorable judgment can cause teenagers to enter a crowded room with the air of regarding themselves as the most attractive and admired human beings alive. On the other hand, sometimes something as trivial as a pimple on the chin can make them wish that they could enter the room invisibly. It often takes several years before this egocentrism declines and the individual can walk into a crowded room without the look of one who thinks he or she owns the world or the fearfulness of one who imagines contempt in every gaze.

Elkind (1974) has suggested that sometimes egocentrism can lead from the possible into the impossible. One example that Elkind gives is the foundling fantasy. In the foundling fantasy, the young people imagine that they are the offspring not of their actual parents, but of much wiser and more beautiful people who were forced to give them up in infancy. Many fix their attention on any of their physical characteristics that their parents do not have and decide that adoption is the most plausible explanation for the discrepancy. Another example is the personal fable through which adolescents imagine their own lives as heroic or even mythical. They see themselves destined for great fame and fortune, discovering the cure for some disease such as cancer, or authoring a masterpiece. Thus, adolescent thought processes are usually a mixture of the abilities to imagine many logical possibilities and to deny reality when it interferes with hopes and fantasies.

Implications for Cognitive Development

The child therapist needs a clear understanding of the typical processes of cognitive development in order to understand that children think differently from adults in many ways. At specific stages, they hold notions of the world that are erroneous by adult standards. It is reasonable that an infant in the sensory-motor stage holds an egocentric value orientation. At that stage, "right" is what feels good and "bad" is what hurts. Later, around age five or six years, in the preoperational stage, children can integrate some understanding of right and wrong providing it is explained very concretely. It is unreasonable to expect most children to perform formal operations, that is, sophisticated interpretation, before about age 11 or 12 years. Understanding can be facilitated within limits by using experiential approaches. Thus, insight therapy, as typically conducted with adults; will have little meaning for most children under 11 or 12 years. Experiential learning, as in play therapy, is more appropriate.

In subsequent chapters, we will present approaches to therapy that claim effectiveness in helping children gain a handle on complex, interpersonal issues. These approaches are only effective if geared to the children's cognitive developmental level. An approach that is effective at one age may be too complicated for younger children and too simple for older children. It is important to keep in mind that the young child has a limited sense of causality. It may be too much for the child to be presented with an intricate set of attributions concerning her or his role or that of her or his parents, in the difficulty they are experiencing. In short, the therapist must probe for the child's level of understanding and begin there in establishing the intervention process.

SOCIAL DEVELOPMENT

The child is expected to learn particular social skills such as using a toilet, dressing, and sharing toys at given developmental levels. The social skills differ greatly from one culture to another. Thus, toilet training begins at about six months in Japan and at about two years within most U.S. cultures. Children first learn from their parents the social skills that they must develop to get along. The quality of the relationship with the parents will affect the child's ability to learn those skills and will transfer to the child's relationships with others. By studying children in foundling homes, Ribble (1945) and Bowlby (1951) illuminated the importance of the infant's continued contact with the primary parent. Bowlby (1951) identified stages of "anaclitic depression." When infants are separated from a primary parent, they protest, then express despair, and finally (if mourning is unresolved) become detached. Detachment may be so great that the child fails to eat, to thrive, or even to survive. We now recognize that these early researchers confounded effects of separation with effects of institutionalization. However, current research supports the tenet that infants need much stimulation and affection. The quality, if not the consistency, of early parenting is critical (Freedman, Kaplan, & Sadock, 1976).

Family and Environment

In time, siblings and extended family members exert influence upon the child's social development. By school age, peer influence becomes critical. As presented in Table 3.2, Freud (1953) identified critical social developmental tasks each child must conquer and has pointed out possible psychological effects of dealing with those tasks. Also in Table 3.2, Erikson (1963) helps us see how the child's solutions to those tasks affect the child's sociability. Moreover, we can identify operational behaviors that suggest a child is entering a particular psychosocial developmental level (Freedman, Kaplan, & Sadock, 1976).

Infancy

In infancy, passive protection by significant others is not enough. Social growth requires active stimulation of the genetically-determined sequence. The handling of the infant's oral needs will serve as a promogenitor of trust with others. A mutuality needs to develop between the caregiver's way of giving and the baby's way of accepting. If feeding is unsatisfactory (for example, if the child is separated from the mother without a proper substitute or if the child is undernourished), the child may grow up with a feeling of loss, of not trusting others, or of being unloved.

Toddler

In the toddler stage, toilet training serves as a paradigm of general training practices. The child must learn self-control to accommodate to social demands. If successful, the child continues to grow with a feeling of autonomy and pride. If not, the child feels doubt and shame. Erikson (1963) tells us that there is a limit to the amount of shame one can endure. If a child feels extremely shamed, the child tends to reject those feelings and to doubt those around him.

From age two to school age, mobility is a key facet of the child's socialization. The child learns to move independently and vigorously. If efforts toward autonomy are encouraged, the child grows in initiative. If the child's independence is discouraged, or if the child feels no support when faltering, self-doubt increases. The child may vacillate between desires to individuate and to remain an infant protected by the mother (Mahler, Pine, & Bergman, 1975).

School Age

During school age, cognition can flourish. If intellectual pursuits are gratifying, the child becomes increasingly industrious. Imagination flowers; friendships build. If efforts at mastery are thwarted, the child begins to see her- or himself as inferior and to act out perceived inferior roles. Competition is expected at this age. The child learns

Table 3.2

Stage of Psychosocial Development

Age	Freud	Erikson	Target Behaviors
O-4 weeks			impassive phase
16 weeks			spontaneous smile aware of strange situation
24 weeks	oral	trust-vs-mistrust	separation anxiety
36 weeks			Stranger anxiety
40 weeks			responds to social play such as peek-a-boo
52 weeks			cooperates in dressing
12 months			
15 months			throws objects begins to choose, to refuse
18 months		autonomy-vs-shame	carries or hugs special toys
	anal		
2 years			dresses self domestic mimicry
3 years			states own sex understands taking turns
	phallic		
4 years		initiative-vs-guilt	plays cooperatively
5 years			plays competitively

Erik H. Erikson
(Author of
Toys and Reason,
Stages in the Ritualization of Experience,
published by W. W. Norton.
Photo by Jon Erikson, 1976, with permission)

to share, but gives up with some difficulty. How the competition is dealt with will help determine whether the child develops a moral system based upon an appreciation of human rights and needs or a rigid moralism. Sexual identification develops during this age, and it also is greatly influenced by social relations. If curiosity is met with age-appropriate replies, the child acquires a positive sense of wonder about life. If curiosity is rebuffed or treated as taboo, the child experiences discomfort (Freedman, Kaplan, & Sadock, 1976).

Parents with problem children often want to know which child-rearing practices "really work." They want to know the "right way." In studying children's social development, we are struck with the dynamic interaction between the characteristics of the child (age, sex, temperament, etc.) and physical and social demands. We can chart the general effect of some social factors upon the child's socialization. There is a correlation between extremes of child-rearing practices and pathological personal, and social development in children (Chess & Hassibi, 1978). On the whole, the factors contributing to maladjustment are so complex that we cannot elucidate a direct link between style of child rearing and a child's psychosocial development. In the rest of this section, we will focus on two aspects of child rearing, the parent-infant bond, and sex role development because they are exemplary and central aspects of normal child development.

The Parent-Infant Bond

The future of an infant is perhaps most importantly determined by the relationship that is established between parent and child commencing with the birth of the infant. The term parent-infant bond is intended to emphasize the psychological fastening that occurs between the infant and, most especially, the mother. Sometimes the bond is referred to as attachment. This bond is revealed by the infant's tendency to maintain close contact with that person. Thus, the infant maintains contact with his eyes; the infant stares intently at his mother, and his eyes follow her as she goes about her chores. As the infant becomes more mobile, he or she tries to maintain physical proximity with the mother. If the child is for some reason unsuccessful in maintaining physical proximity with the mother, the child shows obvious signs of distress. This has come to be known as separation anxiety (Ainsworth, 1973).

The bond between the parents and infant does not develop automatically. Contrary to popular belief, there is no maternal or paternal "instinct." The question of interest then is what factors control the bonding relationship. The most significant variable seems to be early physical and social contact with the infant. Not too many years ago, the usual hospital routine following birth involved the mother's quick glance at her infant at delivery, a short visit with the infant within the next twelve hours, and then about thirty minutes with the baby at feeding every four hours, except at night. Today, it is generally conceded that mothers should have immediate and extensive contact with their infants following delivery. The results of one study (Kennell, Jerauld, Wolfe, Chesler, McAlpine, Kreger, Steffa, & Klaus, 1974) have shown that mothers given extended contact with their infants, in comparison with mothers who had the traditional amount of contact with their infants, spent more time soothing, cuddling, looking, and picking up the infants when they cried. The infants thrived under this attention and scored better on tests of physical and mental development at one year than did the babies who did not have the extended contact. Differences continued to be apparent even at 2 years of age. Mothers who had had more contact with their infants at birth spoke to them more and gave them fewer commands and more encouragement than did the other mothers.

The importance of early mother-infant contact is perhaps best seen in situations of premature infants. Usually when the infant is born prematurely, the mother is allowed only limited access to the infant because of its precarious health for a period of several weeks or months. Quinn and Goldberg (1977) and Leifer, Leiderman, Barnett, and Williams (1972) found that mothers of premature infants are less involved emotionally with their babies than are mothers of full-term infants. They are less inclined to cuddle their babies or hold them. This diminished maternal response after postpartum separation may last as long as nine months (Brown & Bakeman, 1977) and may be a contributing factor to later child neglect and abuse (Hunter, Kilstrom, Kraybill, & Loda, 1978; Klein & Stern, 1971).

The importance of father-infant bonding cannot be ignored. Although the emphasis on attachment to mother is well researched, it is known that the father's presence is as effective as the mother's in making babies feel secure. For instance, a study by Lester, Kotelchuck, Spelke, Sellers, and Klein (1974) indicated that infants whose fathers took an active role in their care were more likely to show an interest in exploring their environment.

A final aspect of the parent-infant bond of importance to the child practitioner is that children who do not develop a strong parent-infant bonding run a higher risk of being abused or neglected by one or both of their parents. "Difficult" children are more likely to be abused than are other children, and parents are more likely to perceive their offspring as "difficult" if a strong bond has not been formed between parents and the infant. Predictors of poor bonding and subsequent child abuse include: parents who have difficulty looking at their infants in the eye or in touching them, parental disappointment over the baby's sex, and displeasure with the infant's physical appearance (Kempe & Kempe, 1978).

Those parents who were rejected themselves as infants are more likely to be abusing parents. These parents seem to lack the capacity to establish a strong bond with their own offspring. Thus, the cycle of child abuse repeats itself from generation to generation. The therapist must be attentive to disruptions in early parent-infant bonding. These disruptions may be the cause of subsequent problem behavior later in the child's life. In a later section, we discuss strategies for rebonding the parents to their child.

Sex Roles and Stereotypes

Parental attitudes and behavior may very well be the determining factor in the development of young children's conception of femininity or masculinity. Children learn about gender very early. Most 2-year-olds know whether they are boys or girls, identify strangers as daddies or mommies, and know that daddy has a penis and mommy has breasts. By age three, children can consistently apply gender labels (Thompson, 1975).

These accomplishments do not mean that children understand that gender is biological. Until age four or five, they are likely to think sex differences depend on clothes, hair, or maturation, rather than on biology, believing that a girl would be a boy if she cut her hair, or that a boy might become a girl if he wore a dress. One preschooler visited the neighbor's new baby who was having a bath. Later, her parents asked if the baby was a boy or a girl. "I don't know," she replied, "It's so hard to tell at that age, especially when it's not wearing clothes." (Stone & Church, 1973).

Given the prevalent notions about female and male behavior in our society and the degree to which colors, clothes, and toys for infants are classified almost exclusively by sex, we assume that boys and girls are treated differently from birth. A number of studies do show different socialization practices for females and for males. Nevertheless, reviews of the research concerning early socialization conclude that, on the whole, the sexes are treated very similarly during the preschool years. Maccoby (1980) concludes that there are two general areas that differ in the socialization of boy and girl children. First, boys are handled somewhat more roughly than girls, and parents indicate more concern about their daughters' physical well-being. Second, boys are physically punished more and given more direction than girls.

One study leading to such conclusions was carried out by Minton, Kagan, and Levine (1971) who observed the interaction of nearly 100 mothers with their 2-year-olds in the homes of these individuals. Both lower-middle and middle class mothers were rather intrusive, interrupting their children every 6 to 8 minutes to reprimand or command them. Sons were reprimanded and physically punished more frequently than daughters, and the lower the educational level attained by the mother, the more inclined she was to be intrusive.

Besides being punished more in general, boys also seem to be punished more than girls for behaviors that are inappropriate for their sex. The masculine role in our society is regarded with greater respect and status. It is more clearly defined than the feminine role, and there appears to be greater pressure for boys than girls to conform to sex-appropriate standards. When asked to respond to sex-appropriate behaviors for boys and girls, parents of young children responded more negatively to opposite sex choices for boys than for girls (Lansky, 1967). Girl children who climb trees and play with toy soldiers are tolerated to a much greater degree than little boys who cry, play with dolls, or like to play at dress-up (especially if it involves dressing up in mommy's clothes).

Because they are punished for exhibiting sex-inappropriate behaviors, it is not surprising that boys are more consistent in their adoption of sex-typed behaviors and adopt them earlier than girls do. When asked whether they would like to be boys or girls, young boys are far more likely than young girls to select their own sex. It is not until the age of 10 that a majority of girls state that they prefer to be female. These results may occur because girls have observed the greater advantage accorded to males and state a preference for their own sex only as a result of pre-adolescent social pressures. An alternative explanation is that because girls are not punished as frequently as boys for sex inappropriate choices, they are therefore less fearful of expressing their honest preference.

A number of theories have been devised to explain sexual identification. We will examine the three most prominent theories of sex role development: the psychoanalytic approach, the social learning approach, and the cognitive developmental approach.

The Psychoanalytic Approach

Freudian theory, which will be discussed in more detail in the next chapter, assumes that physical differences between the sexes predestines them to radically different personality configurations. Psychoanalytic theory stresses the importance of early development in shaping lifelong patterns of behavior, and it does not view sex roles as flexible. Biological and psychological aspects of individuals are the organizing properties for sex role identity which, once crystalized, will be maintained for life.

According to the psychoanalytic position, sex role differentiation appears during the phallic stage of development which involves the resolution of the Oedipal complex (for boys) and the Electra complex (for girls). In this view, a boy desires his mother and becomes a rival of his father. Aware of the father's greater strength and power and fearing castration, the boy renounces his desire for his mother, identifies with his father, and thus completes his gender identity when he passes through this third stage of psychosexual development, around the age of five or six. In this manner, a boy who probably spends most of his time with his mother as his primary caretaker still manages to identify and pattern his behavior after his father. Girls, on the other hand, do not need to switch their identification from their first love object--their mother. According to Freud, they do, however, go through the phallic stage, during which they develop penis envy and desire their fathers. Little girls, like boys, resolve the competition with their same-sexed parent by identifying with that parent and behaving in a sex-appropriate manner. The sex role identity attained at this period will be maintained throughout life, and fixation at this stage may cause lifelong patterns of abnormal sex role identification. Although Freud was the first to report the increased interest in sexual phenomena in children around the ages of four to six, his postulation of the Oedipal and the Electra complexes has proven difficult to test empirically. Furthermore, behaviors observed during this period can be explained by alternate hypotheses. Especially damaging to the psychoanalytic interpretation is the known flexibility of sex role behavior over the life span, as well as the recent trends indicating that traditional sex role differentiations are breaking down.

Social Learning Approach

Social learning theorists such as Bandura (1977) and Mischel (1968) have emphasized the significance of social contingencies and external environmental influences as the main shapers of gender identity. Patterns of reinforcement, verbal instruction, the behaviors of models, and the publically-observable consequences of the model's behaviors (vicarious learning) are the means through which children acquire sex role identification. Through observation of anatomy, children learn that there are two types of individuals, or two sexes, and that all of the forces in the environment indicate that people are differentiated on the basis of these physical characteristics. Children come to have a broad concept of femaleness and maleness on the basis of their experiences. Sex differences are learned, and once this learning takes place, a child's identification is formed.

The Social Learning Approach emphasizes the flexibility of sex role behavior and the potential for changing sex role stereotypes. If the environment is constantly shaping behavior, then alterations in the environment can lead to alterations in attitudes and behaviors of females and males. From this perspective, social changes may lead to changes in early sex role socialization practices. Further, sex role identity is not seen as being laid down indelibly in the first five years of life as is true in the psychoanalytic theory, nor is it seen as being so intimately linked to anatomy.

Cognitive Developmental Approach

On the basis of Piaget's cognitive theory, Kohlberg (1966, 1969) has explained sex role development as a cognitive phenomenon. Whereas social learning theorists view the environment as being the organizing force in sex role identity, cognitive developmental theorists see the organizing force as being the interactions between an individual and the environment. A child's general cognitive level shapes her or his social responses. Sex role development progresses through a series of three stages, beginning with the formation of gender identity--rather than culminating in it--as postulated by psychoanalytic and social learning theories. The stages advanced by Kohlberg are as follows:

1.   Gender identity. The child recognizes that he or she is either male or female.

2.   Gender stability. The child recognizes that boys invariably become men and girls become women.

3.   Gender consistency. The child recognizes that the attributes of being either female or male will not change with changing situations and personal motivations.

By at least age three, the child can accurately label her- or himself and can label the gender of others with some correctness. By age four, the child is partially aware that gender cannot change. It is not until about age six, however, that a firm concept of sex identity is established, based primarily on physical differences of the sexes. This progression follows the more general pattern of cognitive development, and the constancy of gender may be a special case of object constancy. Once basic gender identity has been established, the child actively seeks to shape her or his behavior to match sex identity. With age, the child also relies more on social functions to determine appropriate sex role behavior. Thus, sex role behaviors are influenced by parents, peers, and the social roles played out by men and women in our culture.

Conclusions about Sex Role Research

Recent trends indicate that traditional sex role differentiations are breaking down. Greater numbers of individuals are experiencing discontinuities between early sex role socialization and later life experiences. Females who have been socialized consistently and strongly to favor traditional feminine activities and interpersonal behaviors are likely in later life to experience circumstances or opportunities calling for more traditional masculine role behaviors. Social movements such as women's liberation can be expected to accelerate societal redefinitions of traditional sex roles. Additionally, the changing status of women is having an impact on attitudes about sex roles in young parents and affecting the manner in which they socialize their children. With more and more women entering the work force (almost 50% of mothers of children 18 years or younger), it appears certain that growing numbers of children will develop less rigid attitudes about appropriate sex role behaviors.

A concept, androgyny, has been developed to counter the misconception that femiminity and masculinity are exact opposites--an assumption that leads a great many people to believe that unless one follows the feminine role, the more masculine one becomes, and vice versa. Androgyny, strictly speaking, is the state of having both female and male sexual characteristics and has come to be used in connection with a person's defining herself or himself primarily as a human being, rather than as female or male (Bem, 1974, 1975). In this sense, androgynous men and women share many of the same personality characteristics, instead of following the traditional sex role patterns. For instance, traditional males rate significantly higher than traditional females on a personality trait labelled "dominant-ambitious," but androgynous females and males score about the same, because the men see themselves as less dominant than the traditional male does, while the women see themselves as more dominant than the traditional female does. Androgynous people of both sexes are nurturing and independent, and neither sex tries to be unemotional or passive.

People who are flexible in their sex roles and able to display the best qualities of both traditional stereotypes are more competent and have a higher sense of self-esteem than people who follow traditional sex role behavior (Spence & Helmreich, 1978). This suggests that it is good to encourage children to develop all their potential characteristics letting them engage in rough and tumble play outside as well as quiet play in the doll corner. Instead of saying, "Boys don't cry," or "Girls don't fight," we should simply apply the same standards to both sexes, either advising, "Children should settle their own arguments," or "Nobody fights," as the situation demands.

DISRUPTION OF NORMAL DEVELOPMENTAL PROCESSES

We have confined our overview of normal developmental issues to those topics that are of importance to all children. A growing body of literature identifies factors that disrupt typical developmental processes and can result in abnormal child behavior.

Physical Factors

For instance, certain constitutional factors created by pre- and postnatal experiences have been linked with a variety of childhood emotional problems. Many studies attest that the mother's nutritional status during pregnancy is correlated with infant intelligence (Harrell, Woodyard, & Gates, 1955). Significant malnutrition is associated with infant retardation. The mother's overall health during pregnancy has also been correlated with the baby's birth weight (Erickson, 1978). The low birth weight itself is not pathological, but often may signal undernourishment which can lead to organic lags. Following this logic, low birth weight of a full-term baby is more serious than low weight associated with prematurity as the former is more likely to signal undernourishment.

A number of toxic substances, called teratogens, can be transmitted through the mother to the newborn. The mother's illnesses, especially during the first three months of pregnancy, can affect the embryo's well-being. Viral diseases that are relatively innocuous among adults, such as measles and colds, can cause significant organic impairment, such as retardation, blindness, and deafness. Bacterial infections are also transmitted, although in most bacterial diseases, the infection itself is transmitted rather than the bacteria spurring congenital malformation. The infant can be born with tuberculosis or syphilis or other bacterial illnesses transmitted through the infected mother's placenta. Cigarette smoking and a number of drugs are teratogens leading to prematurity, underweight, undernourishment, and/or malformations in a number of children (Erickson, 1978). Toxemias, such as pre-eclampsia, which affect about 5 % of pregnant women, disturb the embryo's overall health (Chess & Hassibi, 1978).

Several perinatal (during birth) factors affect the neonate's well-being. Anoxia, lack of oxygen during birth, is associated with developmental difficulties and intellectual functioning (Goldstein, Caputo, and Taub, 1976; Drillien, 1970). Prolonged and complicated labor is associated with later retardation, behavioral disorders, and reading problems (Pasamanick & Knobloch, 1966). Premature babies are a high-risk group on a number of vital dimensions (Chess & Hassibi, 1978). A number of postnatal (after birth) factors such as infections of the central nervous system, brain trauma, and malnutrition affect the child's constitutional well-being.

We have described the physical constitutional effects of a number of pre- and postnatal factors. Although the effect of these factors appears first to be physical, these toxic factors are easily and often transformed to temperament and personal disturbances. If the child's constitution is disturbed, her or his ability to develop effective sensory-motor functions will be disturbed. Remember that sensory-motor acquisition is a prerequisite for development of later cognitive ability. Thus, factors in the child's development because of the child's genetic makeup and because of prebirth and birth experiences may impede expected development.

Since determination and treatment of the physical factors that enhance and impede development is primarily the purview of biological medical researchers, we will not discuss these in more detail. In the rest of this text, we consider in depth the temperamental and psychosocial factors that affect child development, as it is within these areas that the child practitioner may have the greatest impact.

Social Factors

A number of social factors may be causative in the disruption of normal development. For example, loss of a parent has been associated with disturbance in normal growth patterns. When children are separated from a primary caretaker, they grieve. The degree of reversibility of the despair or impairment of development depends upon a number of factors such as the age of the child, whether the separation is permanent or temporary, duration and frequency of separation, and the nature of substitute care.

Severe physical illnesses of parents can affect children's development (Glueck & Glueck, 1952). Factors such as divorce and remarriages may also change developmental patterns. We will speak more specifically about how such psychosocial stresses affect children in Unit 4 on children with special concerns.

Clearly, pathology in the parent-child interaction can stimulate maladjustment. Much research has been conducted to ascertain the relationship between parents' emotional problems and those of their children, barring genetic influences. As explained in detail in the chapter on family therapy, the child may be caught in the web of a pathological family system. The child's maladjustment may be the only way to cope within a disturbed world. Too severe, too lax, or inconsistent child rearing have been linked to childhood maladjustment.

Implications about Disruption of Normal Development on Practice

In reviewing the findings on disruption of normal development, we see that the child's biology, temperament, and the physical and social environment can be menacing forces that impede normal development. Some say stress alone causes maladjustment. Others rely on biological explanations. In most cases, maladjustment is probably an interaction of self and environmental factors. Most believe that stress is a trigger that releases constitutional vulnerability (Selye, 1950). As we explore the various theoretical approaches to child therapy in the next unit, you will be aware that each theorist makes certain assumptions about children's motivations. The reader should weigh these assumptions against what is empirically known about child development. As mentioned previously, too often the findings of child development have not been applied to the practice of child therapy.

SUMMARY

This brief overview of child development demonstrates how intricate are the biological, physical, and social forces that lead to the adaptation or maladjustment of a particular child. Thus, an effective psychological assessment of a child needs to consider the child's overall physical, cognitive, and social development in the context of the family and larger social environment. Clinical intervention may be aimed at various spheres of the child's development and various factors in the child's world. Since no simple set of determinants explains the child's behavior and temperament, the tasks of the child practitioner in both assessment and intervention are highly complex, requiring a critical synthesis of empirical data about child development and child therapy and astute sensitivity to the developmental capacities of a given child.

PART TWO
Theories of Child Therapy

PART II

THEORIES OF CHILD THERAPY

As pointed out in Part I of this text, the concept of the child as the focus of clinical treatment has evolved within the last 100 years, spurred by Freud's revolutionary thinking that emotional disorders were often rooted in childhood trauma. Since that time, a vast literature of theoretical expositions and case studies concerning effective means for ameliorating stress in children has developed. Most of these writings and case studies fall into one of the four major theoretical stances to therapy, the psychoanalytic/psychodynamic, behavioral/cognitive, humanistic/psychosocial, or family therapy. The major writings about childhood applications of these theoretical tenets are summarized in Chapters 4 through 7 that follow. Each of these major approaches to child practice that are reviewed report documented effectiveness according to case study analysis and some empirical research. However, experimental verification of each of the theories is limited. At this point, one theory of child counseling cannot be proven to be more effective than any other. Rather, it appears that some combination of the practitioner's training and temperament plus the temperament of the child and specific nature of the child's mental health problems determine the effectiveness of the theoretical modality. Thus, the child practitioner needs a working familiarity with each of the four major approaches to child counseling.

Of course, trying to integrate and apply all of these approaches would be an overwhelming task. It would be ideal is one could integrate the best of each of these approaches into an omnibus theory, but this goal is not viable because several of the approaches rely upon opposing principles and, thus, cannot be philosophically integrated.

In Chapter 8, we have attempted to summarize the important principles that do cut across the varied theories of child counseling and to offer some guidelines for selecting an appropriate theoretical stance for a particular child. In essence, we have attempted to outline a systematic, eclectic approach to child counseling that we believe facilitates the practitioner's listening and responding broadly to the child's and family's needs. Throughout Part II you are presented with numerous clinical examples of the varied theoretical approaches. Chapter 8 ends with an extended case of how we attempt to listen to our child clients.

CHAPTER 4

PSYCHOANALYTIC CONTRIBUTIONS TO CHILD THERAPY

Freud's landmark writing about the case of Little Hans, in which Freud trained a father to help his son overcome a phobia of horses, paved the direction for psychoanalytic work with children, but it remained for a number of Freud's followers, such as his daughter, Anna Freud, Melanie Klein, and Margaret Mahler to describe explicitly how psychoanalytic child therapy could be conducted. As we shall see, the child psychoanalysts differ drastically in principles and techniques. Yet, each accepts some basic tenets of analytic thought.

A major assumption in all child analytic work is that human behavior is determined by the combined effect of one's inherited constitution and temperament and early experiences, particularly with parents during the infancy and toddler stages of development. Humans are conceived of as systems whose energy is expressed in drives, such as the life urge or libido and death wish or destrudo. Most early behavior is motivated by unconscious drives. The development of these unconscious drives, in the id, is shaped by attachment to significant others. The ego analysts, such as Margaret Mahler, accept Freud's precepts about id development but emphasize that conscious processes are also an important domain of human behavior. The child grows from primarily unconscious thought (id) experiencing to secondary conscious thought (ego) through a series of psychosocial stages. Constitutional disturbances and environmental trauma interfere with the child's growth through the stages and with the equilibrium of the id and ego. If the disturbance is relatively tolerable and the constitution strong, the ego may be able to defend against stress, and growth continues. If the constitution is somewhat vulnerable and the stress is repetitive, neurotic symptomatology characterized by inappropriate or over use of defense mechanisms develops. If the disturbance is severe and/or chronic and the constitution weak, the child may exhibit psychotic symptomatology characterized by primitive id and ego functioning.

The child analytic theorists extend Freudian thought by breaking down Freud's oral stage into several more discrete phases. Moreover, they recognize that some emotional problems are unique to children. The child's symptoms are symbolic, but the symbolism is age-specific. The child analysts have described critical differences between adult and child clients based upon their differing language ability and cognitive and physical development. Emotional disturbance is viewed as a defense against unconscious conflicts between impulses that are characteristic of a developmental stage and pressures in the environment that the child has internalized. The child analysts believe that the child will not suffer maladjustment unless he or she has internalized stress.

Further, the child analysts attempt to explain how psychoanalytic theory must be modified when working with children. They believe, that as is true when conducting therapy with adults, "talking through" helps a client resolve conflicts. However, they point out that free association is not possible. Instead, the child therapist encourages the child to use play to express motivations and conflicts. In play, the child reproduces her or his precepts of conflict within the family. These precepts may or may not coincide with the actual family interaction, but the analyst believes that it is these "introjects" (subjective perceptions) that cause the child stress. It is the introjections, not reality itself, that must be modified (Smirnoff, 1971). Keeping in mind these basic commonalities of psychoanalytic approaches to child therapy, let us now overview some unique contributions of the most renowned child analysts.

MELANIE KLEIN: PRINCIPLES OF CHILD PSYCHOANALYSIS

Writing about child therapy as early as 1932, Melanie Klein postulated new concepts about the developmental stages and psychic dynamics in children and offered a systematic means for conducting child play therapy. Klein believed that the first year of life is most critical in the child's personality development. She labelled the first five months as the Paranoid-Schizoid Position and age 6 months to 1 year as the Depressive Position.

The newborn does not sense a difference between her- or himself and the mother, and thus Klein views the infant as in a dim state of awareness. The developing infant learns that all of her or his needs cannot be met. Sometimes the newborn is not fed when hungry. Sometimes the infant experiences discomfort. Thus, he or she feels many fears and anxieties so that Klein perceives the newborn in a somewhat paranoid state.

The depressive phase that occurs from age 6 months to 1 year is catalyzed by the weaning process (Klein, 1937). The infant experiences much anxiety and anger about being left alone. The infant learns to internalize, "introject," central facets of her or his life that are absent. At first, the infant introjects parts of these significant persons, "objects," in the environment. So, the infant introjects breasts or the mother's face. Klein strongly believed that the newborn has a sense of sexual relations so that the infant also introjects partial images of the sexual act. Gradually, the infant learns to introject whole objects, such as a precept of the mother and a precept of the father.

The infant tries to introject only good objects. Thus, he or she learns how to not internalize, to "project," perceptions that the infant perceives as bad. Therefore, the child may introject the "good breast" if the mother is supportive and nurturing or project

Melanie Klein
(Photo by Dr. Hans A. Thorner, with permission)

the "bad breasts" if the mother is cold or her milk is not good. If a newborn grows through the depressive position with basically positive feelings about the objects, the infant will introject a positive ideal object. The positive ideal object serves as a basis of the infant's developing ego and superego, protecting the infant against anxiety and helping to deal with her or his own aggression.

Sometimes processes of introjection and projection become confused or fragmented. The infant may introject bad objects in an effort to control them or project good objects to make the outside person seem safe. If the infant is angry at the parents because many of her or his needs are not met, the infant may never introject whole positive images of the object. Instead, the infant continues to introject "split" precepts, accepting only part of the object he or she experiences as safe. Because of "splitting" of introjects and projects (i.e., only internalizing part of the precept of an object), the disturbed infant does not develop healthy id and ego functioning. The child has an inability to tolerate frustration and to inhibit sexual impulses and does not see others accurately and completely. The infant may be overly aggressive or riddled with anxiety and guilt.

Changes in the infant's family will not help the disturbed child because the child's introjects are split and disturbed. These confused and split introjections and projections,then, are the target of therapy. Klein wanted to help her child clients introject accurate perceptions of the objects in their lives and to reduce the splitting of significant objects into all positive or all negative introjections and projections (Smirnoff, 1968).

Klein developed a systematic play therapy approach to help her child clients understand their motivation and develop more realistic images of others and themselves. At first, she conducted therapy by visiting the homes of her child patients. Later, she saw children in her office (Alexander & Selesnick, 1966). She presented toys of a "primitive kind"--little wooden people, trees, houses, paper, pencils, scissors, running water, and tumblers (Klein, 1960). She believed that if the therapist adopted a very neutral stance, transference occurs in which the child reacts to the therapist as the child perceives significant persons in her or his life. Each repetitive activity in play therapy is viewed as a representation of the child's unconscious conflicts. The more impulsive the play, the more likely it represents a past conflict (Feigelson, 1974). Klein advocated immediate and direct interpretation of the child's unconscious play activity. She felt that children would understand her statements unconsciously and was not deterred by the lack of overt response to her interventions. Her interpretations dealt with themes such as the child's desire to kill the mother, father, or siblings; to incorporate the mother's breast or father's penis; or the child's interest in the primal scene. She believed play material and play activity held symbolic significance. For example, a child might view sticks as penises, bumping toys as sex, water as a symbol for sperm, fear of water as a fear of castration, and nosepicking as an anal attack on the parents. She cautioned, however, that the therapist needed to know the child before interpreting the meaning of play objects and activities. The key to the symbolic import of the toy is not in the toy itself, but in the child's use of the play material (Klein, 1960). She felt that deep interpretations about the child's introjects enabled the client to develop more integrated views of her- or himself and to be more spontaneous and less inhibited (Smirnoff, 1968).

Klein defined the role of the therapist as one of friendly reserve. The therapist participates as little as possible in the play situation, but instead notes interpretations from a neutral, distant perspective. Klein's only adaptation of interpretation with children was the use of the child's vernacular. She interviewed mothers prior to therapy and asked them for the special words which the child used to describe excremental processes, sex, genitals, and masturbation. An example of Kleinian interpretation follows:

Case 4.1. The Case of Rita

Rita (age 2 years, 9 months) put a triangular brick on one side and said, That's a little woman;' she then took a little hammer' as she called another long-shaped brick, and hit the brick box with it exactly in a place where it was only stuck together with paper, so that she made a hole in it. She said, When the hammer hit hard, the little woman was so frightened.' Hitting with the hammer stood for coitus between her parents which she had witnessed until she was two years old. Klein's interpretation was, "Your daddy hit hard like that inside your mummy with his little hammer, and you were so frightened" (Klein, 1960, p. 162).

Although many analysts adopt Kleinian approaches in dealing with adult clients, her system of child analysis has been subject to much criticism. Many feel she is amiss in not focusing upon the child's actual relationship with the parents. She presented a singular, sexual view of children's motivation and was not open to other evidence. Kanner (1962a) discusses Klein's Case of Little Erma who was seen in unfinished play analysis for 575 hours over 2 1/2 years. He writes sardonically (Kanner, 1962a, p. 239):

> We are told she suffered from megalomania, paranoia, pseudologia, severe depression, sadistic and cannibalistic impulses, masochism, homosexual tendencies, anal love desires, a desire to be seduced and a few other signs of an extravagant and uncurbed instinctual life.'--Her parents did not bring her back for the 576th play session.

Even if we choose to disregard many of her interpretations, Klein helped clinicians see that children's behavior could be analyzed and that clinicians could interact with children in a therapeutic manner that is distinct from parenting or teaching. We should give Klein credit for developing a system in which children's behavior can be interpreted to them. Moreover, she helped clinicians see that children do experience emotions of anger and anguish. Importantly, she emphasized that children's subjective perceptions of reality must be taken into account if we are to assist them.

MARGARET MAHLER: A POIGNANT VIEW OF GROWING UP

Beginning her writings in the 1940's and continuing to the present, Margaret Mahler (1968) has built upon the more viable constructs of Kleinian analysis. She has refined explanations of children's development during the first 2 years of life. Her stages of autism, symbiosis, individuation, and rapprochement are described below.

Mahler explains that the newborn strives to replicate the homeostasis experienced in the mother's womb. From birth to 2 months, the newborn is in an autistic state, a state of absolute primary narcissism (i.e., the infant is totally preoccupied with her or his own well-being). The newborn feels no differentiation between her- or himself and the primary nurturing figures. Mahler explains that this autistic phase is normal and healthy. If the child's needs are comfortably met during this time, the child moves smoothly into the symbiotic phase at about age 2 months.

From about 2 months to 1 1/2 years of age, the infant is in a twilight state of symbiosis. During this period infants are only vaguely aware of the boundary between themselves and their nurturing figures Mahler explains that the mother and other nurturing figures also experience the symbiotic state. The child and parent feel a mutual physical and psychological interdependence.

From a period of about 16 months to 3 years, the child enters into the stage of separation/individuation. Concomitant to the child's development of locomotion, the infant moves into the differentiation subphase of separation--individuation. He or she develops a clear sense of self. Gradually, the child develops into a practicing subphase. The child tests the environment and the mother. Thus, the child plays games of hide and seek, or the child may refuse to cooperate with the parent's request. Through such "practicing," the child learns to function in an autonomous fashion.

While the child is pulling away from the mother, the child also wants to maintain close ties with the mother. "As the toddler realizes his or her power and ability to physically move away from his mother, the toddler now seems to have an increased need and a wish for his mother to share with him every new aquisition of skill and experience" (Mahler, 1968, p. 25). If the nurturing figures encourage these explorations and remain supportive, the child develops positive feelings about functioning on her or his own.

Some mothers overprotect and overcontrol the child during the individuation phase. Others are very rejecting of their children once they begin to assert themselves. These mothers may feel rejected by their children's stubbornness, refusal to cooperate, or tendency to run away, and so these mothers withhold any support to their children once they enter the individuation phase. Children who experience faulty upbringing at this stage may become overly dependent and shadow the maternal figure or become insulated from others because of the fear of engulfment. If the parent-child relationship is satisfactory during the separation-individuation phase, the child achieves a sense of autonomy.

Around age two, the child then moves into a rapprochement phase. Object constancy consolidates, and the infant can tolerate more time away from the primary caretaker. The father becomes important as a channel to the excitement and challenges of the external world. Comfortable with her or his own boundaries, the child approaches the parenting figures more affectionately and consistently. A "honeymoon" state in the parent-child relationship may continue for several years. It ends when the child enters school and begins to struggle with feelings of competence and adequacy.

Mahler has used her paradigm of infant psychosocial stages to explain the etiology of neurosis and psychosis. She postulates that the autistic child's development is blocked within the first few days of life. If the infant experiences physical ailments, social trauma, or poor mothering, the infant may perceive the mother as bad and be blocked to her. The child functions in the totally narcissistic state in which he or she was born. Psychosis may occur if the child does not successfully enter into the individuation stage. The psychotic child remains in a symbiotic state in which her or his sense of self is dimly perceived. The growth to individuation may be blocked by malfunctions of biological systems or by inadequate mothering. Some children may be predisposed to not use effectively their mother's nurturing. Neurosis may develop if movement through the individuation phase has been traumatic because the parent is over- or underprotective. The neurotic child longs for reunitement into the safety of the symbiotic phase, but does not want to lose identity. Thus, the child wavers between longing for symbiosis and fear of reengulfment (Mahler, 1968). The following case example illustrates Mahler's unique style.

Case 4.2. The Case of Violet

Violet explored the insides of the piano in a way that made one feel that the piano represented the mother's body: it was reminiscent of the way in which an infant of about ten months will carefully examine and inspect the mother's face and her body, in his attempts to differentiate himself after his emergence from the symbiotic phase. . . For instance, one day, before a Christmas vacation, Violet chose to play a Clementi sonata on the piano. She took all the repeats over and over again, and thus did not bring the piece to an ending. The interpretation was made to Violet that she did not want the piece to come to an end, just as she did not want her time with the therapist to come to an end. Violet's crying and tantrums indicated that this interpretation was correct (Mahler, 1968, pp. 204-205).

Mahler bases the direction of her therapy upon her evaluation of the child's development. If the child is very autistic, Mahler views therapy as a "beginning period." The primary task of the therapist is to establish contact with the child and then to move the child through a symbiotic parenting stage, finally encouraging the child's striving for autonomy. If the child is psychotic, Mahler attempts to create a corrective parenting experience. The therapist provides support akin to healthy symbiotic parenting. The therapist allows the child much freedom, intercedes in any self-destructive play, and reassures the child that he or she is safe and loved. Once the child feels close, the therapist gradually gives her or him feedback that it is all right to pull away, that the therapist will remain a friend although the therapist and child must function as separate beings. With the neurotic child, the therapist must replay the traumatic separation, offering feedback that encourages the child to assert her- or himself and allowing the child to ask for assistance when needed.

Mahler offers a broad conceptualization of early development; however, she does not delineate specific therapeutic approaches derived from her developmental framework. Her theory allows for broad psychodynamic descriptions of a client. Although very eloquent, the relationship between these abstract descriptions and effective therapeutic interventions is not always clear.

ANNA FREUD: ELUCIDATION OF PSYCHOANALYTIC PSYCHOTHERAPY

Anna Freud began extending her father's writings to child analysis in the late 1920's and developed a coherent system for child therapy by 1940. Like Melanie Klein, she perceived child therapy as distinct from adult analysis because of children's developmental and conceptual limitations. However, her proposals for dealing with these developmental limitations differed radically from Melanie Klein. Whereas Klein believed analysis could be completed through play, Anna Freud felt analysis of the unconscious was not completely possible and often not necessary. Because the child's superego was not fully developed, Anna Freud proposed that a complete transference relationship would not develop. Children would sometimes see the therapist as a parent figure, sometimes as a real figure, and some- times as a projection of the children themselves. Anna Freud suggested that the techniques of child therapy must be tailored to the degree of pathology and the degree of ego and superego development.

She agreed with her contemporaries' assessment of the importance of psychosocial stages of development and incorporated the stages posited by Klein and Mahler into her theoretical framework. She viewed the infant as moving through the stages of autism, symbiosis, and separation/individuation. She accepted Klein's tenet that from birth to 3 or 4 months of age infants were in a need-fulfilling stage in which the object is partly introjected. From about 4 months onward, the child develops object constancy which allows for a positive inner image of the object to be maintained irrespective of satisfaction or dissatisfaction. She stressed the importance of the object-centered phallic and oedipal stages, as identified by her father, Sigmund Freud, which are characterized by possession of the opposite-sexed parent and jealousy and cruelty toward the own-sexed parent. Anna Freud perceived the period of latency and pre-adolescence as a very important time in which the child learns control over her or his body. She believed that children's personal growth could be stymied by internal or external events at any stage, but she stressed that a certain amount of ego regression is expected and normal. Development of aspects of personality is uneven so that a degree of egocentrism and disequilibrium is typical in childhood.

Anna Freud proposed that since development is uneven, maladjustment cannot be diagnosed through the child's impaired functioning. Further, she proposed that the presence of suffering is not a reliable index of pathology because a certain degree of anxiety is a normal facet of development. Instead, Anna Freud maintained that maladjustment must be assessed by looking at the relationship of the child's id, ego, and superego functioning. Maladjustment is signalled if: the id is out of ego control; the id is in conflict with the superego; the ego control is rigid allowing limited spontaneity; regressions are permanent; anxiety is internalized regardless of external events; frustration tolerance is low; and ability to sublimate and master anxiety is limited.

The goal of child therapy as perceived by Anna Freud was the alleviation of anxiety and neurotic symptomatology. She felt that this goal is difficult to accomplish because the child cannot free associate, because the ego is not fully developed, thereby limiting transference, and because the child does not voluntarily seek or understand treatment. On the other hand, she believed that the child's instinctual desire to grow was the therapist's greatest aid in therapy. Although the child may not choose to get well, the child will choose to develop. The successful child therapist exploits the child's natural desire for growth and autonomy.

A diagnostic procedure recommended by Anna Freud (1965) provided a comprehensive internal and external profile of the child. The external profile included referral symptoms, description of the child, family history, and information about significant environmental influences. The internal profile consisted of a personality assessment. The child was analyzed to determine if he or she had developed to his or her age-adequate psychosexual stage. Regression, fixation points, and levels of aggression were noted. Ego functions, as evidenced by memory, speech, control of motility, and reality testing, were examined in detail.

To Anna Freud, the first step of child therapy is the establishment of a warm, positive relationship—what she referred to as a "positive transference relationship." The therapist provides the motivation for therapy by winning the child's respect and pointing out how therapy will help the child grow. The therapist then acts as an "auxiliary superego" to help the child evaluate the consequences of her or his thoughts and acts. The therapist encourages the child to discard ineffective defense mechanisms and teaches more appropriate sublimations. The therapist does interpret transferences and resistances when clearly present; however, Anna Freud believed that most children's problems reflected difficulty dealing with a reality, rather than replication of events from the child's past. Thus, Anna Freud, unlike Melanie Klein, would not offer deep interpretations to children experiencing reactive stress, e.g., maladjustment spurred by external events such as divorce or death in the family. In cases of reactive stress, the therapist encourages the child to function more effectively in reality. Only when symptoms are deeply rooted and exacerbated by internalized distortions does the therapist attempt systematic analytic uncovering of id material. For example, if a child in play therapy competitively bumped two toy cars against one another, Melanie Klein might react by interpreting the behavior to the child as a reflection of her or his repressed sexual fantasies. For most children, Anna Freud would view this activity as indicating the child's realistic concerns about the dangers of life. Only when consistent sexual conflict is apparent would Anna Freud venture a "deep interpretation."

Whereas Melanie Klein developed a theory for conducting psychoanalysis with children, Anna Freud presents a model for doing psychoanalytically-oriented psychotherapy. Freud explained that psychoanalytic psychotherapy was more appropriate for the majority of childhood disorders which are reactive, precipitated by external stresses. In sum, psychoanalytic psychotherapy encourages the child's natural urge for growth. The causative factors of the child's distress are carefully considered. The therapist looks for means of aiding the child in overcoming issues and tapping her or his own potential.

SUMMARY

The historical contribution of psychoanalytic theory to the field of child therapy is enormous. The psychoanalysts proposed a number of constructs about psychosocial development that are accepted broadly by child specialists:

1. Childhood is critical in the development of human personality.

2. Aspects of child personality are biologically determined.

3. Much motivation is physiologically and unconsciously catalyzed.

4. Acceptance and love in childhood are necessary for healthy personality development.

5. Family and cultural conditions can prevent or distort the normal expression of unconscious drives.

6. Childhood traumas can become deeply entrenched, blocking further development.

7. The sex drive is natural and powerful.

8. Using play, children's unconscious motivation can be understood.

9. Unconscious drives can advantageously be brought to the surface of the conscious so that they are understood and controlled.

10. By analyzing and interpreting children's motivations, crippling anxieties and defenses can be redressed.

Many child therapists hold that psychoanalysis remains a very viable way of explaining, predicting, and modifying children's behavior. Anthony (1970, pp. 706-707) writes,

> There is also no other set of constructions as clinically useful in elucidating different aspects of personality development....The theory is at its best when showing how instinctive motivation operates in the production of thoughts and feelings and it contains an elaborate and sophisticated theory regarding the ways in which the instincts lead to thoughts and feelings and then on to behavior.

The major criticisms of psychoanalytic child therapy are leveled at the abstraction of the terms, some of which are not clearly defined and consequently cannot be empirically tested, and at the lack of specific psychotherapeutic techniques construed from the theories. Other criticisms are based upon an incomplete understanding of analytic thought. For example, many claim that psychoanalytic precepts must be employed for years in the therapeutic process before clients demonstrate significant change. However, Anna Freud helped us understand that through psychoanalytic psychotherapy, reactive maladjustment, spurred by external stress, may be treated rather rapidly. Moreover, therapists of varied persuasions agree that true personality reconstruction requires years of intervention. Critics of psychoanalytic therapy are apt to claim that insight is not necessary for behavioral change. The psychoanalytic psychotherapists do perceive insight as an important facet of the therapeutic process even though insight may not be a prerequisite for symptom removal. Insight allows clients to understand and control their motivations and operate freely and spontaneously. Many psychoanalytic psychotherapists, such as Margaret Mahler and Anna Freud, recognize the importance of other therapeutic techniques. Besides interpretations, they stress the importance of the therapeutic relationship and of a corrective emotional experience within the therapy hour. Another criticism concerns the validity of interpretations (e.g., especially those symbolic interpretations recommended by Klein). These criticisms seem valid. It is quite a jump from a child playing with pick-up sticks to an interpretation of the child wanting to incorporate the father's penis. On the other hand, often times the ineffectiveness in child therapy is due to poor or inaccurate interpretations rather than the use of interpretations per se.

Before a clinician can effectively employ analytic approaches to child therapy, the therapist must become very knowledgeable in analytic thought so that the interpretation of a client's psychodynamic responses recognize the depth and complexity of human motivation and stress. Analytic techniques can be a powerful contribution to the child therapy armamentarium if the therapist is scholarly in her or his approach to the theory and cautious and deliberate in using the techniques.

CHAPTER 5

BEHAVIORAL AND COGNITIVE CONTRIBUTIONS TO CHILD THERAPY

The behavioral and cognitive approaches to be discussed in this chapter differ markedly from the psychoanalytic approach discussed in Chapter 4 and from the psychosocial approach to be taken up in the next chapter. The behavioral approaches are linked directly to the psychology of learning and have their roots in the work of Pavlov, Watson, Thorndike, and B. F. Skinner. The cognitive approaches are tied to the newer developments in cognitive psychology with roots in information processing, linguistics, and problem solving. Some readers may wonder about the appropriateness of discussing both the behavioral and cognitive approaches within one chapter, and some disagreement regarding the nature of their relationship can be found in the literature (Ledwidge, 1978). Our premise here is that they do possess certain similarities, and that over the years, some of the concepts from cognitive theory have been incorporated into behavior therapy. Leading cognitive behaviorists such as Mahoney, who wrote *Cognition and Behavior Modification* (1974), and Meichenbaum, the author of *Cognitive-Behavior Modification* (1977), refer to cognitions or "self-statements" as classes of behavior. Thus, whereas psychotherapy was and still is considered to be the process of changing a person's mind through verbal methods, changing an individual's self-statements involves changing behaviors--the goal of behavior therapy. Because of this similarity, both approaches are included in this chapter, although they are discussed separately.

BEHAVIOR THERAPY

Historical Foundations

Behaviorism began as a revolt against the subjective influence prevalent in psychology at the turn of the century. John B. Watson in 1913 argued for a scientific psychology based on the objective study of behavior. In establishing behaviorism as the modus operandi of psychology, Watson adopted Pavlov's classical conditioning model as the way in which psychologists should proceed in their study of behavior. According to Watson, all behavior was learned through the principles of classical conditioning. This model of conditioning is today called respondent, Pavlovian, or classical conditioning.

Watson was joined by numerous other American psychologists in his call for an objective, scientific psychology based on behavior. Edward L. Thorndike as early as

1898, for instance, was advocating a psychology based on the Law of Effect. According to Thorndike's Law of Effect, a behavior is learned as a consequence of the "satisfying state of affairs" or reward that follows the response. Similarly, a response ceases to occur if followed by an "aversive state of affairs" or punishment (Thorndike, 1898). One major advocate of both behaviorism and the Law of Effect has been B. F. Skinner. In his now classic book, *The Behavior of Organisms,* published in 1938, Skinner argued that although respondent conditioning was important, more of our everyday behaviors are shaped through operant conditioning. This is a conditioning paradigm in which the rate of the desired response or behavior is contingent upon the consequence. Focusing on operant conditioning as the major type of conditioning, Skinner and his students have sought to show that principles of learning discovered in the laboratory are applicable to a wide range of behavioral problems. The application of these principles to behavioral problems is known as behavior modification or behavioral engineering.

In addition to the operant and classical conditioning models, another approach can be included under the auspices of behavior theory, that of social learning. This approach, developed primarily by Bandura (1969), claims that much behavior can be learned on a vicarious basis through the observation of the behavior of others. The technique of modeling is used, often in conjunction with various operant procedures, to gain therapeutic effects.

Behavior Therapy: Principles and Techniques

Behavior therapy is based on the premise that all behavior is learned and that behavior can be changed through the principles of learning. Behavioral therapists propose that behaviors judged to be adjusted or maladjusted are learned according to one or more of the three behavioral approaches (respondent, operant, or social learning). The subjectively-felt outcome of well-adjusted behavior is a sense of personal well-being. The subjectively-experienced outcome of maladjustment is anxiety. To the behavior therapist, therapy is a special learning environment. The client is not viewed as sick, but rather as lacking in adaptive skills. Behavioral therapy stresses that clients are capable of and must ultimately assume an autonomous, effective way of living. As the client learns to respond appropriately, maladjustment and subjectively-felt anxiety decrease. The behavioral child therapist is concerned with identifying the links between the environment and the child's responses. The behavior therapist is willing to actively intervene and to change the stream of events in the client's life. Target behaviors are increased and decreased using a variety of techniques within a supportive therapeutic relationship (Keat, 1974). The client's autonomy is increased as a result of learning (Fullmer & Bernard, 1972).

The first step in behavior therapy as in other approaches is to establish a comfortable therapeutic relationship (Schwartz & Goldiamond, 1975). The client must feel open to talk to the therapist about the extent and ramifications of the problem for which help

B. F. Skinner
(Photo by Hans-Peter Biemann, with permission)

is being sought. Then, the behavior therapist works with the client to clearly identify those behaviors to be changed and to define the desired behaviors. Those factors that maintain the dysfunctional behaviors or that prevent the occurrence of functional behaviors are then identified. Next, the resources that are available in the client's environment, or elsewhere, are discussed. Finally, the therapist considers those procedures or techniques that are most likely to have an effect on the identified behaviors (Fischer & Gochros, 1975).

One of the distinguishing features of behavior therapy is that the intervention techniques used can be evaluated as to their effectiveness in a variety of settings and with different types of problems (Pinkston, Levitt, Green, Linsk, & Rzepnicki, 1982). Before the intervention is introduced, a baseline of desired target behaviors or dysfunctional behaviors is carefully developed. This baseline is obtained by noting the frequency of these behaviors over some definable period of time, such as hours, days, or weeks. With the introduction of the intervention technique (which is itself clearly operationalized), this record of behaviors is maintained and provides both therapist and client with an indication of the relative effectiveness of the intervention.

The behavior therapist has a wide variety of techniques from which to choose, and as mentioned above, the therapist selects the most appropriate technique as a part of the assessment process. These techniques are based on the principles of either the operant, respondent, or social learning behavior theory approaches.

Operant Conditioning Techniques

These techniques involve the processes of reinforcement and punishment. Reinforcement maintains and increases the probability of a behavior; whereas, punishment decreases the probability of a behavior. Both reinforcement and punishment involve either adding something to the environment (positive reinforcement or punishment) or removing something from the environment (negative reinforcement or punishment). As a general rule, positive reinforcement is the technique of choice, although the others can also be very effective under the correct circumstances (Fischer & Gochros, 1975).

Reinforcement Techniques

In the use of reinforcement, it is important to determine what is reinforcing for that particular child. In early behavioral therapy, a limited number of reinforcers were used, e.g., food, praise. It is now recognized that a variety of reinforcers are feasible, and these vary for each client. Thus, praise may be reinforcing for one child, but another might feel embarrassed if, for example, he or she is praised in front of peers. This attention then actually serves as a punishment and has the effect of decreasing the frequency of the desired behavior. Keat (1979) recommends asking children about their likes and dislikes before implementing behavioral counseling. Building a list of the child's preferred reinforcers is known as a "reinforcement menu." Some unusual activities such as being left alone, watching other people, or reading may be potent reinforcers to some children.

Once the child's reinforcers are determined, they can be systematically applied by parents, teachers, or in some cases by the child. Among older children, a token or point system can be implemented. Tokens can be given each time the appropriate behavior is carried out. The token can later be "cashed in" for the reinforcer the child prefers. Token systems have been effective in many different setting, including homes, institutions, and schools. In addition, they seem effective in dealing with a wide range of problem behaviors (Kazdin, 1977).

In many cases, it may not be sufficient to simply tell the child what behaviors are desired and which ones will be reinforced. The desired response may not be part of the child's behavioral repertoire. In these cases, the reinforcement technique of shaping can be used. Small steps of the desired behavior or successive approximations are reinforced as they occur. For example, in some cases of primary encopresis, the child needs to learn appropriate toilet behavior. Each of the steps involved in this behavior, such as attending quickly to body signals, going to the bathroom, removing clothes, sitting down, and releasing sphincter control are reinforced.

Extinction in behavior theory refers to a situation where the consequences that have been previously reinforced or punished a behavior no longer occur. As a result, the behavior either increases or decreases. A characteristic of extinction is the extinction curve, which is characterized by an increase in undesirable behavior before the client is able to discriminate the new contingency system. For example, a child demands much parental attention, displaying temper tantrums at bedtime and insisting his parents not leave the room until he goes to sleep. Extinction of the parents' attention was carried out which resulted in the child crying for 45 minutes the first night, 20 minutes the second night, 10 minutes the third night, and finally no crying. Extinction should be used with caution and should preferably be used in combination with reinforcement. Differential attention is given in which the undesirable behavior is ignored and the desirable behavior reinforced. Children's aggression has been treated successfully this way (Pinkston et al., 1982).

Another reinforcement technique is that of behavior rehearsal, which involves the child practicing the complex verbal and/or physical desired behaviors in the safe therapeutic environment. Thus, the rehearsed behavior is systematically reinforced in vitro. In time, the child will feel confident to express this complex repertoire in the natural environment, and parents and teachers can be alerted to reinforce this behavior when it occurs in vivo.

Contingency contracting is a reinforcement technique which involves the child client, therapist, and other participating adults (for example, teachers) drawing up a written agreement specifying the therapeutic process. The contract includes the child's goals, the desired behaviors, and preferred reinforcers. If the contract is broken by any party, a joint meeting is held to determine the reason for the broken contract. Renegotiation takes place. Contingency contracting usually involves the use of positive reinforcement, although sometimes punishment-based techniques are used.

Punishment Techniques

These techniques are used to decrease the future probability of undesirable behaviors. As with extinction, no punishment techniques should be used alone as the result may be withdrawal by the client or the development of some emotional problems. One punishment technique involves the presentation of an aversive event (something that is unpleasant to the individual). Extreme cases of self-destruction and aggression can be decreased by this intervention (Lovaas & Bucher, 1974). Response cost involves removing an event to decrease the future probability of a behavior (compared with negative reinforcement which also involves removing a reinforcing event but with the intent of increasing a behavior). Response cost works particularly well in combination with a token system. Hall, Panyon, Rabon, and Broden (1972) reduced whining, complaining, and crying by removing free tokens contingent upon the occurrence of these behaviors. Time out is another form of punishment. The child is removed from a reinforcing situation following an occurrence of the undesirable behavior. This is a technique that has been effective with aggressive, acting-out children (Bostow & Barley, 1969).

Respondent Conditioning Techniques

A number of techniques have been developed from the respondent model of behavior theory. Many of these techniques are based on the concept of counter-conditioning; the assumption is made that some emotional responses cannot occur at the same time as other responses, in other words, they are incompatible.

Systematic desensitization is probably the most widely used and best known respondent technique which is based on counter-conditioning. A response of relaxation is paired with an anxiety-producing stimulus such that the bonding results in the stimulus evoking relaxation rather than anxiety. In the therapeutic application, the child is taught to relax during situations that elicit anxiety and maladaptive responses. The originator of systematic desensitization who referred to the underlying principle of this technique as "occupational inhibition" was Joseph Wolpe (1961). Using the method with adults, Wolpe described the process of desensitization as the method consisting of presenting to the imagination of the deeply-relaxed patient the feeblest item in a list of anxiety-evoking stimuli—repeatedly, until no more anxiety is evoked. The next item in the list is presented, and so on, until eventually, even the strongest of the anxiety-evoking stimuli fails to evoke any stir of anxiety in the patient (p. 191).

Keat (1974) recommends that a potent way to teach children how to relax is through systematic deep-breathing exercises. The breathing exercises can be practiced individually or in group sessions. Practicing isometric exercises also is effective in helping some children learn to identify and create relaxation. Once the child learns to identify the subjective feeling of relaxation and knows how to create these sensations, he or she can pair relaxation with the anxiety-producing situations. The child insomniac can practice deep-breathing upon retiring; or the child who is afraid to speak in class can practice isometric hand clinching before beginning to deliver a speech and during the speech if any anxiety reappears.

Wolpe's (1969) approach of systematic desensitization has the broadest research and empirical support of any behavior therapy technique and has been successfully implemented with children. However, several child behaviorists (e.g., Erickson, 1978 and Keat, 1974) have pointed out that it is difficult to teach children to relax systematically, construct a fear hierarchy, and imagine specific scenes. Keat (1974) suggests that it is often more effective with children to practice the increasingly anxiety-producing situations in vivo rather than in vitro, relying upon the child's imagination. Thus, Lazarus, Davison, & Polefka (1965) successfully treated a child with a school phobia by exposing the child gradually to the school environment, systematically reinforcing the approach to school behaviors.

Another widely used respondent conditioning-based technique is assertion training. Here, the intention is for the client to reduce the anxiety that inhibits expression and at the same time increasing assertive behaviors. The expression of assertive feeling then inhibits anxiety (Wolpe, 1969). The child who is bullied by peers may be taught how to look angry and how to fight. Assertion training often consists of a combination of techniques, for example, the use of positive reinforcement and modeling.

Social Learning Techniques

Modeling procedures can be used to teach both new skills and new ways of combining old skills. Modeling results in new behaviors being elicited which can then be reinforced using operant techniques such as positive reinforcement. Feedback, which stresses the positive aspects of the client's performance, and rehearsal by the client can also be used in combination with modeling and reinforcement. This combination has been used successfully for parent training programs (Nay, 1979). Bandura (1969) has carried out extensive research on the use of modeling for a variety of behaviors, and its effectiveness as an intervention technique appears to have been confirmed.

The case of Michael which follows exemplifies the use of humanistic core conditions and modeling of spontaneous behavior to assist a rigid, withdrawn child. The authors have coined the term "expansion training" (Kaczmarek & LeVine, 1980) for the eclectic approach demonstrated in this case that is particularly suited to anxious children. The primary principles of expansion training can be summarized as:

1. The practitioner avoids reflection, insight, interpretation, and other feedback that may reinforce anxious thinking.

2. The practitioner models spontaneous, playful behavior in the counseling sessions and assures that such behavior does not merit punishment.

3. The practitioner does not actively involve parents or teachers to reinforce or monitor the child's behavior. Changes are gradual, appropriate, and self-reinforcing.

4. The practitioner verbally reinforces any active and spontaneous behavior that the client exhibits in sessions (as long as it is not dangerous to the client or to others), whether or not the behavior is goal directed.

5. The practitioner designs one or more relatively innocuous conflict situations in the counseling sessions and then models alternative ways of handling those dilemmas.

6. As counseling progresses, the practitioner models conflict situations that more closely illustrates a client's concern and again models alternative behavior for handling the dilemmas.

The case provides a brief overview of the symptomology leading to Michael's referral by his classroom teacher to the school counselor. The activities of several exemplary sessions are then overviewed.

Case 5.1. The Case of Michael

History

Michael, an 8-year-old boy, was referred for counseling by his father, a school counselor. Michael was an only child who lived with his father and stepmother. Michael's father was concerned about his son's lack of friends, maintenance of a power struggle in the home, and rigidity in completing tasks.

Before our meeting, Michael had participated in a client-centered, peer-counseling group, where he initiated a power struggle. According to the group facilitator, Michael used the group to discuss his own issues. He talked about his lack of friends and accused the other group members of not liking him. Michael became emotional, sometimes screaming at his peers, often crying and ventilating hostility toward his father. "I hate my father. I have the world's worst father." After two sessions, Michael became an unwilling group member. He complained about coming and used the excuse that he was falling behind in his schoolwork. In the words of the group facilitator, "I was not pleased with the results."

Michael's third-grade teacher reemphasized his lack of friends. According to her, Michael was hesitant to approach other children, but when he did, he tended to alienate his peers with "his subordinate attitudes and his agitated behavior." Michael rarely went out for recess, and on the few occasions when he did, he played alone.

Sessions II and III

The counselor decided to follow Michael's lead in determining the activity to use for modeling spontaneous behavior. His favorite classroom activity, drawing with colored markers, was his choice. Michael's first drawing was a desert landscape that took him two sessions to complete. He outlined the mountains, the sun, and the moon before he proceeded to methodically color them, using predominately blue, brown, and black. Atop the highest mountain peak, he drew a rock and a yucca tree, both placed precariously near the edge. After he had completed the picture, Michael wrote the words Help, OK, and Never.

Michael gave rigid attention to detail and took a very careful approach to drawing. Whenever he took a marker from a box, he would slip a pencil in its place. He would stop the tape recorder while drawing because he could not draw and speak simultaneously.

During this session, the counselor purposely did not put the caps back on the markers as a way of demonstrating more spontaneous behavior. Michael slapped the counselor's hand and stated, "You don't leave caps off markers. They'll dry up." The practitioner also noticed that Michael froze when he accidentally drew on the table. He wiped the table clean immediately because he believed that he would be reprimanded. During both sessions he left after only 20 minutes had elapsed.

Session IV

The counselor concentrated on modeling freer methods of drawing. Michael had begun work on a house when the counselor dumped all of the markers onto the table and began to make bold strokes on the paper.

Counselor: I am going to draw with my eyes closed.

Michael: You cheat; you just make lines.

Counselor: I just make whatever I feel like making.

Michael: You never know what you're making until you're done.

Counselor: I don't like to know what I'm making. It's fun to figure it out when I'm done. And if I don't really make anything, that's all right too.

Time passes (15 minutes)

Michael: I want to make what you're making, it looks more interesting.

Michael put the house drawing aside and began to draw with his eyes closed. He also started to imitate the counselor's choice of color. Then Michael exhibited spontaneous behavior beyond simple imitation by drawing with three colors at once. The completed picture was a conglomeration of circular colored lines that were thickly massed in the center and thinly massed as they moved away from the center. Michael finished the session by writing the word happy on his drawing. The counselor had to remind him that the session was over.

Session V

Because Michael had shown fear when he accidentally wrote on the table, the counselor decided to model an alternate way of dealng with a similar situation. The counselor broke one of Michael's favorite markers on purpose.

Michael: What happened to the marker?

Counselor: It was on the floor and I stepped on it.
It was an accident - no big deal.

Michael: Won't it cost a lot of money to get another?

Counselor: Not really.

Michael: This sure is your bad luck day.

Counselor: Bad day - no. It was just one of those things
that happens. It's really no big deal.

In this session Michael remembered having drawn with his eyes closed, and he expressed a desire to repeat the experience. The counselor followed Michael's lead and ended up with a series of multicolored marks on her paper. Michael looked at the counselor's picture and decided the marks were actually "dots." Taking a black crayon, he quickly connected the dots to form a creature with two distinct heads, one on each side of the paper, that joined in the middle of the paper. Each of the appendages was given an eye and Michael proudly announced that he had drawn a "dragon walking backwards."

Results

The counselor saw Michael for 30-minute sessions each week for one semester. It was difficult to find a measurable index to monitor results. His curriculum had been individualized, and it was not possible to compare the number of assignments given and the number completed. The only index available was the number of times that Michael went out to recess. In February, before counseling was initiated, Michael did not go out to recess at all. Even though his teacher sent him out, he would sneak back into the room to work on assignments. By the end of the semester, Michael was attending recess at least twice a week. Because the counselor saw Michael during the recess period, the maximum number of times he could go out was four. Also, when Michael did stay in from recess, it was increasingly done to complete art projects, a favorite pasttime of his.

The counselor did not actively involve Michael's parents in the counseling process. Michael's parents, however, did seek out the counselor at the close of the semester to discuss the changes they observed in their son. Michael's five-year struggle with his stepmother had eased considerably. He gradually learned to verbalize his difficulty in adjusting to changes. Now when Michael loses in a game of Monopoly with his family, instead of throwing a tantrum he says, "No big deal."

Implications of Behavior Therapy

A number of studies have demonstrated that learning principles derived from early experimental research with animals and humans can provide a clear and systematic way of helping children modify inappropriate behavior and learn more appropriate alternatives. Research about the efficacy of the behavioral approaches is strong. Some profoundly disturbed children have been helped by behavioral approaches when all other therapeutic techniques have failed (Lovaas, Koegel, Sommons, & Stevens-Long, 1973). One of the most powerful features of behavior therapy is that the method of continuously monitoring behaviors (partly made possible because of the observative nature of child behavior) allows for constant and precise evaluation of the efficacy of treatment (Pinkston, et al, 1982).

A major criticism of the behavioral approach is that the techniques are necessary but not sufficient to ameliorate a range of maladjustment. Some argue that the behavioral approaches are needlessly tedious because they do not exploit children's ability to think. These critics argue that through understanding and/or cognitive restructuring (to be discussed in the next section), complex responses can be rapidly taught. They believe behavioral approaches are limited because they emphasize the development of discrete response sets. Yet, no one could argue that the extinction of extremely maladaptive behavior and development of new appropriate behavior is not an important gain. The issue, then, is not whether behavior therapy works, but how its effectiveness can be extended by combining it with approaches that focus on clients' developing a broad range of new attitudes, behaviors, and emotions. One way in which this combination has taken place has been with the development of the socio-behavioral approach (Thomas, 1977) which uses techniques derived from behavior therapy and social psychology. Another development has been that of cognitive behavior therapy.

COGNITIVE BEHAVIOR THERAPY

Recent years have witnessed a sharp resurgence of interest in cognitive processes. Essentially, cognitive psychologists are interested in studying and understanding complex mental processes such as imagery, symbolic representation of external events, and verbal coding of experience. Perhaps the most dramatic development in behavior therapy in the 1970's was the emphasis on cognitive processes in behavior therapy. The terms "cognitive behavior therapy" and "cognitive behavior modification" are used frequently to describe this recent development. The procedures that have received most attention in the recent development of cognitive behavior therapy and that merit the most attention because of their importance are referred to as cognitive restructuring. The essential notion of cognitive restructuring is that emotional disorders are the result of maladaptive thought patterns and the task of therapy is to restructure these maladaptive cognitions. Let us now examine some of the various techniques that fall under the general rubric of cognitive restructuring techniques.

Rational-Emotive Therapy

Albert Ellis (1962) was one of the first psychotherapists to explore use of cognitive restructuring in his "A, B, C" approach to therapy. Ellis explains that we usually perceive the events at point "A" as causing the negative reactions at point "C." For example, a child may perceive others' teasing on the playground (point "A") as causing him or her to be alone (point "C"). Ellis proposes that it is the child's interpretation of point "A," "Nobody likes me," or "I'll never have any friends" (point "B"), that causes the undesirable state at point "C."

A	B	C
Teasing on Playground	"I must be awful." or "No one ever likes me." or "I can't defend myself." or "Kids always pick on me."	Child now hesitates to interact with others at school; or: Child now acts differently from other children dressing peculiarly, etc., as if to say, "I am awful."

When clients experience maladjustment, to Ellis it is because their self-cognitions at point "B" carry a highly charged self-criticism, "catastrophisizing" the consequences at point "A." Programmed with a new cognitive interpretation of the event, the negative consequences will be attenuated.

A	B	C
Teasing on Playground	"Oh well, who wanted to be friends with them." Or "So they tease me, that's not so awful." Or "Lots of kids get teased. Or "Teasing is attention, and I like attention."	Child still seeks company of others and withdrawal or awkwardness with peers does not generalize.

Ellis' (1962) approach is very directive. He capitalizes upon clients' desires to please the therapist. He suggests, persuades, and bombards the clients with feedback aimed at restructuring their self-cognitions (Freedman, Kaplan, & Sadock, 1976). In the Case of Charlie, Keat (1974, pp. 76-77) employs Ellis' Rational-Emotive Therapy to restructure Charlie's self-destructive messages about his repaired and practically unnoticeable cleft palate.

Case 5.2. The Case of Charlie

Therapist: Let's see what the other children are saying to you. What
            do they call you?

Charlie: Usually two names. Either Bugs Bunny or Lippy.

Therapist: How do you feel when they say this?

Charlie: Bad.

Therapist: Let me guess what you're telling yourself. Other kids
            call me Bugs Bunny or Lippy, so I must be pretty
            funny-looking.

Charlie: Yeah.

Therapist: What's so great about what they think? How do they rate
            to say how you look?

Charlie: Don't know.

Therapist: Well, they're not really so hot. Let's see about the
            Bugs Bunny bit. Look at my teeth (counselor
            shows his crooked teeth). Whose do you think are
            worse? Mine or yours?
            (Some therapists use a mirror at this stage to show the
            client how he looks.)

Charlie: Yours.

Therapist: O. K. That's the reality of it. My teeth are worse
            off than yours. Now what's so bad about yours?

Charlie: Not much.

Therapist: Right. You know the saying "sticks and stones?"

Charlie: Yeah.

Therapist: What's the rest?

Charlie: You know it.

Therapist: Yeah. But I want to hear you say it.

Charlie: What's that again?

Therapist: Sticks and stones will break my bones but. . ."

Charlie: Yeah

Therapist: What's the rest?

Charlie: Names will never hurt me.

Therapist: That's it. But that's not what you're telling yourself.
            Names do hurt you now. But they shouldn't. So now,
            what do you say?"

Charlie: Names won't hurt me.

Therapist: That's right. And also, I feel sorry for others who
            have to pick on you to feel good. It's really their
            problem if they need to make fun of you.

   In this case, four attitudes were restructured cognitively. The child was: (1) told not to value others' opinions so much; (2) confronted with reality; (3) told alternative sentences to say to himself; and (4) taught to project the pathology onto the other children rather than absorbing it as his problem. By using oneself as a guide to one's own feeling of self-esteem, the child has a more stable means for evaluating himself. In reality, some of the most physically beautiful people consider themselves ugly. Marilyn Monroe is a classic example of a person who did not incorporate other's aesthetic evaluations into her own feelings of self-worth. She died a lonely and unhappy woman. Through cognitive restructuring, unsure children can learn that physical attributes are basically what a person tells him- or herself they are. Perceptions are, of course, influenced by environmental feedback, but the crucial dimension is what the person tells him- or herself.

Emotive Imagery

   Another technique of cognitive restructuring is to present emotive imagery to the child (Lazarus, 1976). Images can be physically drawn or verbally presented that help children conceive of their behavior or attitudes in new ways.

Paradoxical Intention

Another means of attaining cognitive restructuring is through the use of paradoxical intention. In paradoxical intention, the therapist greatly exaggerates and encourages the child to overuse his or her symptomology. Symptoms help a client to avoid dealing directly with stressful events. Paradoxical intention seems to facilitate adaptation because it encourages a client to move through a conflict situation and stop the unending repetition of the approach-avoidance behavior. Marshall (1976) presents several creative examples of the use of the paradoxical intention with children:

To a child who says, "I don't know," frequently rather than looking at the consequences of his or her acts, ask the child to develop a list of "Rules for Not Knowing."

To the silent child or one who talks but does not share the true content of his or her feelings, practice being silent.

To the child who tends to dismiss his or her inappropriate behavior as "not important," make a list of "How to Have Fun."

With manipulative children, have them teach you "Rules for Not Winning."

To the mistrusting children, tell them not to come to therapy since you are sure you cannot make it worth their while.

As another example, Caron (1980) worked with a child who had developed a habit of urinating 10 to 15 times per hour. The child constantly asked to use the bathroom whether at home or at school The behavior seemed to be maintained because it created a sense of power in the child. He felt he had maximal control over his significant adults. The practitioner challenged the child, "I bet you couldn't go to the bathroom 20 times an hour. You've never been able to go that often. Let's keep a record. If you can go 20 times in an hour, then I'll be really impressed." The child was placed in a paradoxical double-bind. If he accepted the therapist's challenge, he would be cooperating and thus would lose his power over the therapist's desires. In the first therapy session, he asked to use the bathroom four times. The challenge was reinstated in the next session. "I'm really disappointed you couldn't use the bathroom 20 times in our last session. I really thought you could do it." The client did not ask to use the bathroom during the entire session. The new behavior quickly generalized to other environments.

Self-Instructional Training

This technique, developed by Meichenbaum (1977) has become very popular in recent years. The method resembles Ellis' (1962) approach since it holds that irrational self-talk is the cause of emotional disorders. To make the technique applicable to children, Meichenbaum borrowed from the theorizing of Luria (1961) who has written on the developmental sequence by which children develop internalized speech and exert verbal-symbolic control over their behavior. According to Luria, the behavior of children is first regulated by the instructions of adults; eventually, children acquire control over their own behavior through the use of overt self-instructions which they ultimately internalize as covert self-instructions.

The steps involved in self-instructional training are as follows:

1.   The child is trained to identify and become aware of maladaptive thoughts (self-statements). For example, the child may fear the dark and believe that harm will come to him or her when the lights are turned off. The therapist assists the child to identify this fear of the dark and the self-statements made by the child about dark rooms, etc.

2.   The therapist models appropriate behavior while verbalizing effective action strategies. These verbalizations include an appraisal of task requirements, self-instructions that guide graded performance, self-statements that stress personal adequacy and counteract worry over failure, and covert self-reinforcement for successful performance. For example, the therapist may model that he or she is not afraid of a darkened room by saying out loud, "I am a brave person. I can take care of myself in the dark." Then, the therapist may model that he or she can control the situation by turning lights off and on. Finally, the therapist may model various methods of self-reinforcement for remaining in a darkened room without experiencing fear.

3.   The child is then told to perform the target behavior first while verbalizing aloud the appropriate self-instructions and then by covertly rehearsing them. The practitioner now provides feedback to the child concerning his or her performance as well as aiding in sharpening his or her positive self-statements.

If the training has been successful, the self-statements will replace the previous anxiety-inducing cognitions associated with the situation. Meichenbaum (1977) has shown that the method of self-instructional training can be used successfully to reduce diverse anxiety-related problems, to enhance creativity, to develop methods of coping with stress and pain, and to increase self-control in impulsive children.

Implications of Cognitive Behavior Therapy

The basic premise of the cognitive behavior methods of therapy is that children as well as adults react not to the actual but to the perceived environment. These perceptions may be inaccurate or irrational, in which case emotional distress may be the result. Further, this approach recognizes the importance of what people say to themselves in determining their behavior. Thus, the focus of therapy is on changing the things that people say to themselves, implicitly if not explicitly, which lead to ineffective behavior and emotional disturbance.

It is important to point out that both the theory and actual application of cognitive behavior therapy are incomplete. Numerous questions concern the best way to facilitate cognitive restructuring in children. For instance, what is the best way to teach self-statements to children? Is cognitive restructuring more effective with some types of childhood disorders (phobias) than with others (attention deficits)? Also necessary are studies which focus on the development of an explicit technology for maximizing generality across behaviors, environmental settings, and that have long-term consequences. In addition, because of cognitive behavior theories' tendency to emphasize personal change, more emphasis needs to be placed on how strategies for affecting social factors can be integrated into the theoretical framework. Nevertheless, despite these questions, cognitive behavior theory promises to increase in popularity·in the future.

CHAPTER 6

HUMANISM AND THE PSYCHOSOCIAL PERSPECTIVE

In contrast to the psychoanalytic and behavioristic approaches to child therapy, other practitioners prefer to take a more socially-oriented approach. These approaches focus on the individual as a social being and attempt to understand the family and other relationships that have molded the child's personality and behavior. The socially oriented approaches to child therapy are well articulated by the psychosocial theorists such as Alfred Adler and Rudolph Dreikurs, by various humanists such as Virginia Axline, Clark Moustakes, and William Glasser, and by the Gestalt approach of Virginia Oaklander.

THE PSYCHOSOCIAL APPROACHES

Adler's Theory of Individual Psychology

You probably recall that Alfred Adler was one of Sigmund Freud's earliest disciples. He was a charter member of the Vienna Psychoanalytic Society and later its president. However, Adler developed ideas at variance with those of Freud and the Vienna Society, discrediting the importance of psychic determinism and emphasizing social influence. He resigned as president of the Vienna Society and formed his own group which became known as Individual Psychology (Hall & Lindzey, 1970) . He inspired the establishment of an experimental school in Vienna where neurotic as well as normal children were counseled in joint sessions with parents and teachers (Belkin, 1980).

Adler's break from analytic thought because of its emphasis upon psychic determinism lead to several important theses of great utility to the child practitioner. From his theory of personality emerged techniques of use in adult and family therapy. A number of his students, Dreikurs and Soltz (1964) and Dinkmeyer and Caldwell (1970), extrapolated his tenets to develop useful child therapy techniques.

Basic Principles of Adlerian Child Therapy

Adler proposed that people are inherently social beings. They are motivated primarily by social rather than sexual desires. A good demonstration of Adler's position in this regard can be seen in his reinterpretation of the Freudian concept of the Oedipal Complex.

...it is supposed that children have a tendency to fall in love with their mothers and wish to marry them and to hate their fathers and wish to kill them. Such a mistake could never arise if we understood the development of children. The Oedipus Complex could appear only in a child who wishes to occupy his mother's whole attention and get rid of everyone else. Such a desire is not sexual. It is a desire to subjugate the mother, to have complete control over her and to make her into a servant. It can only occur with children who have been pampered by their mothers and whose feeling of fellowship has never included the rest of the world (Adler, 1958, p. 126).

Because of early experiences, each person is a unique creative being. Adler pointed out that children feel inferior because of their limited physical and cognitive capacities. They strive for superiority, to become competent in personal and social realms. If children meet a number of discouraging situations at home and at school, they become disheartened. Out of their successes and failures, children develop a "style of life," a patterned means of seeking superiority. This style of life is well-established by age four or five.

Much of Adler's research focused upon the roles children adopt within the family. He believed that the eldest child possessed considerable freedom in determining a style of life. Adler proposed that most first born children achieve feelings of superiority through socially-sanctioned achievement. However, the eldest suffer feelings of stress because their power in the family is dethroned through the birth of younger siblings. Subsequent children have less choice in their style of life. Characteristically, they do not choose the same pattern as the eldest because this leads to rivalry and frustration. The youngest child typically experiences some feelings of inferiority by virtue of his or her size and age. Current research has supported some of Adler's predictions about children's roles, but research demonstrates that a number of factors besides the child's position in the family contribute to the child's personality development and personal goals and attitudes (Hall & Lindzey, 1970).

Adler introduced the idea of family intervention when treating disturbed children. In family conferences, he would discuss the target child's and other family member's styles of life. Then, he would host a discussion among family members about ways each one could help the maladjusted child develop socially appropriate behaviors.

Dreikurs' Extension of the Theory of Individual Psychology

Dreikurs' extension of Adlerian principles leads to some very effective means of therapeutic intervention. Dreikurs (Dreikurs & Soltz, 1964) developed a system for characterizing children's faulty goals. He built upon Adler's construct that children intuitively strive for superiority. If they fail to achieve a sense of superiority through socially acceptable means, they will select one of four faulty goals. They may strive for attention, that is, instead of seeking to find a place in the world by cooperation, they seek to be noticed, regardless of whether the attention meets others' needs or their own long-term goals. Some children deal with feelings of social inferiority by seeking power. They feel superior if they win, regardless of the consequences of that winning upon themselves or others. Still other children will seek revenge. They build a style of life centered upon "getting even" with others that they perceive are acting superior. Still other children compensate for feelings of inferiority by displaying inadequacies. They obtain recognition by becoming incompetent, beseeching for help. Each of these faulty goals may be pursued actively or passively. In the active stance, the goal is directly sought. In the passive stance, the lack of activity leads to achieving the faulty goal. Table 6.1 lists the faulty goals and some typical active and passive means of achieving them.

Once the purpose of a child's misbehavior is established, the therapist can work with the child's family and school so that the faulty striving for superiority no longer leads to the desired goal. For the attention-getter, passive and active attempts to be noticed are ignored. For children with a faulty goal of power, the power struggle must be systematically avoided. Dreikurs recommends that the recipients of the child's struggle for power (e.g., parents teachers, etc.) simply not respond. He has even recommended that parents remove themselves from the environment when in a struggle for power with the child. By this means the child recognizes that parents cannot be controlled. For those seeking retaliation and revenge, Dreikurs believes the use of restitution is most beneficial. If the child destroys property, he must mend it or find a replacement. If a child hurts another's feelings, she must apologize. Dreikurs also recommends the use of "natural consequences." In many cases, a faulty goal leads to situations that are aversive. If the adults allow the consequences to occur naturally, the aversive effects provide control over the behavior. For example, if the child breaks confidences of other family members, it is decided in a family meeting that confidences will no longer be told to the child until the child again wins the trust of others. If the child "sets-up" another's misbehavior, he or she is held responsible for the other's act. Dreikurs sees the displaying of inadequacies as a most serious faulty goal. If not remediated, the child who displays inadequacies eventually no longer feels any personal power. The therapist should encourage these children to act constructively. Any constructive act reverses the trend of increasing feelings of inadequacy. Important individuals in the child's life must refuse to accept statements of the child's inadequacy as accurate. These children must be encouraged to seek their competencies, and their successful, assertive behavior should be reinforced. Sympathy from others (e.g., "It's not your fault you're clumsy, not everyone can be coordinated at your age.") fosters the child's belief that he or she can gain a noticeable place in the world by being inadequate.

Table 6.1

**Examples of Faulty Goals to Compensate
for Feelings of Social Inadequacy**

Type of Faulty Goal	Active Examples	Passive Examples
Attention Getting	Getting good grades simply for the attention, not because the child wants to learn; always wanting to perform for family and Friends.	Being excessively quiet; losing or gaining an Inordinate amount of weight; not turning in class assignments.
Power	Always wants to be the leader; openly defies parents, teachers & other authorities.	Soiling & wetting after physiological skill for continence is obtained; refusal to cooperate, to answer a question, or to complete a chore.
Revenge	Physically attacks siblings & other children; is destructive to others' property; makes hurtful comments, embarrasses others, or does not keep confidences.	Sets others up for attack, for example, provoking a sibling into a fight or destructive activity, then refusing to acknowledge his or her own role; encourages peers to report on one another's misbehaviors.
Displaying Inadequacy	Frequent, open criticism of self; frequently asking for help; making jokes at one's own expense.	Withdrawing; frequent crying; forgetting to complete assignments.

Implications of Psychosocial Approaches

In general, the Individual Psychology paradigm helps the therapist label the social factors that contribute to or maintain maladjustment. If these social factors can be clearly identified, remediation becomes a relatively direct task. The precepts and techniques of Individual Psychology can be readily mastered and can be taught to parents. Dinkmeyer and McKay (1976) have packaged materials called Systematic Training for Effective Parenting (STEP) for teaching Adlerian-Dreikurian principles to parents. Through the use of text, charts, and worksheets, principles of Individual Psychology and techniques for avoiding power struggles and using natural consequences are taught in about 8 weeks. Based upon the proposition that behavior is not fully determined by the psyche, the techniques of Adlerian-Dreikurian therapy are highly congruent with those of behavioral tenets of reinforcement. In the Individual Psychology model, much behavior can be explained and predicted with a few basic tenets that provide a comfortable means of communication between lay people and practitioners.

HUMANISTIC CONTRIBUTIONS TO CHILD THERAPY

Although the tenets of humanistic child therapy were not eludicated extensively until the last twenty years, threads of the approach were woven by earliest child clinicians. As explained in Chapter 4, Anna Freud rejected the then strongly held assumption that all meaningful therapy required the development and interpretation of a transference relationship. She emphasized the therapeutic benefit of a warm relationship between the therapist and child. In the 1940's, Allen (1942, 1963) outlined the qualities of a facilitative therapeutic relationship with a child. He stated that the therapist needed to begin "where the patient is" and guide the child toward a more creative acceptance and use of him or herself. He described child therapy as an experience in living rather than a corrective, remedial relationship.

According to the humanistic approach human nature is perceived as being essentially loving, cooperative, wise, and health-seeking. The humanistically-oriented therapist facilitates the client's exploration and discovery of her or his feelings and development of autonomy. Personal growth, rather than the abatement of illness or the reduction of symptoms, is the objective of this approach.

The basic principles of humanistic psychotherapy are applicable to children and adults alike. The humanist maintains that all individuals are motivated for personal growth, wanting to actualize their potentials. Personal growth can be thwarted, however, if "significant others" (family and others with important impact upon one's physical and psychological needs) are judgmental and nonaccepting. Once thwarted, individuals tend to mask their personalities, attitudes, and beliefs. They hide themselves either by withdrawing or by acting out. Therefore, maladaptive behavior occurs whenever individuals through social pressure lose confidence in themselves. Their growth and self-actualization is stunted and indirect.

It follows that humanistic therapy must provide an atmosphere of complete acceptance. If the therapeutic climate is warm and accepting, the clients will no longer limit their potentials and will begin discovering answers to their dilemmas (Rogers, 1951). In a very accepting atmosphere, clients will ponder the existential dilemmas that confront each one of us: What is the purpose of my life? How much control do I have over my life? Why must I die? (Axline, 1969).

A number of theorists have been responsible for translating the basic humanistic tenets for use in child therapy. Axline (1969) developed a nondirective system of play therapy that fosters a therapeutic atmosphere of acceptance. Ginott (1961), Dimick and Huff (1970) and others help to specify the personal qualities the therapist must project in successful play therapy. Moustakes (1973), Glasser (1965), and others have helped to operationalize the nature of the existential dilemma in child therapy. A special application of humanistic theory to child therapy that we shall discuss is gestalt techniques.

Personal Qualities of the Humanistic Child Therapist

The humanists have identified a number of personal qualities in therapists that contribute to a positive, warm atmosphere in therapy. These qualities have been tested experimentally in adult therapy-client dyads (Truax & Carkhuff, 1967). They are accepted by most humanistic child therapists, but are not thoroughly validated against child client populations. In their widely accepted text on child counseling, Dimick and Huff (1970) summarize the important qualities of the humanistic therapist.

Unconditional Positive Regard

The therapist expresses unqualified acceptance and faith in the child and his or her potentialities. This faith is conveyed by encouraging the child to make personal decisions and by accepting and appreciating everything the child says and does. The therapist listens carefully and communicates a desire to understand. All of the therapist's verbal and nonverbal messages establish an atmosphere of, "I hold your peculiarities, your loves and your hates, your mannerisms and your habits in esteem and honor as I do all aspects of your self" (Moustakes, 1959, p.6).

Many words are synonymous with unconditional positive regard-- respect, prizing, altruistic love. To communicate unconditional positive regard, the therapist must hold an underlying commitment to others, a belief in children's intrinsic good nature, and an optimism that the children can change.

Empathy

The practitioner must communicate that he or she appreciates the child's feelings. The practitioner symbolically takes on the child's role so that he or she can reflect understanding about the child's feelings. The practitioner is not sympathetic, that is, he or she does not excuse or sanction the child's bad feelings. Nor does the therapist become an advocate of the child against outside adversaries. An example of an empathic response would be, "You're feeling really bad that your brother keeps breaking your toys." The therapist would not respond, "Your brother is really mean. I don't blame you for wanting him to be out of the family."

Genuineness

The therapist communicates a flexible, open manner. The therapist admits his or her errors and shortcomings. The therapist discloses about feelings of vulnerability. The humanistic therapist may say to a child, for example, "I really missed you when you didn't come to our appointment last week;" or "I'm really feeling frustrated. I'm not sure how to show you that you can trust me." The therapist does not stand in judgment of the child. For example, the therapist would not say, "The trouble with you is ---." Rather, the therapist shares with the child. The therapist might say, "How can I help you change the way you're handling those upsetting circumstances." The therapist is profoundly serious in purpose and intensely absorbed in the therapeutic process. The therapist's voice, touch, and genuine concern communicate active involvement with the child.

Concreteness

The therapist's language is relevant to the child. The therapist does not talk down to the child, but communicates clearly guarding against hidden or double messages.

Ginott (1961) writes that the major therapeutic cement of child therapy is the practitioner's modeling of effective ways of being. To the extent that the therapist is emotionally stable, warm, and open, the child will find the therapeutic environment one in which he or she can grow. To Ginott, the humanistic child therapist is a "responsible anarchistic." The therapist does not impose values on the child, but models responsible living and commitment to the child. The therapist encourages the child to break the shackles of unfair socialization and to make a commitment to personal growth.

Nondirective Play Therapy

A number of humanistic child therapists believe that if a therapist provides a warm, supportive atmosphere, children will resolve their own difficulties. Axline (1969) is the major spokesperson of this nondirective play therapy stance. Axline stresses that the potential to grow and to resolve one's dilemmas is within each child. If the therapist provides a sound therapeutic climate, the child will resolve spontaneously his or her conflicts. Axline lists eight steps that are necessary to create a sound play therapy milieu:

1. Accept the child as he or she is. The therapist should never evaluate or judge the child. The therapist should not teach the child about the consequences of his or her acts, nor should the therapist attempt to offer answers to the child's dilemmas.

2. Establish a positive relationship. The therapist should endeavor to make the play therapy sessions an enjoyable experience. The therapist communicates pleasure to be with the child and likes the child just as is.

3. Be permissive. The therapist should allow for a free expression of feelings. The therapist should not sanction or disapprove of any feelings the child presents.

4. Reflect feelings and content. As the child plays, the therapist observes attentively. The therapist mirrors the child's comments in a manner that facilitates insight. As one reads case studies of Axline and her students, it is apparent that she particularly mirrors the child's affect. Thus, if a child says, "I want to play with the doll house now," Axline may simply watch attentively. If the child says, "I need to play house," the therapist might respond, "The play house is important to you."

5. Let the child be responsible for his or her choices. Again, the therapist interferes as little as possible. If a child wants to smear fingerpaints on his or her clothes, the therapist simply responds, "You want to smear paint now." The therapist would not ask questions such as, "What will your mother think if your clothes are dirty?"

6. Consistently communicate to the child that in play therapy the child can and will lead. If the child wants to terminate the session early, it is terminated.

If the child wants the therapist to play with him or her, only then does the therapist participate.

7. Allow the child to explore feelings at his or her own pace. The practitioner should not attempt to hurry the counseling process by reminding the child of what has happened previously or by prompting the child to try to resolve dilemmas.

8. Establish only those limits that are needed. The therapist would not, for example, discuss an injunction against hitting at the initiation of play therapy. This limit would only be raised if the child continued to assault the therapist. Similarly, the therapist would not demand that the child help clean up the playroom.

Axline's reflective stance is illustrated in the case study excerpt which follows:

Child: I want to drink from the nursing bottle.

Therapist: There it is, over on the shelf.
            Drink from the nursing bottle if you
            want to.

Child: Know what?

Therapist: Hmm?

Child: I want to crawl on the floor and
            drink my bottle.

Therapist: You want to act just like a
            baby. Well, go ahead.
            (Child Hesitates) You don't
            know whether you should or not.

Child: Me little baby.

Therapist: You like to be a little baby.

Child: Ummhumm (Child continues to suck
            on the bottle for the rest of the hour.)
(Axline, 1947, p. 174)

In sum, in nondirective play therapy a child's behavior and affect is accepted as much as possible within the limits of the child's and therapist's physical safety. The therapist is actively attentive, but is a responder, never an initiator of the therapeutic process. Axline (1969) presents many case studies in which children seem to "work through" their hurts and find answers to their own dilemmas within accepting environments. Other therapists, such as Moustakes and Glasser whom we discuss next, argue that the atmosphere of acceptance can be maintained while the therapist is more active. They propose that the the therapeutic process is enhanced by supportive, active therapeutic intervention.

The Existential Dilemma

Several humanistic child therapists emphasize the importance of dealing with existential dilemmas in child counseling. Moustakes (1959) writes that the root of children's maladjustment is "submission and denial of the self." The child relinquishes his or her uniqueness. His play therapy is aimed at assisting children to rediscover their unique values and beliefs and reestablish a purpose to their lives that is based upon those unique competencies. To accomplish this goal, Moustakes (1973) offers feedback to his child clients that helps them see their unique attributes and encourages them to make active decisions about their lives. Further, he explains that the most meaningful feedback can be offered within the therapeutic relationship. The therapist shows his or her reactions to the child: "When you do that, it has no consequence upon me." "When you stick your tongue out at me, I feel like going away." The therapist helps the child client clarify values. "Yesterday, you said you'd like to be a scientist; today, you said you don't like school. How can you become a scientist if you choose not to go to school?" The therapist encourages the child to be responsible, to look at the consequences of his or her acts and to make conscious decisions that are consonant with the child's long-range goals.

The following is an excerpt from a play session with a 7-year-old withdrawn and anxious girl.

> Therapist: In here, if you spill and mess, it is all right...As long as you don't mind, it doesn't bother me. (She spills water on the floor and sand on her dress. She looks at the therapist and begins to laugh.)
>
> Therapist: In here, you can laugh about messing. But what about at home?
>
> Child: No. There I have to keep clean.
>
> Therapist: Your mother doesn't like you to get dirty.

Child: When I play with mud, I keep away from my mother. I try to wash it off before she sees me, but sometimes she catches me and screams "K-A-R-E-N."

Therapist: So, at home ther are some things your mother doesn't like you to do?

Child: Yes, many things.

Therapist: You are not always free to do what you want to do.

Child: No. Not free

(Moustakes, 1975, p. 38)

Glasser (1965) writes further about the importance of teaching the child to make wise decisions. He states that children experience problems if they fail to receive love. Without love, their self-worth diminishes, and they make poor choices. Not just delinquent children, but all troubled children (underachievers, anxious, depressed, etc.) make poor choices.

Glasser stresses that a therapist must become actively involved with the client in order to foster feelings of hope and worthiness within the child. Then, the therapist prompts the child to make a judgment about what he or she is doing that leads to feelings of failure. Following this identification of the problem, the therapist helps the child verbally design better choices. The therapist requests a commitment from the child to try these new choices. The therapist contracts with the child about the consequences that will ensue if he or she breaks the commitment. In Glasser's Reality Therapy, the therapist communicates love, but does not allow the child to escape responsibility for designing a more meaningful, productive life.

The Case of P.W. demonstrates an active humanistic stance in child therapy. The therapist relates personally and intimately with the child. The therapist also plays the role of a significant other, "the stranger," in P.W.'s life, thereby encouraging P.W. to learn new ways to relate to his father who he perceived as a stranger.

Case 6.1. The Case of P. W.

When I first met five-year-old P.W., he was very withdrawn and would not even tell his parents or teacher when he needed to use the bathroom. He cried often and seemed to tremble when spoken to. When Mrs. W. first brought P. to see me, she had told him nothing about me. She deceived him by stating, "I'm just going around the corner; I will be right back." When Mrs. W. left, P. had a look of terror on his face and began sobbing. I brought him to my office and held him while he cried. I responded, "It seems like you don't know whether to believe your mother or not. You feel really scared; you don't know if she's coming back."

Over the next few sessions P. sat idly in the middle of the room and looked at me. I set out some toys that I thought might be of some interest to him, but he did not respond.

One day, I brought out a music box, opened it so that the music would start, and P. inched toward it. I explained, "I would be glad to teach you how to run the music box, and you can use it whenever you are here." P.'s eyes lit up. I showed him how to wind up the music box and how to open it. He began to ask some questions, and I discovered he could express himself very well.

In play therapy, P. frequently took adult male figures and buried them in play dough. Employing a toy castle, he would often throw "the mean man" in the dungeon for a million years and set him on fire.

During the sixth session, I suggested to P. that we become "explorers." We began walking farther and farther away from my office, and I would reinforce P. for his new assertiveness, "Look how brave and strong you are. Look how much you are learning to do." Gradually, P. would walk blocks away from the office with me. His confidence generalized to other environments. He began speaking in class and over the next several months learned his alphabet and numbers from one to ten.

One game that P.W. initiated he entitled, "The Stranger." We would go to utility tunnels underneath the office building. P. requested, "You play the mean stranger. You try and get me." I would chase P. up and down the tunnels. Finally, P. would turn around and shoot me, thus getting rid of the mean stranger. I began asking, "Poor me, I don't want to be a mean person. What can I do to be nice?" P. eventually responded that "to be nice, you have to let me know you."

This game initiated dialogue about how frightened he was of his father. He felt his father spent little time with him, seldom expressed his ideas and thoughts, and did not offer comfort or warmth to P. P. was encouraged to express his feelings about his father over a number of sessions. Once P. better understood his feelings about his father, P. and his therapist role played new ways of approaching him. P. learned to express intimate feelings to his family. His openness was paralleled by increased spontaneity and assertiveness. He became increasingly successful at academic tasks and began to form friendships. Gradually, his father responded to P. W.'s approaches, and they developed a more comfortable and open relationship.

Gestalt Techniques

A special socially-oriented perspective that draws from humanistic tenets of child therapy is gestalt. Akin to other humanistic theories, Fritz Perls, the originator of gestalt therapy, proposed that a key aspect of good mental health is personal growth. The gestalt therapist further believes that humans strive to complete gestalts, to interact as integrated wholes with the environment. When a person is restricted or rigid, he or she is unable to complete gestalts. The neurotic individual plays roles rather than living spontaneously, projects onto others what is incomplete in him or herself, and remains "stuck at an impasse" (Perls, 1969). Therapy focuses upon increasing a client's awareness, thereby enabling a client to "break through" an impasse and live more spontaneously. When the client can react spontaneously, with few roles, that client feels in harmony with the self and the environment and is personally healthy.

The gestalt therapist typically employs provocative "games" (also called "experiments" or "gimmicks") to help clients accept responsibility for, redefine, and reintegrate themselves with the environment. These games, such as "role reversal" and "empty chair technique" can be particularly appealing to older children because they provide an activity base to verbal therapy (Belkin, 1980).

Shostrom (1967) uses gestalt terms to describe some role playing, nonspontaneous life stances that some children adapt. Shostrom talks to children and their parents of "Freddy-the-Fox" who begins life as a crier to get others to take responsibility for him, "Tom-the-Tough" who uses hate and fear to control people, and "Carl-the-Competitor" who views winning as the most important goal in life.

Although many propose that gestalt techniques are particularly viable with children, little empirical research documents this position. Gannon (1972) reported that a gestalt group was effective in increasing openness of high school students. A variety of stimulating games and language gimmicks adapted for child and school counseling are outlined in Passons' (1975) text. In Chapter 11, we describe many of Oaklander's (1978) creative techniques that fall within the gestalt tradition.

Comparing the Humanistic and Psychosocial to the Psychoanalytic and Behavioral Approaches

The early approaches to child therapy were dominated by psychoanalytic theory. The strict application of analytic principles to the child therapy process led therapists such as Melanie Klein to look for the symbolic, primarily sexual, content in a child's play. The early child analysts often worked with their clients several times each week for a period of several years in order to foster and interpret transference so that the child could gain more insight about repressed impulses toward family members and the self.

Gradually, child analysts such as Anna Freud realized that children are not simply "little adults," and the process of therapy must be uniquely designed to meet their needs and their developmental levels of conceptualization. Anna Freud and other psychoanalytically-oriented psychoanalysts have stressed the importance of and the unique ways a child therapist can establish a "positive therapeutic alliance" with a child. With a positive therapeutic alliance, insights can be provided that prompt change.

The demands for psychotherapeutic services, the extensive commitment required for psychoanalytic psychotherapy, and new findings in developmental psychology have created an increased emphasis upon environmental interventions to curve childhood disorders. Through the work of Skinner, Bandura, and others, principles derived in laboratories have been extended to modify children's behaviors. The behavioral approaches provide quick, efficient ways that therapists, parents, teachers, and children themselves can learn to increase appropriate and decrease inappropriate behaviors. The behaviorists have demonstrated that not all insight leads to behavioral change, and that insight may not be necessary for behavioral change. By skillful manipulation of environmental contingencies, children can be helped to change a variety of discrete behaviors as well as pervasive life styles.

No one argues about the success of behaviorism in modifying a range of childhood symptomology, but many decry, "What has become of the child, the child's feelings, and rights to make personal decisions?" The socially-oriented approaches emerged as a third force to counterpoise the depersonalizing, dehumanizing qualities of the strict analytic and strict behavioral stances. The humanists propose that the child must be treated as a unique person first, object of scientific study secondly. The humanists have been quite successful in identifying core therapeutic conditions that help a child client feel that he or she is being treated like a unique person rather than an object of scientific investigation. Many believe that the humanists are defining therapeutic qualities that undercut effective behavioral and analytic therapy as well.

SUMMARY

To the humanists, children need acceptance from others as a basis for their accepting and valuing themselves. With self-esteem, children will be socially-productive members of society. They will learn to fulfill their needs in ways that do not deprive others of their abilities to meet their own needs. With acceptance and positive self-esteem, children will want to be close to others. They will cooperate and accept differences in others. With self-esteem, they will make wise decisions. The analysts first wrote of the "corrective therapeutic experience." The humanists have concentrated on defining the therapeutic qualities and interventions that create a warm, accepting atmosphere. Few therapists of any theoretical persuasion would argue against the core conditions established by the humanists. Most would laud the humanists for their attempts to operationalize the therapeutic qualities that are conducive to client growth.

Criticism of the approach takes several forms. Many believe that the core conditions of an effective therapeutic relationship which are central to humanistic thought are very vague. How can these core conditions be taught? How does the therapist really know if he or she is enacting them. As a whole, the work of Truax and Carkhuff (1967), Carkhuff and Berenson (1977), and associates demonstrate that these qualities can be taught. Further, little of this critical empirical research has been conducted with children. Extensive compilations of research suggest that the humanistic approach to therapy is a necessary, but not a sufficient condition to facilitate client gain. The humanists disagree, but their lofty language and abstract theories make empirical testing of client gain difficult.

CHAPTER 7

FAMILY THERAPY

Family therapy is a very potent means for assisting many child clients. It assumes that children do not and cannot have complete autonomy over their behavior. Children are a part of a family system, and they will act in ways consonant with the social rules laid down by their parents.

Compared to other therapeutic interventions, family therapy is a relatively recent innovation for assisting maladjusted children. During the social diagnostic period (1910-1930), social work was distinctive among the helping professions for emphasis in treating the family unit. Then, a shift in focus to the individual almost totally pushed family therapy out of social work practice until the 1950's (Sherman, 1981). In the 1950's, under the leadership of Gregory Bateson and Don Jackson, family therapy gained prominence among psychologists and psychiatrists. Family therapy combines two bodies of knowledge, personality dynamics and social systems, and thus draws upon theories of psychology and sociology. Just as its theoretical base derives from two sources, so the goals of family therapy are two-sided: to increase autonomy of individuals in the family and to facilitate smooth functioning of the family unit. Family therapists attempt to explain and treat the eternal struggle of family members for connectedness and separateness (Janzan & Oliver, 1980). Behind the basic premise that personal growth can be facilitated by assessing and working with a client's family, family therapists differ widely in theory and technique. A survey of 300 established family therapists revealed differences in their practices ranging from use of family therapy as an extension of individual therapy to only working with family units; from seeing few dangers involved in family therapy to elaborating upon many constraints for its use; and from offering insight interpretations to family groups to emphasizing behavioral prescriptions (Committee on the Family Group for the Advancement of Psychiatry, 1970).

On the whole, family therapists tend to build their approaches from either psychoanalytic or systems theory. Those ascribing to a analytically-oriented family therapy use family interviews to diagnose the etiology of a child's problem. Through family interviews, they decide how much of the child's difficulties are self-perpetuating because of internalized emotional problems and how much of the child's problems are serving as an expression of the parents' pathology. The analytically-oriented family therapist then designs individual and small group procedures to help the child and the parents deal with their part of the family difficulties. Thus, family sessions serve primarily as diagnostic sessions that provide clues to interpretations that will be made in individual therapy with the child or parents. They interact and affect one another, and a child's disturbance is viewed as fulfilling a psychologically-meaningful function for the system. Therefore, changes in the child, the "identified patient," necessitate changes in the entire family system. Otherwise, changes in the child will result in the appearance of new symptoms in other family members or the further destruction of the family as a unit.

Since the psychoanalytic approach to family therapy draws primarily upon principles we discussed in previous chapters, we will not discuss these procedures in detail in this chapter. Rather, most of this chapter will concentrate on the techniques of systems approaches to family therapy. The reader who wishes to conduct analytically-oriented family therapy will nevertheless find many of the suggestions of the family systems theorists applicable.

MAJOR CONTRIBUTORS TO FAMILY SYSTEMS THOUGHT

As stated earlier, family therapy combines knowledge of personality dynamics and social systems. Creative synthesis of divergent ideas is needed for this task. Since the 1950's, a number of very creative social scientists from varied fields such as medicine, social work, anthropology, psychology, psychiatry, and communications analysis have contributed to our repository of understanding about families in therapy. Let us mention some of the major figures in this field, then in following sections of the chapter, we will present ways that their thinking has been united into an organized view of how family systems function and malfunction and how family systems therapy should proceed. A discussion of how family practitioners assess families is in Chapter 10.

Gregory Bateson

In the 1950's, Bateson and his colleagues were instrumental in identifying patterns in family communication that can lead to emotional distress in individuals and disturbance with family functioning. Highly regarded is Bateson's theory about how members of families are often placed in "double binds" (that is, no win situations) by inconsistent communication (Bateson, Jackson, Haley, & Weakland, 1956). Bateson et al, (1956) suggested that schizophrenic youth were often raised by parents who communicated to them in an inconsistent manner. He coined the term "schizophrenogenic mother" for the parent who he believed provoked schizophrenia in her child because her verbal messages were confusing for the child to follow. Bateson et al. (1956) stated that schizophrenogenic mothers create double binds for their children. They communicate untenable requests so that no matter how the child responds, the child receives negative feedback and/or absence of reward. For example, a schizophrenogenic mother might say, "Come here, Johnny. Sit on my lap. You never show your mother you love her." When Johnny comes to his mother's lap, she retorts, "You're too dirty. Get off."

Johnny is in a double bind. If he had originally told his mother that he did not want to come to her (because he was dirty or just because he did not want to come to her), she would have responded, "You are bad; you don't love your mother." Johnny goes to his mother and is rejected. There is no way of Johnny's escaping negation by his mother in this interaction. Through language analysis, such as the "double bind", Bateson's work established the importance of communication in healthy and maladaptive families.

Don Jackson and Associates

In his psychiatric family practice, Jackson (1959) noted that families sought balance or homeostasis in how members relate to one another. For example, the aggressiveness of one family member might be balanced by the gentleness of another. When one family member changes or leaves, the balance is upset and everyone will change to create a new homeostasis. Jackson was a key member of Bateson's Palo Alto group which began family therapy while studying communication patterns of schizophrenic families. Jackson's focus on the dynamics between persons was based upon his belief that behavior and communication are the same. Jackson believed that family rituals and members' repetitious ways of communicating are evidence of a family's homeostasis. Further, because families seek homeostasis, they are slow to change. Change in family systems is a complex process which requires that all members adapt to a new balance.

Lyman C. Wynne

Lyman C. Wynne (1961) expanded upon Jackson's premise that families are slow to change. He suggested that some families create a facade of mutual support, "pseudomutuality." They espouse regard for one another, but in actuality are rigid and tolerate little divergence. Individual growth is hampered in families operating with pseudomutuality.

Murray Bowen

Bowen (1966), trained at the Menninger Clinic, suggested that it is helpful to think of the family system as possessing an ego in a fashion similar to employing the construct of ego to explain individual psychodynamics. He agreed with Wynne (1961) that healthy families allow individuals to be autonomous. Bowen (1966) states that members of healthy families identify with a group ego and have a sense of connection with one another. Many unhealthy families are characterized by "undifferentiated ego mass" in which members lose a sense of autonomy. The family members' identities fuse together. Their lives are enmeshed, and there is little intimate contact with people outside the family. Also unhealthy are families in which members are highly "disengaged." In disengaged families, members feel little identification with a family ego mass. Most intimate contacts are with individuals outside the family.

The concept of triangulation, when one family member tells a third person what he or she thinks of another family member, was developed after 12 years of work with Bowen's own family. Bowen detriangled himself from a series of enmeshed family interactions during a trip home to discuss the family business (Anonymous, 1972). Bowen noticed that effective family systems therapists applied systems theory to their own families. They would return from workshops, and develop a better working relationship with their own family members. In the chapter on family assessment, we review Bowen's system of family analysis in more detail.

James Bell

Bell (1964) studied extensively how members seek autonomy and control in families. He emphasized that children modify parents behaviors by their moods, activity levels, etc. In unhealthy families, members struggle overtly and/or covertly for power and control. In maladaptive families, children express frustration in having to follow rules and claim rules infringing on their freedoms are unfair. Parents, in turn, feel unappreciated and frustrated that they cannot exert more control. Healthy families are characterized by sharing, cooperation, and spontaneity.

Bell's treatment involved group counseling in which open communication among family mambers is encouraged. Bell (1964) explained that families in group counseling grow through various stages. Intervention is carefully planned in coordination with each stage. Serving the family as a group allows for treatment in a social context.

Robert MacGregor

MacGregor (1962) contributed greatly to the field of family systems theory through interdisciplinary models for intervention. Based upon his need to serve children and parents in southeast Texas who traveled many miles, MacGregor assembled a team of psychologists, social workers, and psychiatric residents to provide intense two-day family treatment sessions. In order to assist a family in distress, he recommended that a team of therapists work with the entire family, part of the family, and groups of families, according to their need. He called this multi-level approach to intervention "Multiple Impact Therapy."

Richard Speck

Speck (1967) extrapolated MacGregor's principles and developed techniques for working with an extended family in family therapy. Speck stated that certainly all individuals living with a troubled youngster needed to participate in therapy. He believed further that other significant family members that lived outside the home but had affected the family's values and beliefs needed to participate in therapy. The influence of these family members is felt and reacted to even if they are not present, and a new healthy pattern is best established if they are present in therapy. Speck (1967) encouraged critical family members to attend family meetings. With the cooperation of the extended family, a large "social network" is built that can help in the improvement of an emotionally disturbed family member.

Jay Haley

Haley (1963), an influential member of the Palo Alto Group, agrees with Bell that the primary cause of family dissension concerns control. The usual conflict in families is about rules and who will set the rules. The conflict is particularly severe if the ones who make the rules will not admit that they hold the power. As a communication analyst, Haley has provided sophisticated descriptions of the indirect verbal and nonverbal communication patterns that family members adopt in order to gain covert control. Haley states that a family member with a "symptom" gains control and achieves his or her goal through the symptom, but in doing so perpetuates the covert control characteristic of the family conflict. For example, a wife who is ostensibly dominated by her brusk, aggressive husband may gain attention and feel some control through hypochondriacal symptoms. Although her symptoms win her some attention, they eventually frustrate and alienate family members. As a consequence she feels further unappreciated and powerless, and the family conflict continues.

A major purpose of family therapy is to realign control and power. Initially, the therapist assumes control in order to realign forces. Haley believes that if the family therapist assumes control discretely through paradoxical maneuvers, some borrowed from Milton Erickson, then family members believe the changes are their own ideas and therefore do not resist.

Virginia Satir

A social worker, trained as a Gestalt therapist under Fritz Perls, Satir (1967, 1972) has added a humanistic orientation to family therapy. She believes that difficulties in families are created by a combination of individual and group factors: low self-esteem of one or more family members; poor communication patterns; and/or rigid roles. Satir (1967) identifies four types of persons who seem to frequently communicate in nonproductive ways. The "placator's" remarks indicate that he or she feels no good. Continually, the placator seems to be saying, "You are right; forgive me." The "criticizer" tends to center all communication by blaming someone else. The criticizer's covert message is that others are no good. Some family members are "intellectualizers." By being extremely reasonable at all times, the intellectualizer denies the family members' feelings. Finally, the "irrelevant" one communicates in a dizzy, distracting manner. When family members adopt these faulty communication patterns, successful resolution of difficulties is hampered.

Satir's family therapy involves use of very active techniques (role playing, other gestalt-type games) to help family members become aware of their roles in families. She also imparts information that educates the family members about maladaptive roles they are assuming. She uses communication exercises to help family members learn more open and direct ways of communicating with one another.

Richard Bandler and John Grinder

The base of clinical research by Bandler and Grinder was in analyzing the communication patterns of very successful psychotherapists including Milton Erickson, Fritz Perls, Albert Ellis, and others. Gradually, Bandler and Grinder expanded their work to study healthy and nonproductive communication patterns in and out of therapy. Collaborating with Satir (Bandler, Grinder, and Satir, 1976), they refer to the faulty stereotypical communication patterns that families adopt as "calibrated" patterns. Calibrated interpersonal communications are characterized by incongruency. For example, a specific individual's verbal communication may differ from his or her nonverbal communication. In calibrated communications, listeners tend to mistake part of a message for the whole message. For example, a listener may block out conflicting parts of a message and hear only that part that he or she wants to hear. Calibrated communications are further characterized by "mind reading." A listener assumes that he or she understands an abstract message and does not ask for further clarification. Bandler, Grinder, and Satir point out that we often speak in "nominalizations;" that is, we employ an abstract noun to stand for a multitude of feelings. Unfortunately, such nominalizations are often misunderstood. Thus, a wife may say that she wants more "freedom." A jealous husband assumes that this means she wants to have relationships with other men. She means that she wants to work outside the home. The husband would never have considered this "freedom." They both "mind read" that they know what the other feels. A final characteristic of calibrated communication is that a listener forms rigid, fixed generalizations about other's messages. It is the family therapist's role to uncover calibrated communications and to model and encourage open and spontaneous expression of ideas and feelings.

Salvador Minuchin

Minuchin (Minuchin, Montalvo, Guerney, Rosman, & Schurmer, 1967) have developed a popular, practical application of family system theory based upon his work with low socioeconomic families and at the Philadelphia Child Guidance Clinic. Empirical research, a dedication to training and practical, and direct systematic techniques may account for Minuchin's popularity in the late 1970's and 1980's (Nichols, 1984). The basic structural concepts are boundaries, subsystems, power, and alignments. The model is useful for a number of child problems as it takes into account the individual, the family, and the social context.

Every family has a structure which is revealed when the family is in action (Minuchin, 1974). "Boundaries" regulate the amount of contact between family members and the outside world. Small children repeatedly interrupting parents when they are talking indicates minimal boundaries.

Subsystems help the practitioner understand the functions of the family. If an emotionally abused child is looked to for leadership in a family, then the child is the executive subsystem, not the mother or father. Subsystems are determined by emotional boundaries, allowing autonomy of individuals yet permeable to ensure affection (Minuchin, and Fishman, 1981).

Structured family therapists believe it is important to avoid becoming part of the family, while at the same time gaining trust by accommodating to the family's usual patterns of behavior. Assessment techniques are used to activate existing but dormant structures and to alter alignments and shift power in and between subsystems. Restructuring is concrete, forceful, and dramatic which again may account for the popularity of this approach.

Nathan Ackerman

Nathan Ackerman, an early leader in family therapy, applied psychoanalytical theory learned while working with children at the Menninger Clinic to family practice. As the chief psychiatrist at Menniger Clinic, he followed the traditional model of the 1940's of the psychiatrist working with the child and the social worker assisting the mother. Dissatisfied with this model, he began having the therapist see both the child and the mother together (Nichols, 1984). He believed the therapist's role is to stir up the family interaction so family members break out of traditional roles and begin to relate to each other on deep levels of feeling and understanding (Ackerman, 1966). To accomplish this, he insisted that all persons living in a family attend all family sessions.

He established "emotional contact" with all family members before encouraging an open expression of feelings. Open and honest expressions were shared by the therapist as well. He emphasized the intrapsychic effects upon individual members by the family as a whole. The family helps shape a member's needs and desires and feelings of security and self-fulfillment.

Families may appear unified however, below the surface, they can be split into competing emotional components. The practitioner helps the family understand the factions, interactions, and individual feelings that lie behind the dysfunctional symptoms of individual family members. As each individual understands what he or she is feeling, doing, and thinking, each member can change patterns of behavior, thereby achieving deep intimacy (Thorman, 1982). Ackerman, who died in 1971, did not use a set of techniques but rather became deeply emotionally involved with families he treated, creating procedures for the individual family problem. At times, he worked with extended family members; at other times, he saw members individually. This creative and very flexible process makes it difficult to learn Ackerman's approach (Nichols, 1984).

Carl Whitaker

Colorful, radical, strong-willed, and provocative are terms used to describe Carl Whitaker's family therapy. Trained as a psychiatrist, Whitaker began using cotherapists with couples and children in the mid-1940's. Whitaker let his unconscious direct the therapeutic process to realign family power in more constructive patterns. He did not employ structure or a preplanned strategy (Whitaker, 1976). Whitaker's work has no clear theoretical base which may be why his work is not as well known as other pioneers of family therapy. His emotional "goading" of individual family members aids them in understanding their immediate experience in an environment of warm support. Although his treatment is flexible and unpredictable, he views the common problem of families as their inability to share their feelings (Nichols, 1984). He employed a variety of paradoxical and provocative approaches to encourage family members to drop facades and defenses and to express themselves openly to one another. In accord with basic humanistic tenets, he believed that an openness among family members allowed the family to function more adaptively.

We have reviewed major ideological advances in family therapy. In this new and rapidly growing field of practice, at least 43 distinct family therapy models have emerged. For a more complete analysis of the similarities and differences among the major models of family therapy, the reader is referred to *Mind in Therapy* (Kenney & Ross, 1985). Chapter 10 of this text provides an indepth discussion assessing means of healthy families. Next, we provide some general discussion of the concommitants of healthy and maladjusted families. Then, we will discuss general principles of systems intervention.

DETERMINANTS OF FAMILY HEALTH AND MALADJUSTMENT

Combining the ideas of the varied scholars in family studies, we can gain an overview of the characteristics of healthy families and those that are functioning poorly. Healthy families are characterized by openness and clarity of communication. Members speak precisely to one another. There is a minimum of lecturing or "talking at" one another. People listen and compromise. Leadership is assumed in direct fashion and is shared according to the family needs and strengths of the members. The family is both a source of support and encouragement of self-worth and autonomy for its members.

Of course, as pointed out by Satir (1972), all families experience crises, particularly with significant life events such as pregnancy, childbirth, adolescence, the reaching of adulthood and marriage of children, menopause, grandparenting, and death. In healthy families, crises are met with much mutual support and the flexibility and resiliency needed to make necessary decisions.

In contrast, in maladjusted family systems, communication is often unclear or confusing and inconsistent. Members hold "hidden agendas," trying to obtain power and get their needs met covertly. The family is not characterized by a balance of autonomy and support among members. Instead, members may be overly dependent on one another, that is, fused in identity; or they may feel alienated from one another, demonstrating little mutual empathy and trust. Coalitions may form in which some family members are antagonistic to others. Rather than sharing because of a sense of mutual respect and support, affection and sex are used to bargain and manipulate.

Maladaptive patterns are often self-perpetuating. Members feel hurt and misunderstood and rely upon their inappropriate roles and styles of communication to cover their hurt feelings and to regain some sense of power. As a consequence, members often assume rigid roles. Satir (1972) characterizes four such rigid parent roles. She describes the family "tyrant" who constantly criticizes and attempts to dominate others. The family "martyr" communicates in a placating style, is always deferring his or her needs for others, but eventually tries to make others pay through guilt and attention for the sacrifice. The "great stone face" communicates primarily in an intellectualizing mode. The stone face is always super reasonable to cover his or her feelings of tenderness, fear, and anger. The great stone face hides feelings in order to not be vulnerable in the destructive family system; but, of course, the stone face frustrates others so that they burst forth with the anger which the stone face so much wishes to avoid. Satir also speaks of the inappropriate rigid role of being the "pal." The pal indulges the spouse and children even when discipline or asserting for one's rights is a more appropriate response. Other family members quickly lose respect for the pal and feel their own sense of self-worth diminishing because they are not responding in a loving fashion to the pal.

A review of the clinical child literature suggests that in maladjusted families, children as well as the parents often assume rigid roles. We will discuss the terms "family pet," "family baby," "peacemaker," and "scapegoat" as first coined by Ackerman (1971) to characterize these inappropriate, rigid roles.

The "family pet" is showered with love and attention. However, if the pet role is extreme, the child may not learn to cope with difficult situations outside the family network. Also, if this role is exaggerated, other family members may actually or subjectively feel that they lack affection. These members then assume antagonistic family roles characterized by jealousy and negativism.

The common role of the "family baby" can become so entrenched that even as an adolescent or adult, the child is considered a baby by all family members. Of course, a baby is protected, and his or her misbehavior is tolerated. So, the child placed in a rigid baby role comes to expect protection throughout life, and his or her autonomous behavior is limited. If the child's baby role is extreme, other members of the family may not receive the protection that they need. For example, one of the authors (E. S. L.) worked with a twenty-five year old mother who had physically abused her two children, resulting in the death of one of them. It was learned that the mother was one of twins. Her sister was born second and was very weak. The sister required much special nursing as an infant. Throughout her childhood, the sister's baby role was rigidly maintained. In time, the client was expected to assume responsibility and care for her twin sister. In fact, it was assumed that she would work full-time through her adolescence and young adulthood so that her twin sister could attend college without having to worry about money. By adulthood, the client's rage was intolerable. She projected this upon her own children, and thus the familial pathology continued into another generation.

Another rigid family role expected of some children is that of the "peacemaker." The peacemaker diminishes family stress through a variety of maneuvers such as creating a joke in stressful situations or assuming blame for the family difficulties. The problem is that in time the peacemaker as well as other family members begin to assume that the peacemaker is at fault. The peacemaker experiences inappropriate guilt and feelings of failure. Once the peacemaker begins to label him or herself as a failure, he or she begins to act like a failure and more negative consequences ensue.

Another rigid family role for children is that of "scapegoat." A scapegoat is the object of displacement for another or several other family members' feelings of guilt. The scapegoat is punished so that the other members feel relieved of their responsibility and anxiety. Often, the scapegoat reminds the displacing family member of his or her own traumatic past. The scapegoat, in time, accepts and plays out the rigid role assigned to him or her.

Therefore, in maladjusted families, members relate to one another in rigid patterns. Unique needs are met through disguise and manipulation. The problem in the maladjusted family is in the system, the network of relationships. The family comes to therapy because a member, usually a child, has developed extreme symptoms in order to cope with the pathological system. To the family therapist, the member with the untenable symptoms is the "identified patient," whereas the actual patient is the family unit.

PRINCIPLES OF FAMILY SYSTEMS THERAPY

The principles underlying family systems therapy are drawn from its tenets concerning healthy and maladjusted patterns of family interaction. Framo (1979) summarizes these ideas into seven principles that we expand upon below:

1. Families have unique bondings, rules, communication networks, and myths.

2. People act differently in their family systems than in other environments. The family environment is a unique environment. Employing the principles of Gestalt psychology, we could say that the whole of the family is different from and greater than a combination of the individuals comprising it. The family operates with a personality characterized by particular norms, values, and roles.

3. Families seek homeostasis. Once a system of relating is developed, the family resists efforts of anyone to change it. Changes in families necessitate action to break through the homeostasis.

4. Family members can 'drive each other crazy.' Some members, the "identified patients," develop symptoms in order to reduce the stress in the family. The psychopathology of the individual patient is actually present in all family members. The family projects its stress onto the "identified patient."

5. Family symptoms may be passed through many generations. The trouble in families is the 'attempted solution' that is used in a repetitive, rigid fashion. Families get caught in systems needing change. Due to the pull to homeostasis, change is resisted. Pathological solutions can become entrenched through years and generations.

6. If the "identified patient" changes, another member of the family may become maladjusted as he or she absorbs the family stress. In family systems theory, the child brought to therapy is viewed as a symptom, not the cause of the family stress. As the child changes, he or she will affect the way all family members relate.

7. Effective therapy requires a realignment of the ways all members relate to one another. It is more efficient for the therapist to intervene with the whole family system so that the basic sources of the stress are ameliorated. In that way, another family member will not become an "identified patient," and a new harmonious homeostasis can be built.

As stated earlier, family systems therapists differ in the techniques they employ in order to realign family members. All will use techniques that facilitate open communication. The therapist models clear communication (Satir, 1967) and helps break down calibrated communication by challenging rigid assumptions and unclear nominalization (Bandler, Grinder, & Satir, 1976). The therapist creates an atmosphere in which members feel free to express themselves. Bell (1964) begins family therapy with a joint session with parents in which he gleans their version of the difficulties, including children's developmental history and education. Then, Bell explains that in family therapy, he will serve as a moderator encouraging all family members to talk. Bell (1964) then brings together all family members over age four and reexplains his role in the therapeutic process.

The family systems therapist uses techniques to help members to become more aware of the family dynamics, myths, and rigid roles. Some family therapists are more directive and controlling in order to accomplish this aim than are others. Satir (1972) describes herself as a resource person who is not omnipotent, God, parent, or judge. She sees herself as an "official observer" who gives the family feedback about how members express their autonomy and individuality; what roles are played either overtly or covertly by family members; and whether individual members are congruent in their verbal and nonverbal communication as well as in their behavior. Family therapists point out examples of rigid role taking and how they serve to block individual's personal growth. Gradually, the therapist entreats family members to give one another feedback about how it feels to be in those roles. A variety of exercises and worksheets may be used to facilitate family members' awareness of the family dynamics.

Some family therapists exploit the power inherent in the clinician's role to increase family members' awareness of group dynamics (Haley, 1963; Minuchen et al., 1967; and Whitaker, 1976). Haley (1963) states that the therapist initially makes new rules for the family that will make them aware of how the family functions. The homework assignments and injunctions are designed to break up coalitions and neutralize the effects of symptoms that led to covert control.

Finally, the family systems therapists are instrumental in fostering behavioral changes in the family unit. They prompt members to act in new ways (insight is of secondary importance). They offer behavioral prescriptions. For example, the therapist may tell family members to hold nightly discussion groups (if communication has been limited), to go out on a family picnic (if alienation is high), or for each member to spend one evening out without other family members present (if fusion is intense). The therapist offers new rationalizations for old problems. By "reframing" the problem, using different explanations to describe a phenomena, members may be willing to tackle the problem in a new way. Thus, a family may come to therapy with a presenting complaint that family members are not loving to one another and are spending little time together. The therapist might reframe the problem by stating, "Actually, your problem is that you love each other so much that you are afraid to hurt one another's feelings. I want you to get together for a family conference each evening and lovingly tell each other what you feel and what has been bothering you." The therapist may use behavioral contracts to further ensure that goals are direct. Some family systems therapists use paradoxical statements and behavioral prescriptions in order to prompt family members to work through resistance to change associated with the family homeostasis. Some paradoxical verbal approaches include:

- Go slow approach. The therapist tells the family that they are trying to change too fast. The paradoxical intent is that the clients will resist and therefore change faster.

- Using resistance. The therapist asks family members to accentuate their symptoms, to continue doing what they are doing, but to do more of it. For example, a woman who is hypochondriacal might be told to go to bed, not do any work, and not speak to anyone if she feels the slightest bit ill. The paradoxical effect is that by accentuating the symptomology, covert maneuvers are made overt. Clients become more aware of their actual motivations and resist the therapist's injunctions, thereby assuming power more directly.

- Pleading ignorance. The therapist acts as if he or she does not understand what is happening in a family interaction. This forces family members to assume more responsibility in the session and to openly explain maneuvers.

- Paradoxical decompensation. A client with a debilitating problem is asked to demonstrate the symptomatic behavior in the therapy hour, but in an exaggerated fashion. For example, Carl Whitaker (1980) tells of a family counseling session in which the identified patient was an adult male schizophrenic who believed he was Jesus Christ. Whitaker told the client that his trouble was that he had not been baptized. Whitaker proceeded to recreate the original biblical baptism scene, having family members serve as Mary, John the Baptist, etc. The client soon asked Whitaker to stop the proceedings and stated that obviously his family members were not biblical characters, and he was not Jesus Christ. Thus, the effect of the paradoxical decompensation can be that the exaggerated symptom does not serve its manipulative purpose in the therapy hour so that the client stops it.

- A benevolent sabotage. The therapist collaborates with one member of the family to stage a reaction to other family members in order to break rigid relationship patterns. For example, in a private session with a mother who has been placed in a role of a martyr in a family, the therapist might suggest that the mother return home from the session complaining to the family that the individual therapy upset her so much that she cannot do any work. Whenever family members demand something from the mother, expecting her to play a martyr role, she responds that the therapy was so disconcerting that she simply cannot do a thing. The paradoxical sabotage helps the family member break rigid role expectations without directly defying the family rules.

In the Case of Brad's Family (Heath, 1981), you will read of the use of many of the specialized techniques developed by the family systems therapists. Note that the family sought therapy because of the disturbing behavior of their child, Brad. This child might have been placed in individual therapy, but the therapist gleaned information about the family which indicated that the child's symptomatology was primarily a reaction to profound disturbance in the family system. Therefore, the therapist chose to aim therapeutic intervention at changing family roles and communication styles.

Case 7.1. The Case of Brad's Family

It was easy to tell that Mrs. Jackson was upset when she first called. Her son, Brad, age 9, was having problems in school. Mrs. Jackson was simply terrified that Brad was going to "follow in his brother's footsteps." Ruth, Brad's school counselor and Mrs. Jackson's friend, had referred her. Ruth was also a vigilant member of our agency's Board of Directors. Mr. Jackson was the Chief of Police of a small town in the county. All things considered, the family was scheduled for a counseling session the same evening. Mrs. Jackson was told to bring the whole family so work could begin immediately on this "serious problem."

The family arrived early. Chief Jackson had insisted that Butch (18) and Brenda (16), Brad's siblings, attend. They were both acting unhappy to be there. Chief began in a loud, stern voice, "I will not stand for it." Mrs. Jackson began to sob; Brenda looked out the window; Butch looked for an ashtray; and Brad looked at the floor. When the chaos died down, Mrs. Jackson announced that a teacher had witnessed a marijuana cigarette falling out of Brad's locker. Butch laughed, and Brenda said, "Mom you didn't tell me about this." Then the Chief's pocket pager beeped, and he got up and went to find a telephone. I asked everyone else to wait outside while I talked to Brad. His mother seemed relieved.

Shaking my head I asked Brad if it was always like this in his family and offered him a Coke. He nodded and declined the offer. After some casual conversation I said, "Some kids I see in here get in trouble to get help for their families, but you seem different. You're smart and you don't seem to be crazy. Am I right so far? ("Yeah.") Now I don't know if you're innocent or guilty of the "crime," but you are in trouble with your dad and mom. They think you're turning into your brother, so they'll bug you for weeks, months, or even years. I've seen parents like them push kids into proving them right. You probably don't want it, but I might be able to help you get them off your back. You'd have to promise me that you wouldn't tell them what we're up to. If you did tell them, I'd have to lie, and who do you think they'd believe? Think about it for a while."

The family was called back in. Chief said he had to leave in four minutes. Since Brad had agreed to the plan, I proceeded by instructing the family to do all it could to prove Brad guilty for the next few days before our next session. "After all," I said, "It is better to be cautious when the stakes are this high. We have to nip this problem in the bud." Another session was set for a week later.

The second session was spent talking about other problems in the family. They had grown tired of trying to prove Brad guilty and argued that it was unfair. I told the family that my consulting psychiatrist had recommended that Brad meet with me every other day for individual therapy. In this way we could get at any underlying problems. Since it was important that Brad knew that the whole family wanted to help him, I continued, they must take turns driving him the 15 miles to the agency. Eventually all agreed to the treatment plan.

The individual sessions began. We talked about the weather, sports, minor problems, and occasionally about different ways to act in his family. We also climbed out the window now and then and walked to the ice cream store. After six such sessions, Mrs. Jackson and Chief were convinced that whatever I had said to Brad had helped, and that they didn't want to bring him over anymore if the therapy had worked. Even the school counselor was pleased. Just to make sure everyone was convinced, I cautioned them that change takes time and saw Brad for six more sessions. At follow-up, Mrs. Jackson reported that "everything" was fine and asked what we had talked about. Neither Brad nor I would say. Ruth remained watchful over the agency's services, and we continued to get referrals from the Chief's police department.

In the Case of Brad's Family, the therapist placed focus upon problems in the family system as a whole. The therapist is concerned about members stereotypical expectations of one another and about the general commotion in the family unit. The therapist intervenes in the family system by changing alliances. He forms a covert pact with Brad, the identified patient, so that Brad and the therapist agree to convince family members that they must prove Brad guilty. Also, notice the frequent use of paradoxical statements. The therapist states, for example, "You probably don't want it, but I might be able to help." No matter what Brad says, he is complying with the therapist. If he refuses help, he validates the therapist's statement. If Brad accepts the help, he is developing a therapeutic alliance.

ISSUES IN FAMILY THERAPY

The family therapy literature is extensive, and empirical studies of its effectiveness are increasing (Knopf, 1979). For example, in one controlled study, family systems intervention increased the number of positive responses among family members, decreased the frequency of undesirable behavior, and facilitated more spontaneous interaction among members (Hardcaste, 1977). There is a need for empirical studies which tie down the precise psychological problems for which family therapy is preferred.

The early family therapists believed that all children's problems were best dealt with by intervening in the family system. Some still ascribe to this position, but a number now agree that the difficulties of the identified child patient may become so internalized that individual therapy is preferred. In other cases, family members besides the identified child may be so disturbed that individual therapy with them must precede effective family intervention (Framo, 1979). Wynne (1961) suggests that family therapy is contraindicated if conditions prevent the establishment of a working relationship with the family. Ackerman (1966a) is more specific. He states that in family systems intervention is not preferred if one or more of the following conditions exist:

- There is an irreversible and malignant trend towards break-up of the family.

- One or both parents are psychopathic.

- One or both parents are consistently dishonest in therapy.

- A valid family secret might be revealed inappropriately in therapy.

- One or more family members has rigid defenses that may break under family therapy.

- Organic disease prevents participation by one or more critical members.

- The family expresses an unyielding prejudice against family therapy intervention.

Some see a goal conflict in family therapy. The practitioner hopes to increase individual autonomy, but also aims to facilitate family harmony. Sometimes these goals are incompatible. For example, an adolescent may feel that to be happy he or she needs to live in his or her own apartment. The parents, on the other hand, feel better if the adolescent comes home at an early hour each evening. In this situation, there is a conflict between the adolescent's need for autonomy and the parent's need to protect the adolescent. The family therapist must be honest with the family about his or her beliefs in what will facilitate family growth.

Some practitioners and theorists question the ethics of paradox and manipulation by the family systems therapist. It has been suggested that the paradoxical meaning may be confusing to very disturbed clients who have been raised on and are vulnerable to double binds. The family systems therapists employing these approaches reply that their use of indirect techniques is appropriate because they are benevolent in helping their clients. They see their double binds as therapeutic, having the long-term effect of increasing a client's sense of autonomy and control. The reader needs to consider the ethics of this important issue before deciding to use or not use a family systems approach.

SUMMARY

A systems approach to family therapy began about 25 years ago when a few maverick therapists began to treat entire families. This approach is based upon the principle that the family is a system which has a unique structure. The family attempts to maintain its structure and thus resists change. Those therapists adopting an analytic framework in family therapy employ different techniques than those who prefer a systems approch. The analytically-oriented family therapist holds the individual as the primary client. The family systems theorist sees the total system as the difficulty. Analytically-oriented therapists use family meetings to form interpretations about individual psychopathology. Family systems theorists use the group sessions to point out inappropriate processes and how members relate to one another. They point out double and unclear messages by members and ask them to clarify their meanings. They help identify rigid roles assumed by family members. Homework assignments are given in which members are asked to play new roles. At times the family seeking homeostasis refuses change. Therefore, paradoxical techniques may be implemented. By exaggerating the rigid, maladjusted pattern of relating to one another, new dynamics among members emerge, and the symptomatic way of interacting can be diminished.

All family theorists agree that families function better when members are aware of the group dynamics, communicate spontaneously and openly, and assume direct responsibility for behavioral change. All family theorists agree that childhood maladjustments are often a manifestation of parents' problems or problems in the family as a whole. Thus, the effective child therapist is always concerned about the family and draws all or part of the family into therapy as necessary. Family therapists have been very creative in their development of therapeutic techniques. The effectiveness of these techniques and the conditions under which they are preferable to other therapeutic interventions are presently under empirical investigation.

CHAPTER 8

A SYNTHESIS OF THEORIES AND APPLICATION

Our review of the major theories of child counseling and therapy reveals a multiplicity of ways to conceptualize childhood maladjustment and a variety of techniques to facilitate personal growth. Since each of these theories of childhood personality development is based upon partially untested assumptions about the nature of human beings, the absolute validity of the theories cannot be ascertained. Rather, the theories must be evaluated according to their consistencies, thoroughness, expansiveness, and usefulness. Although our review of each theory of childhood personality and therapy is brief, we have tried to delineate each one's respective strengths. Each provides a profitable means of conceptualizing the problems of some children. Each has been found to predict some children's behaviors. Each has been widely employed by practitioners.

Almost a century ago, practitioners committed themelves to the ideal of prevention of insanity in childhood and eradication of delinquency in adolescence (Richmond, 1917). Yet, with the theoretical advances in child theory and therapy, much remains to be done. Kanner (1973, p. 219) coined the expression "salvation of the splinter group" to describe those who zealously support a new therapeutic technique as the answer to all childhood problems. Some believe that the explanation of childhood maladjustment lies in infantile sexuality; others expound that the key is a faulty mother-child relationship; some propose that the answer is inappropriate conditioning; while still others hold that childhood problems are neurologically based. Kanner asks (1973, p. 218):

> Have the theories brought about the abolition of fratricide, tyranny, greed, and prejudice? They have not.---This is because the basic goal has been split off into a variety of single approaches' each claiming the sole possession of the key to redemption. Ideals degenerated into ideologies, the Golden Rule into iron-fisted injunctions.

It would seem most profitable to integrate the various approaches of child counseling and therapy into an overall system so that clinicians could select systematically the best approach to employ with a given child. No doubt, accepting only some aspects of each theory and removing those tenets from their respective whole minimizes the overall meaning of those constructs. However, if the constructs are placed in a new inclusive paradigm, they gain in their expansiveness and overall usefulness. Unfortunately, a total integration does not presently seem possible because the theories are based upon such differing assumptions about humans and discrepant views of how people change. Some of the theories are descriptive, and the techniques of child counseling and therapy that flow from them are means of fostering natural growth. Other theories are explanatory, attempting to show positive factors that predict childhood behavior. The techniques emerging from those viewpoints are more directive. A full integration of these theories will require a broader paradigm about human behavior that works concomitantly to explain behavior and mental events (Anthony, 1970). It seems that a total integration of the theories of childhood personality development and child therapy is not yet possible. Yet, the effective child clinician needs to be open to discoveries emerging from various approaches.

We think that some principles can be drawn from the theories of child counseling, social work , and psychotherapy that can aid the child practitioner in his or her selection of techniques. We are not suggesting that these principles constitute a new theoretical integration of all the approaches. Rather, we present these principles as guidelines that reoccur throughout the varied theories reviewed in preceding chapters.

PRINCIPLES FOR ASSISTING CHILDREN IN CRISIS

1. Early life experiences are critical.

    The newborn reacts to various stimuli with a circumscribed set of responses. The newborn watches, smiles, coos, cries, and kicks. The infant may respond to light, food, warmth, hunger, surprise, and a variety of other stimuli within the same limited repertoire of behavior.

    The newborn's perceptual and psychomotor skills specialize soon after birth. The infant learns to distinguish him- or herself from the environment. Responses become more specific. The infant may cry without kicking, smile without cooing. The infant learns to focus attention more specifically on given objects and events. Responses are tailored to particular people and occurrences. Thus, the child smiles more to the presence of the mother than to strangers. The child wants to control responses in order to obtain desired reinforcement from the environment. Cooing may bring the desired attention of one parent, while crying impacts significantly the response of another. Increasingly, environmental factors modify the child's behavioral repertoire and responses become specific to particular environmental cues.

2. <u>The infant is born with certain constitutional traits and vulnerabilities.</u>

Infants differ along a series of dimensions from birth, and often these differences persist throughout the life of the individual. For instance, some infants are more distractable than others; still other infants show more marked activity levels than most; and some infants appear to be far more affected by new objects or people in their environment. Also true is the fact that infants and children differ in how they experience and express elation and sadness as well as in their openness to others. It is important to recognize individual differences in working with children since each child brings to therapy a unique set of characteristics that must be dealt with by the therapist.

3. <u>Growth proceeds in an orderly fashion.</u>

The burgeoning research in developmental psychology demonstrates that growth in the physical, cognitive, psychomotor, and psychological spheres emerges in a predictable, interlocking order. For example, a child must develop a certain degree of physical muscular strength before he or she can demonstrate the psychomotor skills of grasping and holding objects. Similarly, a child must develop abstract cognitive skills before he or she can begin to develop a depth of emotional reactions. Being empathic of others necessitates a sophisticated cognitive ability of conceptually "taking on" another's role (Mead, 1934). Developing a conscience, that is feeling good about one's positive acts and guilty or remorseful about wrong-doings requires the complex cognitive abilities of being able to remember and evaluate one's past acts and to predict future consequences.

4. <u>Children develop through successive stages whose order is relatively immutable. The exact age at which children pass through the developmental stages varies from child to child.</u>

The exact age a child passes through a developmental stage and masters specific skills depends upon an interaction of the child's biological makeup and social environment. The keener the child's perception, the more spontaneous and relaxed his or her temperament, and the more stimulating and supportive the environment, the more rapidly and easily the child passes through developmental levels of growth.

5.   <u>A certain amount of anxiety in childhood is expected.</u>

Whenever an individual attempts a new and challenging task, he or she experiences a degree of anticipatory anxiety. This psychologically-felt anxiety is associated with psysiological changes (such as increased arousal and quicker reaction time) that mobilize the person to maximize performance. Thus, anxiety is part of a holistic, organismic response that allows a person to invest his or her best efforts for new challenges (Selye, 1950). If a child feels no anxiety, the child is not testing limits and growing to potential. What the child practitioner is alert to and attempts to ameliorate is massive anxiety that is chronic and not associated with challenges but instead overwhelms the child and impedes action.

6.   <u>The well-adjusted child is characterized by spontaneity, creativity, self-awareness, curiosity, caring of others, autonomy, and a positive and realistic self-concept. Children do not, however, demonstrate all these traits all the time.</u>

The different child theorists vary in their definitions of children's mental health. Some speak of positive self-concept or self-esteem; others speak of positive family and social relationships; still others focus upon the child's ability to meet his or her needs in an adaptive fashion. However, when one reviews clinical work from each of the persuasions, the mentally healthy child is described in similar terms of being spontaneous, curious, with a positive ability to care for others and for self. Of course, no child can exhibit these traits at all times. Furthermore, under times of crisis, it is expected and appropriate that the child would display reactive emotions and behaviors such as depression, nightmares, and acting out, that are part of the organism's recuperative efforts against stress.

7.   <u>The maladjusted child is characterized by one or more of the following traits that are present so much of the time that the child's overall psychosocial development is impaired: withdrawn behavior, impulsiveness, self-destructive behavior, inability to obtain positive reinforcers from significant others, negative and unrealistic self-concept, lack of identity, discouragement, and lack of initiative.</u>

As stressed previously, all children display reactive (that is, nongrowth enhancing) behavior at times. It is self-protective to react to stress by temporary withdrawal or acting out. Furthermore, no one is well adjusted all the time. The maladjusted child is one who behaves in reactive ways for extended periods of time. Because of their chronicity and intensity, these behaviors no longer serve self-protective functions but instead are self-destructive. Thus, if a child's pet dies, it is an expected response that the child will grieve the loss by crying, withdrawing, and other reactive behaviors. These reactive behaviors allow the child to discharge the hurt and also elicit support from others. Contrast this response with that of a child who says she hates school, cries every morning on the way to school, and is reclusive and withdrawn during the school day. This protracted reaction no longer serves a successful discharge function. Nor does it help this child deal with the stress she feels about school. The child must attend school and is not focusing upon constructive ways of approaching it. Furthermore, her reactions become frustrating to others and may elicit criticism from them. The intensity, duration, and chronicity of this child's reactions indicate maladjustment.

8. <u>Children raised in warm and supportive environments characterized by consistency in discipline are more likely to be well adjusted.</u>

There can be no perfect formula for raising children. Children are born with certain constitutional traits and vulnerabilities and born into particular familial and social environments. The most effective child-rearing techniques for a particular child will be very individualistic, based upon the child's needs, ways of enhancing the child's particular strengths and the expectations of the family and culture in which the child lives. Thus, a child of aggressive temperament may respond well to firm discipline. A very sensitive child with strong esthetic interests may flourish better in a quiet environment that gently encourages the child to explore and use his or her capacities.

Yet, despite the child's idiosyncratic needs, all children profit from encouragement and support. A warm and supportive environment helps develop a positive view of oneself. While punishments and restrictions can curb nonproductive and maladaptive behaviours, reinforcement and support are required to help a child grow and enhance his or her strengths (Rogers, 1951; Azrin & Foxx, 1971).

Once an appropriate style of child-rearing is identified, it is important to maintain it with some consistency, for inconsistency and erratic discipline and expectations can be very confusing to children and prompt emotional disturbance (Bateson, 1972). Of course, the child-rearing should be modified as the child grows and the child's needs change, but these modifications should be logical to the situation and systematic rather than haphazard and frequent.

9.   <u>Children's healthy development is facilitated by an open communication with parents and significant others.</u>

A distinguishing characteristic between human beings and all other animals is the extent to which humans rely upon cognitive abilities. A child's overall well being is critically dependent upon the development of cognitive abilities. For the baby, communication verbally and nonverbally with one's caretakers is the primary mode through which the child learns to think about him- or herself and to interpret the environment (Chess, et al., 1978).

As the child grows older, open and frequent communication helps the child refine his or her understanding of the world. Healthy families are characterized by open, clear, and frequent communication. These families are able to help one another with their problems and to work through conflicts. In disturbed families, communication is closed and/or confusing, and the children's abilities to expand their cognitive abilities are impeded (Satir, 1972).

10. <u>Children need a balance of evaluative feedback concerning their socially appropriate and inappropriate behaviors and acceptance for their individuality.</u>

Much humanistic child-rearing literature stresses the importance of supporting the child, praising his or her accomplishments, and encouraging his or her individuality. Other child-rearing specialists write of the importance of setting appropriate boundaries and limits (Mahler, et al., 1975, and Spock, 1960). In fact, all children need both encouragement and limit setting. Children are not born knowing all the appropriate limits to their safety and the expectations of their culture. Thus, it is the caretakers' responsibility to set guidelines and maintain them. However, when the environment is supportive and encouraging, children have a desire to please and to model appropriate behavior. Thus, when a child is supported and encouraged from birth, less limit setting is needed, and the child is more likely to grow to his or her potential and to be a productive member of the family and society (Adler, 1927).

11. <u>Children's maladjustment may occur as a consequence of constitutional vulnerabilities, disturbed family life, life crisis, natural disasters, and/or faulty learning. If of intense magnitude and duration, any one of these factors could result in maladjustment. However, most maladjustments are caused by a combination of such factors.</u>

The child practitioner must create a dynamic explanation of the child's behavior by integrating therapeutic observations of the child with those of peers and family members and by piecing together background information provided by the family and school. In order to ascertain the etiology of the child's maladjustment, the child practitioner must rely upon some theory of childhood personality development that offers a full explanation of how psychosocial factors affect the child. Analytic, behavioral, and humanistic theories attempt to answer such questions, and the reader must decide which paradigm seems to provide the most fruitful explanations. Clearly, the child practitioner must be very scholarly in his or her understanding of the theoretical framework employed because he or she will use that theory to build important formulations about the child. It is crucial that the perceptions and interpretations reflect accurately the child's dilemmas. If not, therapy might increase the child's confusion.

12. A necessary condition for child counseling is a warm and supportive relationship between the child and practitioner in which the child feels respected, accepted, and understood.

Although the different child theorists stress varying formulations of the causes of a child's maladjustment and employ different techniques for ameliorating the problems, all concede that successful counseling is dependent upon first establishing a trusting relationship with the child. The child must view the practitioner as someone who has his or her best interests in mind before the child will begin to disclose about problems, to listen to the practitioner's interpretations or advice, or to model the practitioner's behaviors or suggestions. Children will not automatically trust the practitioner because they are told that the practitioner is a helpful person. The trust must be earned. In the initial sessions, if the the child practitioner listens very carefully and is supportive and nonjudgmental, an ambience of being understood is created, and the child will begin to trust the practitioner and the counseling setting (Rogers, 1951).

13. An important ingredient in counseling with children is activity (e.g., play therapy, role playing), which can be used as a medium for expression of ideas and reinforcement for appropriate behavior.

Many feel unsure about how to communicate concepts with young children of no or limited language facility. Some falsely assume that since these children cannot talk, they do not understand concepts. They view analytic and cognitive therapy approaches as inappropriate for the preverbal child.

The effective child practitioner can bridge the language barrier and communicate constructs to young child clients through the use of activity. The practitioner observes the child's play pattern and then verbalizes observations and interpretations about the meaning of those patterns to the client; or the practitioner may engage the child in specific activity so that the practitioner can demonstrate dynamic principles that will be helpful to the child.

14. Effective child counseling and therapy include work with parents and others significant to the child.

The child spends about an hour or so weekly with the child practitioner but the majority of time with family and school personnel. The child, more than the adult client, must be a respondent to the significant adult figures in the family and school. It is logical, then, that the child practitioner's effectiveness is increased when the practitioner's treatment approach is consonant with the approach of other significant adults in the child's life. Child theorists disagree somewhat upon how these significant adult figures should be brought into the counseling process. Some suggest that they be viewed as "consultants" to the child practitioner and that they should help plan a treatment strategy (Moustakes, 1973). Others recommend bringing the parents into treatment themselves (Klein, 1960). A number of child theorists stress the value of having at least some of the sessions as family sessions in which system's issues are addressed. What is clear is that the impact of family and significant adults in the child's life should not be ignored. We believe that the child practitioner must assess the level of parents' psychological functioning in order to determine the best way to include them in the counseling process. If one or both parents are very disturbed, individual counseling for them may be appropriate. Dependent upon the particular case and the practitioner's theoretical persuasion, the child practitioner must decide whether to serve as a consultant and/or teacher to the significant adults or whether to bring them into the counseling process.

15. Child practitioners must often seek ways of incorporating other support systems (e.g., school, human services department, juvenile justice system) into the helping process through case management if the child is to be served.

We have stressed throughout this text that the needs of children are often not listened to. The effective child practitioner must be a child advocate and, as such, cannot restrict clinical practice to the office. It is crucial to understand how the child functions at school since the child spends so many hours of his or her life in that environment. If the child's home or social environment is disruptive, then the practitioner best serves the child by enlisting the aid of appropriate agencies. Because these agencies are often riddled with bureaucratic complexities that block effectiveness, the practitioner must remain engaged with the agencies, following up on referrals to assure that appropriate services are provided.

16. Analytic approaches are designed to foster a child's spontaneity and self-awareness. Analytic approaches are most appropriate when a child has reached a developmental level where he or she can conceptualize about personal and family dynamics.

If the child's maladjustment seems deeply tied to the child's overall personality so that the conflicts are internal and self-sustaining, analytically-oriented uncovering techniques may be preferred. For example, if a child demonstrates excessive fear of her father and other males, it may be necessary to help her understand the inappropriate dynamics concerning her father and other males that she has integrated. It is in this particular kind of problem that analytically-oriented therapists view their strength in assisting child clients.

17. Therapeutic approaches from the theory of Individual Psychology are designed to foster social competence and caring for others. This is often accomplished when group therapy is conducted for the child and significant adults.

In the Individual Psychology approach first advocated by Alfred Adler, the therapeutic situation is oriented toward an examination of the client's interpersonal relationships. Here, the child's evolving lifestyle is studied. The child is helped to become aware of his or her social interests and to learn cooperative strategies for social interaction. Further, the ordinal position of the child within the family constellation frequently provides valuable information about how the child relates to others in the family. As a result, the child's self-esteem is enhanced so that neurotic striving for superiority over others is eliminated and replaced by cooperative social behaviors.

18. Humanistic approaches emphasize the development of positive and realistic self-concepts. This approach claims particular effectiveness in maximizing a child's potential and creativity.

Within a warm, supportive environment, the child is prompted to try new responses. Within an accepting play therapy environment, the child can test the consequences of various acts and thereby refine his or her discrimination. Thus, for example, a humanistic approach might be very effective for a 5-year-old with the primary symptom of encopresis, which is signalling an over controlled, rigid personality and suppressed anger toward perfectionistic parents. Within the permissive, accepting relationship, the child can explore ways of expressing suppressed anger and behaving spontaneously.

19. <u>Behavioral therapies are oriented toward the elimination of self-defeating, self-destructive, and/or socially inappropriate behaviors, and the shaping of autonomous, assertive, and socially appropriate behaviors. A strength of this approach is its applicability for children of any age.</u>

For infants and children who have regressed to primitive behaviors, behavioral modification is very effective. Through systematic reinforcement, grossly simplified and inappropriate behaviors can be shaped into more complex behavioral repertoires. Working with children at this state of development, the practitioner initially responds somewhat like a parent, satisfying basic needs for hugging, feeding, etc., and thereby reinforcing bonding. Gradually, the therapist encourages the child to initiate autonomous behavior. Systematic behavioral reinforcement techniques help the therapist reinforce this autonomy.

Sophisticated behavioral approaches may be useful for older children with behavioral maladjustments. Techniques such as shaping and modelling can encourage a child to learn new adaptive behaviors. For example, the encopretic child can be taught positive and assertive ways to respond to parents' requests.

In short, if the child is basically adjusted, but has demonstrated discrete maladapted behaviors, behavioral approaches which lead to quick, definable gains may be preferred. Thus, behavior modification might be the treatment of choice for a nail-biter or a child who is afraid to speak in class but appears otherwise adjusted.

20. <u>Family theorists recommend systems intervention when a child's problems appear to be emeshed in disturbed family relationships.</u>

In some cases, maladjustment does not seem to be internalized into the child's personality structure. Rather, the maladaptive behavior seems to be a situational response to faulty family relationships. In these cases, family systems intervention is preferred. Generally, verbal children ages 8 or older are able to comprehend and integrate their experiences derived through sophisticated, language-oriented family systems approaches.

21. <u>Cognitive restructuring therapies argue that language plays an instrumental role in the child's adjustment. By modifying the child's internal speech, subjective comfort and appropriate behaviors can be fostered.</u>

As children develop cognitively, they begin to integrate more complex precepts of their relationships to their environment. With increasing cognitive development, the child's sense of conscience emerges. By about 4 years of age, the child begins to evaluate the consequences of his or her actions, and the rudimentary aspects of morality begin to appear in the child's behavior. With the concommitant acquisition of language during early childhood, the child is able to communicate with others at a level different from the preverbal child. With the ability to communicate with others, the child can learn to "take on" the role of others and to internalize how others feel in given situations. Thus, by the time the child reaches the age of 4 or 5, he or she is able to empathize with others. By modifying self-speech, the child can be taught positive feelings about self and others, and behaviors will change accordingly. This is the basic theoretical tenet of cognitive restructuring therapies

22. <u>Regardless of which therapeutic approach is selected, the practitioner, with the child and significant others, must identify target goals and means of measuring progress toward those goals.</u>

It is incumbent upon the practitioner to assume responsibility for identifying target goals and to relate these to all critically-involved parties. Too often, counseling has proceeded without a clear understanding by the parties involved of the goals of the sessions. In such cases, the child may be unaware of the purpose of the counseling and unaided or confused by it. The purpose of counseling should be explained to the child over a number of sessions to assure the client's understanding and cooperation.

At times, the parents' implicit goals may not be consistent with those of the practitioner or child. Differences in goals may be especially apparent if a referral is placed by an outside agency. In such cases, for example, the practitioner may view the most adaptive goal for the child to change some aspect of the family dynamics, while the parents may initially want to maintain a status quo and want the child only to change. When the critical parties hold different goals for the counseling, an essential aspect of the early counseling should be to work towards the establishment of compatible expectations. Equally important as the transmittal of goals to the child and significant others is the practitioner's use of explicit goals to help guide in the solution of therapeutic techniques and to chart progress. Of course, the goals may change as the practitioner gleans more information about the family and/or as the child and family change. It is important for these changes to be discussed with family members.

23. Therapy, regardless of approach, is not static. The techniques must be modified as the child approaches the target goals.

The theory and techniques employed in therapy with children should be continually reevaluated and modified to fit the child at each stage of development. Thus, counseling may, for example, begin with systematic behavioral shaping of a variety of behaviors, move to a humanistic approach in which the child is given freedom to try and test out the consequences of new learnings, gradually evolving into a rational discussion of the effect of the child's acts and culminating in a mutual discussion of the dynamic forces the child must cope with at home and at school.

24. Considering the multiplicity of human variation and the complexity of maladjustment, the practitioner should draw upon a variety of theories and techniques.

Although good research about counseling outcomes with children is limited, that research which is available indicates that effective counseling can occur when the child practitioner adopts any one of the major theoretical persuasions. Furthermore, techniques associated with particular theories appear best suited for children suffering specific syndromes of maladjustment. Thus, phobic children respond quite well to desensitization techniques. Family therapy appears essential in cases of limited child abuse in which the goal is restoration of the family. It is our contention that a child practitioner artificially limits effectiveness if he or she employs one approach to the exclusion of all others. We recommend adopting a systematic eclectic approach, in which the theory and techniques employed are based upon a judicious understanding of the child's needs and problems and the empirical research about the clinical theory and techniques under consideration.

25. It is the practitioner's responsibility to evaluate client's progress after termination of the therapy relationship. A significant limitation in the field of child therapy is the failure to evaluate the intermediate and long-term effectiveness of therapeutic approaches.

Any aid the child practitioner provides to a child in feeling better about him- or herself, in functioning better at home and with peers, and in performing at school is most worthwhile. However, as Klein (1960) explained, many of children's psychological problems go into periods of latency, especially during the middle elementary years. Thus, the ultimate effectiveness of the clinical interventions with children rests upon the children's abilities to function as productive and content adults. Yet, there are only a handful of longitudinal studies of the effectiveness of child therapy. If child practitioners would assume responsibility for assessing the long-term gains of the clinical interventions, we would quickly gain a wealth of data about which intervention approaches hold enduring consequences for given children and which psychosocial problems are most amenable to our clinical techniques.

APPLICATION OF PRINCIPLES

In this chapter we have synthesized a general set of principles that emerge from our review of the major theoretical approaches to child therapy. In this section, we want to illustrate the application of these principles by means of a case analysis. The Case of Todd Wilson that follows was taken from the files of the author (E. LeVine) who worked with Todd for a period of two years. The case was selected because all the principles can be illustrated. Actual case material is presented first, followed by discussion that highlights the application of various principles. We hope that this interspersing of case material and discussion proves to be helpful to the reader who wishes to have a better idea of how child therapy is actually conducted.

Case 8.1. The Case of Todd Wilson

Mrs. Wilson called me requesting an appointment for her son. She stated that her 6-year-old, Todd, had experienced significant personal problems since he was an infant. "He has always been difficult for me to manage. Now things are absolutely out of hand. The teacher called me yesterday and said that she cannot handle him in her special education class. He is destructive with class material and hits and kicks other children. The teacher also said, He won't listen to anything I say.'"

An overview of Todd's social history was elicited from the mother during the phone conversation. Todd, a child adopted in infancy, lived with his mother who when Todd was 2 years old divorced his adopted father. Subsequently, when Todd was 4, the mother remarried, and her husband adopted Todd, thereby becoming his second adoptive male parent. At the time that therapy began, Todd's family consisted of his parents and an older sister. Todd also visited with his first adopted father, whom he called "Dad," one weekend monthly. His relationship with all family members was stormy. He would defy their injunctions and state that he "couldn't stand them." Despite medication with Ritalin (recommended by the mother's psychiatrist), his attention span was very short (maintaining given activities for less than two minutes at a time).

Because the crisis precipitating Todd's referral to therapy concerned his school behavior, I decided to visit him in the school environment.

> In this initial contact, Principle 11 is implemented. The therapist begins to integrate a dynamic explanation of the child's behavior by gleaning varied information. As outlined in Principle 7, some signs of maladjustment are evidenced, such as impulsiveness, destructive behavior, and inability to obtain positive reinforcement.

My first encounter with Todd was observing him playing with his peers on the school playground. Todd kicked a peer who would not hand him a ball (even though it was not Todd's turn). The teacher reprimanded Todd. He ran to the corner of the playground and covered his ears, closed his eyes, and shouted, "I don't want to hear about it. I won't listen."

> Principles 14 and 15 are implemented. The therapist quickly involves significant others into the therapeutic process. The therapist seeks information from parents and teachers and establishes rapport with them so they will be willing to cooperate in the therapeutic programming for Todd.

> Observation of Todd at school further illustrates aspects of Principle 7, that maladjusted children may reveal discouragement and lack of initiative. Todd's behavior suggested that he had difficulty discerning the needs of others. When his request for the ball was not met, he reacted by closing his eyes and covering his ears.

A full psychometric battery was administered at the initiation of therapy. Physical signs of the mental status exam generally appeared typical except that Todd constantly moved his hands and legs in an awkward, frenzied fashion. Orientation and judgment were appropriate, but some distorted thinking was apparent. Todd spoke of "alligators in my stomach that are eating at one another" and of "wanting to die."

Todd's performance on the WISC-R demonstrated an above average ability to deal with conceptual tasks. His high scores on the Similarities and Comprehension subtests were viewed as good prognostic signs indicating his ability to conceptualize and thereby profit from verbal therapy.

Aptitude testing revealed that Todd had achieved reading and numerical skills typical at the pre-primer level. Learning disability testing indicated some minor difficulties in figure-ground discrimination (corroborated by a relatively depressed score on the

Block Design on the WISC-R) and significant auditory discrimination problems. Upon further auditory screening, Todd's auditory disability was localized as a problem in attending that was exacerbated by background noise. His ability to discern sounds and integrate them was intact when he concentrated well.

His answers to the Rorshach, Children's Apperception Test, Sentence Completion, and Draw-a-Person Test portrayed a very anxious child who viewed the world as hostile, difficult to understand, and impossible to change. Todd saw himself as helpless, the subject of unfair attack, and unlovable. On the Draw-a-Person Test, he drew himself in miniature compared to other family members and without hands. Of further note, he drew earmuffs to cover his ears. His mother and sister were characterized by large mouths with sharp, jutting teeth. To the sentence completion item, "Dad and Mom,"he answered, "hate me." To the sentence fragment, "My family," he added, "goes around in circles."

Todd's emotional and behavioral problems seemed primary and more profound than his academic difficulties. Observation, interviewing, and psychological testing created a portrait of Todd as a highly distraught youngster whose anxiety and low self-esteem led to difficulty concentrating and performing at school. He seemed to feel so afraid of and to be so unable to defend against interpersonal difficulties that he withdrew into personal daydreams, literally and symbolically covering his ears.

> Principles 1, 2, 3, and 4 are demonstrated. Through results of the psychometric battery, the therapist begins to identify life experiences and constitutional traits leading to Todd's maladjustment. The mental status and psychometric results enable the practitioner to identify Todd's levels of development in the cognitive, affective, and behavioral domains. Information about his developmental accomplishments and lags will aid in the selection of appropriate therapeutic techniques.

I called Mrs. Wilson's psychiatrist to learn more about the medication he prescribed for Todd. The psychiatrist had recommended a minimal dose of Ritalin, "primarily to take the edge off of Todd's rambunctiousness." The psychiatrist indicated that his physical examination of Todd did not reveal signs of hyperactivity and therefore the psychiatrist had not recommended further testing for organic impairment.

> Here, Principle 15 is carried out. Advice and support is sought from another support system relevant to the Wilson family, Mrs. Wilson's psychiatrist.

The following treatment plan was established:

1. Curb destructive behavior to other persons and objects. This goal would be accomplished by systematically shaping and reinforcing socially appropriate behaviors within the therapy hours and by instructing parents and teachers to carry out a similar procedure.

2. Once aggressive behavior is minimized, establish a therapeutic alliance in which Todd and the therapist begin to relate to one another in an open, supportive fashion. A humanistic therapeutic stance would aid in accomplishing this goal.

3. Encourage Todd to talk and sort out his feelings about varied family members. Todd would be particularly prompted to explore his reasons for feeling that family members hated him and were attacking him.

4. Help Todd learn new ways to respond to family members, school personnel, and peers so that he could receive more positive responses from them.

5. Aid Todd in developing a more positive, realistic self-concept. This goal involved Todd's learning to value his competencies and to recognize and change his self-defeating patterns.

Observable evidence of growth towards these goals would include:

1. Less reprimanding by teacher and parents for aggressive, destructive behavior.

2. A decrease in fidgety behavior.

3. An increased ability to spontaneously explain the sources of his distress.

4. Less covering of his ears.

5. Understanding of ideas and directions when stated only once.

Since it was hypothesized that Todd's school problems were secondary to his emotional distress, it was predicted that his auditory learning disability would decrease, and his school performance increase as gains in therapy accrued.

These goals were discussed with Mr. and Mrs. Wilson and weekly therapy sessions with Todd were initiated.

> Principle 22 is fully employed. Short-term and long-term goals were established. Means of monitoring progress towards these goals were delimited. The target goals were discussed with and agreed upon with Mr. and Mrs. Wilson.

The first few times Todd came to psychotherapy, his behavior was highly uncontrolled. He moved around the room in a wild fashion, grabbing a bag of blocks and pounding them against the floor and walls. The practitioner explained to Todd that he was "free to use the play therapy as you wish, the only rules are you cannot hurt yourself or me." Soon afterward, Todd looked defiantly at the practitioner and started to throw the blocks at her. She rose calmly and explained that since the rule was broken, play would have to end for the day.

In the next session, frenzied activity and block-throwing continued. After about ten minutes, Todd stopped, looked at me, and swung the bag of blocks at himself. The play therapy injunction was repeated for Todd. "You may not hurt yourself or me while you are in here. I'm going to help you take care of yourself until you learn how to care better for yourself. Therefore, our session must end for today." Todd protested and began to cry. The practitioner held him and stated, "I can see you are sad and need some help. I offer to help you just as long as you need, but we are finished playing for today." The practitioner and Todd sat quietly next to one another for about ten minutes. They engaged in some casual conversation. At the end of this period, Todd was less agitated, and the session was terminated.

> Principle 13 is shown here. Activity in the therapeutic process is provided by working with Todd in a play therapy milieu.

> Principle 19 is also employed. One aspect of the early treatment would be behavior modification of Todd's obstreperous behavior. The practitioner used the play therapy situation and her attention as contingencies to modify Todd's self-defeating, self-destructive behavior.

> Then, Principle 12 was initiated. Once limits were established, the practitioner offered support and warmth in order to build a therapeutic alliance. Todd's basic needs for protection, physical, and emotional support were met, and he would gradually be encouraged to display more autonomous, self-directed behavior.

Over the next few sessions, Todd involved the practitioner in a number of punitive play themes. Through symbolic games, he would put the her in jail for a "hundred-thousand years." Several times a session, he would place her in a "spanking machine" and severely reprimand her. "I'm pouring boiling hot water all over you." The practitioner would respond, "Oh, I'm so sad.... I must be so bad. What have I done that is so bad?... How can I be better so that I won't have to be in a spanking machine anymore?"

> As is true of some maladjusted children, explained in Principle 7, Todd did not demonstrate a clear sense of identity. In fact, at times he seemed to project onto and confuse his ideas and feelings with those of the practitioner's. Initially, the practitioner did not attempt to make insight interpretations about Todd's punitive play. Todd's self-perceptions were so blurred that it would be difficult for him to comprehend that he was displacing his frustrations about himself onto the practitioner. Thus, as explained in Principle 18, the practitioner maintained a humanistically-oriented psychotherapeutic approach. She responded to Todd's play, rather than interpreting it. Gradually, she helped him understand how an individual who is so severely punished might feel. Importantly, the practitioner suggested to Todd that he could change. He could learn behaviors so that punishment against him would be diminished.

In the next six sessions, Todd progressed to play in which good and bad were dichotomized, such as in games of war and cowboys and Indians. Sometimes, Todd would be the "good guy," but generally he chose to be the "bad guy" and instructed the practitioner to play the "good" role. Regardless of whether he adopted the good or bad role, Todd always won the game. The practitioner pointed out to Todd that it was very important to him to win. Then, she tried to help Todd understand his developing view of the world. "To you the world is made up of good guys and bad guys. You want to win and don't know whether to be good or bad in order to win."

> Todd's play of dichotomized good-bad themes reveals some growth toward adjustment as explained in Principle 6. Todd now portrays a clear sense of himself in relationship to the practitioner, and he struggles to define his identity as good or bad. The practitioner continues the humanistic stance. She offers warmth and acceptance and reflects the content and affect of Todd's play. Thus, she encourages Todd to check out the effects of his newly acquired world views.

In the next four months of therapy, Todd began to request that the practitioner put him in the spanking machine and lock him up for a hundred years. She responded,

"You feel very bad about yourself. You think you should be punished. I think you are a special friend. You are my special friend. I would like to help you if you are sad, but I won't lock you up. You can change if you are sad, and I'll help you." Todd insisted defiantly that the practitioner lock him up. She consistently refused, repeating the previous explanation.

> As described in Principle 18, the practitioner maintained a humanistic-existential stance over the next few months. She communicated her acceptance and caring for Todd. This catalyzed an existential dilemma in their relationship. Todd seemed to be asking, "How do people care for one another? Are you going to punish and scorn me?" The practitioner employed some concepts of Individual Psychology as discussed in Principle 17 to demonstrate to Todd that she was committed to him. It would behoove Todd to change in some ways, and the practitioner would not cooperate in play and talk that was destructive to Todd. She understood his negative feelings and was willing to help him sort them out through further play and communication. Implied also was that the therapist would not reject Todd regardless of whether he maintained this intensity of friendship or became more intimate.

Todd began to invent games involving family members. He requested that the practitioner play his sister. Then, he would get angry and throw the sister in the spanking machine. Then the practitioner would query, "What did I do wrong? How can I get out of here?" Todd said that the sister was bad and took his toys. She responded, "I'm glad you told me. I'll try to do better." Later, he stated, "You always get what you want from Mom." The sister (practitioner)) answered, "I don't think so. Mom won't let me stay out as late at night as I want to." Todd continued to sort out his attitudes about his sister through this role playing. In time, his anger toward her began to dissipate as evidenced by his developing play themes in which he and his sister went swimming and shopping.

> As stated in Principle 23, therapy is not static. As Todd's adjustment is fostered, new therapeutic techniques are appropriate. As described in Principle 21, rational, cognitive approaches helped Todd analyze and reassess family dynamics.

Todd began placing the practitioner in the role of "Pop," his second adopted father. He developed a game where he would stab Pop with a knife and the practitioner, playing Pop, would cry bitterly. Then he would take the same knife and stab himself and would not be hurt at all. He was joyful about this game, and the clinician responded that it was really important to him to be able to upset Pop and to not get hurt himself.

One day, a plane roared overhead and Todd explained, "That's my father flying that plane." He had never used the word "father" before; he had always referred to his current male parent as "Pop." Thus, the practitioned asked him several questions about his father--"What is your father like?" Todd responded, "He is safe--my father is safe. My life is a whirlpool, but my father is safe." As his feelings about his father were explored, it became apparent he was referring to his biological father. This came as a surprise since Todd had never before mentioned his biological father whom he had no knowledge of. It seemed that he had created an entire image of his natural father that was ever-present in his imagination. The image affected him as much as his adopted male parents whom he called "Dad" and "Pop," respectively.

> As explicated in Principle 21, Todd continued to develop, and his language, cognition, and symbolic communication became increasingly important. The practitioner needed to be sensitive to the meaning he attached to words. His language, which he now used in a highly sophisticated fashion, held keys to the nature of his conflicts. The practitioner used Todd's language to help identify his underlying conflicts. Gradually, using a cognitive restructuring approach, she helped him change the meaning of some of his terms so that he could feel better about himself.

From about the eighth month through the twelfth month of psychotherapy, Todd often requested that the practitioner play the role of his Pop as he endeavored to work out his conflicts about his parents and confused and negative feelings about his own adoption. She willingly consented to play the role of Pop but asked also to play his father. Todd continued to be very angry towards Pop, stabbing him with a knife. Once, when the clinician played his father, he cried out, "Where did you go? I'm no good." In many therapy sessions, the following theme was played out by the practitioner in the father role: "Todd, I love you, but I just couldn't take care of you. I asked that you be adopted because I loved you and wanted you to have a good home."

> The practitioner now combined analytic and cognitive restructuring approaches as defined in Principles 16 and 21. She asked to play father because she wanted to facilitate Todd's uncovering deeply repressed conflicts. Todd's deeply rooted traumatic anxiety, that he was no good because his natural father rejected him, was uncovered. The practitioner then began to help him redefine himself as good, giving him new symbolic explanations about why his natural father had given him up for adoption.

In similar fashion, his angry feelings towards his mother were worked through. When the practitioner played the role of mother, he would first attack her with pillows and other objects and then hug her. She (the therapist) responded, "I don't know whether you love me or hate me."

> A similar analytic and cognitive working-through was conducted concerning Todd's reactions to his mother. As posited in Principle 24, a variety of theories and techniques were employed to help Todd deal with the varied facets of his personal dilemmas.

In a psychotherapy session that occurred about a year after initiation of therapy, Todd stated, "You be the mother and I'll be the father. I don't want to be the little boy anymore. He proceeded to play the role of father, calling the practitioner "honey,' taking her hand and flirting with her in an adult fashion.

At this point, several discussion sessions with the parents were initiated. The mother explained that Todd often played an adult role with her. When Pop was out of town, Todd would state, "Now I can be the man around the house."

In a few emotionally tense sessions with the parents, the mother began to identify that in some ways she was reinforcing Todd for playing this adult male role. She was placing upon him many of her unsatisfied needs in her marital relationship.

Her relationship with Todd had many sexual overtones. He loved to wrestle with her, liked to watch her get dressed, and would walk into her room in the mornings stark naked saying such things as, "Look at me, Mom."

When these interactions were discussed, concomitant with the parents' discussion of their relationship, the mother began to view her own behavior as inappropriate. Therefore, the advisability of marital therapy was agreed upon.

In the marital therapy sessions, the couple worked hard to reduce their conflicts with one another and to become more effective in meeting one another's needs. The mother began to modify her behavior towards Todd, making it clear to him that his special role in the family was that of son, not surrogate husband.

> Todd's play seems to indicate some concern about his sexual identification and/or confused role in the family. Through the application of Principle 20, the practitioner met with the parents to see if this recent play therapy session indicated internalized conflict or whether Todd was responding primarily to stress in the family system. As explained in Principle 14, the therapist must decide whether to serve as a consultant

to the parents or to bring the parents into therapy. In this case, diagnostic discussion sessions with the parents illuminated a need for marital therapy.

Marital therapy helped foster Principles 8 and 9 in Todd's home life. Marital therapy increased the consistency in discipline and appropriate support that Todd received. Principle 10 also came into play after Mrs. Wilson's needs for companionship were more successfully met with her husband. Now she was able to give Todd realistic feedback for his behavior: support when appropriate, reprimands when necessary.

At this point, one year and three months after therapy had been initiated, Todd was much calmer and able to express his feelings more spontaneously. He bounded into his session about Christmas time, picked up a bag of blocks and exclaimed, "Remember how I used to use these? I used to throw them around the room. Now they are Santa Claus' bag. Come sit on Santa Claus' lap and tell me what you want for Christmas." The practitioner was aware that Todd's request would probably provoke sexual feelings, but she was ready and felt it was appropriate to deal with them. When she sat on his knee, Todd stated, "Can I spend the night here with you?" The practitioner stated, "What about Mrs. Claus?" Todd became visibly upset, stating, "You make me so mad!" He got on his sleigh and went back to the North Pole. He carried on a conversation with Mrs. Claus in the corner of the room, then he returned on his sleigh and stated, "Well, I can stay with you now because Mrs. Claus and I have gotten a divorce." The practitioner responded, "Divorce isn't that easy. I can see we need to talk about divorce quite a bit more, Todd. You're mother has been divorced, and this must be hard for you to understand." Over the next few sessions, Todd and the practitioner discussed his confusion about male and female relationships, and about his mother's need to get a divorce. In time, Todd was able to accept that he was not a causal force in his mother's divorce. "You were a very little boy. Just as little boys are too young to go to work and do other things grown-ups do, little boys are too young to cause divorce. Your parents caused their divorce and that was sad for you. Now, you've gotten these sad feelings out, and you can go on and grow up and put this all behind you."

The new family system, that is, a better relationship between his parents, helped Todd stabilize his behavior and his role in the family. However, some of his concerns lingered on. From the initiation of therapy, Todd had expressed feelings of being "no good" and of being abandoned by his parents. Now he hints that he somehow feels tied into his parents' relationship problems. Principle 5 points out that all children experience anxiety. Todd's sensitivity to his parents' marital discord probably intensifies natural Oedipal strivings.

Todd now communicates well in a dialogue fashion. The play serves primarily as a platform for identifying his remaining conflicts. After the conflicts are identified through play and role-playing, therapy is conducted in an almost strictly verbal fashion.

A cognitive approach is implemented in therapy. The logic and illogic of his perceptions are discussed. He is offered a metaphor about "little boys" to help him restructure his thinking concerning his role in his mother's divorce.

After a year and one-half of psychotherapy, Todd returned to a regular educational classroom. In the regular classroom, Todd's behavior continued to improve. Therapy was continued for several more months, so that it was clear that gains toward all target goals established at the initiation of therapy were firmly maintained.

At biannual follow-up sessions gains were maintained. At the final, three-year follow-up, he was performing above average in all school work. He was participating in several sports and was particularly effective at football. He spoke with delight about his three "good pals." His parents reported that he continued to be very active, but that his energy was now constructively channeled.

Here we see that Principle 22 is followed. Todd's progress toward therapy goals is charted. Specific target goals such as decreased reprimanding by significant others, decrease in fidgety behavior, increased ability to talk about his feelings and to concentrate are achieved. In addition, secondary goals of improved school performance are noted.

Of course, as explained in Principle 5, Todd is not completely free of anxiety. However, Todd exhibits many overall signs of adjustment elaborated in Principle 6 such as spontaneity, self-awareness, autonomy, curiosity, and caring for others.

Finally, the therapist is committed to Principle 25. Effectiveness of therapy is reevaluated every six months for three years following termination of therapy.

PART THREE
Developing a Treatment Plan for the Child and Family

PART III

DEVELOPING A TREATMENT PLAN FOR THE CHILD AND FAMILY

So far in this text, we have been speaking of the child in theoretical terms. When the practitioner meets the child client, the abstract of children's mental health issues and theoretical approach to child treatment must be translated to specific goals and procedures. The intent of Part III of this book is to help set forth concrete strategies for assisting each child with mental health needs. An essential part of developing treatment plans is to identify the working hypotheses about the nature of the child's problems. Then, the practitioner can decide what type of treatment to provide for the individual and for the family. Chapter 9 overviews the means of assessing the nature of the child's problems and Chapter 10 overviews means of assessing the family as a unit. Chapter 11 discusses specific ways of setting up treatment to meet the needs of the family and the child.

CHAPTER 9

CHILD ASSESSMENT

Two processes are involved in clinical assessment. The first refers to the diagnosis of the gravity of the child's problems. Here, the therapist attempts to determine how the overt symptoms and feelings of subjective discomfort interfere with the child's personal growth and adaptation to the environment. The second aspect of assessment is evaluation of the predisposing and precipitating conditions. The therapist attempts to ascertain how familial, school, physical, intrapersonal and/or interpersonal factors contribute to the child's problem.

Done well, assessment facilitates communication. Most importantly, the results obtained from our assessment help us determine the course of action. Despite this important function, many professionals view assessment with some degree of doubt especially in the area of intellectual assessment. The prevailing negative attitude about psychological assessment and especially standardized testing is often so potent that new findings in the field are not evaluated objectively. A lesser number of professionals defend the use of assessment and may not be open to criticism about psychological evaluation. It seems that the topic is occasionally difficult to discuss objectively. We feel that it is important to begin this chapter by sharing our view of assessment.

Given our definition of assessment (diagnosing the gravity of the child's problem and the predisposing and precipitating conditions), we believe a child therapist must not assess. Therapists differ in how systematically they acquire expertise in assessment techniques, but if the therapeutic procedures are to be based upon client needs, then some assessment of the client's problem are required. We see the need for a relatively systematic assessment procedure. When the procedure is systematic, it is easier to obtain knowledge about all the needs of the child's development (physical, cognitive, affective); and the chances of missing a potentially important variable diminish. The procedure need not be excessively formal, for it is often impossible to gain information from children in a formalized structure. What we recommend is that the child therapist be guided by a relatively systematic format so that the therapist knows what information he or she will try to obtain at appropriate points in the assessment interview(s).

Used appropriately, the assessment devices are guides for the therapist, but they can be misused. For example, it is misuse to assess a child and not propose a plan for therapeutic or remedial help. In this case, assessment labels a child without providing needed intervention. For example, we all have heard statements such as, "Johnny is so hyperactive that there is no use in putting him in a regular school classroom." Conscientious practitioners do not support such uses of assessment since it is a therapist's responsibility to be of assistance rather than to reinforce inaction.

Results of assessment are ill-used if all children are compared to a single norm. Cultural, class, sex and socioeconomic factors as well as the child's individual temperament must be considered in any effective assessment procedure. In assessing ethnic minority children, issues of relative reliability and validity must be carefully coordinated.

Naturally, the practitioner should not employ tests that he or she is not skilled to administer. This latter misuse of testing is rarely mentioned, but does occur. Many assessment instruments require much training in their administration and interpretation, and it is the therapist's responsibility to be certain that he or she possesses necessary prerequisite skills. There is a difference between a "reading" knowledge and "administrative" knowledge of assessment devices. The effective child therapist needs a broad reading knowledge about the types of assessment devices available. This broad knowledge is necessary for understanding psychological reports, research articles, for communicating with other professionals and clients' parents and teachers. The therapist need not and practically could not know how to administer all available assessment instruments. It is better to know the fine points of administering and interpreting a few tests than to have superficial knowledge in the administration of a broad range of instruments.

We have organized this chapter by first discussing diagnostic interviews and the kinds of information the child clinician will want to obtain and observe from parents, teachers, and the child. Then, we review a number of psychometric instruments. Rather than simply listing tests, we divide the review of assessment devices into the domains of screening for organicity and cognitive assessment (including intelligence, achievement, early childhood, and learning disability testing) and social and personality assessment (including measures of overt behavior, standardized, and projective personality testing). By this organization, we hope to show how a battery of test results can be combined to shed light on a child's problem areas and how such information can be employed in identifying the most constructive means of intervention. We cannot provide an extensive review of the reliability, validity, and administrative procedures of each device, but we attempt to familiarize the reader with the types of instruments that can comprise a child assessment battery. We will also present the strengths and limitations of various test formats.

ASSESSMENT INTERVIEWS

Gaining Background Information From Parents

Depending upon one's theory of counseling, the amount of background information desired will vary. Nevertheless, we have demonstrated earlier that the most child psychopathology is catalyzed by a combination of biological and psychosocial stresses. Certain background information is critical to understand these stresses.

Some therapists like to have parents fill out a written questionnaire about the child. They may use this written questionnaire in place of or as an adjunct to the verbal interview.

Some therapists prefer to ask parents for background information in structured interviews. In these background interview sessions, it is important to be open and nonjudgmental with parents. The therapist will want to withhold possible interpretations about the child's problems until all necessary background information is obtained. If interpretations are offered early, parents may have a tendency to offer only background information that fits into the proposed interpretation. It is helpful to ask parents to give very concrete examples of target difficulties. That way, the therapist is able to better discriminate problems that are the child's from those that are the parents'.

An informal parent interview is conducted like a brainstorming session. The therapist encourages parents to generate all information that may be relevant to the child's present functioning. The therapist does not judge the ideas presented, but does encourage parents to be as operational as possible. Later, after these interviews are terminated, the therapist looks for consistency among the parents' statements in order to formulate themes about how the child and family function (Chess & Hassibi, 1978). A broad range of questions about the child's past and present functioning in the physical and social domains should be gleaned. Combining information about the mother's pregnancy, progress through developmental landmarks, illnesses, and medical exams, the child therapist can begin to form hypotheses about the potentiality of organic impairment. Naturally, if organicity appears likely, the clinician will refer the child to a medical professional for further assessment. The therapist will also ask questions to determine the child's social relationships with family members, peers, and other adults. By asking about the client's relationship with siblings and other peers, parents and other adults, about how the child deals with responsibility at home and in other environments (doing chores, following directions, etc.), and about specific disruptive behaviors (temper tantrums, obstinance, etc.), clear themes about the child's strengths and problems emerge. For example, the clinician may learn that the child gets along well with parents and other adults, but does not relate well with siblings or peers; or the clinician may discover that the child's relationship with all family members is stormy, but that the child's social behavior at school and in other environments is consistently appropriate. In the first example, the child therapist begins to suspect that the child's problems center upon personal/social difficulties relating to other children. In the second example, the therapist would formulate the hypothesis, awaiting further substantiation, that the child's difficulties are intimately tied into problems in the family system. In one way or another, it is very important that the child therapist obtain information about the client's functioning in each of the developmental domains.

Very possibly, parents' recall of developmental landmarks may be somewhat distorted; and of course, they present their view of the child's problems which may not coincide with the opinion of the child or of other significant adults. Although some information may lack absolute accuracy, very unusual behaviors tend to be remembered with relative precision. If the responses are viewed as the parents' perceptions of the child, not as absolutes, meaningful trends emerge about how the parents' view the child's problem and their role in provoking or ameliorating the child's stress.

Interviewing The Child

In the initial sessions with the child, the therapist wants to glean information about the child's perception of his or her problems, remembering that the child may have a different perception for coming to therapy than the parents. Therapists agree that great skill and patience is required for assessment sessions with children. Freedman, Kaplan, and Sadock (1976, p. 1038) explain that the therapist must be a "responsive human being. It is virtually useless to push diagnostic questions at a child who is unready or unable to lower his guard." By responsive human being, Freedman, Kaplan, and Sadock (1976) mean that the therapist waits for a cue from the child that allows asking relevant question. Thus, if a child asks, "Where is my mother now?" an opportunity is available to learn more about the child's relationship with his or her parents. Similarly, if a child says, "I have a toy like that at home," questions about the child's daily activities might be asked. If specific questions need to be asked quickly (for example, if the child is experiencing some crisis at school that requires prompt resolution), it is usually helpful to begin by asking simple questions first to help the child feel at ease. Questions about likes and dislikes, pets, and hobbies, etc. can facilitate communication (Chess & Hassibi, 1978).

Information about the child's overall development falls into seven primary areas: size and appearance, social/emotional adjustment, motility, coordination, speech, thinking processes, cerebral functioning, and sensory acuity. Some of this information can be obtained by direct observation while short activities and games may help determine other developmental data. Table 9.1 presents the major areas in a child's mental status examination, that is, the major developmental areas that need to be investigated (Goodman & Sours, 1967) and some activities or observations that help in making the assessment (Keat, 1974).

Table 9.1

Mental Status Examination with Children

Target Area	Specific Indicators	Significant Activities
Size & Appearance	Nutrition Color of Skin Dress Habits Mannerisms	
Social/Emotional	Friendly Happy Mature for Age	Is child easy to engage in conversation? How does the child handle separation from parents?
Motility	Hyperkinesis Hypokinesis Tics	Does the child sit still when asked to for three minutes?
Coordination	Posture Gait Balance Gross Motor Coordination Apraxia	 Ask child to walk stairs & to throw a ball to an object while hopping. Pick-up sticks, make a fist, play jacks, unwrap candy, use a toothbrush, play "Simon Says"

Table 9.1

Mental Status Examination with Children (continued)

Target Area	Specific Indicators	Significant Activities
Speech	Dysrhythmias Pitch Modulation Neolosisms Mutist Aphasia	Have child name things in room. Have child repeat a sentence, give meaning of a sentence.
Thinking Pattern	Very Fragmented Bizarre Concepts Merging Lapses of Attention Cognitive Errors (attaching literal meaning to figurative words) Idiosyncratic Views Blurring of Reality & Fantasy Obsessions Repetitive Talk Dysphasia	Name & hide objects. Have child find them sequentially.

Table 9.1

Mental Status Examination with Children (continued)

Target Area	Specific Indicators	Significant Activities
Sensory Acuity	Vision	Hold up fingers at various distances. Note ocular muscle.
	Hearing	Ask child to identify when he/she hears stop as you approach.
	Taste	Ask about any negative feelings for foods.
	Agnosia	Ask about any "scary" experiences. Have child close eyes & touch & identify common objects. Note any indifference to pain; loss of tactile experience.

On the basis of a directed observation of the child conducted along the guidelines suggested in Table 9.1, the therapist can gain needed information about cerebral functioning, the so-called "hard" signs and "soft" signs of organic pathology. The "hard" are indicative of specific brain damage and include disorders of ocular muscles, indifference to pain, lack of tactile sensation, and convulsions—especially those with associated vertigo or vomiting (Chess & Hassibi, 1978). Neurophysiological referral is in order if these signs are present. "Soft" or nonfocal signs are sometimes indicative of organicity, but do not imply anything about the area of neurological malfunctioning. "Soft" signs include hypotinicity (flacidity and limpness of muscles), fine and gross motor coordnation difficulties, signs of aphasia, dysphasia, agnosia and apraxia (Chess & Hassibi, 1978; Goodman & Sours, 1967). The presence of several of these "soft" signs signals the need for further psychophysiological testing, especially if these results confirm findings from the parent interview (Chess & Hassibi, 1978).

If neurological consultation reveals no organic syndromes to underlie these "soft" signs, it is then important for the therapist to work with teachers, speech pathologists, and other related professionals to help remediate the motility, coordination, speech, or acuity disorders. Since the child's physical and psychological development are intimately interwoven, remediation of psychomotor difficulty is integral to therapeutic gain. Clearly, the child's emotional harmony is hampered if he or she is unable to play or compete with peers at psychomotor tasks or if sensory/motor deficits hamper effective adjustment to school.

If the systematic observation of the child reveals that most difficulties are in thinking processes, the practitioner will want to explore the extent of the thinking disorder. Psychometric testing may be helpful in this regard.

Since a child is usually brought to counseling because his or her behavior is quite disturbing to some significant adults, many clinicians like to observe the child and significant adults interacting at the initiation of therapy. By watching how significant adults and the child interact, the practitioner may gain new hypotheses about how they are provoking disturbing responses from one another.

Summary of Interview Data

Regardless of theoretical orientation, the child clinician needs information from the child and significant adults about the child's overall functioning, strengths, and problem areas. Specific questioning about developmental history aids the clinician in assessing the probability of organic impairment and in targeting problematic areas of personal and social functioning. Observation of the child, significant adults, and their interaction provides essential information about intrapersonal problems related to emotional and physical development and interpersonal difficulties that are provoked by maladaptive patterns between the child and significant adults.

Because the child's and significant adults' behaviors and attitudes will change as therapy is implemented, the informal interview process should continue through various phases of intervention so that new information and procedures can be incorporated into the management plan as needed.

PSYCHOMETRIC INSTRUMENTS

Psychometric instruments can offer another sample of a child's behavior. At best, these results offer further clinical hunches for therapy. If there is a discrepancy between the parents' report of a child and clinical observation or a discrepancy between the child's stated feelings and overt behavior, test results may suggest the motivational factors underlying the child's behavior. Some tests can be useful for screening organic pathology. Others help delineate the relationship between emotional and academic problems. The results are most likely to be helpful when the test is selected wisely to help shed light on a specific concern.

When a therapist tests a child, it is very important to allow plenty of time to establish rapport. Generally, we can motivate our adult test examinees verbally by suggesting that the test is important or asking them to do their best. With younger children, tests may not seem as intrinsically important. To a preschool child, testing may be an alien experience. These children are likely to be frightened by the therapist telling them they must do their best. Often the child's performance depends upon the relationship with the therapist. The child is willing to cooperate with the therapist's requests because of the rapport between them. Some behaviorally-oriented therapists attempt to increase the child's motivation to perform well by offering a reinforcement after completing segments of the task. This approach works well with many children, providing standardization procedures are not compromised in the process.

Children's performances are also contingent upon how interesting they find the work to be. They look at the task like a game and want to quit when the game is no longer fun. The therapist must be sensitive to the child's level of interest in the task. Generally, it is a good idea to terminate the testing when the child's interest wanes as indicated by increasing fidgeting, changing the subject, or negativism. Several testing sessions may be required to obtain a valid measure of the child's true functioning.

The child's response to the test situation is often as important as the actual answers to the questions. The therapist will want to know the child's response to the first question as an indication of how the child responds to novel tasks. Also important are repetitive response patterns. Of course, these response patterns should be considered in relationship to the child's overall behavior, but do provide one more clue under relatively standardized conditions about how the child thinks and behaves. Thus, how the child responds to not knowing an answer and being wrong may be clues about how the child responds to errors at school and at home. If the child frequently requests assistance, this may suggest that the client is hesitant to act on his or her her own and may indicate strong dependency ties. If the child frequently asks, "Am I right?" the therapist might postulate that the client needs much reassurance or is questioning her or his judgment. The child may respond differently to one test than another, and certain tentative conclusions can be drawn from this behavior. For example, a child may work fast and smilingly on an achievement test and very haltingly on the Rorschach. In this case, the therapist may hypothesize that this child prefers structured tasks. Thus, the therapist notes all test behavior and adds this to other assessment findings.

A vast number of tests are available, and the reader should be familiar with the Mental Measurement Yearbooks which review all standardized tests in print (Buros, 1972). In the remainder of this chapter, we will attempt to overview types of assessment devices widely used today. Our review is by no means exhaustive. We have attempted to organize this review around functions served by the tests: screening for organic problems, cognitive assessment, and social and personality assessment. Some tests are used for more than one of these functions and may be mentioned more than once. In many cases, numerous books have been written about a single instrument. Yet, we have time and space to write only a few paragraphs. Our review will emphasize how a child therapist might benefit from the type of test results, and we will refer you to further reading in the various areas.

SCREENING FOR ORGANICITY

We have stated that "hard" or "soft" signs of neurological impairment may be obtained through the clinical interview with the child and his or her parents or other significant adults. A number of psychological instruments can offer further confirmation of organicity. We will review two, the Bender-Gestalt and Weschler tests, which child practitioners often use. The reader is reminded that many other screening devices are available. Then, we review briefly neuropsychological batteries that are administered by child practitioners who specialize in assessing organicity in children. We demonstrate that the organic assessment devices range greatly in reliability. The combination of test and administrator sophistication determines the precision in identifying organicity.

Bender-Gestalt Test

Psychometrists commonly use the Bender-Gestalt Test (Bender, 1962) as a rough means of screening for organic brain dysfunction among children. The nine cards with geometric designs were developed by Lauretta Bender in 1938 based upon the belief that there is a tendency to perceive and complete the designs according to principles biologically-determined by sensory-motor patterns of action. Children before age four scribble with little resemblance to form. Lines are drawn in primarily radial directions with few horizontal movements. Around preschool age, children begin to form loops. Circles are drawn for dots. By age six, good reproduction of form is expected. Bender (1938) posited that children with organic brain syndrome will draw on more primitive levels than expected by their chronological age; that is, she believed that organic brain syndrome would be demonstrated by infantilized or regressive drawings. She further posited that these "errors" are distinct from the distortions of an emotionally-disturbed child.

Koppitz (1964) developed an objective scoring system normed to 1,200 public school children between the ages of five and ten. Administration is in three phases. In the first phase, the administrator simply states, "I have nine cards with designs on them for you to copy. Here is the first one. Now go ahead and make one just like it." The child copies the nine designs handed to him or her in turn as the directions are repeated. In the second phase, the child is requested to draw as many designs as can be remembered. In the third phase, the child is presented with a design seriously distorted in the first phase. If the child makes the same error again, the card is laid next to the child's drawing, and the child is asked if he or she can perceive the difference between them. In the Koppitz (1964) scoring system, points are given for regressive drawing that may be indicative of organicity. In general terms, the scoring system attempts to discriminate the following types of errors:

Errors Indicative of Organic Brain Syndrome	Errors Indicative of Psychological Problems
Rotation	Overabundance of vertical movement
Distortion	Fluidity of pattern
Fragmentation	Loss of Boundaries Between designs
Oversimplification	Destruction of the gestalt by elaboration
Use of angles for curves	Embellishment with own ideas
Perseveration	First few forms good, then deterioration
Collision and overlap of form	
Circles for dots	
Lines that do not meet	

Figure 9.1 is a reproduction of the 9 cards of the Bender-Gestalt. Following this reproduction are protocols completed by two 5-year-old children. Protocol A was produced by a child diagnosed as brain-damaged, while Protocol B was drawn by a child referred to counseling because of her insomnia and frequent tearfulness. Naturally, this brief review of the Bender-Gestalt does not prepare us to present a scoring of these protocols; but it might be helpful for the reader's broad understanding to visualize how Bender-Gestalt protocols differ in production. On Protocol A (Figure 9.2), completed in eight minutes, several factors associated with organicity are demonstrated, such as fragmentation and oversimplification, distortion, and overlap of forms. In addition, dots are not clearly formed, and angles and curves are not differentiated. In Protocol B (Figure 9.3), forms are rather meticulously completed, but in many cases appear overworked. Protocol B showed many erasures. Note that Figure 4 of the Bender was attempted twice. Dashes and circles are carefully formed, but at times circles are made rather than dots as in the original cards. Notice the child's embellishment, such as the heart around Figure 3 and the face in Figure A. The child

Figure 9.1. Nine of Wertheimer's
Original patterns used by him
for research in visual gestalt
psychology have been selected and
are offered to the individual to be
examined for copying. Figure A
is used as an introductory figure (with permission).
Published by the American Orthopsychiatric Association.

Figure 9.2

Figure 9.3

preceded these embellishments each time by stating, "I didn't do that one right." The child worked slowly and meticulously at the task (a total of 20 minutes); yet did not place the drawings in the sequential order (as if she were so concerned about completing each drawing correctly that she did not pay attention to the broader gestalt).

The validity studies of the Bender-Gestalt Test have not been totally favorable. Tolor and Schulberg (1963) reviewed thirty years of research and reported that the test did not have high validity coefficients with organicity. Practitioners often disagree with conclusions that cast doubt on the Bender-Gestalt Test. Our recommendation is that the instrument be considered only only as a rough screening device for organic brain syndrome (Chess & Hassibi, 1978).

The Wechsler Subtest Scatter

A series of intelligence tests developed by David Wechsler have been used to screen for organicity. The tests used with children are the Wechsler Intelligence Scales for Children - Revised or WISC-R (Wechsler, 1974) which is normed for children between the ages of 6 1/2 to 16 1/2 years, and the Wechsler Preschool and Primary Scale of Intelligence or WPPSI (Wechsler, 1967) which was developed for children ages 4 to 6 1/2 years. Each test was standardized on a broad cross-section of the population (Anastasi, 1976). Both scales require considerable training to administer and interpret. The skill of the test administrator can greatly affect how the child performs on the test.

The use of the WISC-R or WPPSI in identifying possible organicity lies in the comparison of subtest scatter. The WISC-R is comprised of twelve subtests. The Verbal scale is made of the following subtests:

1. information
2. comprehension
3. arithmetic
4. similarities
5. vocabulary
6. digit span

The Performance scale includes:

7. picture completion,
8. picture arrangement,
9. block design
10. object assembly
11. coding
12. mazes

The WPPSI is also comprised of twelve subtests, most of which are modifications of the WISC-R tasks. The Verbal subtests include:

1. information
2. vocabulary
3. arithmetic
4. similarities
5. comprehension
6. sentences

The Performance subtests are:

7.	animal house	10.	geometric designs
8.	picture completion	11.	block design
9.	mazes	12.	animal house retest

In general, a 15 point discrepancy between the Verbal and Performance scale scores, especially if the Performance exceeds the Verbal scale score, is suggestive of possible organic pathology. The test protocol is more suspect if block design, object assembly, and digit symbol are the lowest performance subscales (suggesting possible right hemisphere damage leading to difficulty interpreting figures), if the similarities subscale is significantly lower than vocabulary (suggesting concreteness that is characteristic of organic brain syndrome), and if digits backward is considerably poorer than digits forward (suggesting difficulty in transposition, also characteristic of some organic brain syndrome) (Friedman & Barclay, 1963; Lutey, 1977). Experts study the Wechsler protocols for more subtle indicators, such as noting the number of rotations and perseveration of the geometric designs subtest of WPPSI. The interpretation of organicity from the Wechsler tests is covered extensively in Lutey (1977) and Sattler (1974). In this chapter, we want to simply illustrate that with specialized training in interpretation of the Wechsler tests, they may serve as relatively reliable screening instruments of organicity. Over time, the greatest use of the Wechsler tests may not be as measures of global IQ, but rather as more discreet measures of intellectual thinking processes.

Clinical Neuropsychological Assessment

Although the child practitioner would not administer neurological tests, she or he will often make referrals for neurological evaluations when organicity is expected. This branch of human neuropsychology emphasizes use of objective psychometric methods in the assessment of higher cortical functioning to determine the presence and nature of organic impairment. Both psychological (memory, cognition) and neurological (sensation, perception) levels of analysis are included (Meier, 1974). Originally the domain of physicians (neurologists and psychiatrists), it is now common practice for therapists of varied clinical backgrounds and advanced training to administer and interpret neuropsychological assessment batteries such as the Reitan (1964) or the Gardner (1979) batteries.

The clinical neuropsychological assessment batteries are employed to identify the nature and extent of brain damage. Ideally, the results suggest directions for treatment and remediation of sensory or learning disorders. Thus, if a child therapist suspects organicity to be a cause of a client's behavioral or academic difficulties, the therapist may conduct or refer a child for further clinical neuropsychological assessment.

When neuropsychological assessment first began to be practiced in the 1940's, instruments were employed simply to identify the extent of impairment. With our increased understanding of the specialization of various cortical loci, clinical neuropsychological assessment has become exceedingly complex. A number of sophisticated instruments are administered to identify the area as well as the extent of brain damage. For example, the Reitan (1964) battery integrates results from the Wechsler-Bellevue (Wechsler, 1944) Wide Range Achievement Test (Jastak & Jastak, 1965), several other standardized instruments plus a number of tests developed by Reitan. The Reitan battery has been remarkably more effective than chance in diagnosing organicity that has later been confirmed by surgery. The battery is also useful since it can be used effectively in localizing the brain damage as left or right hemisphere, and whether it is motor or sensory related (Reitan & Davison, 1974).

Not all clinical neuropsychological assessment batteries are concerned with identifying the point of brain lesion. Others attempt to target the type of impaired functions. Thus, Gardner's (1979) battery provides a means for identifying the sensory and motor processes impaired in minimal brain dysfunction. His battery includes selective use of a parents interview form, Wechsler Intelligence Scale for Children (Wechsler, 1974), standardized tests of coordination, visual and auditory processing, plus several tests he has developed, particularly the Steadiness Tester. The Steadiness Tester requires the subject to place a stylus in holes of a metal board, and the number of times the stylus touches the perimeters of the holes is recorded. The instrument is used to diagnose steadiness and impulsivity. It can also be employed to determine the effectiveness of amphetamine treatment for a given client by determining a baseline steadiness rate, administering the medication, and retesting in six hours.

It is important to recognize the importance that age plays in the manifestation of symptoms resulting from brain damage. It cannot be assumed that brain damage will have the same effect in an adult, a school-aged child, and an infant. Clearly, the pattern of impairment may vary as a function of the age at which the injury is sustained. The behavioral effects depend upon the learning and intellectual development that has occurred prior to the injury. Research on preschool children, for example, indicates that at this age level the brain-injured tend to be deficient in all intellectual functions (Graham, Ernhart, Craft, & Berman, 1963). Another study by Graham, Ernhart, Thurston and Craft, 1961 of young children with a history of prenatal or birth trauma demonstrated lower IQ test performance on a variety of standardized intelligence tests. It is suggested that the intellectual impairment may be due to the diffuseness of the brain damage or to critical deficiencies in language and/or attentional control which hinder the acquisition of cognitive abilities.

Summary

The broad screening for organic assessment is not highly reliable, so referral for neurological evaluation should be considered when organicity is suspected. The assessment of neurological impairment is very complex. Reliable neuropsychological instruments require much training to administer and interpret. The age at which the damage occurred, the age at which the children are assessed, and the duration of the pathological condition are all critical in the interpretation. For the most part, the child practitioner will conduct only rough screening for organicity based upon her or his observation and broad testing of the child. It is important for the practitioner to be aware of the range of neuropsychological tests that are available so that referrals can be made when appropriate and so the practitioner can understand reports returned from these referrals.

INTELLECTUAL ASSESSMENT

Intelligence is an ill-defined term used to describe mental ability. Operationally, the term is defined as the score on a test of intelligence. There are numerous tests of intelligence some of which will be discussed here. Before beginning our discussion, it must be noted that the question of measuring mental capacity has been heatedly debated by social scientists and politicians alike. The central issue of this debate concerns the inheritability of intelligence and the possible bias in the tests that favor white middle class children. Repeatedly, the issue is raised of how test scores are analyzed by educational personnel. There is no question that IQ scores have been misused in a variety of ways: to maintain students in special education classes; to track ethnic minority students into vocational, rather than academic programs; and to overgeneralize about favorite students' capabilities. These are just a few of the abuses perpetrated with these tests. Yet, used judiciously, the tests have long been an aid to child therapists. Here are two examples of cases in which IQ results combined with other data served functional purposes.

A couple brings their 3-year-old daughter to you because she has been slow to learn to talk. The mother was ill with an unidentified flu virus during the first trimester of pregnancy. The parents are worried that their daughter may be retarded. You assess the daughter with a battery of tests including a mental status exam and a Weschler Intelligence Test and record lags in gross and fine motor coordination, and an intelligence score 1.5 standard deviations below the mean. You note that the child's attention span is extremely short, from 1 to 2 minutes duration. You help the parents identify an educational nursery school program to work on the problems identified and to increase intellectual stimulation. You recommend further neurological testing. You plan a systematic behavior modification program to be administered by the parents to increase the daughter's attention span.

Seven-year-old Johnny is brought for therapy upon the recommendation of the teacher. During the assessment session with the parents, they explain that Johnny is a delight at home, always quizzical and willing to assume responsibility. At school, Johnny is not completing work and is engaged in much attention-seeking behavior such as blurting comments without being called upon and moving his desk around, thereby creating much noise. In the initial interviews with Johnny, he tells you that he does not have any problems, but he just does not like school. Johnny surpasses expected developmental landmarks on all mental status areas examined and is a verbally facile child. You decide to administer an intelligence test and several psychological inventories. The inventory results suggest that Johnny is a very ingenious child who likes to work independently and plays with only a few close friends. He enjoys the company of adults. The WISC-R (Wechsler, 1974) results reveal an IQ of 130 with exceedingly high subtest scores on similarities and block design. You recommend that Johnny be placed in a program for gifted children and/or be given opportunity for self-directed, small group study.

School Age Scales

A large number of IQ tests are available for the child therapist's use. The Wechsler Intelligence Scale for Children-Revised (WISC-R) and Wechsler Preschool and Primary Scale of Intelligence (WPPSI) provide reliable measures of a number of skills associated with intelligence for children ages 6 to 17 and 4 to 6 1/2 respectively (Wechsler, 1967, 1974). In addition, the Stanford-Binet Intelligence Scale (Terman & Merrill, 1973) is a frequently used instrument with children. The Stanford-Binet can be used with children as young as two years of age. Like the Wechsler scales, the Stanford-Binet is a standardized test that has been shown to have high test reliability and validity. The test, unlike the Wechsler scales, yields a single IQ score which is the composite of both verbal and performance items. For a complete description of these tests, see Anastasi (1976).

Many clinicians regard the intelligence tests not only as a standardized test of intelligence, but also as a platform for behavioral observation and clinical interview. The tests allow the examiner to observe the child's work methods, approaches to problem solution, activity level, self-confidence, persistence, and ability to concentrate. Obviously, the qualitative observations made in the course of administration should be interpreted with caution because they are less standardized. The value of the administration as a clinical interview will depend to a large extent on the skill, experience, and sophistication of the examiner, as well as on his or her awareness of the limitations imposed by the test on this type of observation.

Both the Wechsler tests and the Stanford-Binet require much training to administer. Testing must be done individually, and generally requires at least an hour. A number of short-form tests have been modeled after these scales. Most of the short-form tests elicit answers through a single sensory channel (Palmer, 1970). Thus, all questions may be verbal or pictorial. Often, the breadth of skill measured and thus the reliability of the score is diminished with these short-form instruments. One such instrument is the Peabody Picture Vocabulary Test (PPVT) which was constructed by Dunn (1965). The PPVT can be administered to children from 2 1/2 years to 18 years and consists of a series of 150 plates, each containing four pictures. As each plate is presented, the examiner provides a stimulus word orally, and the child responds by pointing to the picture on the plate that best illustrates the meaning of the stimulus word. The test requires only 10 to 15 minutes to administer. The raw score can be converted to mental age, deviation IQ, or percentile. The PPVT correlates moderately well (correlations in the 60's) with individual and group intelligence scales. Although useful as a quick assessment instrument especially with handicapped children, the retarded, and in some cases with ethnic minority children, the PPVT is limited because of its reliance on verbal knowledge only.

The Leiter International Performance Scale (Leiter, 1959) is a nonverbal test of intelligence that can be used to evaluate children with sensory or motor deficits who have difficulty speaking and reading. Among the tasks included in the Leiter are: matching identical colors, shades of gray, forms, or pictures; copying a block design; picture completion; number estimation; spatial relations; memory for a series; and classification of animals according to habitat. The test is administered without time limitations and the score can be converted to mental age and IQ. Correlations with the Stanford-Binet and Wechsler tests are usually between .50 and .90. The Leiter is purported to be relatively culture free, although this claim and the adequacy of standardization have been questioned (Sattler, 1974).

Another short-form test is the Columbia Mental Maturity Scale (Burgemeister, Blum, & Lorge, 1972). Originally developed for use with cerebral-palsied children, this scale consists of 92 items, each of which is made up of 3, 4, or 5 drawings printed on a large card. The child is required to identify the drawing that does not belong with the others. This test requires no verbalization and is not dependent upon the child's vocabulary as is the PPVT. The test is lauded for the usefulness of the approach, but further documentation of its standardization is needed (Sattler, 1974).

Infant Scales

A number of scales have been developed to assess infant cognition. Two of long-standing usage are the Cattell Infant Intelligence Scale (Cattell, 1940) and the Bayley Scale of Infant Development (Bayley, 1969). The Cattell is a downward extension of the 1937 Stanford-Binet and is appropriate for infants age 2 years to age 30 months. Because of infants' restricted behavioral repertoire, most of the tasks are of an essentially motor type. Standardization of the instrument is old (1930) and limited to 274 infants of middle-class families. In many settings, the Cattell scale has been replaced by the

Bayley Scales of Infant Development (Bayley, 1969). This instrument has been designed to assess the developmental status of children between the ages of 2 months and 2 1/2 years. The Bayley scales consist of three components. The Mental Scale samples such functions as perception, memory, problem solving, the beginnings of verbal communi- cation, and rudimentary abstract thinking. The second component, or Motor Scale, provides measures of gross motor abilities, such as sitting, standing, walking, and manipulatory skills of hands and fingers. The final scale, the Infant Behavior Record, is completed by the examiner after the other two parts have been administered. This scale is designed to assess various aspects of personality development, emotional and social behavior, attention span, persistence, and goal-directedness.

As a whole, the infant scales are not as reliable as scales of intelligence for older children and adults. Importantly, they are generally not good predictors of later per- formance on intelligence tests since intellectual development is susceptible to many intervening factors (e.g., illness, loss of a parent, etc.) that make long term predictions deficient. However, there is some evidence that infants with very low scores do perform poorly when retested with the Stanford-Binet or Wechsler series at a later age (Erickson, 1978). Perhaps the value of the infant scales is that they are most helpful in the early detection of sensory and neurological defects, emotional disturbances, and environmental deficits (Anastasi, 1976).

Summary

Used judiciously, the intelligence scales can aid a practitioner in determining if a child's adjustment difficulties are related to unusually high or low cognitive functioning. Perhaps more important than the actual IQ scores, these instruments can serve as a standardized format against which to view the child's cognitive and overall functioning.

ACADEMIC ASSESSMENT

Child practitioners frequently see children whose academic performance is below that expected for their age and grade level. Many schools employ educational spe- cialists who are trained in diagnosing the specific types and possible causes of learning deficits. Yet, in some cases, these children are not identified in the schools, and it falls upon the child practitioners to identify the child's academic problems for the school personnel. Moreover, sometimes school counselors and diagnosticians assess a child's educational lag and then refer the child to a therapist because they believe that the primary block to the child's academic performance is emotional. Or the school personnel may refer a child with academic deficits to a child therapist because the child's frustration with learning has prompted inappropriate school behavior, such as not completing assignments, refusing to come to school, or reacting to school tasks by crying, stubbornness, or attention-getting behavior. For a variety of reasons, then, the child practitioner should be familiar with the principles of academic assessment and types of instruments available. For a very extensive review of individual and group tests of school aptitude and achievement, the reader may wish to consult Anastasi (1976). We will now elaborate on the basic principles and purposes of these instruments.

Reading Tests

A very large number of academic difficulties can be traced to reading problems. Most school activity is dependent upon reading comprehension. A child with a reading deficit struggles to complete assignments, may not be able to follow written instructions, may not understand what is written on the blackboard, and may miss many items on exams because he or she cannot read them, even though knowing the correct answer. It is no wonder then that many children with severe reading problems behave inappropriately in school. They have few means of constructive involvement in the academic tasks. Two commonly used achievement tests employed in the schools that include measures of reading skills are the California Achievement Test (Tiegs & Clark, 1970) and the Metropolitan Achievement Test (Durost, Bixler, Writestone, Prescott, & Balow, 1971). However, since these written tests require students to read complex sentences and passages in order to respond, those children with extreme deficits may become very distraught and little meaningful information may be obtained from these instruments.

A number of individually administered oral reading tests have been developed that allow examiners to assess the child's reading competence in a more informal fashion. Oral tests such as the Durrell (1955), Gray and Robinson (1967), and Woodcock (1973) are comprised of several sections. The child's listening comprehension level is tested. Then the child's ability to read single words is examined. The child then reads passages orally beginning with paragraphs containing words more basic than his or her tested sight vocabulary. Gradually, the subject is asked to read and answer questions to passages containing higher level vocabulary so that an "independent level" of reading (the child can read this material on his or her own), an "instructional level" (the child can read this material with the teacher's support and assistance), and a "frustration level" (the child experiences too much difficulty for productive learning to occur) can be evaluated (Lerner, 1971). The oral reading tests are an efficient way of assessing the child's encoding, decoding, and comprehension skills and thus help pinpoint types of reading difficulties.

Achievement Tests

A variety of standardized achievement tests such as the Wide Range Achievement Test (Jastak, Jastak, & Bijou, 1965) and the California Achievement Test (Tiegs & Clark, 1970) are available for assessing children's academic performance in key educational areas such as reading, arithmetic, and language arts. Typically, the child's performance on the achievement test is compared to performance on a standardized intelligence test. In this way, assessment is made about the relationship of a student's potential for learning and actual achievement level. If a discrepancy is noted in a particular academic domain, special diagnostic tests in arithmetic, spelling, spoken language, and written expression can be administered.

Some typical diagnostic tests are: Key Math Diagnostic Arithmetic Test (Connolly, Nachtman, & Pritchett, 1973), Houston Test for Language Development (Crabtree, 1963), Gates-Russell Spelling Diagnostic Test (Gates & Russell, 1962), Lincoln Diagnostic Spelling Tests (Lincoln, 1955), and the Picture Story Language Test (Myklebust, 1965). These tests help define remedial education programs. Remediation is based upon the specific interlocking of the child's academic strengths and deficits. For example, Johnny achieved a superior IQ score, high reading, and arithmetic proficiency. However, his spelling skill is extremely low. On the WISC-R, the coding subtest showed a significant number of reversals. Johnny seems to possess superior analytic ability and skill in reading and comprehending material in context. The Lincoln Diagnostic Spelling Tests (Lincoln, 1955) might be administered to pinpoint his specific spelling deficits. Results of the spelling diagnostic test might suggest, for example, that Johnny needs extra training in left-right sequencing and figure-ground discrimination. In contrast, another child, by the name of Sally, has a WISC-R score that is one standard deviation below the mean with no significant subtest scatter. Oral reading tests and spelling achievement reveal consistent performance about one year below expected grade level. Sally's remediation will be more broadly based. Most likely, she will profit from special instruction in reading and will need texts aimed at the instructional reading level indicated by a reading test.

Early childhood

Several tests are available for screening children's school readiness. Two such tests are the Boehm Test of Basic Concepts (Boehm, 1971) and the Denver Development Screening Test (Frankenburg & Dodds, 1970). The early childhood screening tests may be administered individually or in groups and generally do not require extensive training. These tests attempt to measure children's performance in affective, language, and motor domains in the hopes of identifying children with significant developmental lags that may prevent their successful adaptation to school. Of course, the early identification needs to be followed by special preschool training. Many of these tests provide limited standardization data. Moreover, most of the preschool training programs are too recent for a reliable measure of their effectiveness. Current research suggests that these preschool programs are most effective when parents are taught to stimulate speaking and behavior in identified deficit areas. The stimulation needs to be specific to measured deficits, and the remediation pursued within the child's primary environment, the home (Hunt, 1975).

Learning Disability Assessment

In discussing achievement tests, we noted that educational researchers have been particularly concerned about children for whom there is a large disparity between measured intellectual potential and academic achievement. We mentioned that emotional problems have been posited as preventing full academic growth for some of these children. Sociological factors such as lack of stimulation in the home or poor and inconsistent educational experiences have also been proposed to explain this discrepancy among children.

A group of educational researchers (Frostig, Lefever, & Whittlesey, 1964; Kirk, McCarthy, & Kirk, 1968; Minskoff, 1975) have suggested that some of these children may be experiencing deficits in sensory or motor integration. Although the visual and auditory acuity and the musculature of these children is intact, they may not be efficient in processing information. Thus, a child may have 20/20 vision, but not be able to discriminate significant forms from background or may experience difficulty orienting objects in space. Another child may have no hearing loss but still be unable to concentrate in a room with background noise. Other children with normal reflexes may be inefficient learning fine motor tasks such as writing. Clearly, children with problems of processing sensory and motor stimuli may experience difficulty completing typical school tasks. The term "learning disability" is used to describe these children and is broadly defined as a learning difficulty characterized by a significant disparity between measured achievement and intellectual ability with no associated organic pathology or loss of acuity.

Perceptual motor, auditory discrimination, and psycholinguistic tests have been designed to identify learning disabilities among children. Commonly used tests included the Frostig Developmental Test of Visual Perception (Frostig, Lefever, & Whittlesey, 1964), Auditory Discrimination Test (Wepman, 1958), and the Illinois Test of Psycholinguistic Abilities (Kirk, McCarthy, & Kirk, 1968). These tests offer extensive reliability and validity data and are normed to a broad range of children of different ages and ethnic groups. Materials have also been developed for school personnel to teach processing skills once deficits have been identified.

However, there is much controversy among educators about whether mastery of the processing skills improves academic performance. Hammill and Larsen (1974) argue that task analysis is more effective than perceptual motor testing and remediation material in measuring and teaching to process deficits. In task analysis, the academic difficulty is operationally analyzed into discrete subtasks. Children are taught the discrete subskills that are requisite to the target learning deficit through the sensory modalities with which the child is most adept, under systematic reinforcement conditions.

Others argue that testing of perceptual motor deficits and teaching of process skills is helpful for some children with specific disabilities. They state that learning disability testing and remediation is effective under specific conditions, but that research findings are yet too limited to predict which children will profit most from the training (Minskoff, 1975).

Summary of Academic Assessment

The field of academic testing is becoming increasingly complex. A number of sophisticated instruments have emerged and concommitantly a number of controversies have arisen pertaining to the usefulness of testing and the devising of remediation programs to correct academic deficits. The child therapist may find it useful to gain mastery of one or two academic tests of each of the major types. Again, the therapist needs to be aware of the range and possible uses of academic assessment instruments so that clients can be referred for appropriate educational diagnosis when necessary.

SOCIAL AND PERSONALITY ASSESSMENT

A number of instruments used for assessing children's affective reactions and behaviors are adaptations of adult scales while others have been developed specifically for children. In either case, administrative procedures must be built upon developmental levels and different responses can be expected according to the child's cognitive and social sophistication. In general, the younger the child, the fewer and more concrete the responses will be. Moreover, with young clients the examiner must typically assume an active role. Thus, there are few self-administered, standardized personality tests for children. In general, the childhood personality assessment devices can be divided into measures of overt behavior versus underlying psychological dynamics.

Measures of Overt Behavior

These tests attempt to assess children's individual and/or social behavior and do so with varying degrees of objectivity and standardization. Although not a formally standardized test, behavioral assessment is a very important systematic means of recording children's overt reactions. In behavioral assessment, several target behaviors are operationally defined. The examiner decides upon the target behavior after interviewing parents and the child. When interviewing each party, the examiner keeps in mind that their perception may be distorted by their experiences. Thus, the examiner encourages each person to be as specific as possible in describing the problem that led to the referral. The environment in which the difficulty occurs is delimited. By talking with the child, the examiner attempts to gain a picture of reinforcers and punishing agents associated with the target behavior. Then, the examiner observes the child's target behavior in the problem-ridden environment. The duration and frequency of the behavior for whole periods of time or systematic intervals is recorded. The behavior is observed under baseline conditions and under hypothesized reinforcing and punishing conditions. Of course, observer reliability must be considered. It is often helpful to chart other children's behavior in the environment in order to gain a comparison measure (Erickson, 1978). The behavioral assessment helps the therapist determine the conditions prompting the problematic behavior and more appropriate behavior and thus provides a very objective guideline for therapy.

Sociometry can be used as a measure of children's social behavior. This approach is useful if the problem behavior appears at school or in some other social situation. The client and peers are asked to name children they prefer to participate with for various activities such as working on school tasks, playing a game, leading an activity on the playground, or sitting next to on a bus. In this way, a measure can be gained of how other children relate to the client. Sociometric measures can offer an alternative view to the child's perception of his or her problem. For example, a child may report that he or she has no friends. Yet, classmates may state that they like to play with the child. Therapy might then focus upon helping the client gain a more realistic appraisal of his or her interpersonal skills. Sociometric measures are also a useful index for assessing therapy gains (Keat, 1974).

A number of questionnaires are available for assessing children's interpersonal skills. Generally, these scales are completed by important adults in the child's life. Perhaps the most renowned social questionnaire for chidren is the Vineland Social Maturity Scale (Doll, 1965). This instrument is administered orally to parents. Questions concern the child's self-help skills (eating, dressing, walking), ways of occupying time, communication skills, and socialization with adults and peers. Answers are scored according to whether the child demonstrates the behavior at home and for the examiner, only at home, or not at all. The overall score is computed by comparing the child's tested social maturity age to chronological age. Other scales such as the Burks' Behavior Rating Scale (Burks, 1969) are completed by teachers. The difficulty with most of these scales, as with the Vineland, is their limited objectivity. The informant (usually one of the parents) is not asked to keep a systematic record of target behaviors as in behavioral assessment.

Informants may define target behaviors differently. Thus, what one teacher considers "angry outbursts" may not be congruent with another's perception. In a study by Erickson (1978) parents were asked to respond on a questionnaire about how counseling related to their child's attendance at school. The parents reported that attendance increased with counseling, while actual review of school records revealed that attendance had decreased. Overall, results of behavioral and social questionnaires tend to have low interrater reliability as well as low reliability for a single rater over time. In addition, the validity of such measures is also open to question.

Some scales have been developed in which behaviors are operationally defined and informants are asked to systematically observe children's responses to the various criterion questions (Erickson, 1978). Yet these scales are generally research instruments that are cumbersome to administer and are not widely available or employed.

Measures of Psychological Dynamics

These tests attempt to assess the child's intrapsychic functioning. Each relies upon a set of theoretical constructs about how personality develops and what constitutes adjustment and maladjustment.

Apperception Tests

The Thematic Apperception Test (Murray, 1943) and Children's Apperception Test (Bellak & Bellak, 1971) are comprised of a series of cards portraying people (TAT) or animals (CAT) in ambiguous social situations. The child is asked to tell a story to each card. Interpretation is based upon the notion that subjects will reveal much about their perception of social relationships and their needs as they create stories to the ambiguous stimuli.

The TAT is widely used with adults. Bellak and Bellak (1965) developed the CAT because they felt children would find it easier to compose stories about animals than about people. In practice, most therapists agree that some children prefer the human figures and others the animals (Chess & Hassibi, 1978). Thus, the examiner may need to experiment with a card from each set to determine which is more appropriate for a particular child.

Elaborate schemes for scoring motivation and attitudes about parents, peers, and siblings are available. The CAT cards are further scored to determine the child's attitudes about heroes, concepts of the environment, significant conflicts, nature of anxiety, defenses versus fears and conflicts, adequacy of super ego and integration of ego. Reliability of the scoring system is low, barely above zero in most studies (Palmer, 1970). Many therapists prefer to view the test results in a more casual fashion, looking for common themes that run throughout the stories. The results are used for clinical hunches that must be confirmed with further interviewing and assessment.

Figure drawing tests

The Human Figure Drawing Test was originally developed as a measure of intelligence (Goodenough, 1926). However, a revision by Machover (1949) is frequently employed in personality assessment. First, the child is asked to draw a few human figures under very open-ended directions. Then, specific inquiry is made: "What is the child or person in the picture doing?" "What is the best (worst) part of the boy?" "Does he have any friends?" "How much does he enjoy his family?" "How much does he like school?" According to Machover (1949), stylization of drawings and response to inquiry questions hold symbolic significance. Thus, lack of arms or hands might reflect feelings of guilt about actions or an inability to act. Drawing a person of the opposite sex may represent confused sexual identity (Machover, 1953).

Research has not consistently supported Machover's thesis. The child's experience and skill at drawing greatly affect results. Koppitz (1968) compared human figure drawings of normal and disturbed children on thirty dimensions suggested as most significant in the literature on human figure drawing. Only four were shown to be significant:

1.   poor integration of body parts in girls above 6 and boys above 7
2.   shading of body parts and limbs for girls above 7 and boys above 9
3.   slanting by 15 degrees or more
4.   drawing a tiny picture.

Koppitz (1964) noted further that omission of major body parts and grotesque figures were so rare that statistical analysis was not possible. Thus, despite wide use, the human figure drawing does not seem to be a reliable measure for discriminating types of emotional disturbance among children before age 6. Moreover, among older children caution must be exercised in attaching particular symbolic significance to small distortions.

Also commonly used is the House-Tree-Person Test (Buck, 1950). Extensive guidelines for scoring results are offered; but caution, as suggested with the Human Figure Drawing, needs to be exercised in interpretation. As a whole, the drawings should be employed to offer clinical hunches, not definitive statements, about children's attitudes and behavior.

The Rorschach

Of course, it is not possible to relate the major constructs of Rorschach testing in this brief review. Nor can we begin to elucidate the pros and cons and reliability of the Rorschach protocol. The interested reader is referred to Palmer's (1970) thorough review. The Rorschach is aimed at assessing the child's preconscious and subconscious experiences. Whether or not the reader accepts this tenet or finds such results valuable, depends of course upon his or her theoretical approach to counseling and therapy. We will attempt to show through some brief examples of scoring issues how the content of responses to the Rorschach cards and perceptual modes are viewed as indicators of the child's emotional dynamics. The same underlying rules of Rorschach assessment are applicable to children as with adults. However, in the children's Rorschach, developmental trends are emphasized. Thus, for young children, magical thinking is not as diagnostically significant as with adults. Color responses are common and are believed to reflect the more spontaneous emotional character of children. Fewer texture responses are expected since children's experience of anxiety is more diffuse and less introspective. The average number of responses for children ranges between ten and twenty, considerably less than for adults. Inquiry and testing the limit responses to the last card are considered diagnostically significant about how the child deals with separation (Halpern, 1953).

Sentence Completion Test

Sentence Completion Tests tend to be used with older children because the young child's limited linguistic development circumscribes his or her repertoire of responses. Rotter's Incomplete Sentence Blank (Rotter, Rafferty, & Schachtitz, 1965) offers a systematic way of scoring responses for degree of resistance and degree and nature of conflicts for children 13 years and older. Although linguistically simpler sentences can also be constructed for the younger clients, if the examiner administers the sentences orally, the test is more appropriate for the young child. Although many such forms are available, a difficulty is that most incomplete sentence blanks are not built upon a consistent rationale (Palmer, 1970). The range of responses is limited by the nature of the incomplete sentences presented. Unless the responses are carefully interpreted, it is easy for the test creator's bias to appear as the child's primary concern.

An semiprojective test that is quite appealing to young children is the Rosenzweig Picture Frustration Study Form for Children (Rosenzweig, 1950) which can be used with children between the ages of 4 - 13 years. In this test, children look at cartoon figures which are portrayed in difficult social situations. One cartoon figure is portrayed as making a comment (e.g., "I'm not going to ask you to my birthday party.") The style is akin to that in a comic book. The child is asked to complete the comment for the other figure in the space provided. The results can be scored on one primary personality dimension of aggression--extrapunitiveness or intrapunitiveness. Extrapunitive is aggression turned outward toward the environment, while intrapunitive is aggression turned inward on the subject.

Standardized Personality Instruments

Compared to the voluminous number of standardized personality instruments available to assess adults, there are very few comparable instruments for children. For the most part, children lack the cognitive ability to answer the kind of questions upon which standardized personality profiles are drawn. For example, the California Psychological Inventory (Gough, 1969) is one of the most widely used standardized personality instruments employed with youth, and its youngest norms are for children 13 years and older. The CPI consists of 480 items answered as either true or false and yields scores in 18 scales. The scales provide scores in such personality dimensions as Dominance, Sociability, Self-acceptance, Responsibility, Socialization, Self-control, Femininity, Achievement-via-independence, etc. The overall test reliability is relatively high, and intercorrelations among scales are relatively high. The CPI has been used to predict delinquency, high school grades, and high school dropout (Anastasi, 1976).

Tests of self-concept are rather widely used. The Piers-Harris self-concept scale (Piers & Harris, 1969) can be individually administered to children under grade three and group administered for older children. Coopersmith's (1967) Self-Esteem Questionnaire which attempts to measure the child's feelings about self in relation to parents, school, peers, and personal interests has also been used widely with children in grades 5 and above. These questionnaires tend to report moderate reliability coefficients, but their validity is limited by questions about the underlying constructs they are measuring.

Summary of Social and Personality Assessment

As a whole, the reliability and validity coefficients of the personality instruments employed with children have been relatively low because of the children's developmental limitations. In some cases, the instruments have not been subject to close empirical scrutiny. Most likely, validity increases when a test battery rather than a single instrument is employed in the assessment of a child. In contrast, behavioral assessment techniques appear to be highly reliable and valid. It is not surprising that this approach is gaining wide use by therapists of various theoretical persuasions. The sensitive therapist can probably make good use of information obtained from personality assessment instruments; however, it is important to also obtain and use more objective information about the child's behavior prior to attempting a diagnosis.

SUMMARY

Usually therapy with children begins with assessment so that the therapeutic process can take a meaningful, specifiable direction. Interviews and tests can be useful in obtaining needed information about the child. The reliability of interviews are limited by the subjective perceptions of the clients and informants and the practitioner's biases and limits of understanding. The reliability of the information obtained on a test is limited by the boundaries of standardization as well as by the practitioner's skill in administration and interpretation. There is much room for error. Referral for specialized testing (e.g., for suspected organic interference or learning deficit, or because the test administration requires extensive training) should be considered, keeping the child's best interests in mind. If we search for cues to a child's maladjusted behavior through the accumulation of test results, employing a variety of carefully chosen assessment techniques, the chances of discovering the breadth of the child's problem increased. If we look at assessment as an ongoing process and continually reevaluate the client's progress as well as the therapeutic goals with the client, assessment becomes an integral part of therapy.

We have discussed theories of child adjustment and therapy and looked at a variety of ways of assessing for the presence of those problems in the individual client. We will now consider ways of assessing the family dynamics and determining the relationship of the child's problems to the family's overall functioning.

CHAPTER 10

FAMILY ASSESSMENT AND CASE MANAGEMENT

Knowledge about patterns of behavior within a family is critical in alleviating many children's problems. Understanding how this information is gathered and implemented necessitates a grounding in family theory and research. Identifying the present phase of functioning in a family's overall development provides important clues for a successful treatment. Further, various theories attempt to explain how families function, and each offers guides to the selection of techniques for assessment. This chapter identifies critical assessment points in a family with examples based upon three theoretical perspectives. The process of case management helps child practitioners to effectively interact with agencies that may serve the same family.

FAMILY ASSESSMENT

Theory Guides Assessment

An examination of mental health and social service practice raises the following questions:

Do theories explain why an assessment technique works?
Do practitioners develop theories first and then development assessment techniques?

Very often it appears that practitioners select assessment points and devices in a somewhat idiosyncratic or arbitrary fashion. They then employ theory to justify their approach. If family theory is an explanation of the interrelationships of variables in family interaction, then it is important to understand the specifics of the theory as a framework before we can analyze the dynamics of a given family. On the issue of inference, Richmond writes, "Inference, then, a passing from known to unknown facts is the reasoning process most familiar when it takes the form of drawing a conclusion from the relation existing between a general truth and particular incident" (Richmond, 1917, pg. 81).

The problem-solving process or scientific process assures a close application of theory to practice. The problem-solving process includes gathering information, assessing that information, planning for change, change, and evaluation. Some suggest that these steps are interrelated and continue concomitantly. Others believe you must take each of these steps one at a time before beginning intervention.

A theory of family functioning is the way we give a logical explanation of how variables or facts are related and the theories of family therapy were presented in detail in Chapter 7. Assessment, information gathering, and analysis are critical steps that must take place in applying a theory of family dynamics to clinical assessment of the family framework. Analysis or assessment then becomes a way to make sense out of the data we have collected. Treatment techniques and intervention strategies should be based upon a logical connection with theory.

Family Life Cycle

As the family develops, it grows through distinct developmental phases, and particular developmental tasks must be completed (Solomon, 1973). For example, the birth of the first child thrusts a family into a new developmental stage. A couple must readjust from the partner role to the parent role. Another example is the grieving process at the departure of the oldest child from the family to college or the military. Identifying the stage of a given family in the family life cycle offers clues for assessment and intervention planning. This identification helps to focus attention on presenting problems within the family and the resulting problems for a child. Further, the stage of family development can provide a focus to begin assessment. The importance of each stage will vary with every family and culture; however, the following events commonly prompt significant changes in most families' development (Bloom, 1984).

Stages of Family Development

1.   Courtship. This period is sometimes called the unattached young adult stage. The young adult is dating, exploring sexual and moral behavior with the opposite sex. The adult begins to examine relationships with partners for their long-term potential. Friendships are established which may lead to more permanent relationships.

2.   Marriage and Couplehood. Marriage publically identifies the young unattached adult as a member of a couple. Young adults experience separation from their families and begin to invest in each other. The couple begins to explore living with another person and adjusting to a partnership role. Alternative family forms such as gay units may emerge at this stage (Harry & DeVall, 1978). There is a shift from the idealized wish for a perfect partner to compromising and relating intimately with a realistically-held view of the spouse. Also during this time adjustments are made within the extended family, as inlaws accommodate to the new marital relationship.

     Conflicts that typically arise during this stage are associated with the couple's relating intimately as the increased close contact may expose incompatibilities. These conflicts can cause breaks in the relationship or push the dyad to deeper levels of intimacy.

3. <u>First Child.</u> The transition to parent includes accepting the childbearing role. Preparation for child birth provides a new definition to the role as spouse. Further, sexual behavior is altered or interrupted during pregnancy. The birth or adoption of the first child impacts the extended family as well. In many cultures, the role of parent increases one's status.

    Bonding and attachment hold important consequences for the child in later life. Effective parents are sensitive to the crucial importance of bonding and to the developmental phases of the child and adjust their lives accordingly. The parents must establish a home environment that will accommodate both the roles of spouse and parent. New limitations to privacy and mobility imposed by the child's needs present areas for adjustment. The marital dyad has now become a triad with all the complications and issues involved in group dynamics.

4. <u>Growth of Children.</u> In this phase, additional children are born into the family. Older children are introduced to community institutions, such as school, church, and social development groups. Children seek their own roles and pass through developmental phases. Many of the individualized roles, however, are not based upon the family responsibility but upon community and social needs. The child looks at the parents' actions even more than words for guidance of the child's moral behaviors, so that it becomes important for parents to carefully monitor their responses. The issue of discipline becomes an important topic of parental discussion and parental joint efforts. The sharing of affection between child and parent may become important gratification for parents. During this time, family financial resources may be stretched, adding further stress and responsibility upon the parents.

5. <u>Departure of Oldest Child.</u> In adolescence, peer groups become important and are powerful competitors to the parents for the youth's allegiance. Erratic behavior by adolescents at home and in peer relations may be spurred by lack of knowledge amd experience about their emerging sexuality. Child rivalry may become intense as children enter the teenage years and begin to assert their independence to parents and siblings. When the family begins to release young adults, optimally they maintain supportive relations (Duvall, 1971). The family is particularly prone to stress at this stage as the family is more likely to face problems such as illness and career change.

6. <u>Aging Family or Retirement.</u> This stage is reached when all children have left home, and the couple returns to a dyad. This is a time for renewing the

marital relationship. The couple's relationship may be strained if either or both are distressed over the loss of work. Feelings of isolation may increase if the couple experiences less social systems available to them. How to deal with leisure time may require adjustment in the marriage roles. Earlier retirement may result in mid-life crisis for career persons and has been associated with higher divorce rate among this group. Adult children may continue to visit, and the extended family may now include grandchildren and younger generations. Parents grieve the departure of children and establish new relationships during this final stage. Parents may need to accept their roles as elders and transfer business and central social responsibilities to adult children. Although the drastic changes and losses pose much stress for the couple, their relationship can be deepened by the lifetime of shared experiences and the problems resolved. The death of one partner later in this stage marks the end of the family cycle.

Evaluation of Family Life Cycle

The above discussion of family life development can be helpful in focusing thinking about the stresses family members incur but may reflect the myth about the American family. Few American families complete this total life cycle today. About 60 percent of all children born now can expect to live with only one parent for sometime during their lives (Kamerman, 1985). The traditional dyad of leadership in a family is rapidly becoming nonexistent.

The life cycle paradigm does have some utility in understanding traditional families where conflicts or serious child-related problems exist. For example, it points to the concept that the more children in a family, the more complex the dynamics of that family. However, it is inappropriate for a practitioner to consider families that fall outside this paradigm as abnormal.

The family life cycle is of little utility to some theorists. Behaviorists have a limited need to examine the family life stages, as they consider family behavior to be most crucial at this time.

Critical Assessment Points

A number of factors determine which information the family practitioner attempts to collect in the assessment process. These factors can be considered along the dimensions of a longitudinal development versus present functioning; internal forces in the family versus external factors affecting the functioning; and factors promoting health versus factors prompting illness in the family. In the sections that follow, we will explore the points of interaction that would be the focus if one were to adopt extreme positions at each end of the continuum. In reality, the practitioner does not need to make a choice of techniques at either extreme, but may choose a point along the continuum (Reiss, 1980).

Development Versus Present Situation

In determining critical assessment points in the family, some consider the longitudinal development of an individual family (Bowen, 1960). The longitudinal assessment examines the family history and is the least used approach in family diagnosis.

Others focus upon the current family functional level. In this second approach, current patterns of behavior that cut across the developmental stages of a family are analyzed. The examination of the stage of the family in the family life cycle is considered of little functional utility (Reiss, 1980).

Assessment techniques used for assessing the family's functioning differ widely if one ascribes to a developmental rather than a present situation orientation. The following brief discussion of the psychoanalytic and behavioral processes of family assessment illustrates the types of data one would obtain from the developmental and present situational orientations, respectively.

In assessing a given family dilemma, the psychoanalytic approach assumes surface phenomena or variables only hint at the underlying experiences and motives of the family. These underlying phenomena are inaccessible to the client system and can only be discovered through the help of a clinician. Treatment encourages family therapists to search for causes which are not apparent to the family. Assessment is only the beginning in identifying solutions for the family problem.

Behavioral assessment consists of determining the events just prior to or just after an incident that influences the frequency and force of a behavior. Patterson (1971) studied the frequencies of certain classes of behavior and then measured these behaviors by using trained observers or the spouses themselves. Baseline information was gathered. A precise program was developed to reduce the force and frequency of the behavior.

Intra Versus External Family Factors

According to one's orientation, one may focus upon internal family functioning or the sociological or external world in which the family grows and copes. In the intra-family assessment, the family/community interaction is considered subtle, primarily directed by strong intra-family functioning patterns. The family is united against the world.

The sociological approach gives more consideration to the environmental impacts upon the family and is more a traditional social work approach. As an example of research conducted from the sociological approach, Bott (1971) examined family networks. She noted that families which rely upon only one set of friends may be more subject to familial problems and are more likely to follow traditional sex roles. Families with different sets of friends are more egalitarian in their power system. The setting for the collection of information is dictated by the weight practitioners place upon the environmental impact. If the practitioner adopts a more sociological perspective, he or she may suggest a meeting with the family in its home and community.

Illness Versus Health

Practitioners are often polarized around the dimension of viewing the family from an illness or a health perspective. According to the illness or medical model, the practitioner should focus upon a disorder and symptoms within individuals. This approach is employed extensively in the literature. The health orientation involves examining the competence of the family to meet problems. The competence, or health model, addresses family resources, including economic, emotional, social (Howells, 1971), and cognitive (Reiss, 1980) supports. For example, a study of returning World War II husbands (Hill, 1949), determined that how a family dealt with crisis and what experience the wife had outside the home influenced the adjustment of postwar families.

The health perspective also points to the importance of considering the adaptative style of the family in understanding how families tend to cope with crises. For example, a study of Puerto Rican versus Anglo middle class persons (Spiegel, 1981) found that Puerto Rican families tended to stress loyalty to the family and a present time orientation. Anglo families, on the other hand, stressed individualism and delayed gratification. The Puerto Rican families felt like they were subject to nature, while the American families felt capable of mastering nature. Cultural styles are important in assessing a family. For example, according to the research by Spiegel, one might expect a Puerto Rican family to rely more upon extended family members in times of crisis than an Anglo family.

According to the health orientation, the following characteristics determine healthy family systems:

1. Power balance is understood and accepted by all family members.

2. Each member has rights and autonomy is encouraged.

3. Each member can tolerate separation, and members support one another through losses.

4.   Members perceive reality in compatible ways.

5.   All members are free to express their feelings.

Based upon these characteristics, Lewis developed a scaling procedure to help determine the potential of a family to deal with a crisis (Lewis, Beavers, & Gossett, 1976).

Some Technical Measurement Decisions

Three measurement decisions must be made before initiating the family assessment. First of all, one will glean different information if the assessment is totally completed before intervention is begun than if assessment continues at the same time as intervention. If a behavioral approach is used, the assessment must be completed before any intervention is introduced. On the other hand, psychoanalytic practitioners begin intervention during the information gathering stage.

The selection of the site of the assessment is a critical issue that is often not carefully considered. Most psychologists, counselors, and psychiatrists assess families within clinical settings, while social workers may use home visits. O'Rourke (1963) found the office was seen as men's turf and might introduce more conflict between father and son. The home was seen as the woman's turf, which exposes more mother-daughter conflicts. Informality versus formality of the assessment, time of day (for example, as soon as dad gets home from work), and the environment are all critical aspects to consider in family assessment.

The choice of measurement techniques in assessing the family is a critical determinant of what one will learn. The practitioner must decide whether to conduct an individualized or a standardized assessment of the family. A fully individualized assessment will not provide the practitioner with any comparative data and is subject to a lack of objectivity. On the other extreme, an assessment which relies completely upon standardized measurement fails to note some uniqueness in the family and might set the stage for unsuccessful intervention.

An example of measurement, which relies upon some individualized approaches and some standardized techniques, is Goal Attainment Scaling (Compton & Galaway, 1984). Goal Attainment Scaling is an individual, quantitative process which is used to assess family process. Individual objectives for each family member are ranked on a five-point weighted scale. Goal Attainment Scaling helps clinician to be sensitive to clinical change within each family member. The importance of the goal to the family is not evaluated with Goal Attainment Scaling.

Standardized tests may also be used with families. An excellent example is the Parent Attachment Structured Interview (P.A.S.I.) (Roll, Lockwood, & Roll, 1980). The

P.A.S.I. is used to gain a better understanding of how closely the child is bonded to each parent and other significant adults by assessing the dimensions of (R) responsiveness, (S) security, (C) confidence, and (H) hostility to each significant adult. The child is asked 50 basic questions regarding daily interactions with each parent and other attachment figures. Some examples are:

> Who likes to put you to bed?
> Who is too tired to play?
> Who helps with your homework?
> Who breaks promises?

The answers show the range and degree of positive attachments.

Clinical research has advanced to the point where theoretical and technical family assessments can be tested for reliability and validity. A cross-sectional rather than developmental clinical tool used by Costell and Reiss (Reiss, 1980) in their research laboratory has individual family members sort cards. Although family members cannot see each other (they are in separate booths), by using earphones and microphones, they can communicate during performance of the task. How do they work--as a group or an individuals? Do they see the task as solvable? The answers to these questions can be objectively measured. Then a classification system of families can help predict the usefulness of clinical treatment (Straus & Tallman, 1971).

One of the difficulties of employing standardized tests in family assessment is the ability of the practitioner to provide feedback to the family in a useful manner. Another difficulty is the general problem of classifying complex social units such as the family. You as a practitioner must balance the need for standardization with an understanding of the unique factors of every family.

Outline For Family Assessment

Based upon the previous discussion, we find information regarding the family life stage, patterns of behavior, and the environment important variables in making an assessment of family functioning (Thorman, 1982). The following outline can serve as a guide for gathering information of significance for clinical intervention.

I. Family life cycle stage.
   In this assessment, the practitioner determines the family life
   cycle phase, critical points of conflict, and potential growth
   within this phase.
   A. Relationship of the couple within the phase.
      1. sexually
      2. emotionally

      3. role definitions
      4. power balance
      5. division of labor
  B. Children's interaction with the community.
      1. academic issues
      2. peer group
      3. extra-curricular activities
      4. learning disabilities/or other physical problems
  C. Family constellation
      1. children's roles
      2. children's and parents' responsibilities
      3. intensity of bonding and mutuality of attachments
      4. use of resources (economic, social, societal)

II. Family patterns of interaction
  A. Family structure
      1. How are decisions made?
      2. Democratic parenting?
      3. Family history
      4. Is this a "blended" family (children and parents
         joined from previous marriages)?
  B. Individualism
      1. Can children and parents express themselves safely?
      2. Is everything done as a family or can individuals act
         independently?
      3. Do children have a sense of self-identity?
      4. How is affection shared?
      5. Are children allowed to mature and grow at appropriate
         developmental stages?
  C. Interaction and communication
      1. How do families resolve conflicts?
      2. Who starts the conflict resolution?
      3. Are conflicts addressed or ignored?
      4. Are certain conflicts left to brew?
      5. Do family members clearly understand each other?
  D. Crisis intervention
      1. When faced with a problem, is the family adaptative?
      2. How does the family restore equilibrium after a crisis?
      3. What resources can be brought to bear upon a crisis?
      4. What process does the family use in coping with a crisis?

III. Family environment
  A. How is the home arranged?
      1. shared or own bedrooms?
      2. arrangement of bathrooms

      3. privacy
      4. parents' view of neighborhood
   B. What resources does the community provide?
      1. upwardly mobile job
      2. school
      3. fire protection
      4. recreation
      5. boy scouts, girl scouts
   C. Family social status
      1. additional career activities
      2. child care
      3. friends
         a. father's
         b. mother's
         c. children's
      4. activities
      5. extended family

This outline elucidates broad data to be gleaned in each family assessment. These data will help identify the areas which may require a more in-depth assessment for an individual family.

Assessment Process According to Family Theory

   The family assessment approach employed by a practitioner is greatly dictated by the theoretical basis for treatment. Spiegal (1981) lists three common assumptions held, to some degree, by the majority of family therapists. First, the family system is critical to working with an individual client. Second, observed behavior is considered as a presenting problem, which is only symbolic of deeper structures and patterns of behavior. The third common assumption is that effective family treatment depends upon interdisciplinary orientation. The openness to outside professional influence is characteristic of family therapy.

   Despite these commonalities, a closer examination of family therapy highlights a divergence among family theories and assessment. To gain a better insight to different approaches to family assessment, we present three specific (of more than forty-three recognized models of family therapy) approaches to family assessment based upon a behavioral, Adlerian, and Bowen ideological analysis of family functioning.

Behavioral

   The assessment of a family according to a behavioral theory is based upon the relationship between a stimulus and a behavior in the environment of a family. The assessment focuses upon identifying specific outcome behaviors, the clients' capabilities, and the impact of behaviors upon individuals with the family. Direct observations of behaviors and related antecedents are made when feasible. Behavioral assessment is an ongoing endeavor which continues to correct the intervention while evaluating progress. The assessment in behavior modification is a process that answers the following questions:

1. What aspects of the problem are due to specific behaviors of the individuals involved?

2. What specific behaviors are to be changed?

3. What factors maintain the disfunctional behaviors or prevent the occurrence of functional behaviors?

4. What resources in the client's environment are available for changing the behavior?

5. What intervention is most likely to have a positive effect on the target behaviors? (Fisher J. & Gochros, 1975)

Although these questions may be rather simplistic, the method of obtaining precise information on a client's behavior at a specific time is a complicated task. Multiple sources of information are needed to obtain an accurate picture of the relevant behavior. Parental accounts of a child's behavior may be quite inaccurate (Evans & Nelson, 1977). Many variables may produce a behavior. The behavioral basis for assessment is that a behavior may be understood only by breaking down a general behavior to very specific parts. This information may be gathered through:

1. check lists,

2. inventories, such as marriage inventories, and

3. schedules, such as sexual survey and reinforcement schedules.

A short schedule for identifying potential reinforcers for children with school problems, developed by Blackham and Silberman, is as follows:

1. What games would they buy, if they could?

2. What three things do they like to do in their classroom?

3. What three jobs do they most like in their classroom?

4. What would they most like to buy with 25 cents?

5. What other kinds of things do they enjoy doing in school? (Blackham & Silberman, 1971, pp. 173-174)

The behavior family therapist attempts to change observable behaviors; therefore, behaviorists do not focus upon the history of a family. A distinction is made between the description of a behavior and the functional analysis of a behavior. A parent may describe a five year old as hyperactive. The mother is asked exactly what these hypactive behaviors are, when they occur, and how intense they are. In functional analysis, the therapist must identify the events that influence and maintain the behavior. The assessment focuses on identifying the relationship between the behavior and its reinforcement. Because most behavior is determined as response to the environment, the behavior therefore can be changed by modifying elements in the present environment. This orientation does not preclude the assumption that patterns of behavior develop over a period of time, but emphasizes that by examining current problems in detail, a planned intervention is incorporated into the current environment.

Fisher and Gochros (1975) list twelve basic steps in behavioral assessment:

1. an evaluation of the presenting problem

2. a survey of the patterns of the client's behavior in an environmental context

3. discussions with the family

4. identification of specific behaviors for targeting for change

5. collection and analysis of base line information on the target behavior

6. identification of behavior just prior to the target behavior and the resulting experience

7. development of terminal goals and intervention objectives

8. selection of an intervention plan by the family and the therapist

9. specification of modification techniques

10. evaluation of potential reinforcers for the intervention

11. selection of potential reinforcers for the intervention

12. collection and analysis of data on the changes in behavior after the intervention

Behavioral assessment also considers cognitive, cultural, physical capabilities, or emotional factors that may facilitate or limit the outcome behaviors (Gambrill, 1981).

If some critera are not established for the collection of behavioral information, the practitioner may spend all of his or her time in the assessment phases. A filter that is helpful is to determine whether targeting the behavior will address the following questions:

1.   Will it help decide which problems are of concern?

2.   Is intervention about this behavior necessary?

3.   What specific behaviors should be pursued?

4.   How should they be pursued?

5.   How will progress be monitored?

6.   How can positive change be maintained? (Gambrill, 1981, p. 77)

Adlerian Family Education

As explained in Chapter 7 on the socially-oriented perspective to child counseling, the Adlerian/Dreikursian family education model is a form of family counseling based on the premise that behavior is purposeful. If a family can identify the causes or goal of a child's misbehavior and the parents' reaction to it, then appropriate interventions can be identified. A primary task of Adlerian/Dreikursian assessment is that of identifying the goal of a child's misbehavior. These goals revolve around four principles: (1) attention-getting behavior, (2) power struggle with the parent, (2) revenge, and (4) displays of total inadequacy (Dreikurs & Soltz, 1958).

During the initial steps of assessment, the therapist may ask the family to recount the previous day beginning with a specific description of getting up. The child's behavior, what went wrong, and the feelings of the parents are discussed. Many times the child's nonverbal answers are keys to assessing the goals of misbehavior under this model.

Jimmy, aged 12, cannot be awakened by his mother, who continually goes to his room while cooking breakfast to beg, plead and then scream at him to get up. Jimmy and his parents are questioned alone by the practitioner to identify the goal of misbehavior. Jimmy's eyes widen and he smiles when the practitioner asks if he wants to show Mom he is the boss. The mother confirms a power struggle by stating she feels "powerless when it comes to getting Jimmy up."

Adlerian therapists can often identify the child who is responsible for the unpopular task of taking out the garbage after a brief discussion with the family. This may be the older child or the youngest depending upon the family interaction. By guessing the child who takes out the trash, the therapist has a validation of his or her assessment and gains legitimacy with the family. This assessment is possible through careful attention to the family consultation. Comments about the children indicate the child or parent who is most unpopular in the family.

Bowen Family Systems

Assessment is a major undertaking for a client and practitioner using the Bowen Family Systems approach discussed in Chapter 7. The client does most of the work with the practitioner serving as a coach by providing guidance and making suggestions (Hartman, 1981). The assessment process covers two major dimensions. One is the study of the intergenerational family over 4 to 6 generations. The second dimension is the current family emotional system. Ann Hartman has added a mapping process to the intergenerational family, the eco-map. The eco-map is a combination of the genogram, which maps the family's resources, and emotional strengths and weaknesses (Hartman, 1978).

The family history provides an opportunity for the client to learn about current family functioning by understanding family history. The family history

1.   organizes facts,

2.   clarifies distortions,

3.   demystifies mysteries,

4.   identifies major events in the family, and

5.   identifies issues and themes that continue to be addressed by the current generation.

Examples are the family's attitudes toward work, sex, parenting, religion, and the handling of crisis. Most individuals in the family comply completely with the family tradition or rebel and do the exact opposite.

The genogram is a precise family tree, which includes important social data. As demonstrated in Figure 10.1, male is indicated by a square, a female by a circle and connected by a line during marriage with *m* and the date of the marriage. Offspring are shown beneath the marriage with the date of birth. An x through a circle with a **d** and a date denotes the death of a female. A dotted line is drawn around family members who comprise a household. The generations are portrayed in a linear fashion. The reconstruction of the family tree is complex and time consuming. A genogram may be up to 30 feet long with small type. Figure 10.1 depicts six generations of a family as a small example of this process.

The impact of world history and major world events is readily apparent. The family's responses to these crises provides insight into the type of family.

Occupational patterns may also be useful. An example is a workaholic husband. A genogram reveals four or five generations of high achieving males who moved West and worked night and day to achieve their dreams.

Figure 10.1

The genogram may become rather complex. It may contain a great deal of information and therefore be difficult to read. To structure the investigation, Hartman (1979) suggests an examination of the inner generational identification and transmission The child processes. How do individuals identify with other individuals in the family? For example, a child is born at the same time as another person in the family dies. becomes a replacement for that person and carries the emotional burdens and expectations of the deceased person. Transmission takes place when parents identify their children with others who occupy the same birth order in the parents' generation (Hartman, 1981).

Another way of making the genogram relevant is to explore its personal relevance to the current generation. What are the family themes? For example, is there continual Western Movement or do the women marry husbands who then move them from their family's homes?

As another example, a professional woman's husband may leave her after the children are grown. Her daughter, another professional woman, sets the stage for her husband to leave after the children are grown. Such patterns may be transmitted through several generations. Overall, the assessment process under the Bowen Family System is to step outside of the family and help them become aware of the innerlocking relationships through the generations.

CASE MANAGEMENT

Definitions

While not critical to clinical treatment for all children, the process of case management may prove extremely helpful to practitioners as they communicate with third parties including agencies, insurance companies, professional groups, and the human service agencies. Case management provides support to children when family support is unavailable or insufficient. Society must act as the parent in these cases. The case manager articulates the needs of the family, coordinates services to them, and advocates on their behalf (Johnson, 1985). Case management emphasizes decision-making, coordination, and service.

The knowledge, skills, and roles of a case manager include:

1.   Knowing the resources available

2.   Holding expertise in the particular area of practice such as child abuse, incest, and neglect, mental health, or developmental disability

3.   Employing the interpersonal and group skills to interact as a colleague with other professionals

4.   Being able to coordinate services to the client and provide an overall service plan

5.   Educating the community on needs for additional resources and services or duplication of services (Mayhall & Norgard, 1983)

The major components of case management identified by the Joint Commission on Accreditation for Hospitals are:

1.   assessment,

2.   developing an individualized plan,

3.   linking and coordinating,

4.   monitoring, and

5.   advocacy (Johnson, 1985).

Historical Roots of Case Management

Casework

Case management has evolved from social casework, group work, and community organization. Social casework's early roots are found in the pioneer work of Mary Richmond's Social Diagnosis, published in 1917. During the 1930's the functional approach, first developed at the School of Social Work at the University of Pennsylvania, viewed change as coming from the client, not the caseworker. The purpose was to give focus, direction, and content to the social worker's practice. Casework was seen as a way of providing social services with a psychological understanding and skill in helping the individual client. Social caseworkers were agency-based (Smalley, 1971). In the late 1950's, Helen Harris Perlman, at the University of Chicago, introduced the problem solving approach to social casework. This approach taught the client how to solve problems he or she faced through life. The client's ability to perceive, grasp, remember, control impulses, judge, and perform other skills generally associated with ego functioning are critical to the problem solving process (Perlman, 1957).

Thomas (1977) stated that the behavior modification approach is a valid approach to casework because social caseworkers frequently are involved in altering or stabilizing a client's behavior. The behavioral approach is a highly specific conceptualization of human behavior with specific techniques for assessment and modification. Evaluation of practice is also critical to this approach.

Group Work and Community Organization

The roots of case management are also tied to social group work, family theory, and community organization. Environmental impacts on children, such as poverty, racism, or lack of services, may be outside the power of their parents to control. Therefore, a case manager may be required to mobilize change at a macro level, in the legislature, in a school system or professional group. The impact of policy on child practitioners is discussed in Chapter 15.

Settings

Case management has evolved in a number of settings as a highly desirable approach to working with clients. The child clinician will no doubt be involved with case management services at some point in time. Case management is being used in the child welfare system, the mental health system, systems for the developmentally disabled, and in institutional structures for the elderly. We will address the first three of these.

Child Welfare

Protective services to children across the country are adopting the case management system as a method of involving many support services to keep children in their own homes. A number of studies (Fanshel & Shinn, 1978) have shown the detrimental effect of long term foster care upon children.

One model for avoiding foster care is home-based services (Hutchinson & Nelson, 1985). A key to this model is early identification of abuse and neglect, provision of relevant treatment and societal services. In order to provide these services, a case management model is necessary. The role of the case manager in protective services is to develop a service agreement with the parents which is approved by the court. This agreement is time-limited and notifies the parents that failure to comply with the service agreement might result in termination of their parental rights and placement of their children for adoption. A child clinician may be called to provide an evaluation and therapy to the child during this stressful period of change.

Model Format for Case Management

A format for case presentations developed for student interns is presented below. The case is a military family who has recently relocated.

1.   Demographic Data and Source of Referral.

      Example: This is the case of Mrs. W, a 21-year-old Catholic Caucasian woman and her four children: Elizabeth, age 5; twins Tony and Larry, age 3; and Marianne, age 2. Mrs. W is newly separated from her husband who is a 23-year-old PV3 in the Military Police unit at Ft. Bliss. Mrs. W was referred to Social Work Services hospital OB-Gyn Clinic after her first visit for prenatal care in the fifth month of this pregnancy.

2.   Presenting Problem(s).

      Example: Mrs. W is in the second trimester of a complicated pregnancy and is expected to have her second set of twins. She has a history of spontaneous abortions x 2. Upon initial examination, the referring M.D. noted old bruises on her abdomen and upper forearms. Client admitted to a marital problem but stated her husband is a "good man" who "sometimes" becomes violent when he drinks too much. Their recent separation occurred after a quarrel about his drinking during which he "beat her up." When she reported this to her husband's CO, he confined the man to the barracks "until he sees a social worker." Mrs. W says "they can make him go but nothing will change." She is afraid he will be released and harm her again. The W family is about to be evicted from their three-room apartment for failure to pay the rent.

3.   Brief Family History.

Example: The W's met in high school and have been married seven years. Mrs. W and the children came to El Paso from Boston against Mr. W's wishes three months ago. Although he is a high school graduate, until Mr. W joined the Army the family was on and off welfare as he could not hold a job for long "because of his bad temper."

Both Mr. and Mrs. W are the youngest children of large working-class Catholic families. Most members of their respective families of orientation reside in the Boston metropolitan area. Just prior to their coming here, Mrs. W and the children had been living with her oldest sister and her husband. This couple financed their plane fare to El Paso. Several of Mr. W's siblings are said to be alcoholics. Mrs. W blames their strained relationships with her family on her husband saying, "They think he's no good, just like his brothers."

Mrs. W has a pretty face but is somewhat obese and needs dental work. She was a high school dropout at 15 and has never held a job outside her home. She is proud of the fact that she is "very good with kids" and has done a lot of babysitting to earn extra money. She draws well and "always wanted to go back to school and study art."

4.   Psychosocial Evaluation.

Example: These young, overwhelmed, multiproblem parents who are geographically distant and emotionally alienated from family and friends now face compounded interpersonal, social, and financial problems in accordance with previously established patterns.

5.   Case Management Goals/Objectives.

Example:
a.   Strengthen family relationships.
b.   Build community support system.
c.   Assist family with basic human needs.
d.   Coordinate agency services.
e.   Enable parents to assess strengths, evaluate current situation, and establish future goals and objectives.

6.   Psycho-Social Treatment Plan.

Example:
a.   Explore military and civilian community resources.
b.   1 x 1 counseling support to Mrs. W.
c.   Coordinate with social worker responsible for family violence cases; offer conjoint/marital counseling to the W's.
d.   On-going consultation with referring M.D. and with Mr. W's CO.
e.   Refer W children to Pediatric Clinic for health assessment.

7.   Progress Evaluation (for up-date and future discussion).

Example:
a.   Strengths assessment.
b.   Problem areas/resolutions.
c.   Case management issues.
d.   Revised/on-going treatment plan.
         (Gloria Shipley, TCSW, ACSW, with permission)

Mental Health and Developmental Disabilities

Public Law 95-602 of 1978, the Developmental Disabilities Training Act and Public Law 96-398 of 1980, the Mental Health System Act, have incorporated case management requirements (Johnson, 1985). Case managers must coordinate services, provide support, and advocate for disabled clients. New York, Minnesota, Georgia, and Utah have already created case management systems, and other states such as Florida and New Mexico are giving it serious consideration.

Many of these services are modeled after the Fountain House in New York City. There are now 180 programs in the United States that resemble the 19th century settlement houses in Britain and the United States (Johnson, 1985). The settlement house workers' philosophy of reform, democracy, and working through existing social structures are key.

Case managers rarely should conduct the child psychotherapy (Austin & Caragonne, 1981). At times, case managers are referred to as social brokers. As such, they are aware of the resources in a community that can be matched to the client in a customized fashion. An example of how a case manager successfully organized a range of services for a family is Case 10.1 of the Salazar Family.

Case 10.1. The Case of the Salazar Family

A Hispanic family from northern New Mexico was referred to the Social Services Division because their children were found on several occasions by the police outside, poorly clothed for climatic conditions, and begging food from the neighbors. Mrs. Salazar, age 21, and Mr. Salazar, age 24, frequently smoked marijuana. They were absent from their home for a period of two or three days every other week. The social worker, using the case manager model, gained legal custody of the children through a court hearing as a first step toward protecting the children. The case manager worked with the District Attorney to prepare the case.

Mr. Salazar was unable to hold a job because of his drug habit, although he expressed interest in returning to work as an auto mechanic. The case manager contacted the local mental health center to provide drug abuse treatment. Then she contacted the employment office and enrolled Mr. Salazar in a training program to update his skills. After four weeks, he received on-the-job training.

Mrs. Salazar and Mr. Salazar began attending parent education classes through the public health services. The children were evaluated by a physician and a psychologist for physical and psychological problems. No physical problems were found; however, the psychologist found signs of detachment and began re-attachment therapy. The Salazars expressed some marital problems and were referred to a clinical psychologist for marriage counseling.

After a period of 6 months, Mr. Salazar was employed as a mechanic. The couple had completed the parent education program and were more effective as parents. Attachment became apparent between the children and the parents as role functions were restored. The clinical psychologist continued to work with the Salazars concerning their marital problems but closed the children's cases. The case manager assumed the role of monitor and continued to check on the Salazars for the next six months. At the end of one year, the case was closed with the approval of the District Judge.

Conclusion

On a typical day, a case manager may perform an assessment of a new case, monitor a number of other cases, work with a self-help group in the afternoon, and present testimony before a legislative committee in the evening. This "switching of hats" makes the job of the case manager very interesting but also makes it extremely difficult for most clinicians. A case manager must have a broad knowledge base and be well versed in legal, social, psychological, and economic theories. He or she must be aware of the interaction necessary to work with a system of agencies and other professional groups.

The largest profession performing case management is social work. Often job descriptions require social work education for classified positions (Johnson, 1985). Nevertheless, it is important for all helping professionals to be aware of the case management system and its importance in working with children.

Public and private funds may continue to decline for direct human services. Continued interest in deinstitutionalization will require a case management approach in communities. A case management system will more efficiently use available resources.

SUMMARY

A good family assessment provides the practitioner with critical insights regarding the internal and external functioning level of a family. The framework for understanding the family is based upon the theoretical perspective used. Since family therapists work with the family as the basic unit of intervention, understanding the family dynamics, patterns of behavior, and life cycle stage enables the child practitioner to be more effective.

We have stressed the importance of a theory-based assessment and through examples, we have applied three different theoretical assessments to cases. Critical assessment points help guide us to a consistent, objective method of collecting information. The information obtained during the assessment determines the intervention or treatment plan. A well-planned and well-executed assessment clearly states the family's and the child's problem. A well-stated problem is half the solution.

Case management is a comprehensive process to link and coordinate all involved parties working with a child or family. Steeped in the tradition of casework, group work, and community organization, the process is being used in developmentally disabled programs, mental health, and child welfare services. A child practitioner may serve as a case manager or more likely as a member of the team working with the family.

CHAPTER 11

SELECTION OF CHILD TREATMENT MODALITIES

The selection of child treatment modalities refers to the structure and attitudes adopted by the child practitioner to facilitate communication with the client and to preclude behavior that is counterproductive to the treatment goals. How the practitioner initiates and terminates the session, sets limits, selects styles of therapy (play therapy, group, etc.) and when the practitioner seeks adjunct services or refers the client are all part of the treatment plan (Frankel, 1977). The treatment plan must be consonant with the practitioner's theoretical position, but a number of treatment issues cut across sessions regardless of the practitioner's theoretical persuasion. The treatment plan must be adjusted to individual client's needs and vulnerabilities. The plan will be unique to each client and change with progress in treatment.

In this chapter, we will discuss issues of treatment modalities in broad terms as guidelines for integration in your approach to therapy. First, we will consider issues about the child's development that help the practitioner to select treatment modalities (whether play therapy, bibliotherapy, etc.). Then we will overview the various stances the child practitioner may adopt when working with parents. Next, we will analyze the stages of the helping relationship. A number of specific approaches (such as art therapy, play therapy, storytelling, bibliotherapy) that are appropriate at the various stages will be overviewed. Part of the treatment plan involves the practitioner's decision about whether the child will profit more from individual or group therapy; therefore, the purposes and structures of group therapy will be discussed. Effective treatment requires the practitioner to carefully monitor and manage his or her own reactions to the child and the child's family, for the practitioner's effectiveness is limited by the level of his or her own adjustment. In a section titled Professional Issues, we will identify key factors that may alert the practitioner of personal concerns that are interfering with the clinical progress. Finally, the issues concerning referral are reviewed. The last section of this chapter overviews reasons for and sources of referral.

DEVELOPMENTAL FACTORS THAT DETERMINE THE PLAN

As emphasized in Chapter 3, the child practitioner must be knowledgeable of developmental processes in the social, cognitive, affective, and motor domains. A good understanding of developmental psychology will assist the practitioner in making important decisions concerning the course of treatment.

The practitioner must first consider the child's social developmental level. The young child is highly dependent upon the parents. Typically the parents or teachers choose therapy for the child. The child may not feel he or she has any problems. If the child is aware of difficulties, most likely he or she externalizes the cause, stating, for example, "School is hard; My parents yell a lot;" or "They did it first." Thus, consideration of the child's social developmental level helps the child practitioner judge the child's commitment to the therapeutic process (Freedman, Kaplan, & Sadock, 1976). A prime goal of the treatment plan with a child client is to create motivation for therapy, and we will look at ways of instilling motivation in the following section.

The child's social development must be considered in order to assess if there are issues concerning the child's separation from parents. For example, if a child of 3 or 4 is brought to therapy and is too frightened to leave a parent, this is not unusual. The practitioner may want to begin by seeing parent and child together. If, on the other hand, a school phobic child of 11 is unwilling to come into the therapist's office alone, although the child has shown social independence in a variety of other ways (e.g., joining the Boy Scouts or going to the store alone), a very different approach may be used. In the latter case, the therapist may want to insist upon the child coming in alone. Or, the therapist may enact a behavioral shaping procedure, rewarding the child for entering the therapist's room alone for progressively longer periods of time.

The method and extent to which the therapist includes parents and other significant adults in the treatment plan depends in part upon the child's social development. If the child's difficulties involve developmental and/or social events such as eating, going to bed, or relating with teachers, effective intervention may necessitate the practitioner's working closely with significant adults in the child's environment (Ornstein, 1976). On the other hand, sometimes children are overly dependent upon parents, as in the case of the 11-year-old school phobic child mentioned previously. In these cases, the practitioner may choose to focus most intervention upon the child as a way of building the child's self-reliance. The interaction of the child's social developmental level with the quality of the social influences in his or her life must be assessed and used to therapeutic advantage. The practitioner's relationship with the parents can vary not only in the amount of contact, but also in the purpose of the contact.

In the next section of this chapter, we will overview the stances a practitioner can assume when working with parents. At this point, we want to emphasize that the way the child practitioner decides to manage time with the parents and child depends in part on the child's developmental capacities and liabilities.

An important facet of the treatment plan with children is to incorporate ways of dealing with the clients' developmental capacity to conceptualize. Because of children's limited conceptual ability, they may not be able to fully understand the purpose of therapy. Their initial willingness to attend sessions may not be built upon hope for change, as is typically true of adult clients, but rather upon seconday factors such as liking the practitioner, enjoying the special attention, or being reinforced by parents for going to see the therapist. The therapist must find some way of enlisting the child client's interest in therapy, and great skill and sensitivity is often required for this feat.

Evaluation of the child's level of conceptualization will also affect the type of counseling employed. For children under 4 years of age, interpretations may not be meaningful because the child may not completely comprehend certain relationships that are beyond his or her symbolic ability. A young client most likely can understand and name certain feelings. Thus, help in labeling feelings or identifying a wish or fantasy which serve as the stimuli for emotions may help a young child sort out diffuse feelings and contribute to the child's adjustment. The therapist working with a very young client will want to create a therapeutic medium such as play therapy that is conducive to the clinician's identifying and helping the client label feelings and behaviors (Lester, 1975).

As children reach school age, their ability to understand and to sit and talk with the therapist increases. However, they also recognize the asymmetry of talking with an adult and often become much less conversant than if talking with a child of similar age. For these children, techniques such as role playing, use of a tape recorder, or storytelling are useful (Lester, 1975).

The child's level of affective development must be carefully considered in the treatment style. The young child tends to act spontaneously upon feelings. Feeling and behavior are not perceived as distinct until conceptual ability to introspect about oneself has developed (Chess & Hassibi, 1978). The more limited the developmental ability to conceptualize about feelings, the more action-oriented therapy must be. At the earlier affective developmental levels, the therapist learns much about the child's feelings from the child's behavior. However, the therapist must decide just how much acting to encourage. It is countertherapeutic for traumatic feelings and events to be re-enacted so globally that diffuse distress is expressed (Freedman, Kaplan, & Sadock, 1976). Thus, the therapist must create a treatment plan in which enough action is encouraged to provide understanding of the child's problems. Then, the therapist can identify and label these for the child and develop programs for change. However, the therapist must provide enough structure and limits to activity that self-destructive behavior or pervasive anguish is not elicited. In fact, if ego functioning is significantly impaired, the therapist may want to use the sessions to help the child distinguish play and reality (Freedman, Kaplan, & Sadock, 1976). In such cases, the therapist may terminate activities if the child seems to perceive the acting as reality.

Finally, the practitioner needs to assess the child's level of motoric development in evolving the treatment plan. At earlier developmental levels, much diffuse motor activity is observed, and attention span is short. Sessions need to be of shorter duration for younger children. The preschooler may be seen for several weekly sessions of 20-30 minutes duration while most children of age 10 or older can handle a 45 minute or an hour session. Less goal-directed activity should also be expected for younger children. As we have discussed previously, from infancy, children differ in motor activity. Generally, this difference in activity level between children continues through to adulthood. Thus, in addition to assessing the child's motoric development, the clinician will also want to plan treatment strategies in relationship to the child's motoric temperament. For the extremely nonreactive child, a medium will be picked that encourages activity so that behavior and feelings are expressed and can be identified for therapeutic purposes. For the highly active child, activities should be chosen that increase control, and at the same time reduce total activity so that introspection and insight can be achieved.

In general, when aspects of the child's development are carefully considered, the client will feel and act more positively about the sessions, and the potential for establishing a positive relationship between practitioner and client increases. Moreover, when the structure of therapy takes into consideration the child's development in the cognitive, affective, social, and motor domains, the child's developmental strengths can be maximized while opportunity is provided for the child to develop skills that are immature or blocked. Of course, the child's development should not and will not remain static over time. Thus, the treatment issues will change as therapy continues, and the treatment structure should reflect these changing needs.

ROLE OF PARENTS IN THE TREATMENT PROCESS

As you read in detail in the unit on theories of child counseling, child theorists prescribe vastly different recommendations concerning how much and in which ways parents should be engaged in the treatment process. On the one hand, strict classical analysts believe that treatment should focus upon the child and that parents should be excluded from the therapy process. The classical analysts maintain that this focus upon the child is necessary to maintain confidentiality and the child's trust. Further, the analysts believe that the parents' emotional problems have contributed greatly to the child's distress and that the parents are unable to be therapeutic until they complete extensive personal therapy. As a consequence of this stand, some classical analysts such as Bruno Bettelheim (1967) suggest that preferred treatment often involves removing the child from the home and placing the client in residential treatment. Other theorists, especially some of behavioral persuasion, maintain that effective intervention can be completed by working primarily with the parents. Some behaviorists work exclusively with the child client's significant adults such as teachers and parents to set up elaborate behavioral modification schemes to change the child's socially maladaptive behaviors.

Each of these extreme positions is subject to certain limitations. Those who work almost exclusively with the child and very little with the parents seem to be ignoring the reality that the parents spend many hours with the child and will continue to exercise tremendous influence over the child. Furthermore, as we have stated, the parents are generally responsible for initiating and bringing the child to the sessions. If the practitioner does not engage the parents into the treatment process, they may withdraw their support and may withdraw the child from therapy. Most parents who bring their child to therapy are open to feedback and can be helpful therapeutic allies. Their perception of the child's problem is significant, even if distorted by their own problems and needs, because their perception of the child is clearly affecting their interaction with the child and the child's life. The practitioner can best understand the child's total milieu by gaining knowledge about parents and their perceptions of the relationship. Moreover, if parents are unaware of the practitioner's goals with the child, they may unwittingly sabotage therapeutic efforts.

On the other hand, those who work almost exclusively with significant adults and not the child may err by not recognizing the child's needs, feelings, and rights. As you read in the chapter on the humanistic and the psychosocial perspective to child therapy, most child theorists agree that when a child is treated with positive regard and respect during the therapeutic process, the child is more likely to become more motivated to change and may have many answers to his or her own dilemmas. Furthermore, severely limiting the child's role in the therapeutic process ignores the child's rights to privacy in his or her interactions with the parents.

It is not surprising, then, that most child practitioners adopt a moderate position in which they work with both the child and parents. Yet, even within this moderate orientation, theorists and practitioners differ greatly in how they approach parents. Some child practitioners of the humanistic persuasion recommend that the practitioner should adopt a supportive, clinical role with parents. The parents are viewed as distressed about their child and their relationship with the child and needing support to work through their feelings about the child and their own parenting skills (Axline, 1969; Ginott, 1961).

Many theorists and practitioners see their roles with parents as advisors and consultants. For example, Dreikurs and Soltz (1964), Moustakes (1973), Keat (1979), and others adopt a problem solving strategy with the parents in which they help the parents plan more appropriate ways of interaction with the child. Models of child therapy have developed in which parents are trained in therapeutic techniques so that they respond as "paraprofessional" practitioners to their own children (Guerney, 1964; Ack, Beale, & Ware, 1975). We will discuss these approaches in detail in the chapter on preventive mental health. Those theorists and practitioners ascribing to a family systems viewpoint assist the "identified patient" by working with the family as a unit. As one more example of the variety of orientations for working with parents, Gardner (1975) recommends seeing the parents and child together for the first session in order to foster a sense of openness about the child's problems and to communicate to the child that the therapist will attempt to adopt an objective position concerning family issues. Following this initial contact, Gardner (1975) may meet parents separately in order to gain a systematic history about the child's difficulties. Then, Gardner conducts somewhat traditional individual therapy while the parents remain in the room.. The parents' roles vary from passive observers to active participants during the sessions.

Given the wide range of orientations proposed by child theorists, it is difficult to draw definitive conclusions about how the practitioner can best interact with the child's significant adults. Empirical data about the relative efficacy of these approaches are lacking. At the minimum, it is advisable to talk to parents about the goals and process of therapy. The parents will be interested in learning about the therapist's strategies (such as play therapy, story telling, etc.), about changes they might expect during the therapy, and about how long the therapy is likely to continue (Haworth, 1964). Clearly, the practitioner's orientation with the parents should be congruent with his or her overall theory of treatment. The theorists and practitioners agree that parents can be valuable allies or formidable blocks to the change process. Within the framework of his or her theory, the therapist should give careful consideration to the best way of engaging particular parents into the counseling process. The therapist should review in his or her thinking the variety of stances that can be adopted when working with parents and select an approach that seems most likely to foster the child's movement toward their goals.

STAGES OF CHILD THERAPY

As we have stated, the therapy sessions should be characterized by change as the child uses the sessions to further growth and development. The exact changes will depend upon the child's personality and specific personal difficulties. Nevertheless, certain issues are characteristic at the intial, middle, and final stages of child therapy and should be considered in the treatment plan.

The Initial Sessions

Several treatment issues are critical at the initiation of therapy. The practitioner needs to establish him or herself as a person that can be trusted by the child, parents, and other significant adults. The practitioner must help their child clients understand why they are receiving this special intervention. Importantly, the treatment must enlist the child's committment to the therapy. Frey, Heckel, Salzburg, and Wackwitz (1976) correlated a number of dimensions of children's personality with therapists' views of gain in psychotherapy as indicated by reduction in target symptoms. The child's motivation for psychotherapy correlated most highly with therapists' perceived change in symptoms. Yet, we have said few children choose therapy voluntarily. Thus, stimulating a child's interest in and motivation for therapy is a major goal of the initial sessions.

To begin with, the therapist must set a tone of neutrality. As the practitioner meets the child and parents, the practitioner communicates to both that he or she will try to understand all viewpoints. Even when expressing an opinion in controversial issues between the child client and parents, the therapist attempts to communicate a respect for all parties. The clinician quickly sets the tone that he or she will not offer quick advice or get angry, but rather, will try to understand the child's behavior. It is important to remember that the child is seldom the initiator of the treatment. The initial clinical task is to win the child's cooperation for the therapy process. In his text on psychotherapeutic approaches to the resistant child, Gardner (1975) offers many helpful and creative suggestions to enjoin the child's cooperation. In the initial contact with parents and child, Gardner explains that he employs "seductive reasoning," that is, he attempts to make the sessions seem appealing and fun to the child. He begins by asking the child relatively innocuous questions ('Where do you go to school? What is your favorite game?' etc.). He shows the child his "clinical wares" (games, videotapes, music, magic tricks). He gradually moves into a discussion of problematic concerns while monitoring that the child's resistance is not increasing. If resistance does build, Gardner (1975) resorts to other "seductive" strategies.

Once the child's willingness to participate is gained, the child practitioner must help the client understand about the process and goals of therapy. The practitioner communicates that the practitioner and child will be working together, that they will be actively engaged in a joint discovery about the child (Ornstein, 1976). Statements such as the following may be made:

"This is your time to do and say whatever you would like to."

"You seem like a child who has a lot to say. This is a place where you can do that."

"I'd like to ask you some things about yourself because I'd like for us to know each other better."

Early in the sessions the therapist helps the child identify a reason for coming (Freedman, Kaplan, & Sadock, 1976). The therapist may begin by posing a question to the client-- "Do you know why your parents brought you here?" Yet, the therapist must be cautious about telling the child that he or she is coming because of others' complaints. The child may not know he or she is considered a problem. Most likely, the child feels some discomfort and wishes the practitioner would do something about those things and people that are perceived as the cause of the problem. Thus, the presenting symptom as labeled by others may not be the child's concern. For example, it may be countertherapeutic to tell a child, "Your parents brought you here because they can no longer tolerate the many fights you have with your sister." It is generally more productive to determine if the child is concerned about any aspect of his or her life. Almost always, the therapist can gain the child's interest by treating the sessions as a way of helping a child with concerns about growing up. The offer of aid for the difficult task of development is almost always enticing to the child (Freud, 1965).

McConville (1976) coined terms for three opening styles to aid different children in their growing up concerns:

1. "What's In It For You"--To be used with children who are aggressive or experiencing difficulty dealing with authority, emphasize what the child may personally gain in therapy. For example, "In therapy we can help you not get thrown out of school and then you can stay in the club with the guys. Think you might be able to get an office in that club?"

2. "How Can I Help You - Or Take 'Good Enough' Care of You?"--To be used with children who are very anxious and pursue very destructive patterns, the therapist may adopt a stance communicating, "I will help you grow up less painfully." For example, the therapist might say, "As you tell me about how those kids pick on you and what you do about it, I will help you find ways of dealing with them. We will help you learn to protect yourself."

3. "What's It Like Being You?"--Works best with a very withdrawn child where the practitioner may need only offer counseling as a place where the child can begin more open and spontaneous expression. Here, the therapist may say, "The point of this time is for you to have a place where whatever you want to do or not do is ok."

The child will also profit from an explanation of how therapy works. Imagine children's puzzlement when they are told that therapy will make them feel better, make friends, etc. without any explanation of how it works. No doubt many children wonder if they will be taking medicine, if they will be asleep, or if therapy is some kind of magic. Practitioners have tended to minimize explanations about the child therapy process to their clients because they feel the children would not understand or would not be interested. Yet, several recent studies indicate that children prepared for the process of therapy through "training sessions" are perceived more positively by their therapist (Jennings & Davis, 1977) and are more able to report information about therapy, show more reduction in target symptoms and drop out of counseling at community mental health centers less frequently (Urie, 1975). The practitioner should explain to the child that in therapy:

■   Play and fantasy will be considered communications about him or herself. This explanation minimizes the child's feeling that clinical interventions are an intrusive attack.

- Talking and/or playing together increases the child's awareness about him or herself.

- Through increased awareness, the child's ability to grow and mature can be nurtured.

- Through some specific activities that practitioner and child plan together, the child's problems can be decreased.

During the initial sessions, the therapist should talk about confidentiality. Most young clients will not mind if their parents know about their activities or conversations in the therapy sessions, but a few clients do (Gardner, 1975). The therapist should be honest about issues of confidentiality. Total confidence should not be promised if it cannot be delivered. In many cases of referral to child practitioners (for example, if the child is highly disruptive at school or in determining child custody cases), total confidentiality is practically impossible and/or not in the child's best interests. Generally, the therapist can make a commitment to not disclose information about the sessions without first informing the child. If the child remains upset about the possibility of disclosure, the therapist might recommend that the child be present if critical issues must be discussed with the parents.

Structural limitations of the sessions should be set early and maintained consistently. Most clinicians agree that causing physical harm to self, the therapist, or other clients is not permitted (Axline, 1969; Moustakes, 1959; Dimick & Huff, 1970). However, therapists differ greatly in how much nondestrictive activity they allow. The important point seems to be to distinguish wild behavior which serves no therapeutic purpose from activity in which the child can be assessed, understood, and assisted. In the first case, the behavior is labeled "acting out" because the child acts upon his concerns and frustrations with little conscious awareness of the emotions or the stimuli precipitating them. In the latter case, activity may be very active or highly charged, but sufficient control is maintained that the child is helped to understand the behavior. Generally, if the therapist is very responsive to the client, acting out behavior is short-lived, and arbitrary controls will not have to be established frequently.

Ornstein (1976) explains that if acting out cannot be controlled by the therapist and significant adults through support and sensitive interpretation, then limits must be set as a palliative measure. The limit setting may not in itself stop the client's problem, but is necessary for the client and others to look at and resolve the child's concerns.

If issues of establishing rapport, identifying goals, and setting limits are given careful attention within the initial sessions, the therapeutic process is greatly enhanced. The therapist and client work together to accomplish these goals. Thus, the initial treatment tasks well completed builds a "therapeutic alliance."

The Middle Phases

Once a therapeutic alliance is established, the therapy moves into a "work phase." With adult clients, Carkhuff and Berensen (1977) have identified this therapeutic work phase as: (1) helping a client understand the nature of his or her conflicts and (2) aiding a client in developing action plans that will change maladaptive patterns. Applying the Carkhuff and Berensen (1977) scheme to child therapy, it can be seen that child practitioners employ a variety of activities to help their clients move through the understanding and action phases of therapy.

Numerous activities for child therapy have been described in the child literature, and almost all writings are expository in which an activity is described and applied to a clinical case. Each activity seems to offer advantages for helping specific children express their difficulties directly or symbolically. Some activities such as art therapy seem particularly helpful in clarifying an understanding of a child's dilemmas. Other activities, such as role playing, are particularly effective in stimulating a child to act in new ways. Of course, the activities will only be helpful to the extent that the therapist competently uses the findings that emerge in those sessions. It would be impossible to review all the techniques employed with children in this text, but in this section we will attempt to describe the major ones.

Play Therapy

Almost all child therapists use play as a technique in their treatment approach. The medium of play provides a very practical way of forming an alliance and learning about a child. Play, as compared to the recreation of adults, serves a practical function for children. Erikson (1963) explains that the play of children is preparatory for life. Through play, the child attempts "to synchronize the body and social processes within the self" (Erikson, 1963, p. 211). The child practices mastery of himself or herself and of the world through this "internal reality between fantasy and actuality" (Erikson, 1963, p. 212).

Play was first introduced into therapy by Hug-Hellmuth in 1913. She stated that the analyst paves the way for analysis by sharing in the play activities (Kanner, 1962a). As we have discussed in detail in an earlier chapter, Melanie Klein and Anna Freud employed systematic play therapy techniques in the 1930's. Erikson was the first therapist to systematically observe differences in children's play throughout their development and to identify differences in play between males and females. He noted that the toddler's play is mainly "autocosmic," a way of bringing material to the child. The preschooler's play is "microspheric," in that the child begins to move toys to replicate the child's view of the world. Erikson reported that male preschoolers' play often deals with themes of 'high' and 'low.' He builds towers and rockets as he works out his Oedipal concerns. Erikson noted that girls' play often deals with themes of 'open' and 'closed,' for example, building and designing interiors of houses. Erikson believed girls were working through their Electra concerns, practicing for the female roles they will assume. He believed that if a disturbed child were allowed to express these themes with an accepting adult therapist, the child would gain "play peace" (Erikson, 1963). Today, most therapists do not accept the premise that play activity is aimed at the child's working through oral, anal, and phallic conflicts. However, most do hold to Erikson's concept that the child begins to experience subjective comfort when play activity is watched and responded to by an accepting adult.

A number of other purposes of play therapy have been posited. Kanner (1962a) sees the primary advantages as catharsis, to drain off excess energy, and self expression, as a means of satisfying needs before the child is skilled enough to directly impact the world. Ginott (1961) and others see added advantages of play therapy in helping the child learn new life skills, providing means for interpreting a child's behavior and for evaluating gains in therapy. Dimick and Huff (1970) emphasized that play provides a very effective way of facilitating the therapeutic alliance. While the child is playing, he or she tests limits with the therapist and in doing so learns more appropriate ways of relating to the therapist and others. Therefore, play therapy is an activity that can facilitate movement through all major phases of therapy from acceptance and forming a therapeutic alliance, to understanding of the problem, through action and practice to termination.

Clinicians are surprisingly consistent about the materials they recommend for effective play therapy. A room about 10' by 15' is preferred. This size allows activity and yet is small enough to provide some natural control to acting out and to keep the therapist and child in relatively close proximity (Dimick & Huff, 1970; Keat, 1974). Generally, toys should be picked that allow a child to create, to project his typical behaviors and thoughts (Axline, 1969). Thus, structured games are generally not as effective as dolls, puppets, paints, trucks, and animals.

A problem that often arises in play therapy is that children may want to "borrow" some material and take it home with them. Again, on this matter, most therapists agree. The child should be allowed to take home his own creations, such as paintings and clay models, but not to take toys home. As a whole, keeping material in play therapy is considered an important structural limit for teaching children about the role of therapy within their lives.

There is much more controversy on how the therapist should respond in play therapy than there is in how to set up the play therapy environment. The therapist's theoretical orientation affects how active he or she is in the play therapy session. As discussed earlier, Axline (1969) popularized a nondirective approach to play therapy. The play therapy atmosphere is very permissive. Only acts injurious to the child or therapist are limited. The therapist conveys understanding without interpretation.

Axline (1969) maintains that first unrealistically negative, then unrealistically positive, then appropriately mixed emotions about the child's significant adults and self will be expressed in this permissive atmosphere.

Other therapists are more interpretive or active in play therapy according to their theoretical underpinnings. For example, Moustakes (1973), identifying himself as an existential therapist, actively responds to the child in play therapy in order to remediate the child's previous experiences and to form a close, constructive relationship.

The research about the efficacy of play therapy is controversial and limited. Sabatani (1976) compared the effects of participating in individual play therapy to watching films about social interactions for a random group of elementary school age children. Play therapy facilitated more popularity (according to sociometric choice) than the systematic watching of films. In contrast, when 26 children were divided into a experimental play therapy group which received 15 weeks of 45 minute individual play therapy sessions and a waiting list control group, no differences were found on six primary dimensions of adjustment (Barrett, 1976). With the paucity of research findings, it is clearly too early to try to evaluate which approach to play therapy is most effective. The somewhat bleak findings clearly suggest that a therapist should not assume he or she is doing therapy with the child; that is, helping the child, simply because they are playing together. With the lack of empirical guidelines, it becomes even more important for the therapist to carefully delineate the purpose of the play therapy, to develop a directive or nondirective approach consistent with theory and treatment goals and to assess progress towards those goals.

Art Techniques

A great range of art techniques can be employed. Some therapists encourage free drawing sessions. Others like to have the child draw pictures of their families, themselves, their neighborhood, etc. An approach developed by Winnicott (1971) called the "Squiggle Technique" in which the client and therapist draw lines alternately and discuss them has become quite popular. Stein (1976) has found it useful to have her clients make "funny books" of their drawings and discuss them.

In her highly creative text, *Windows to Our Children,* Oaklander (1978) offers a wide range of drawing techniques that she implements from a gestalt perspective. Oaklander (1978) assists children to become more aware of their sensory experiences and through sensory enrichment, more cognizant of their feelings. For example, she asks children to complete individual or group paintings on large poster boards with car paint. "The flow of the paint and the sensuous feel of it, as well as the sheer enjoyment of the activity, open the child up to sharing some deep feelings and this leads to his talking about some problems in his life which in turn leads to a discussion of his options in resolving that problem" (Oaklander, 1978, pp. 60-61). Employing finger paints or clay, she may direct her child clients to become aware of the sensation of pulling, tugging, and smoothing the milieu to increase their sense of control and mastery. "Bunch it up. Tear it. Tear little pieces and tear big pieces... Bunch it up. Pick it up and throw it down. You may have to peek for this... Do it again. Do it harder. Make a loud noise with it. Don't be afraid to hit HARD" (Oaklander, 1978, p. 70). She then encourages the children to move from a discussion of their sensory experiencing to their overall personal experiences.

Almost always, the drawing is seen as an adjunct to therapy that aids understanding of thoughts and feelings. The therapist offers commentary about the drawings and encourages the child to talk about them. The drawing techniques are particularly useful in the middle phases of therapy. Most therapists do not look for universal symbolism to the drawings since the child's developmental level, culture, and experience all affect art work. Rather, comments are usually intended to lead children to talk more about the drawing and thus to tell what it means to them. For example, statements about firmness of footing, size of body parts, that a certain color is preferred, and questions about what a certain part of the painting is, may facilitate further verbal therapeutic exchange (LeRoy & Derdeyn, 1976).

Oaklander (1978) offers a number of guidelines by which the therapist can employ art media as a backdrop to clinical intervention:

- Ask the child to share the experience of drawing, his or her feelings about doing the task, how he or she decided to approach it.

- Ask the child to discuss the drawing itself, giving it a title, etc.

- Ask the child to elaborate upon parts of the picture, describing shapes, forms, colors, people, and objects in it.

- In accord with gestalt principles, encourage the child to describe the picture as if the picture were the child; for example, 'I am this picture. I have curvy soft lines. I have hard lines. I am mostly blue.'

- Pick specific parts of the picture and ask the child to identify with it. For example, 'Be that lion in the picture. Describe yourself. What do you look like? What are you doing?' Then ask the child to elaborate further about that part. For example, Where would the lion rather be?'

- Prompt the child to dialogue between two parts of the picture. What does the mouse say to the lion?'

- Encourage the child to pay attention to the colors. What does blue mean to you?'

■   Watch for missing parts or empty spaces in the drawing and ask about them; for example, "I wonder why the mother has no hands?"

The use of drawings as an adjunct to verbal therapy requires a sensitive response to small nuances of the child's creation while avoiding over interpretation. In the Case of the Ill-Tempered Artist that follows, the therapist used drawings to move through the first several stages of treatment (Caron, 1980). By allowing the client to draw quietly, without forcing verbalization through the first few sessions, a therapeutic alliance with this guarded youth was established. Using the drawings as a topic of conversation, a dialogue between the therapist and client emerged gradually, leading to a discussion of the referral problems.

Case 11.1. The Case of an Ill-Tempered Artist

Reason for Referral: This 12-year-old client was referred for psychotherapy primarily due to problems in controlling his temper. He reportedly was breaking school windows, lying, writing obscene notes, and refused to accept responsibility for his actions. Although previous intelligence test results indicated low average intelligence, the school diagnosticians determined that he was five or six grade levels behind his peers. Additionally, he was thought to be oppositional, guarded, and inaccessible to contact from the outside world.   .

Intervention Strategy: This client was guarded, quiet, and inactive during initial sessions. The utilization of art therapy provided the client with a safe way to begin to communicate in a monologue fashion. Art provided a method of developing a therapeutic relationship. Eventually, a therapeutic dialogue emerged. Within the therapeutic dialogue, the client talked about the meaning of some of the pictures and eventually discussed his school problems.

Therapy Progress: The first four pictures were of birds. Two of the four birds looked quite aggressive (See Figure 11.1). Picture five was a stylized desk, and picture six was once again a bird, but not particularly aggressive. The bird's reflection resembles the lower part of a naked man. For the seventh picture, he drew a ram with a human mask-like face. This is the first sign of a person in any drawing. Next a van with a C.B. radio was drawn (See Figure 11.2). Through the front window one can see the obscured face of a person. Lines around the antenna indicate communication. Next, he drew the first clear person. He chose to reproduce a picture hanging on my wall. This was seen as a good prognostic sign as it indicated the youth's sense of connection to therapy and to the therapist. The tenth picture was probably the most unusual of all the pictures. The client stated that it was the skeleton of an animal in a casket. This fictitious animal lives in the forest and chased people. The people were afraid of it because they didn't know what it was. Then one day while crossing the road the animal was run over and

Figure 11.1. First Picture, "Bird"

Figure 11.2. Eighth Picture, "Van"

Figure 11.3. Last Picture, "Man"

killed by a truck. The people placed its body in a casket. For the next picture he drew a somewhat aggressive cartoon character. He chose not to draw in future sessions, but rather played air hockey and even brought a friend to participate. It seemed as if he had symbolically buried a wild aspect of himself and was reaching out to peers and the therapist. A month later he brought five additional pictures consisting of three birds, one walrus, and a man's face (See Figure 11.3). The pictures were seen as less aggressive and healthier.

Behavioral Progress: When therapy began, the client was being disciplined in the school office almost daily. After about one month of therapy, he quit having to go to the office. He continued to write an occasional obscene note, but was now usually willing to admit his guilt when caught. He was somewhat more verbal and spontaneous.

Six month follow-up: In a six month follow-up interview with the mother, she stated that he had maintained the behavioral gains in school and with his peers. She felt that temper control was no longer a problem.

Writing Approaches

Some child clients respond well to invitations to write about their life circumstances and feelings. Children can be encouraged to write stories about themselves, others, or fictional characters. The stories about others and fictional characters are seen generally as a child's projection of his or her own life views. According to the clinician's theoretical persuasion, these stories can be responded to in a variety of fashions. The child may be asked to talk about his or her feelings about the story, to expound upon various characters' responses, etc.. The therapist may offer explanations or interpretations about the characters' actions.

Oaklander (1978) encourages her child clients to write poetry. She devised a modified version of the Japanese Haikus which she has found most of her children are able to enjoy writing. The modified Haikus consists of five lines. The first and fifth line are the same single topic word. Line two is a two-line descriptor of the topic word. Lines three and four are three- and four-word descriptors correspondingly. For example, a child might write:

Mothers
Very Nice
You Love Them
Make You Feel Safe
Mothers

or

School
Very Hard
Not Enough Play
Summer, Please Come Soon
School

Again, the therapist can use the children's poetry in a variety of clinical fashions.

Structured Interpersonal Approaches

Naturally, all child therapy involves stimulating intimate interaction between the therapist and child. In traditional play therapy, the interactions grow in depth through a relatively unstructured format. Several practitioners, with Richard Gardner as a leading proponent, have created structured strategies for engaging children and deepening the therapeutic relationship. Gardner (1971) originated a storytelling technique involving several steps. First, the child is encouraged to tell a story and give it a moral. Gardner videotapes the child's story. He may create a fantasy situation about the tape recording, for example, telling the child to pretend that he or she is a famous storyteller and is about to broadcast a story through a national television circuit. Gardner then introduces the child storyteller to the "listening public" with a flamboyant, complementary opening..."Today, ladies and gentlemen, we have for your enjoyment, Bobby who will be telling us a story on our show. Bobby, tell the folks a little bit about yourself..." If the child is hesitant to begin a story, Gardner offers nondirective verbal leads. He tells the child that he will begin the sentences and the child should finish them. Gardner's leads are open prompts such as:

"Once upon a time, a _____"
"Then the animal _____"
"Afterwards he felt _____"
"And lo and behold, right then _____"

Gardner consistently requests the child to end the story with a moral. It is Gardner's thesis that the child will reveal frustrations and conflicts through the dynamics of the tale.

On the assumption that the child's story is really about the child, the therapist listens, asks for clarification, and tries to understand the psychodynamic meaning. Then the therapist makes up a story selecting one or two of the same themes, but providing an ending moral that represents a higher level of adjustment. No doubt, you will enjoy Case 11.2, The Case of the Unsure, Angry Eight-Year-Old that follows in which the storytelling technique is exemplified (Furgeson, 1981).

Case 11.2. The Case of the Unsure, Angry Eight-Year-Old

Eight-year-old Sandy lives with her mother, father, older sister and brother, and a younger brother. Her school problems go back to being suspended from her four-year-old preschool class for hitting and biting. Currently, her third grade teacher finds her behavior unacceptable. She does not complete her independent work and disturbs others. Sandy has a poor self-concept, accepts herself as a problem child, and does not feel that she can change her school behavior.

At home, her parents find her temper tantrums very difficult. Sandy erupts with uncontrolled anger, screaming and yelling, at what seems to be the slightest provocation. These tantrums are often unexpected, and her parents have not been successful at either preventing or stopping them. They feel that Sandy knows her tantrums are unacceptable, but that she feels unable to change her behavior. Her family considers her their difficult member, and Sandy seems to feel trapped in that role.

At her third session, Sandy told her therapist, Juli, the following story about their visit together.

Sandy's Story

> Once there was a girl named Sandy. She was a cheerleader. One Sunday afternoon, she went to her brother's soccer game. He was only five, and the team was called the Super Jets. Sandy's sister Lynn who is 11 always calls it Blue Jets. Then Sandy says, "No, it's Super Jets." While Sandy was cheering, she saw a lady named Juli. Sandy got very embarrassed because she thought Juli would get mad at her because she wasn't very good. After the soccer game, Juli and Sandy went to Swenson's where Sandy had a chocolate ring-a-ding. It was in a really high glass, a Parfait glass. And after that, Sandy said she was freezing. And Juli said, "Do you want to go wait out?" and Sandy said, "No." And then Sandy got her shirt dirty from cheerleading, and she's going to get in trouble, don't worry. She's going to have to clean it herself, by hand. Sandy wondered if Juli knew any ladies who got in trouble when she was a girl. Sandy and Juli went riding in the car. Sandy knows a boy in her class who gets in lots of trouble. Then they went through a green light. Then they went over a big hill into the telephone wires and b-o-i-n-g the storyteller's brain stopped again, and nobody would talk to her. The moral of this story is, "Nobody likes a storyteller."

The therapist decided to focus on Sandy's poor self-concept as represented by Sandy's cheerleading, her dirty shirt, and the boy who got in trouble in school. In the story, the therapist suggests to Sandy that she accept her behavior and herself as a likeable person and consider that as she grows, she will change. The therapist's additions to Sandy's story are underlined.

Therapist's Story

Once there was a girl named Sandy. She was a cheerleader. One Sunday aft- ernoon she went to her brother's soccer game. He was only five and the team was called the Super Jets. Sandy's sister Lynn who is eleven always calls it the Blue Jets. Then Sandy says, "No, it's Super Jets." Sandy felt pleased to be right, to get noticed for being right. While Sandy was cheering, she saw a lady named Juli. Sandy got very embarrassed because she thought Juli would get mad at her because she wasn't very good. What she didn't know, or maybe she'd for- gotten, was that Juli would still like her even if she wasn't very good. She'd still take her to Swenson's. After the soccer game, Juli and Sandy went to Swenson's where Sandy had a chocolate ring-a-ding. It was in a really high glass, a parfait glass. And after that Sandy said she was freezing. And Juli said, "Do you want to go wait out?" and Sandy said "No." And then Sandy got her shirt dirty from cheerleading, but she knows how to clean it herself. Sandy and Juli went riding in the car. Sandy wondered if Juli was like her. Sandy was afraid Juli wouldn't like her if she knew how much trouble she got into. But Juli knew girls like her and as they grew up, they changed and didn't get into trouble. Then they went through a green light. Then they went up a big hill over the telephone wires and landed on the top eating ice cream. The moral of the story is, "It's more fun to watch yourself as you grow and change than to be mad at yourself."

The case of the Unsure, Angry Eight-Year-Old demonstrates how a child at the concrete operational level can be helped to rethink her approach to life. It probably would not have worked to offer this 8-year-old interpretations about her tendency to repress feelings and cover her errors, but she learned about her ways of defending against anxiety and her personal dynamics in the storytelling technique.

An infinite variety of modifications to the storytelling approach are possible. For example, the therapist can create an open-ended story representing a conflictural area for the child, and have the child finish the story (Keat, 1974). Words can be written for favorite songs. The child's needs often prescribe the exact storytelling approach.

Related to the structured storytelling technique is the use of bibliotherapy in child counseling. Published books on relevant themes can be read together. Stories can be useful discussion guides in group counseling sessions or can be given to the child to read at home. If the practitioner wishes to conduct a relatively unstructured verbal or play therapy session, it may be unwise to keep the bibliotherapeutic material in the therapy room. Some resistant child clients may begin reading as a way of avoiding interaction with the clinicians   Table II.1 lists a number of bibliotherapeutic references that the child therapist may wish to employ.

Table 11.1

Bibliotherapeutic Material for Children

I. Books that Foster General Self Awareness

Carr, R. *Be a frog; a bird, or a tree.* Garden City, N.J.: Doubleday, 1973.

DeMille, R. *Put your mother on the ceiling.* New York: Walker and Company, 1967.

Gardner, R. *Dr. Gardner's stories about the real world.* Englewood Cliffs, NJ: Printers Hall, 1972.

Hazen, N. *Grownups cry too.* Chapel Hill, NC: Lollipops Power, 1973.

Leonni, L. *Fish is fish.* New York: Pantheon Books, 1970.

Pearson, J. *Begin sweet world: Poetry by children.* Garden City, NJ: Doubleday, 1976.

Preston, E. *The temper tantrum book.* New York: Viking, 1969.

Silverstein, S. *Where the sidewalk ends.* New York: Harper and Row, 1974.

II. Books that Teach about Effective Interpersonal Relationships

Guilfoile, E. *Nobody listens to Andrew.* New York: Follet, 1957.

Gardner, R. *The boys' and girls' book about divorce.* New York: Jason Aronson, 1970.

Lobel, A. *A frog and a toad are friends.* New York: Harper and Row, 1970.

Waxman, S. *What is a boy? What is a girl?* Culver City, CA: Peace Press, 1976.

III. Self Concept and Ego Building Readings

Charlie, R. & Moore, L. *Hooray for me!* New York: Parents Magazine, 1975.

Gibson, M. *What is your favorite thing to hear?* New York: Grosset and Dunlap, 1966.

Gibson, M. *What is your favorite thing to touch?* New York: Grosset and Dunlap, 1966.

Kraus, R. *Leo the late bloomer.* New York: Young Readers Press, 1971.

Simon, S. *I am loveable and capable.* Niles, IL.: Argus, 1973.

The therapist may want to use structured games with some child clients. Gardner (1975) has devised a number of games that foster intervention. Very well known is his "Talking, Feeling, dnd Doing Game" (Creative Therapeutics, 155 County Road, Cresskill, NJ 07626). In this board game, the clinician and client compete to reach the end point by throwing dice and moving on a pathway. The players land on squares which signal them to pick up either talking, feeling, or doing cards. The cards request players to describe or act out ideas of potential clinical relevance (for example, "What is the worst thing a child can say to a mother?" "Say something that tells about a feeling." "Pretend you are having a temper tantrum." "Why are you so angry?"). If the player responds at all to the request on the card, he or she receives a chip. The player reaching the end point first receives five extra chips. The winner of the most chips can select a trinket from the prize jar. Gardner (1975) reports that highly resistant and reticent clients are quite responsive to this structured approach. Through these relatively nonthreatening activities, the children reveal their attitudes and feelings, which allow the clinician to prompt for further explanations and to offer interpretations.

With N. L. Kritzberg, Gardner (1975) devised another game, "Board of Objects," which the clinician can set up with inexpensive play material. Small figurines are placed upon each square of a 64 or 100 square game board. One face of each of two dice is painted red. Players throw the dice. If a red face lands up, the play is to select an object from the board. If the player can say anything about the object he gets one chip. If he can make up a story about the object he receives two chips. This game allows the clinician to gain insight and offer feedback about very young clients.

Some popularly published games may also hold therapeutic value. For example, Gardner recommends the use of Scrabble for Juniors (Selchow & Richter, Bay Shore, NY) and the Campbell's Bowl of Soup Game (Multiple Toymakers, 200 5th Avenue, New York, NY 10010) as easy games which elicit children's personal thoughts and can be used as props for therapeutic intervention.

Many therapists employ a variety of role playing techniques with children with great success. The basis for and theory behind developing such techniques was discussed fully in Chapter 5 on cognitive behavioral approaches in child counseling. Lazarus (1976) has written avidly about the approach and reported that behavioral rehearsal was twice as effective as direct advice and non-directive treatment. His research has been criticized because he personally administered all three treatments while clearly holding a bias in favor of the behavioral approach. However, Lazarus' findings have been replicated in a variety of closely related studies (Smith, 1976). The role playing may be casual in which the clinician and client play out a conflict situation. Roles may be reversed so that the child learns how significant others are feeling. Role playing may involve watching stimulus films or acting out roles in structured plays or unstructured psychodrama. The role playing may be employed in group sessions to practice a particular personal/social issue, such as learning to be more assertive or learning to talk with divorced parents. Role playing techniques can be particularly effective in later phases of counseling because they facilitate action, the adoption of new beliefs, and practicing of new behaviors.

A variety of other structured techniques can be incorporated into the treatment plan. The therapist and child can act out open-ended plays, respond to film vignettes, produce puppet shows, etc. Some child-practitioners employ relaxation training fairly regularly during sessions to help the children feel more comfortable about themselves and about discussing their concerns (Keat, 1979). The structured techniques can be particularly effective in the middle and later phases of therapy. They can facilitate understanding of the client's and significant others' values, ideas, and problems. These techniques also provide a means for integrating new cognitive understanding and practicing new verbal behaviors, thereby helping to move clients through the action phase of counseling.

Summary of Activity Therapy

As we look at the variety of activity therapies, several points emerge. The activity is a means to therapy, not therapy itself (Stein, 1976). Although the therapist may recommend an activity for a child, the activity will not help facilitate a therapeutic alliance unless the child finds the activity of interest. Children differ in the degree to which they like to be active or talk with the therapist. The clinician must use the strategy to accomplish specific clinical aims. Therefore, some degree of clinical verbal communication between the therapist and child should occur during or after the activity is completed in order for counseling to progress.

The beginning clinician often wonders which approach to use with a particular client. Although there is no single answer to this question, several guidelines can be offered. The nature of the child's development and presenting complaints guide the choice of technique. For example, a withdrawn child might respond well to the low-threat Talking, Feeling, Doing Game (Gardner, 1975). An overly active child might respond well to acting out a play. The high action in this case would help delimit nontherapeutic movement. Building upon Lazarus' (1976) Theory of Multimodal Therapy, Keat (1979) follows the acronym BASIC ID to select techniques that will strengthen the child's adaptive functioning within each of the following modes:

Behavior
Affect
Sensation
Imagery
Cognition
Interpersonal Relationships
Drugs and Eating Habits

Table 11.2
An Example of Multi-Modal Profile for Johnny

Multi-Modal Scheme from the Basic Acronym	Johnny's Problems	Treatment
Behavior	Difficulties relating to father after divorce	Bibliotherapy, read books on children of divorce
Affect	anger, fears of abandonment	relaxation training role play talking with father
Sensation	has interest in art	draw family picures then and now and discuss
Imagery	hesitant to reveal feelings about self	Talking, Feeling, Doing Game
Cognition	has stopped completing school work since parents' divorce	family conference, behavioral contracting
Interpersonal Relations	area of strength, no apparent difficulties	not applicable
Drugs & Eating Habits	Johnny and Mother eat at erratic times since divorce	nutritional discussion and bibliotherapy

Keat (1979) completes an analysis of the child's functioning in each sphere and then selects relevant techniques to strengthen the child's functioning. An example of such a multimodal profile is presented in Table 11.2.

We suggest that the various techniques tend to be appropriate for different phases of the therapeutic relationship. Some techniques serve broad purposes and may be employed through several stages, while others are particularly useful at discrete phases to help resolve particular problems. The phases overlap as movement through those therapeutic stages may be uneven. Overall, therapists' selection of treatment techniques should reflect the child's particular needs and movement through the therapeutic process.

Terminating Therapy

The timing and method of termination is at least as important as the initial meeting procedure in affecting clinical gain. Much therapeutic benefit can be lost if a child feels rejected by the therapist or if separation from the therapist causes great anxiety.

Of course, no simple guidelines can be given about when to terminate. A growing body of literature suggests that short-term therapy of eight weeks or so duration is often as effective as long-term therapy that lasts a year or more (Ewing, 1976; and Kissel, 1974). Thus, it is likely that in some instances therapists are keeping children in therapy longer than parents and children believe necessary or beneficial. The more clearly the therapy goals are defined, the more this situation can be avoided.

Of course, child therapists of different theoretical persuasions suggest very different criteria for deciding when to terminate. Humanistically-oriented therapists speak of terminating when children feel good about themselves and when they talk more positively about themselves. They maintain that the child client generally tells the therapist when he or she is ready to terminate. Such broad goals usually require 4 months or longer to accomplish. The behavioristically-oriented therapist, on the other hand, looks for extinction of symptomatic behavior which is often accomplished in less than a dozen sessions. The analytically-oriented therapist is concerned about children's ability to interpret their own play and to play less stereotypically and defensively. Again, such goals require relatively long-term treatment. In interviewing 1200 clinicans, Weissman (1975) reported that the primary factor listed for termination was development of effective coping mechanisms and problem solving strategies. Along these lines, we believe that the decision for termination should involve evaluation of the child's developmental progress. Termination is appropriate if the child's cognitive, affective, social, and motoric development is moving forward in a systematic fashion. The developmental sequence laid down in earlier chapters offers a systematic way of evaluating the appropriate point for termination. The therapist should not assess this development only within the sessions. The new personal skills learned with the clinician should have transferred to the child's normal environment.

Once the child practitioner believes termination is appropriate, it should be discussed with the client. Most likely, the clients will need several sessions to fully deal with their attitudes about termination. These final sessions should be employed to assess that new skills are firmly established in the child's everyday life (that they are not reduced once the therapist begins to discuss termination). It is the therapist's responsibility to raise the termination issue over a number of sessions. After all, even constructive parting can be difficult to handle. Learning to deal with the parting constructively becomes an integral part of the therapeutic process. The child may need assistance is talking about feelings toward leaving. In some cases, new reinforcement systems may need to be established in the child's everyday environment. The practitioner must also be very closely attuned to his or her feeling of loss. Some children want to know that the practitioner will remember them, that their relation had an impact upon the therapist. Whereas most clinicians will not take or give presents or toys during the therapy process, some do exchange gifts at termination. As the child and practitioner work out a constructive approach to termination, child clients will learn effective ways of parting that will help them in many later life experiences.

With termination, the treatment plan has almost ended. Whenever possible, the therapist should include follow-up sessions to the overall treatment plan to ascertain that gains are maintained. Direct contact visits are advisable at three to six months following treatment. Many renowned therapists attempt to follow their client's progress for several years (Axline, 1969; Moustakes, 1959). Klein (1960) has stated that the real test of treatment success cannot be evaluated until puberty when the client's full identity unfolds.

GROUP THERAPY

So far we have been discussing primarily individual approaches to child therapy, but group counseling is often employed and preferred. In reviewing outcome studies of group therapy, Abramowitz (1976) reported that a variety of techniques (activity, play, verbal, and behavior modification) and outcome measures (self-concept, academic performance) have been employed. About 1/3 yield positive results, 1/3 negative, and 1/3 mixed findings. On a comparative basis, the most positive results were obtained through behavioral approaches.

Among therapists there is relative consensus about the children who will profit most from a group therapy experience. Weissman (1975) sampled 1200 clinicians with a twenty-item questionnaire and found that group therapy was preferred for children who need to address themselves to social inhibitions or to impulsive acting out behavior.

Thus, group therapy provides an excellent medium for children with interpersonal difficulties who need to learn to identify their mistaken interpersonal goals (Keat, 1974a).

Group therapy has also been shown to be useful with socially withdrawn children (Axline, 1969). When sociometric choice was used as a criterion of change, those students who were judged by their peers to be of low social acceptance and who received a model reinforcement counseling program made significantly more gain in social acceptance than similar students who received counseling without models or a control group that did not receive counseling (Hansen, Niland, & Zani, 1969). Models in this study were students who had been accorded high social acceptance by peers. The high and low social acceptance students met together and therapists merely reinforced ideas, insights, and suggestions relevant to acceptable social behavior put forth by both groups of students.

Group work may also be preferred for dealing with children who have all experienced a similar situational stressor. Thus, groups for children of divorced parents or for children experiencing the stress of having to move are recommended (Weissman, 1975).

Practitioners recommend that children's groups should be carefully structured. A group of four to six members if usually cited as the appropriate size of maximize constructive social interaction (Abramowitz, 1976). However, dual group therapy has also been used. In dual group therapy, two children are placed together because it is believed that their personal or interpersonal difficulties are compatible yet different enough that they may be of assistance to one another (Fuller, 1977). For example, one of the authors worked with two children in dual therapy who were both grappling with the knowledge that they had been adopted. Each child had learned about the adoption in a disturbing way (in one case by a peer and in the other by a sibling). Each felt inferior to their siblings. One had responded by withdrawing from family and peers. The second child seemed to mask her concerns by constant activity; but her activity was so frenzied that she too had few friends. The children reached each other on common issues. The second child, feeling befriended, became more controlled, and the first one began to model the second child's gregariousness.

In group therapy, the length of the session should vary with the children's ages. Children between five to eight years should generally meet for no more than about 40-60 minutes. For children from nine to twelve, groups may last longer, from one to one-and-a-half hours (Keat, 1974). As for the frequency of sessions, younger children may need to meet more than once a week to maintain changes, while older children can usually assimilate ideas from weekly sessions.

Attention must also be paid to group composition. In the early days of child counseling, therapists recommended single sex groups (Dimick & Huff, 1970). This idea has not been supported by most current writers unless the children comprising the groups are particularly conflicted about issues of sex roles and sex identification. It is also important that children be at about the same cognitive and social developmental level. Developmental homogeneity is more important than absolute age (Keat, 1974).

As a whole, more communication rules need to be set with groups than in individual therapy with children. Dimick and Huff (1970) recommend telling the children that the groups are an opportunity to really listen to one another and to look at problems and find solutions. Keat (1974) tells his child group members that they will be expected to cooperate with one another. Additionally, he insists that children must listen to one another and not interrupt, that only one person may talk at a time, and that the group will stay on one topic until all agree that they have finished talking about it. The therapist should also spend considerable time making certain that the children realize the importance of keeping group activity confidential and that they know what the concept of confidentiality means.

Again the therapists' theoretical approach will guide the leadership style (Shulman, 1979). Group therapists and therapists differ in how much they interpret conflict or how much they allow children to "work through" conflicts for themselves. According to Abramowitz's (1976) review, although the behavior modification approach resulted in more positive outcomes than the other approaches, it is impossible to conclude that this approach is significantly more effective in all cases. Regardless of how directive and/or interpretive the therapist is, it is generally perceived to be the leader's responsibility to define and set group goals, help the children move towards those goals, and maintain the group's limits (Keat, 1974). Since most children's defensive structures are not well-developed, the leader may also need to actively stop or prevent a member from being rejected or verbally attacked (Axline, 1969).

A variety of activities may be used in conjunction with the group discussion. The leader may direct group work with art, writing, reading, or structured interpersonal activities. A number of group games may facilitate interchange. For example, the children may be told to look in a mirror and describe what they see, what they like and dislike. Children may be told that they can go to a "magic store" and purchase anything they want. Group discussion follows about each member's choice. Published group counseling programs such as Methods in Human Development (Bessell & Palomores, 1973) may be employed. This program incorporates use of the well-known Magic Circle in which the children are encouraged to express their feelings and assured that someone within the group will react to their feelings in a constructive, caring fashion. Recorded music can be used to establish a mood or provoke discussions about the ideas of a song. For a group of inhibited children, creating music with bells and drums, etc., can facilitate interaction (Keat, 1974). Open-ended play therapy may be employed. Highly unstructured groups such as open-ended play therapy groups are usually comprised of fewer members, about three or four, and highly aggressive children are generally excluded (Ginott, 1961). As a rule, the more disturbed the members of the group, the more structured the group should be (Freedman, Kaplan, & Sadock, 1976).

Research about group effectiveness with children is relatively encouraging. Yet, the variety of approaches makes the task of empirical investigation quite overpowering. The groups differ in all combinations of size, composition, age, activities, and leadership style. Ultimately, research needs to focus more specifically upon techniques appropriate for specific children.

PROFESSIONAL ISSUES

We have talked about plans to facilitate client expression of affect and constructive activity. The effective child practitioner must also monitor his or her own attitudes and behavior. As we discussed in Chapter 6, the humanistic theorists have written adamently and prolifically about how important the practitioner's overall adjustment is in determining the clinical progress. Their research about the importance of the core conditions is now broadly accepted as a necessary (though not always a sufficient) condition for effective therapy. Gardner (1975) summarizes characteristics about effective child practitioners. They like children; they can project themselves into the child's situation; they can react and use insights from their own memories about growing up; they have the capacity to express warmth and excitement; they are nurturing and can express strong parental impulses; they are flexible and creative; they tolerate frustration and can accept failures. On top of projecting these overall qualities, effective child practitioners consistently monitor their feelings and behavior to assure that they are not responding to particular clients in countertherapeutic ways. As another way of conceptualizing this issue, the child clinician checks that he or she is not falling into a countertransference mode where actions and statements reflect the clinician's needs, not the child's. Child therapy places special stress that may elicit countertransference. It is very easy to respond to a child client as a parent, especially if these needs have been thwarted or frustrated in the practitioner's private life. The therapist may find himself or herself responding like an angry or critical parent. The therapist may become over-solicitous, similar to a smothering or over-protective parent. Another signal of countertransference may be the clinician's feeling frequently bored during the sessions. The boredom may indicate that the practitioner is expecting his or her own needs to be met in the sessions.

It is also very easy for a child clinician to regress along with the child. The younger the child, the more likely is countertransference regression to occur (Azima, 1976). In these cases, the child practitioner begins playing with the child instead of responding therapeutically to the child's play. One signal of regression spurred by countertransference may be the therapist's making childlike reflections or interpretations (Kabcenell, 1974). Or, practitioners may realize that they are feeling very defensive. Many children are intially negative or hesitant about counseling. The therapist should

Richard A. Gardner, M.D., P.A.
(with permission)

be able to analyze these responses in the context of the child's total adaptation. For example, the child may feel anxious about the clinician's stance of neutrality if the child is used to being told what to do. Other children may feel uncomfortable about the lack of structure in therapy. If the therapist finds himself or herself responding defensively to the child's hesitancy, possibly the therapist's own childlike needs for security and acceptance have been provoked.

When a child specialist recognizes signs of countertransference, he or she should include professional consultation in the case treatment plan. If these reactions cannot be successfully resolved, referral of the child client to another clinician may be in order.

Referrals

A critical aspect of a treatment plan is knowing when and to whom to refer. Child clinicians may refer a client to another clinician, as exemplified in the previous section on countertransference. The clinician may also refer when psychophysiological intervention may be helpful and when milieu therapy seems needed. There are a variety of psychophysiological and milieu approaches, and we shall summarize the major aspects of each.

PSYCHOPHYSIOLOGICAL APPROACHES

The psychophysiological approaches assume that at least part of maladjustment is organically-based and that once pathology is expressed, psychosocial stresses exacerbate the symptomatology. The psychophysiologically-oriented child practitioner probably accepts one or more of several basic assumptions: (1) psychological and physiologic treatments are not mutually exclusive and are often additive; (2) relief of a child's suffering (from depression or anxiety, for example) is a worthwhile goal, even if "the cause" of the problem remains unknown and unknowable; and (3) a child cannot achieve optimal functioning if the possibility of organic functioning is ignored (LeVine, 1985). The healthy child prompts less negative reactions from others. As others become warmer and more accepting to the child, symptomatology decreases further. Reduction of the physiological disturbance curbs the child's destructive cycle of interaction with others. Most psychophysiological approaches can be included under the rubric of shock therapy, psychosurgery, or psychoactive drugs.

The psychophysiological approach of shock therapy in child treatment was pioneered by Loretta Bender (1955). As early as 1940, she employed electroshock therapy with schizophrenic children. She theorized that shock stimulated maturing and patterning of undeveloped nervous systems. She claimed many gains and that 25 % of her treated children demonstrated higher long term adjustment than the nonshock control group. Nevertheless, a high percentage of her experimental group was schizophrenic on follow-up so that many believe her use of shock therapy to be unsupported and of questionnable ethical value. Today, electrical shock therapy is not used to treat schizophrenics, but is sometimes prescribed for depression and manic conditions. No authorities advocate its use in children, and experts disagree about its appropriatness for treating depression in adolescents (LeVine, 1985).

Psychosurgical approaches with children were initiated by Narabayashi (1972). Severing a part of the amygdala or posterior hypothalamus, Narabayashi (1972) reported calming effects on some uncontrollably aggressive children. No doubt the reader can quickly generate the sharp ethical issues psychosurgery has aroused. Can there be an appropriate reason for permanently severing nervous tissue in a child's brain? Moreover, how can the relative effectiveness of these approaches be assessed since it would be unethical to conduct sham surgery with control children?

Psychotropic medication is basic to treatment for a number of organically-based disorders such as epilepsy and some forms of hyperactivity. In treating many syndromes, psychiatrists who specialize in psychopharmacology have not developed a systematic theory about what medication and quantities to employ. In fact, the mechanisms by which many of the drugs affect children's behavior is little understood. If the medicine ameliorates symptoms, it may be that physiological imbalances are being corrected. So far as is known, psychotropic drugs ameliorate symptoms, just as aspirin relieves the pain of a toothache. The relief may be of value for its own sake, but the diseased tooth has not been corrected. Increasingly, the drug effects are providing clues about psychologic mechanisms involved in mental symptoms and behavioral disturbance (LeVine, 1985).

The psychophysiologically-oriented therapists offer several guidelines for employing psychopharmacological treatment with children. First, they point out the importance of teaching parents about the uses and limitations of the drugs. Thorough parent education helps to ensure that parents will administer the appropriate dosage to children. Parents have been known to alter dosages given to children because of their own needs. The dosage of a tranquilizer may be increased, for example, when a parent "is having a difficult day." Parents are also educated to watch for possible side effects associated with particular medications. In this way, the parents help the therapist decide upon the best type and dosage of medication (Chess & Hassibi, 1978). Psychotherapists who specialize in psychopharmacology explain to parents and others that the amount of medication must be carefully measured when treating the child. Children tend to vary more in sensitivity and reactions to the drugs than adults. Recommended dosages must be uniquely determined, beginning with small amounts and gradually increasing dosage until the desired effect is achieved. Feedback about the effect of the increasing dosages should be systematically sought from parents, teachers, and others closely involved with the child. Most specialists recommend that children be given "drug holidays." Every few months, preferably when the child is out of school and his or her quality performance need not be demanded, all medication should be terminated for several days. The drug holiday seems to help prevent the development of side effects and to assure whether or not the psychopharmacological treatment needs to be continued (Freedman, Kaplan, & Sadock, 1976).

Although nonmedical child therapists cannot prescribe psychotropic drugs, all child clinicians need familiarity with the types of drugs and their effects so that they can communciate intelligently with other professionals and clients' parents about the efficacy of psychopharmacological treatment with a given child. With some understanding of the possible uses and limitations of these drugs, the child practitioner or therapist can make wise decisions about when to refer a child to a physician for possible drug intervention.

Stimulants

The most frequently employed pharmacological agents in child therapy are stimulants. In 1937, Bradly identified the "paradoxical effect" of stimulants upon hyperactive children. He reported that the disruptive acting out of 50 % of his hyperactive patients decreased with stimulant therapy. Stimulants are the most widely used treatment for hyperactive children today. Between 500,000 to 600,000 children are estimated to take stimulants for an average of 3 to 5 years (Sprague, 1977).

The most commonly prescribed stimulants for hyperactive children are Ritalin (methylphenidate hydrochloride), Dexedrine (dextroamphetamine sulfate), and Cylert (pemoline). Ritalin is not recommended for children under age six. A beginning dosage is usually about 10 milligrams per day, and the medication may be increased to a maximum of 60 to 80 milligrams per day. Dexedrine should not be administered to children under age three; beginning dosage is about 5 milligrams, and it can be titrated up to 30 to 40 milligrams per day. Cylert dosages vary from about 37.5 to 150 milligrams. Ritalin and Dexedrine are fast-acting and fast-dissipating drugs and thus are given about three times daily. A slower acting drug, Cylert is administered one or two times daily (Barkley, 1977).

Between 73 to 75% of children are said to "respond" to these medications while only 39% "respond" to placebos, but what is meant by "respond" is a complex pheonomenon. Earlier, physicians believed that the good candidates for stimulant treatment could be identified through the results of electroencephalograms. Their success in identification has not been as efficient as desired. If the EEG reveals severe organic involvement, stimulant treatment holds a high probability of success. For most of the hyperactive children with slightly abnormal EEG's or normal EEG's, the basis for success or failure for organic treatment with stimulants has not been identified. Stimulant medication is attempted on a trial and error basis (Chess & Hassibi, 1978). Summarizing 120 studies of stimulant therapy on children, Barkley (1971, p. 418) concludes that the "stimulant therapy produces a reliable increase in on-task behavior (attention) in the classroom as well as a reduction in disruptive behavior, such as vocalization, noises, motor recklessness, and social integration." Barkley (1977) further adds that these psychotropics are equally effective as behavior modification programs, but that the two in conjunction are not particularly more effective than each one singly.

It was assumed that since the children on the medication were attending better in school, handing in more assignments, and cooperating, their academic performance was improving. Several investigators report salutary effects on IQ, especially on performance subtests (Conners & Rothschild, 1968; Knights & Hinton, 1969). However, in his broad review of the stimulant studies, Barkley (1971) reported that only 17 of the 120 empirical investigations assessed academic achievement, and the majority of these failed to note any improvement in academic performance regardless of type of drug or duration of treatment. Routh (1979, p. 185) concurs that "the behaviors correlated with learning disabilities can be influenced by treatment including drugs, behavior modification, and changes on environmental structure. What has not been demonstrated is any effect of such treatment on academic achievement." Barkley (1971) posits that limited academic effects may indicate that hyperactive children are more likely than nonhyperactive children to have related difficulties of lower IQ, lower socioeconomic status, and more neurological soft signs—all of which correlate with depressed school performance.

The stimulants are contraindicated for autistic and schizophrenic children. Possible side effects include weight loss, gastrointestinal disturbance, insomnia, and less commonly, headaches, drowsiness, sadness, tics, dizziness, and nail biting. There is new evidence emerging that these drugs may decrease socialization with the mother below typical levels (Barkley, 1977) and adversely effect growth in terms of height and weight (Safer, Allen, & Barr, 1972; Quinn & Rapoport, 1975). Cylert has a unique side effect of prompting nose picking by some children. Minor side effects should extinguish in about four weeks. If not, discontinuance of the medication is advised. Given the possible side effects and limitations of effectiveness, Barkley (1977) recommends that:

- Stimulants should not be used as a sole method of treating hyperactive children.

- Special attention should be paid to the learning problems of hyperactive children.

- Parents must be educated about the limitations and side effects of drug treatment.

- School therapists should monitor side effects and ascertain if learning as well as attention are improving.

Most experts consider drug holidays particularly appropriate for children on stimulants in order to monitor effectiveness and potential side effects (LeVine, 1985).

Major Tranquilizers or Neuroleptics

The use of neuroleptics with children is generally reserved for the most seriously impaired. Most recommend use of verbal and behavioral techniques before implementing these powerful medications (Freedman, Kaplan, & Sadock, 1976). Drugs may be used to combat aggressiveness, acute anxiety, hypermotility, excitability, insomnia, and stereotypical behavior, delusions, and hallucinations (Campbell & Small, 1978).

The reaction of children to the neuroleptics tends to be varied and must be carefully monitored. Two to 4 week trials are needed to establish efficacy (Chess & Hassibi, 1978). At this time, there is no consistent literature to support the use of one neuroleptic over another in treating childhood maladjustment. Chess and Hassibi (1978, p. 424) write that "neuroleptic selection is dependent upon clinical judgment and the degree of familiarity of the clinicians with the particular drug."

The most common side effects are drowsiness and lacissitude. These effects should disappear in a few days. If they remain, options are to reduce dosage, change to another neuroleptic, or discontinue usage of the neuroleptics. Among adults using phenothiazines, extrapyramidal side effects (twitching, shuffling gain, odd head and neck movements) sometimes occur. These effects are quite rare among child users of neuroleptics. Tardive dyskinesia (involving rhythmic muscular movements, with protrusions of the tongue, chewing movements of the chin, and contractions of the neck) has been noted to occur in a few children following sudden discontinuance of the drug. Whereas tardive dyskinesia may be irreversible among adult patients, it is not as refractory among children and tends to disappear spontaneously in 3 to 12 months. Nevertheless, the psychological risks from these effects are profound, and the risk of permanent tardive dyskinesia, though small, is not zero. Photosensitivity and weight gain are common side effects when employing neuroleptics with children, but these side effects appear relatively harmless and reversible (Chess & Hassibi, 1978, Knopf, 1979). Overall, neuroleptics should be regarded as serious drugs for serious conditions, and an assessment of relative benefit versus risk should be made before starting a child on any of these agents. Children taking them need careful observation for side effects, drug holidays, and regular reviews of need for continued treatment (LeVine, 1985).

Minor Tranquilizers

Control trials of minor tranquilizers with children show equivocal or minor gains, but these medications continue to be prescribed for a variety of anxiety states in children. The side effects of the minor tranquilizers with children are minimal, but apparently so are the gains. Experts do not agree about what if any are the indications for sedating children (LeVine, 1985). Nevertheless, some continue to prescribe tranquilizers to relieve school phobia, night terrors, anxiety attacks, eneuresis, encopresis, insomnia, muscular tension, tics, hypochondriasis, sexual preoccupation, and depression (Freedman, Kaplan, & Sadock, 1976). The tranquilizers most commonly prescribed for children are Benedryl (diphenhydramine), Librium (chlordiazepoxide), and Valium (diazepan). Although types of minor tranquilizers, they spur agitation and disorganized thought among children. It is critical that they not be used in place of direct intervention to reduce the child's anxiety (Knopf, 1979). Recent research indicates that the minor tranquilizers may be of greater use in muscle relaxant therapy than for reducing anxiety states (Chess & Hassibi, 1978).

Antidepressants

The last 5 years have brought an increasing interest about childhood depression. It appears this childhood state can be diagnosed as reliably as adult depression, referring to symptoms such as disturbance of sleep, appetite, energy, concentration, mood, and suicidal thoughts. Depression in childhood is as responsive to antidepressants as adult depression.

Tofranil (imipramine) has been used with success in the treatment of eneuresis. Some children have taken dosages of 50 to 75 milligrams per day for 6 to 8 years in order to control wetting, and few serious side effects have been reported. Bedwetting appears as responsive to this medical intervention as it is to treatments based upon behavioral procedures (such as, for example, the bell devices that ring when a child wets the bed pad during the night). Imipramine has been used to treat school phobia, and in these cases, the drug appears to be reducing depression associated with the school fear (LeVine, 1985).

Side effects of antidepressants are similar to those found in adults: sedation, dry mouth, blurred vision, constipation, and lightheadedness. Treatment with antidepressants is often monitored by blood tests to assure that an adequate amount of the drug is present. Research will need to demonstrate them of significant usefulness to counter their potential dangers (LeVine, 1985).

Ethical Issues in Drug Use

Over 600,000 children are taking psychotropics. For many, painful and socially disturbing behavior is curbed with the medication. In other cases, children are taking strong medications that have potentially very negative side effects without clear documentation of their physiological disorder and of the expected gain. Ladd (1973) has mentioned a number of potential dangers that should be considered in psychotropic treatment of children:

- There may be long-term physiological and psychological side effects.

- The practice may encourage positive attitudes among parents and children towards the use of pills as a means of solving problems.

- The children may begin to believe that their behavior is out of their own control. .

- Insisting that children take such drugs may infringe upon their rights, leading to adverse effects on their temperaments and towards society.

Psychotropic drugs have been recorded as critically useful in cases resistant to other treatments. The Office of Child Development extensively studied the use of psychotropics in the treatment of childhood disorders and concluded that drugs are very useful and preferred treatment for a number of specialized cases (Chess & Hassibi, 1978). The child practitioner should maintain an open consultative position with a child psychiatrist so that cases can be referred in which organic impairment seems likely and pharmacological intervention is a treatment of choice (for example, in cases of epilepsy). In addition, if the practitioner maintains a consultative relationship with medical personnel, difficult cases can be discussed and the advisability of psychotropic medication assessed cojointly.

MILIEU THERAPY

In the milieu approaches, the daily environment is ordered as a partial or complete psychotherapeutic program. The therapist refers a child to these programs when the child and/or family is too disturbed to be assisted by short-term outpatient interventions. Types include residential living centers, special education classes, and therapeutic summer camps.

Residential Treatment

One poignantly difficult decision that a child practitioner periodically faces is, "Should this child be institutionalized?" The child specialist may encounter this question when parents or teachers no longer feel able to cope with the child or when the specialist's interventions have created little noticeable impact. Unfortunately, the decision to institutionalize is usually based upon negative rather than positive reasons. The child is institutionalized because all else has failed.

Before the therapist and family decide to institutionalize the child, they should consider several factors. First, the child needs contact with nurturing parents. In residential treatment, adult figures will hopefully respond positively to the child, but they cannot provide the ongoing interaction of natural parents. If the child is separated from parents, feelings of loss and depression about separation from parents generally emerge, and these emotional problems must be dealt with as well as the previous emotional problems. It should also be kept in mind that in residential treatment, a child's interactions with peers is usually limited to his or her own age group. The child is separated from experiences of dealing with older and younger siblings. For this and other reasons, Freedman, Kaplan, and Sadock (1976, p. 1138) write, "Cure, whatever that may mean, is rarely an attainable goal for children in residential treatment." In one study, Lovaas, et al. (1973) reported that even among autistic children, those raised at home improved more than those raised in institutional settings.

Ideally, the residential center should include specific programs for the child that foster development in the cognitive, affective, personal, and social domains. Unfortunately, many centers are merely custodial while others offer no more than hospital maintenance and a regular visit to a therapist. Given the above limitations, are there any possible reasons for institutionalizing a child? The answer is a cautious "yes." If the family system is very pathological and the family members indicate an unwillingness or inability to change, it may be preferable to live away from the home (Chess & Hassibi, 1978). Even so, foster care placement which maintains the sense of a family unit may be preferable to institutionalization. If the family can afford a highly specialized program offering much individual attention such as Bettelheim's (1967) orthogenic school, residential treatment may facilitate a child's working through critical traumas and developing socially appropriate skills. Redl (1972) states that a good residential treatment center is characterized by:

- staff roles that are clearly delineated to the children

- daily routines that are a part of the therapeutic goals

- placing children in living groups so that their problems will not be exacerbated by one another, but instead so that they will be able to assist one another

- positive morale among staff

- lots of space and a variety of activities

As a whole, the child should be managed within the home as long as the family is able and willing to cooperate in treatment. Residential treatment is best viewed as a stopgap measure for breaking destructive family patterns. Once new adaptive patterns can be established, plans should be enacted to return the child to the home.

Summer Camps

Knopf (1979) recommends that therapeutic summer camps can offer a compromise in which a child lives in a structured therapeutic environment for part of the time while not being removed entirely from the family. The camps may be day treatment or residential. Ideally, they offer opportunity for the child to develop social, personal, and physical skills, thereby increasing their sense of independence. They may be beneficial in helping some children learn to get along with peers without added academic stress of the school setting.

Special Education Classes

It seems logical that children may profit from help in special education classes if their problems lead to difficulties in getting along with peers, learning disabilities, attentional problems, or academic lag. The difficulty is that we do not yet know which emotionally disturbed children are best served in what kinds of special education classrooms (Knopf, 1979). For example, there is a high correlation between hyperactivity and learning difficulties so that hyperactive children are often referred to special education classes with highly individualized instruction. However, it is not well documented that these children learn more in such environments. Apparently, they seem less different in individualized classrooms (probably because other children are a active in these open environments as hyperactive children). The academic accomplishments of hyperactive children are less than other children in both environments (Routh, 1979).

Before recommending a maladjusted child to be placed in a special education class, Knopf (1979) asks therapists to consider the following questions. Does the child feel a significant social stigma by being isolated from peers? Will the child's social development suffer because of a lack of healthy, adjusted peers to model? Is the special education classroom structured to allow gradual mainstreaming back into the traditional classroom so that the "hot house" effect, of a child losing gains once returned to the traditional setting, can be controlled? With the answers to these questions in mind, referral may be appropriate if the child's adjustment is so impaired that he or she is abused by or abuses peers or if the maladjustment is so significant that the child's ability to learn academic and social skills is largely blocked.

SUMMARY

In developing a treatment plan, a variety of information must be synthesized. The therapist will consider various facets of the child's development that have been gleaned through observation, formal interviews and informal assessment of the child and parents. The child's and parents' values and their goals for treatment must be clarified. Once the therapist has accumulated extensive background information, he or she selects therapeutic structures that offer most promise toward working through the child's dilemmas. A great variety of therapeutic structures are available: individual versus group therapy, play therapy, art therapy, etc.; and a number of specific techniques such as role playing, storytelling, art therapy, and music therapy are possible. The goals of therapy and the stage of the therapeutic process help the clinician select the appropriate technique. The child specialist considers the role of significant others in the child's dilemmas and brings them into the treatment plan for consultation, for group therapy, or for support to the child whenever appropriate. In many cases, the child can be assisted best by seeking consultation or services from other professionals. It is the therapist's ethical responsibility to know when to refer to physicians, special educators, and other professionals. Moreover, the therapist must know him- or herself well to be certain that all proposed treatment procedures are designed to meet the child's best interests, not for the practitioner's or significant others' convenience.

Although each child is unique, therapy tends to follow broad stages from acceptance and forming a therapeutic alliance, to uncovering and understanding a client's problem, to changing maladaptive patterns and practicing new behaviors, and finally termination. Varied therapeutic structures and techniques will be helpful as the therapy progresses through the stages. For example, supportive techniques such as nondirective play therapy may be particularly helpful in building a therapeutic alliance. Storytelling techniques can help uncover and restructure maladaptive thinking. Role playing, behavioral rehearsal, and group therapy can help move the client to new appropriate stages.

The varied structures and techniques that comprise the treatment plan are the strategies that seem most likely to promote working through personal problems with a given client. The strategies provide an environment for but do not themselves create change in the client. Playing with a child, telling stories, and drawing can model good relating, but do not assure that significant conflicts are worked through or that new adaptive behaviors are learned. The amelioration of significant distress requires the systematic application of theoretical principles of human behavior within the strategic therapy setting. The child therapist needs to implement specific verbal and behavioral approaches that are a part of his/her theory of child therapy. In the next chapter, we demonstrate through an extended case analysis, how various treatment strategies and a theoretical approach to child practice can be combined.

PART FOUR
Vulnerable Children

PART IV

VULNERABLE CHILDREN

At this point, you are well aware that our sensitivity in listening to our children and in selecting the appropriate intervention strategies depends upon a number of factors, such as the extent of our knowledge about counseling theories, one's comfort in applying particular approaches, and our expertise in identifying the problem and outlining treatment steps. In addition, our sensitivity and effectiveness is enhanced by our knowledge about particular types of childhood mental health needs. We are more likely to identify a mental health problem if we are fully cognizant of the broad spectrum of children's special concerns. Moreover, certain clinical approaches are particularly applicable to particular kinds of disturbance.

However, attempting to overview the various special concerns of children is a difficult task. Hundreds of attempts have been made to classify childhood disorders, and none have been completely adequate. What we have chosen to do in this unit of the text is to provide an overview of the types of psychosocial stresses that can leave a child vulnerable to maladjustment. Thus, Chapters 12 through 14 identify the special concerns of children that are largely perpetuated by the children's interface with disturbed or adequate familial and broader social environments. These chapters will be of prime importance to social workers and other child practitioners who serve as child advocates. The causes as well as effective modes of intervention in child abuse and neglect are described in Chapter 12. The emotional difficulties for parents and impediments for aligning services for special needs children are discussed in Chapter 13. Chapter 14 identifies situations where children have new families. Major topics include children of divorce, adopted children, and foster care. We will see that in many cases, the child's problems will abate dramatically if we could correct the familial and social disruption.

Throughout Part IV, we will attempt to apply principles presented earlier in the text. We suggest means for setting up treatment plans that are appropriate to the special needs of a given child.

CHAPTER 12

CHILD ABUSE AND NEGLECT

SCOPE OF PROBLEM

Numerous investigators have tried to estimate the magnitude of the problem of child abuse and neglect in the United States. Since the early 1960's, no less tha 20 studies have estimated the number of incidences of child abuse (Mayhall & Norgard, 1983). These estimates vary widely and are based upon different definitions of abuse, different designs to the studies, and varied sources of data. In addition, problems involved in trying to accurately estimate the magnitude of this social problem have to do with differences in the statutory definitions of abuse and neglect, in the ages of children covered by the laws, and in the types of cases.

The estimates range from 4 million physically abused children (Gil, 1970) to more than 14 of every 100 children in the United States (Straus, Gelles, & Steimetz, 1979). A survey by Gelles and Straus (1985) projects that at least 1 million children are abused each year. This is a decline of 705,000 children from 1975 estimates. Gelles and Straus state that in 1975, 3.6 % of all children between the ages of 3 to 17, living with both parents, were severely abused. In 1985, the percentage dropped to 1.9. The decline over the decade is attributed to couples marrying later, having fewer children, and to fewer unwanted pregnancies.

A unique epidemiological study was conducted by Nagi (1977). Using incidence rates for the state of Florida, Nagi extrapolated the reported cases of suspected abuse and neglect to cover the entire U.S. population. In arriving at a national incidence rate, Nagi computed three estimates--a low, medium, and high estimate. Nagi used 1970 census figures to compute his national incidence rates.

Nagi (1977) estimates the national frequency of child abuse from approximately 600,000 (low estimate) to 1,000,000 (medium estimate) to 1,400,000 (high estimate). In his analysis of the demographics of child abuse, Nagi (1977) reports that children under the age of 5 years are the most vulnerable (38.1 %) to abuse and neglect, while the sex of the child does not appear to be a significant variable. There is little difference in the incidence of abuse and neglect by the sex of the child. As for ethnicity, the highest incidence rates per 1,000 children are associated with Anglos, but the incidence rate for Blacks is close behind.

Nagi's statistics from Florida and corresponding population for the United States indicate that allegations in reported cases would place mothers as the most frequent abusers, followed by both parents and then fathers. A sizable proportion of stepfathers are also reported.

Nagi (1977) also compiled data concerning the type of abuse and neglect. Beatings (16.0 %) are the most common form of child abuse. Neglect falls into the major categories of disorganized family life (31.0 %), left unattended (21.6 %), medical neglect (16.0 %), and lack of food, clothing, or shelter (12.5 %). Sexual abuse (2.7 %) is perhaps the least discussed and researched form of child abuse. Little specific information is available about either the incidence of sexual abuse or about the sexual offender. Experts usually concede that the unreported incidence of sexual abuse among children is considerably higher than the reported incidence. An indepth study of 930 San Francisco women identified a history of child sexual abuse (including rape) in 38 % of the women before age 18 (Russell, 1983). A number of other studies establish that sexual abuse affects a sizable number of children (Finkelhor, 1984). Further, the usual victim in sexual abuse is a female child; however, the reported incidence of sexual abuse of male children is on the increase.

In addition, the statistics pale when confronted with a single abused, neglected, or sexually abused child (Chambers, 1980). Few children suffer more emotional and physical pain than abused children. Although there is public concern about this pain children suffer, almost all resources have been directed to treatment of parents (A. Cohen, 1979). A review of the literature on abuse reveals a large number of articles addressing family and parental therapy but far fewer on specific treatment for the child. An approach for children, Reattachment Therapy (LeVine & Frazier, 1983), is presented in this chapter.

DEFINITIONS

Definitions of abuse and neglect vary somewhat from state to state, but Chase's (1975) summary of what is usually meant by these terms can be a useful guide. According to Chase

> Child abuse is the deliberate and willful injury of
> a child by a caretaker--hitting, beating with a belt,
> cord, or other implement, slamming against the wall,
> burning with cigarettes, scalding with hot water,
> locking in a dungeon, hog-tying, torturing, even
> killing. It involves active, hostile, aggressive
> physical treatment. Child neglect is more passive
> negative treatment characterized by a parent or

> custodian's lack of care and interest, and includes
> not feeding, not clothing, not looking after, not
> nurturing. The legal definitions vary in different
> states; so does the degree of harm done to the child.
> (Chase, 1975, p. 1)

While this is a good definition of abuse and neglect, it does not encompass an explanation of sexual abuse. The identification of sexual abuse is relatively recent and few treatment approaches are empirically tested. Definition of sexual abuse includes behavior ranging from exhibitionism to forcible rape. For example, one researcher defined as a sexual attack the exposure of genitals by a male to a child. Another definition required some form of physical contact (Elwell, 1979).

To encompass all forms of abuse and exploitation within its mandate, the National Center on Child Abuse and Neglect adopted the following tentative definition of child sexual abuse:

> Contacts or interactions between a child and an
> adult when the child is being used for the sexual
> stimulation of that adult or another person.
> Sexual abuse may also be committed by a person
> under the age of 18 when that person is either
> significantly older than the victim or when the
> abuser is in a position of power or control over
> another child.
> (Child Sexual Abuse, 1981)

An area of sexual abuse which appears to be on the increase is the use of children in pornography (O'Brien, 1983). An amendment, Subsection 5(3), of the Child Abuse Prevention and Treatment Act of 1974 defines sexual abuse to include the obscene filming of children as follows:

> "the obscene or pornographic photographing, filming,
> or depiction of children for commercial purposes, or
> the rape, molestation, incest, prostitution, or
> other such forms of sexual exploitation of children
> under circumstances which indicate that the child's
> health or welfare is harmed or threatened thereby. . ."

CAUSES

Social and behavioral scientists have looked for the "cause" of child abuse so that it can be eradicated. We now recognize that the types and causes of child maltreatment are multiple. Eradication will require extensive societal changes and intervention in family patterns that are deeply entrenched in our society. "Spare the rod and spoil the child" is a maxim that appears to be practiced still in the United States despite our advanced knowledge about parenting and effective ways of modifying behavior through the use of positive reinforcement.

The authors' clinical experience with abusive families reveals that an older sibling may carry out the abuse of a younger child either through overt or subtle orders from the parent. These attacks are severe and may include attempted drownings, poisonings, and setting fire to clothing. Parents refuse to see these attacks as serious and may shrug them off (Tooley, 1977).

Generally, child maltreatment is spurred by a combination of parents' personalities, children's temperaments, and stresses (e.g., poverty), which overload the family system. There is little consensus about the characteristics of the abusing parent (Starr, 1979). Parents have been reported as disturbed, immature, narcissistic, egocentric, impulsive, or aggressive (Freedman, Kaplan, & Sadock, 1976). However, most abusive parents are not very different from average parents. They love their children and want the best for them. They also get angry at their children and do things they later regret. While child abuse cuts across nearly all social categories, it is especially likely to occur among young and uneducated parents, for their self-esteem is often low and their need for social support is usually high. In their immaturity, they expect too much from their babies. When the infant cries, they interpret the crying as deliberate misbehavior, intended to upset and anger the parents.

Many abusive parents were themselves victims of neglect or abuse as children. Parents without family and friends as resources who have poor interpersonal skills are ill-prepared to parent.

> When a parent is asked to describe the child in detail, a worker may find that the description focuses on how well the child meets the parent's needs. The child is perceived as a "good child " if he is capable of meeting these expectations and as a "bad child" if he does not. In asking for the parents' ideas of appropriate behavior for a child of a given age, one discovers that their perception has little relationship to normal child development. An abusive parent states, with approval, that a four-year-old little girl is good because she has helped to toilet train her two-year-old brother, clean up the living room every morning, and is always watching out for her two

> younger siblings, playing with them and showing concern for their
> safety. Of course she is also expected to take major responsibility
> for her own care.
> (Kempe & Kempe, 1976, p. 122)

When the child fails to successfully complete these parental tasks, the parent strikes out at the child, perhaps in a systematic form of torture. Child abuse is not usually premeditated, nor is it a rational act. Most abusive parents are sorry and display deep guilt after the abuse (Kempe, & Kempe, 1976).

The general public finds it inconsistent that such a loving parent can inflict so much pain on the child. Related health professionals see these parents as being extremely solicitious. Parental low self-esteem, a high need for nuturing, use of alcohol, and isolation are identified as common characteristics of abusive parents (Justice & Justice, 1976).

According to Anderson and Lauderdale (1982), approximately 10 % of the abusive parent population is considered psychotic or aggressively psychopathic. Those that are extremely abusive to newborns are especially prone to psychopathology. Resnick (1969) studied the personalities of parents who killed their infants within 24 hours of life. He reported that 3/4 were severely disturbed. They were often suicidal. They overvalued their children and believed that they killed them as "acts of mercy," or that they had been ordered by God to kill their children.

In some cases, one parent observes and tolerates the abuse by the other parent. In such cases, one wonders whether both parents are psychologically disturbed or whether the primary pathology leading to child abuse comes about only when both parents are together. A persistent trait that appears in a number of studies is that the parents are intolerant of the children they abuse. They spend less time in auditory and tactile stimulation of these children. They are frustrated with their hyperactivity or slow development. Along these lines, Wolkenstein (1977) worked extensively with parents who had a disproportionate fear of abusing their children. He reported that most wanted these children, but began feeling anger toward them even before their birth.

For more discussion of family dynamics, please refer to Chapters 7 and 10. We will now examine the physical, psychological, and developmental impacts child abuse may have on children.

IMPACTS

A backdrop to understanding the impact of abuse and neglect upon the individual child is evaluating the impact of abuse and neglect on societal institutions in a community. Of course, child abuse effects the family, but it also impacts on economics (through foster care payments, loss of work, etc.), health care, education, government agencies, and the media. Somehow child abuse touches everyone in a community.

Physical Impacts

Physical injuries to children range from subdural hematomas (bleeding in the skull), spinal fractures, burns, scalding, to more bizarre injuries. Less obvious injuries are now being identified and reported. Although bruises, welts, and lacerations may quickly heal, the trauma which produced them may permanently affect the central nervous system. Physical blows, shaking, neglect of infections, malnutrition, and water deprivation can cause brain damage or abnormal development. These may result in seizures, mental retardation, hearing and vision loss, cerebral palsy, and learning disabilities (Martin, 1980).

The mistreated child may suffer secondary physical problems because of poorer health care. When abused children are compared to children who have accidental trauma, Gregg and Elmer (1969) noted abused children are seven times more likely to have serious lapses in child care, such as lack of immunizations and proper hygiene. Studying infants in Australia, Oates, Davis, Ryan and Stewart (1978) reported that abused infants have a five times greater chance for significant illness than the control group.

The lack of proper nutrition, particularly with neglected children, may result in anemia. Neglected infants are given bottles with water, Kool-Aid, or juice, which contain low levels of iron. The resulting behavior is a shorter attention span, poor learning ability, and apathy (Martin, 1980). Hearing loss from lack of medical attention for ear infections, below average height, and poor weight gain are more common in abused children (Mayhall & Norgard, 1983). Recent research is documenting increasing links between abuse and subtle physical impairments.

Psychological Impacts

The psychological affects of maltreatment can be devastating. The clinical history of abused children shows failure to thrive, reduced height and weight, poor hygiene, irritability, and repressed personality (Freedman, Kaplan, & Sadock, 1976). The aggressive tendencies of abused children have been widely documented. Analytically-oriented therapists speak of the child's tendency to identify with the aggressor. The analytically-oriented therapists state that these children develop rudimentary superegos filled with violence. This violent superego formed through identification with the aggressor is redoubled by the child's frustration in not getting his or her own needs met. Since expression of the agression would prompt more battering, the child suppresses it and becomes strongly passive and masochistic. As the child matures, he or she is likely to express this rage with his or her own children, and thus the pattern of violence is passed through families (Bender, 1974). Behaviorally-oriented therapists also point to the child's identification with the abusing parent, but in this approach, the explanation is based on the modeling role of the parent. The parent models aggressive behavior, and even though the child is the target of the aggression, the child displays aggressive behavior against objects and other children. Years later, the formerly abused child becomes a parent who abuses his or her own children. Much research suggests that child abuse can lead to lifelong patterns of severe social maladjustment characterized by hostility, alcoholism, drug addiction, sexual difficulties, and inadequate parenting ability (Freedman, Kaplan, & Sadock, 1976).

While many abused children become very aggressive, others are withdrawn, reclusive, or obsequious to others. The child feels alone and must use all of his or her energy to survive day to day. Living a confused, violent life, he or she may retreat to a fetal position and withdraw totally from others. Or the child may become the perfect child always eager to please the teacher as a way of avoiding abuse. This low self-esteem correlates with a higher self-abusive behavior. Green (1978) found that 8.3 % of abused children with a mean age of 8.5 had attempted suicide. A total of 20 % of them demonstrated self-mutilative behavior.

Abused children's emotional development is likely to be delayed in several areas. Kinard (1980) established differences between abused and nonabused children on psychological tests measuring self-concept, aggression, socialization with peers, establishment of trust, and separation from the mother. The test battery included the Piers-Harris Children's Self-Concept Scale, the Rosenzweig Picture-Frustration Study, and the Tasks of Emotional Development (TED) Test.

To summarize, the psychological impact of abuse or neglect is a list of numerous traits and characteristics that stalk a child into adulthood. The child faces parents with unrealistic expectations who do not meet his or her of basic needs, and the child attempts to survive in an environment of fear. The family may be under tremendous economic, social, and psychological stress. In this environment, many children can do little more than survive day to day, leaving little energy or time for normal child development.

Developmental Impacts

Abused and neglected children may also suffer developmental delays in areas such as IQ, learning ability, and language development (Martin, 1980). Developmental delay and deviation have been consistently correlated with abuse, although the exact developmental impact varies from study to study (Mayhall & Norgard, 1983). Martin (1980) reviewed the studies investigating the impact of abuse on intelligence development. While he found a variation of degree of impact, he concluded that abused children have lower IQs, use poorer language, and show less academic progress than nonabused children.

One study of abused children suggests that neglected children have a higher risk of mental retardation, 39 %, than abused children, 24 % (Kent, 1976).

Research on developmental delay is complicated by compounding factors in experimental design as many of the children are receiving education and psychological intervention. Yet, even given clinical intervention, development of these children is delayed. An evaluation of children in three treatment programs reported abused children functioned poorly on motor, language, and cognitive skills (one standard deviation below the mean), but did not have serious delays (Cohen, 1979). The Evaluation of Child Abuse and Neglect Demonstration Projects (1977) states that over 50 % of abused children were behind (one of more standard deviations below the mean) on cognitive, language, and motor abilities. A number of research studies from around the world attest to the impaired cognition in abused and neglected children even as young as 5 months old (Martin, 1980).

Treatments can help children overcome delays to some degree. For example, one study (McKay, Sinisterra, McKay, Gomez, & Lloreda, 1978) suggests that cognitive delays can be overcome through intensive medical and nutritional treatment. Direct, specific therapies for individual children have provided some, but not complete, success according to Martin (1976).

In working with abused and neglected children, a good developmental assessment is necessary to alert the therapist to possible developmental delays. Treatment for these delays may necessitate medical, nutritional, educational, and social services.

TREATMENT OF ABUSE AND NEGLECT

The first and foremost step in treatment to ensure the child's physical and emotional safety is to stop the abuse in the family. A discussion of family interventions is presented in Chapter 7, so here we will address treatments for the child.

Establishing a Relationship

An abused child comes from an environment in which he or she feels isolated and untrusting of adults. This world view tends to create the impression during clinical assessment that the abused child is less capable than he or she really is. Thus, in establishing contact with the child, the practitioner needs to be sensitive to and learn to work around these presenting behaviors.

Martin (1976) identified seven behaviors displayed by abused children which may present difficulty in assessment and in establishing contact. These are as follows:

1. Hypervigilance
   The child may feel threatened by the intense scrutiny inherent in the assessment for therapy. A preoccupation with every move, facial expressions, or other habits of the therapist is common for an abused child until he or she feels comfortable interpreting the therapist's nonverbal behavior. The child is easily distracted by anything that is unfamiliar.

2. Fear of Failure
   The abused child's efforts to avoid failure are tested during any evaluation session. Assessment should begin with simple, easily achievable tasks which progress to more difficult tasks. The child may be overcome with anxiety. The fear of failure may have been imprinted so strongly by parents with unrealistic expectations that the child has failed to internalize any positive feelings about his or her successes. If the child is assured he or she will not suffer punishment for a mistake or for sharing thoughts, then a basis for a relationship can be established.

3. Difficulty Attending to Instructions
   When faced with an evaluation task, most abused children react in one of two extremes. The child may grab materials and become aggressive in an attempt to control his or her environment. The other extreme is the child who withdraws and shuts out instructions. The inability of the child to focus on the task makes following instructions almost impossible.

4. Touching Objects
   Abused children have overlearned the lesson to not touch in many cases. This may result in grabbing toys or test materials in order to possess them. The child may continually glance at the therapist while reaching for a toy trying to read any dissatisfaction or disapproval. Permission to touch at will is usually not permitted by abusive parents who have unrealistic expectations of the children.

5. Verbal Inhibition
   As we have explained, language development may be delayed in abused and neglected children. As a result, assessments which require verbal responses may require the therapist to prompt the child, and pictures are often helpful in eliciting meaningful answers from the child. The child's home environment may have taught him or her that it is dangerous to speak.

6. Failure to Scan

Many abused children impulsively select the first answer they come to, not realizing that a better solution may be found later. Instant direct feedback to a child's correct or incorrect responses may help the child to look for other alternatives.

7.   Passive-Aggressiveness and Resistance
Abused children will rarely confront an examiner by refusing to attempt a task. As the tasks become more difficult and the threat of failure increases, the responses may be weak and may be shrugged off. The child may say "yes" but then do "no." The child may do things he or she wants to do, such as play with a toy when he or she just said "yes" to completing a paper/pencil evaluation. This is clearly a coping mechanism developed at home to do as the child wishes with minimal threat of abuse by the parent. At this point, the practitioner may begin to feel the frustration the parent faces every day.

Martin (1976) suggests therapists convey new attitudes to the child such as:

1.   The therapist likes the child whether or not the child can do things.

2.   The therapist wants to help the child with the problems he or she faces.

3.   The therapist will not reject the child.

4.   The therapist will not be taken surprised by what the child says including detailed discussions of the abuses.

In order to convey these attitudes, the practitioner must possess a good self-understanding of his or her own feelings and abilities to work with abused children. We will now explore these issues.

Professional Self Issues

Martin raises the subject of the practitioner's values and personal abilities to work with abused children and the parents who abuse them. Mayhall and Norgard (1983) list a number of excellent questions the practitioner should honestly assess before working with these clients.

1.   Can I use authority appropriately in the treatment process?

2.   Do I have a strong support system in my personal life and long term relationships?

3.   Can I find a silver lining in every cloud? Am I optimistic?

4.   Can I be objective in assessing situations by identifying pluses and minuses?

5.   Can I handle myself in a crisis and in unfamiliar situations?

6.   Basically, do I think people are good and want what is best?

7.   Can I be accepting of different cultures, values, and child-rearing practices?

8.   Can I plan ahead and stay on a course for a year or more and be able to anticipate the results?

9.   Can I meet my personal needs away from the job so I do not depend on satisfaction from a child or his or her parents?

If the practitioner cannot answer yes to these question, then serious consideration should be given to not working with abused children. The population of abused children and their parents can be very different to work with and the reinforcements for the practitioner's efforts may be few and very delayed. The practitioner's frustration can foster more distress to this vulnerable population. As well-meaning as a therapist may be, if one's professional self is not suited to meeting the above criteria, then other client groups should be served.

Child's and Family's Resources

What strengths and competencies exist within a child and the family in overcoming the abuse cycle? With their developmental delays and possible physical and emotional problems, the strengths on which to focus may not be apparent. However, a very negative assessment may be a product of the therapist's reaction to a painful situation and may not be fully objective (Mayhall & Norgard, 1983). The parents' sincere statements of love and caring for their child should not be ignored. Rebuilding parental self-esteem can be facilitated by the understanding that the parent probably lacked love and nurturing parenting (Schneider, Hoffmeister, & Helfer, 1976). The practitioner may need to look for strengths from the child's personality, from the extended family, and from the community. Treatment goals are based upon an understanding of dysfunctions in the family, the child's maladjustment, and possible strengths.

Reattachment Therapy

We believe the primary unit for intervention for child abuse is the family; however, as cited above, the family has often been viewed as the only point of treatment. The victim, the child, not only may require emotional support and understanding but also assistance in learning coping behaviors. A review of abuse and neglect literature suggests that the child plays a larger role in abuse than previously believed (Friedrich & Borinskin, 1976). Special needs children may develop maladaptive interaction patterns with parents, such as being the scapegoat for family stress or creating strong feelings of guilt in the parents who are resentful or feel responsible for their exceptionalities.

We need to recognize that the children may not change just because their environment changes. Thus, the abused child who harbors much hostility and clings in a passive, aggressive fashion to a parent may continue to provoke hostile behavior from a parent who is attempting to curb an abusive pattern.

We should also keep in mind the tenets of family system theory that teach us that if any member of a family changes, changes in the overall system may occur. Thus, if an abused child changes and learns appropriate ways of assertiveness, he or she may modify the violence in the family. A practitioner may serve a vital role in helping abused children to modify their own behavior so that they do not provoke and instead avoid abuse.

A model, "Reattachment Therapy" (Frazier & LeVine, 1983), has been developed for ameliorating the developmental disturbances associated with early abuse in young victims, as well as enhancing the ability of the child to actively re-establish a more healthy bond with the primary caretaker. "Reattachment Therapy" is accomplished through the use of two overlapping phases of intervention. The first, Attachment Substitution, involves the systematic formation of a substitutive attachment bond between the child practitioner and child so that the youngster can experience relief from symptoms prompted by the lack of a consistent and benign attachment figure. The second, Parental Attactment Inducement, is geared toward aiding the child to comport him or herself in order to elicit attachment behavior from others, particularly the original caretaker.

In the attachment substitution phase, the practitioner employs the following steps:

1.   The therapist creates a benign, permissive, and warm atmosphere. Severely battered children rarely respond immediately to such social overtures. Their experiences have taught them that adults are frequently violent, punitive, and unpredictable. As such, they justifiably have little desire to readily entrust yet another strange adult with their affection. Thus, the establishment of an accepting, warm, and nonpunitive climate is essential to the facilitation of a substitutive attachment bond, and failure to create such an atmosphere jeopardizes further attempts to bring the victims into therapeutic relationships. Refusal to scold, punish, or conditionally accept the young child, especially during this initial phase of treatment, is a basic factor in eatablishing such a climate.

2.   The practitioner stimulates attachment bonding from the child by actively gratifying various development needs. The exact attaching behaviors to be elicited from the child depend, among other things, upon the child's given level of psychosocial development (Schaffer, & Emerson, 1964). From birth to 2 months of age, the child learns to be responsive to adults as opposed to

other objects in the environment. Then, the child begins to discriminate among adults, a skill which normally appears from 3 to 7 months of age. Next the child learns to approach the caretaker when wanting physical or psychological nurturance, and the selectivity of this major step is apparent in the appearance of separation or stranger anxiety about this time. Finally, by age 1 to 3, the child and caretaker enter into a goal-directed relationship in which they actively accommodate their behaviors to one another.

The unique parameters of Reattachment Therapy dictate that the ministrations of basic needs be used so that the child learns that the practitioner and other adults can be helpful in meeting the child's needs. Feedings, treating accidental cuts or scratches, occasionally facilitating sleep, and changing soiled clothes (with a same-sex aid available) are just a few of the ways in which the therapist can facilitate a reparative bond.

The second phase of Reattachment Therapy is a systematic changing of the abused child's behavior so that he or she is a more attractive child, more actively inducing affectionate responses from the primary caretaker. If the abused child is removed from the permanent care of the abusing parent, then the attachment inducement techniques to be described are aimed at teaching the child how to exhibit attaching behaviors toward the new caretakers. The guiding parameters for affecting attachment inducement are:

1. The therapist focuses upon improving the child's physical appearance. The typically unattractive or unusual appearance of the young abuse victim makes him or her a likely target for displaced aggression. Though there are inherent limitations in those dimensions of the child's physical appearance which can be affected in psychotherapy, treatment interventions can be focused toward improving those aspects of the victim's physical appearance which are susceptible to intervention, such as personal hygiene, bizarre body movements, or treatable physical anomalies. For example, one mother, Mrs. B., reported that she often became "disgusted" at her daughter's crossed eyes and stuttering, inaudible speech. The practitioner referred the child for appropriate speech and opthamological care, as well as reinforcing gains in these behaviors during treatment. As the child's speech and wandering eye improved, her mother commented that she was finding Linda much more "attractive and lovable." Additionally, during most sessions, the practitioner washed the child's face and combed her unkempt hair. Occasionally, her hair was even worked into various styles. Linda's mother seemed to have noted and appreciated these appearance improvements, for after several months of this, she began to bring her daughter to treatment clean, with new clothes.

2.   The practitioner reinforces aggression-neutralizing behaviors. Certain attachment eliciting behaviors, such as looking, smiling, laughing, cooing, and reaching tend ot neutralize aggression. Actively rewarded in treatment, these behaviors will serve to retard the overt discharge of the caretaker's violence. For example, Linda's eye contact was systematically reinforced and increased, and this behavior positively transferred to interactions with her mother. Mrs. B. mentioned that Linda didn't seem to be "hanging her head so much lately" at one point in treatment. Further, the child's mother reported that after spanking Linda on one occasion, she "looked into my daughter's eyes and just felt sick. . ." Thus, increased eye contact and other aggression-inhibiting behaviors can help to minimize future abusive episodes.

3.   The practitioner focuses upon decreasing clinging behavior. Clinging behaviors are characterized by desperately holding the caretaker, acting helpless, and crying and throwing fits when the caretaker leaves, even momentarily. To the extent that trust can be re-established during the substitutive phase of therapy, the clinging behavior will subside, since the roots of this difficulty lie with the desperate need for bonding (Harlow, 1958). Once the major task of establishing trust between the child and practitioner is accomplished, shaping of the child's behaviors toward psychological individuation (Mahler, Pine, & Bergman, 1975) from the attachment relationship can proceed. The practitioner encourages the child to attempt novel activities, and also points out and reinforces the youngster's autonomous behaviors with praise. For example, the therapist once commented to Linda, "Today I am sitting farther away from you, and you are doing just fine." On another occasion, the therapist pointed out that, "Today I had to leave the room for a moment and you were such a big girl and stayed by yourself--you knew I would be back!" Even attempting a novel puzzle was responded to with such individuation-oriented remarks such as, "Look how fast you have figured out that new puzzle—and you'd never even seen it before. It was new, and you weren't even afraid of it!"

The practitioner focuses upon eliminating behaviors in the child which frequently preceded the abusing parent's attacks. These behaviors are typically described by the abusing parents with such phrases as, "When he does that, I could just knock his head off;" or "It's almost as if her were just begging for it, so I gave it to him!"

For example, Linda's self-mutilation and refusal to go to sleep at night without an emotional outburst greatly provoked her mother, and the removal of these behaviors relieved this pressure, decreasing the probability of further abusive episodes. The removal of her stuttering verbal style had a similar effect. As another example, the child's mother described to her therapist that, "I always lose it when Linda wets her pants—she's just a big baby." Linda re-enacted these traumatic episodes in play therapy. When the therapist suggested that the baby doll had wet her pants, Linda began to yell, "Bad girl!" at the toy and hit it with the larger doll. At this point, the practitioner took the large doll from the child and began to "point out" to it that the baby doll had simply gone a very long time without being able to go to the toilet and that severe punishment is uncalled for. The child hesitated momentarily, then moved away from the toys. A few moments later, however, she walked over to the mother doll, picked it up, and said to it, "Mommy, it's OK if baby wets her pants, it's not so bad." Now Linda could view her own wetting in a realistic manner, and thus could openly talk about the topic, making appropriate toilet training more possible. Omission training, as well as nonpunitive ministration of the situation when "mistakes" occasionally occurred in therapy, gradually led to a decrease in the amount of times that the young girl urinated in her clothes, thereby decreasing the overall possibility of an attack being incurred by this situation.

4. The practitioner terminates when the child has become reattached to his or her caretaker and normal developmental processes have been restored. The final phase of attachment inducement involves the practitioner's gradually fading the intensity and frequency of contacts with the child, while encouraging the child to reestablish bonding with the original caretaker. This termination must be accomplished very gradually, so that trust and affectional bonds formed with the treating person are not disrupted prematurely, restimulating original feelings of rejection. The child needs time to talk about the upcoming separation and to work through emotions prompted by it.

In "Reattachment Therapy," as in any collateral treatment, the counseling of family members should be coordinated. For example, at one point in treatment of Linda's mother, her therapist noted that Linda was displaying signs of potential depression. The child was seen for daily therapy sessions until the crisis period had ended. The termination of treatment for Linda was planned, to some extent, to coincide with the resolution of Ms. B's own issues in treatment.

Play Therapy

It has often been said that play is children's work. Children use play as a natural method of expressing their feelings and problems; therefore, play may be a useful assessment and treatment modality. The practitioner may provide guidance and interpretation of play for the child, or the child may direct play in a nondirective approach. If abused children with low self-esteem are difficult to manage in therapy sessions, are depressed or aggressive, they may greatly benefit from instituting play therapy. Children who are frustrated by limitations imposed by special handicapping conditions can use play therapy to vent their feelings without danger to themselves or other children. As a caution, the behavior of a severely disturbed abused child may become very volatile in a totally unstructured play environment. Thus, the practitioner needs to balance the creation of a free and supportive environment with the structure required because of the child's temperament and problems.

SEXUAL ABUSE AND INCEST

Sexual abuse and incest are now considered separate from other forms of child abuse and neglect. The sexual abuse literature has matured from personal and case descriptions to theory development and research. Reports of sexual maltreatment have dramatically increased--from 1,975 in 1976 to 71,961 in 1983 (American Humane Association, 1985). Because of the societal taboo against adult/child sex and the limitations child victims have in exposing the crime, the number of incidences reported is probably a small percentage of the actual cases. Three major studies suggest that between 3 and 9 % of all men and between 12 and 28 % of all women have sexual contact with an adult before age 16 (Finkelhor, 1984). Much sexual abuse is perpetrated by close family members over a period of between 3 and 5 years (Sanford, 1980). Most victims are unable to tell anyone of the sexual abuse and may suffer substantial and-long lasting emotional scars (Finkelhor, 1984).

Affects of Sexual Abuse

The use of children for adult sexual stimulation, whether through child pornography, abuse, or incest damages the child in seven basic ways (O'Brien, 1983).

    1.   Psychological
The introduction of sexual activity too early in a person's development strips part of the childhood. Children are not prepared for strong emotional feelings associated with sex (Kempe & Helfer, 1980).

    2.   Low Self-esteem
Sexual abuse produces withdrawal from friends, depression, and is personally degrading and destructive. The child's attempts to gain self-respect are confused by the continued love/hate relationship with the parent.

    3.   Exploitation
By the very definition of sexual abuse, the child is being used by an adult to meet the adult's own needs. Some perpetrators may try to blame the child for their actions, but this should hold no more weight than blaming a child for any crime an adult may commit.

4. Creates Vulnerability
    Children are dependent upon adults, so children are vulnerable. The use of
    the child sexually creates more pressure, and anxiety, so that the child be-
    gins to interpret dependency as dangerous.

5. Distorted View of Sexuality
    Although some children do not realize it until they mature, sexual abuse
    creates an abnormal view of the sexual relationship. Victims of child
    pornography may relate to a later sexual relationship strictly in terms of
    sexual performance.

6. Violates Child's Privacy
    Pornography violates a child's privacy every time a magazine or film is
    viewed. If an incestuous relationship is discovered, the child's privacy must
    be invaded by police and child practitioners.

7. Distorts Moral Development
    As a child's knowledge of right and wrong develops during the time he or she
    may be a victim of sexual abuse (age 9-11), inappropriate moral development
    may occur. Many cases of incest occur in church-going, disciplined, rigid
    families (Sanford, 1980), creating a sense of hypocrisy and confusion among
    the victims about what constitutes morality.

Few persons fail to recognize that sexual use of children affects their normal,
healthy development. Children are not prepared to cope physically, emotionally, socially, or intellectually with an adult sexual relationship regardless of how the child may
feel about the experience.

Factors Affecting the Impact of Sexual Abuse

Several variables affect the intensity of the impact of sexual abuse upon children.
Boys who have been sexually abused usually have greater problems adjusting than
girls (Kempe & Helfer, 1980) as some theorists believe it is culturally more acceptable
for girls to have sexual experiences with adults than for boys (Mayhall & Norgard, 1983).
The longer the duration of the sexual abuse the greater likelihood for severe damage.
The age of the child at the time of discovery of the sexual abuse in part determines the
psychological effects. Kempe and Helfer (1980) argue that younger children do not understand the mores of society, and therefore, sexual abuse may create less problems
for a young child than for a sexually abused adolescent. Sexual abuse ranges from violent physical attacks upon the child to caressing and hugging. Thus, the amount of
force or violence used by the perpetrator may greatly affect the prognosis for the child.
The manner in which the perpetrator encouraged silence and cooperation may determine whether or not the child assimilates the experiences as highly destructive and

permanent. How professionals and significant others react to the situation once the sexual abuse is revealed greatly affects how the child will react.

The literature differs on the degree of psychological trauma suffered by the child, depending on whether the perpetrator is a significant other or a stranger (Mayhall & Norgard, 1983). There is agreement, however, that the closer the child and the perpetrator, the greater the chance of a continued incestuous relationship. Children may have a better chance of recovery if the perpetrator is a stranger rather than a family member (Finkelhor, 1979).

Causal Theories

Four major theses about the causes of sexual abuse have dominated the public literature (Finkelhor, 1984).

1. The popular public image is that the abuser is a sexual degenerate who must be punished for his or her crimes. Current research does not support this explanation.

2. The classical Freudian model postulates that the sexual abuser has suffered impairment in his or her sexual development during the Oedipal phase. Very little research substantiates this theoretical perspective.

3. Other theorists maintain that early learnings of sexual abusers reinforced their fixating on sexuality. They reach adulthood with no prohibitions against having sex, even with children. Some research from the social learning perspective supports this thesis.

4. A final viewpoint sees sexual abuse as part of a larger maladaptive lifestyle. The adult may be influenced by a number of problems including alcoholism, marital problems, sexual problems, and lack of close friends. The adult's sexual relationship with a child is promoted more as a need for closeness than sexual gratification. Social system and family theorists ascribe to this thesis of the cause of sexual abuse.

These four theses assume the child is in a biological family; however, national reports (Child Sexual Abuse, 1981) indicate biological parents are far less involved than step parents and other adults (such as boyfriends).

Research from a family and social psychological perspective is adding valuable information about etiological factors that contribute to sexual abuse (Cohen, 1983). A new live-in boyfriend or step family usually create strong sexual undertones in a family. Teenage children may not feel secure with the new adult and may use seductive behavior to ensure affection. Sexual acting out may occur because of the weakened incest taboo (Visher & Visher, 1979).

Generally, the family ambience contributes to the conditions under which incest or sexual abuse occurs (Justice & Justice, 1976). Often, the nonsexually abusing parent contributes to the pattern by ignoring it or remaining silent to signals of the abuse, being absent, subtly encouraging the abuse, or by not assuring the child's safety. A child may be at risk of sexual abuse in a family with a strained marital relationship in which divorce is not seen as an option. The father turns to the daughter for sexual gratification, many times with the willingness or complacency of the mother (Mayhall & Norgard, 1983). A family where one parent is often left alone with the child while the other parent is at work or pursuing a hobby may set up a situation for incest. Role reversal may take place where the mother tells a 12-year-old girl, "Be sure and take care of Daddy tonight." An overly protected child where the parent tries to isolate the child from other contacts within the family and community may indicate an incestuous parent fearing the child will tell or will take another partner.

A family with potential for sexual abuse may do everything together and have very little outside contact. The father is seen as all-knowing. The family can totally depend on him. Such symbiotic family ties, especially in conjunction with the factors discussed above, can create fertile ground for an incestuous relationship between the parent and child (Sanford, 1980).

Other theorists (Justice & Justice, 1976) suggest that high stress levels created by loss of work, death of a significant other, moving from one town to another, serious personal illness, or other stressors may rob the family of the energy to invest in meaningful relationships in the community. Therefore, the father or mother may turn to the son or daughter for affection and eventually, for sexual gratification.

Treatment

Much attention and research is being completed on the treatment of perpetrators, although we find little substantial research on the effect and treatment of the victims. Some research has suggested that it is not the sexual assault upon a child that creates the most profound trauma, but rather the other adults' and professionals' reactions that foster severe psychological distress. Conte (1984) refers to this phenomena as system-induced trauma. He states that medical, legal, mental health, and social work professionals are aware of the possibility of creating system-induced trauma. However, many children are subject to insensitive interviewing by professionals who do not understand the dynamics of sexual abuse. The physical examination, which may be necessary, may create additional trauma to the child. To further intensify the trauma, parents may create a crisis atmosphere (Elwell, 1979).

Often, the child is blamed for the abuse. Appropriate crisis intervention is necessary to work with victims of sexual abuse. As long as the sexual abuse is stopped immediately upon discovery, therapy can take place with less crisis orientation. The "normal" panic response of parents and professionals may be unwarranted, as the child may not see this as a crisis.

Hoorwitz (1983) points out several general steps to take in the treatment of victims of child abuse. The first step is to clarify the therapist's role with the other involved professionals, including the court so the therapist can present him- or herself accurately to the family. As in the treatment of child abuse, it is important to assure that the child is adequately protected. A choice of last resort should be removing the child from the family home. A preferred approach is to remove the perpetrator if necessary.

Research has shown that children rarely make up serious allegations of sexual abuse, and even if they do, some type of dysfunction exists within the family (Giarretto, 1976 and Finkelhor, 1984). However, the denial of the abuse is of utmost concern to most perpetrators and their spouses. The therapist needs to ensure that the question of the veracity of the allegations of sexual abuse does not dominate the communication to the point that the child's needs are not addressed. Often, it is helpful for the practitioner to emphasize that the child who claims sexual abuse is in serious distress and that family problems are evident. This distress must be addressed. The therapist needs to ensure that there is a commitment to treatment. Several hours with the child may be necessary to build a lasting and trusting relationship. O'Brien (1983) outlines important messages a victimized child needs to hear from the therapist.

1. It is all right to talk about the abuse with the therapist. The child may feel guilty for "turning in" the offender because he or she liked the adult or was told he or she would be severely harmed if "our little secret" was ever told. The therapist should try not to focus upon the actual acts which occurred but rather upon the child's feelings. The child may not view him- or herself as a victim and may be puzzled about questions on the subject.

2. The children must understand that the therapist believes him or her. Even though the child may not be able to give specific information such as dates, times, and other details, through the use of anatomically correct dolls and description, he or she may be able to give a very clear description of the sexual abuse.

3. The therapist must assure the child that he or she is safe with the therapist. Although the child may not have experienced fear during an incestuous relationship, discovery may create anxiety. Children need assurances that no matter what has happened in the past, they are now safe. The end of abuse through the efforts of the police or the therapist will begin to build trust in the

child. The child must feel that it is all right for him or her to feel. Children may suppress feelings of guilt, hurt, anger, and confusion. The opportunity to express these feelings honestly, in an atmosphere of trust, begins a sense of security.

4.   The child needs to be assured that under no circumstances is he or she responsible for the abuse. Children may or may not know that they have been abused, but regardless it is important that they understand the abuse was not their fault as a way of relieving present or future guilt feelings. An explanation of the adult's problem deflects blame from the child. An example is explaining to a child that sometimes adults don't have adult friends so they make friends with children. What they do to the children is unfair. The adult needs help so that he won't do this again to anyone else.

Many times children have a distorted view of why the sexual abuse took place, linking it with some minor misbehavior on their part. To address this concern, the therapist should let children know that bad things happen to everyone at some point in time. The example of Cinderella as cited by O'Brien (1983) is a story of how someone who lived a good life was mistreated by her stepmother. It wasn't Cinderella's fault that her stepmother treated her badly.

The therapist needs to be very empathic, to express deep concern about the abuse. The therapist may tell the child that he or she wishes this had not happened to the child. The therapist communicates that while he or she regrets what happened, it is important to continue to move on in one's life. The therapist, through words and behavior, emphasizes that the child can count on the therapist as long as the child needs help. Hoorwitz (1983) suggests eliciting a family member as an ally for the abused child.

During the therapy, a number of special topics need to be addressed. The child's feelings about the parents must be explored. Very often, the parent/child roles have been distorted as the child plays a surrogate spouse role. Clarification of role confusion may require extensive therapy. The child may feel a lack of support from the nonabusing parent, so very negative attitudes about each parent may surface. The issue of trust and the child's sense of well being are also subjects for treatment. After years of sexual abuse, the child may begin to blackmail the parents by extracting bribes and privileges. This distorted method of relating to adults must now be addressed and and corrected if present. Treatment of long term effects of sexual abuse includes understanding the child's sexuality and how comfortable the child is in his or her sexuality. Future sexual relations may produce anxiety, deep fears, and images of the sexual abuse, unless negative feelings about one's sexuality are discussed.

Adult victims of child sexual abuse report that they are confused about their sexuality and feel sexually stigmatized (Meiselman, 1978). Finkelhor (1984), in his study of possible effects of sexual abuse on sexual feelings and behavior, found a statistically significant difference between victimized women and nonvictimized women in his sample of university students. Victimized women stated they felt awkward in sexual situations. Men who were sexually abused as children stated they were very dissatisfied after sexual experiences. Some research about the long term effect of child sexual abuse indicates that the victim is likely to become involved in homosexual activity. The premise is that boys who are molested by men will become homosexual. Women who were sexually abused by men will turn to women for sex because sex with men brings back terrible images (Finkelhor, 1984). Finkelhor did find a connection between childhood sexual abuse and adult homosexual behavior for boys. However, he did not establish this relationship for girls. Boys who were sexually used by older men are four times more likely to be homosexually active as adults than nonvictims.

The clinical treatment of sexual abuse victims only recently developed a theoretical and research base to guide practice. Child practitioners can help children deal with emotional trauma of discovery and prosecution by developing an attitude in the children that they are believed and now safe. Individual child therapy should be conducted in conjunction with family therapy that addresses the immediate family and sometimes the extended family and the factors that may have led to a high risk situation. The institutional approach to treatment of the perpetrator is a heterogeneity of therapy and criminal prosecution which makes it difficult to integrate child and family treatment. The number of children reported as sexually abused will likely climb as the general population becomes aware of the problem. Determination of appropriate treatment for the perpetrator, victim, and family is critical.

SUMMARY

The first and foremost aim of treatment is to stop the abuse within the family. So far, the most success has been achieved by group therapy for parents combined with social case management in which parents are taught new ways to handle family stress. The most successful groups seem to be the self-help groups sponsored by Parents Anonymous. Many communities have established telephone hotlines for parents to call when they find themselves losing control as well and around-the-clock crisis nurseries where parents in need of a few hours' peace can drop off their children. Experts agree that most child abuse and neglect can be prevented:

- If parents can reach out for the help they need to cope with the stresses in their lives.

- If professionals and agencies that provide services to families can be attentive to families who are having particular difficulties in the demanding task of raising their children.

- If communities can support preventive programs to help families in stress, such a Parents Anonymous, family stress centers, parental stress hotlines, and crisis nurseries.

A combination of volunteer groups, hotlines, crisis nurseries, and social case management has led to some alleviation of this problem. Unfortunately, we still have no good base rate of remission to compare with these treatment gains. Evaluation of treatment modalities is as difficult as determining the many causes of abuse. Studies that report high success rates often have biased subject selection processes. None of the studies thus far has been conclusive. Many of the findings appear contradictory (Mayhall & Norgard, 1983).

Prevention of child abuse has taken several directions. Broad educational programs are helpful in making parents cognizant of their violence to their children and of places where they may receive help. Some screening instruments attempt to identify the potential for violence in parents, but these tests produce many false positives (that is, they do identify a large percentage of the potentially abusive parents, but they also include a significant number of parents who are not violent). Even if the tests were more reliable, it would be nearly impossible to force the potentially abusing parents into treatment (Starr, 1979). Some social scientists believe that we need to eradicate all types of corporal punishment. As long as corporal punishment is accepted in the school, many parents will continue to believe it is all right to beat their children (Starr, 1979). Prevention of child maltreatment rests on major social reforms. Only to the extent that we are able to alleviate the causes of child abuse, e.g., poverty, inadequate parenting behavior, mental illness of a parent, etc. will this significant social problem decrease. Until we reach this ideal goal, child practitioners must work closely and intimately with both perpetrators and victims of abuse so that the cycle can be interrupted as swiftly as possible, and healthy family functioning can be restored.

CHAPTER 13

SPECIAL NEEDS CHILDREN

In this chapter, we will review the emotional development of "special needs children," those with limiting conditions imposed by their biology and/or social experiences. We will discuss the stresses and needs of retarded children, those who are gifted, those with physical illness, and those who are deaf. Many of the physical problems are especially precipitated by conditions associated with being poor, such as malnutrition, poor housing, and limited prenatal care. Because of these predisposing conditions and the unusual stresses of being raised in a low socioeconomic environment, these are also considered special needs children. Although more types of special needs children could be discussed, we have limited our review to those conditions that are most frequently manifested. We hope the reader will find that many of the ideas presented are applicable to other special needs children.

MENTALLY RETARDED CHILDREN

The term mental retardation has been employed to describe a wide range of intellectual abilities ranging from minor deviations from the norm in tested IQ to limited functional ability that requires the individual to be totally dependent on others for basic care. Within the past decade, the term developmentally disabled has increased in usage to describe persons who are mentally retarded, autistic, brain or central nervous system damaged, such as those who are epileptic or cerebral palsied, or who have a learning disorder such as dyslexia. Although a number of treatment modalities described below apply to developmentally disabled children, our discussion in this section will focus on mentally retarded persons.

Definition

The prevalence of mental retardation has been estimated as ranging from 3 % (American Psychiatric Association, 1980) to 20 % of prepubertal children (Robinson & Robinson, 1970). Rapid industrialization may be catalyzing a higher reported incidence as people with borderline IQ scores and adaptive skills find it increasingly difficult to cope with the demands of a technological society such as that in the United States.

Historically, mental retardation was considered a unitary deficiency in some genetic component of intelligence, and it was assessed by the unitary score of an intelligence test. In 1959, the American Association of Mental Deficiency (Heber, 1959) laid down the more expansive criteria used today. The criteria place less stress on the IQ score per se and more emphasis on functional skills. Mental retardation is diagnosed if three factors are present:

1.   Significant subaverage intellectual functioning as measured by a score on an individually-administered IQ test resulting in a score of 70 or below.

2.   Concurrent deficits in adaptive functioning.

3.   The developmental period is between ages 1 and 19 (Grossman, 1977).

As clear as this definition sounds, determination of mental retardation in practice is often complex. It is often difficult to ascertain if the measure of IQ represents the subject's maximum performance (or if instead performance was limited by experience and adjustment). Similarly, it can be difficult to assess the subject's competency especially if she or he has been abused, neglected, or is experiencing concomitant emotional problems. Below, we review some of the complications in assessing the three factors associated with retardation. An indepth discussion of measurement is found in Chapter 9.

IQ Assessment

Dickerson (1981) lists three psychometric instruments that are most frequently used when assessing IQ.

1.   Cattel Infant Intelligence Scale (1940): This test is used primarily with children between the ages of 3 months and 30 months of age. It assesses imitative behavior, motor skills, language, and perceptual development.

2.   Stanford-Binet Intelligence Scale: This test of IQ can be used with children of 2 years through adulthood. The global assessment of IQ is assessed through subtests requiring verbal and psychomotor reactions.

3.   Wechseler Intelligence Scale for Children Revised (Weschler, 1974): this test is designed for children between the ages of 5 and 15 years of age. In addition to the global assessment of IQ, discrete analysis of verbal and perform-ance (psychomotor skills) is provided.

Although the standardized tests are helpful to the practitioner to determine general intellectual functioning, without an assessment of cultural and social skills and adaptive behaviors, dangerous conclusions may be drawn, as in the case of Jose below. Case 13.1 is drawn from actual case material brought to the attention of the second author of this text.

Case 13.1. The Case of Jose

Jose, a Yaquis Indian, lived on a reservation in rural southern Arizona until age 9. In the 1950's, he was brought to an institution for the mentally retarded. Speaking in Spanish (a second language for Yaquis), Jose's mother explained that he "was difficult to care for." The staff administered the Stanford-Binet test in English, Jose's third language. Jose scored 57 on the verbal scale and 71 on the performance scale. The state of Arizona considered scores below 80 IQ officially within the range of mental retardation, so Jose was institutionalized. When Jose was 13 years old, he tore some ligaments in his knee while working on the institution's ranch. A doctor in the nearby town of 2000 operated on the knee and, unfortunately, permanently damaged the ligaments. Jose, who grew to 6'3" and 235 pounds, could not do physical labor from then on.

In the early 1970's, at age 22, Jose was moved to a new community residential facility in Tuscon. Every new resident received a totally new assessment, including adaptive behavior and IQ tests. Jose was retested (for the first time since age 9) with the Stanford-Binet, this time in Spanish, his second language. He scored 91 on the verbal and 82 on performance. Because of the years of sheltered living with few expectations or assistance in developing social skills, Jose's adaptive tests showed he needed to live in a highly supervised group situation.

The state of Arizona was faced with the problem of institutionalizing a young adult who was, according to the standardized IQ testing, not retarded; yet, after a life of institutionalization, could not function outside of a residential setting. Some staff spoke of a law suit against the first hospital for institutionalizing Jose as retarded.

The next week, Jose hit his girlfriend in the face several times. Quickly and quietly, he was transferred to the state hospital with the diagnosis of mental illness.

Assessment of Adaptive Functioning

Because mental retardation describes a functional status and adaptive behavior of an individual child, a person may meet the criteria of retardation at one point in his or her life and not at another (Mandelbaum, 1977). In 1973, the American Association on Mental Deficiency continued to refine the definition of mental retardation as, "Mental retardation refers to significantly subaverage, general intellectual functioning existing concurrently with defects in adaptive behaviors and manifested in the developmental period" (p. 56). Subaverage general intellectual functioning means the child's score on an IQ test is 2 or more standard deviations below those of other children of the same age. The term, adaptive behaviors, refers to age-appropriate behaviors necessary to function in a family and as a social being within the community. It also incorporates an assessment of the sensory motor skills, communication skills, and developing vocational skills (Grossman, 1977).

The measurement of adaptive behavior is difficult and often subjective. The 1974 revision of the adaptive behavior scale published by the American Association of Mental Deficiency (Nihira, Foster, Shellhaas, & Leland, 1974) is most frequently employed. Based upon interviews with persons knowing the child well, the adaptive behavior scale (Nihira, et al., 1974) attempts to quantify behavioral development in 10 domains (independent functioning, economic activity, memory of time, domestic activity, responsibility, and socialization) as well as tabulating maladaptive behaviors and use of medication. Unfortunately, the adaptive behavior scale was normed only to the institutionalized retarded children and thus is not adequate for assessing the behavior of the retarded children who live at home.

The Vineland Social Maturity Scale (Doll, 1965) assesses infant or young children's motor, cognitive, and social skills. The scale assesses the ability of an older child to function autonomously regardless of her or his physical handicaps, language usage, verbal comprehension, or use of social skills. The skill level of the person interviewing the suspected retarded child has been shown to affect results of adaptive skill assessment. Thus, questions of the appropriateness of the test instrument, relationship of scores of varied instruments, skill of the assessor, developmental changes over time, and compounding psychological and social factors make it difficult to reliably assess adaptive behavior.

Development During Childhood

The third criterion for classification of the mentally retarded is that this functioning be manifested in childhood. If a low IQ score and minimal adaptive behavior is not apparent until adulthood, the symptoms are labeled an organic brain syndrome.

Classifications

Based upon the assessments mentioned above, retarded children's abilities are usually classified as follows:

Mild. Commonly referred to as educable, mild retardation represents the IQ range between 51 and 70. This child can grow to be fairly independent and maintain a job.

Moderate. Commonly referred to as trainable, this group represents an IQ between 36 and 51. Through specific training, these children can live in group homes or live semiindependent lifestyles. They experience delayed development.

Severe. These children will fall into an IQ range of between 20 and 35 with delays in speech and motor skills and will require a supervised, protective workshop environment. These children may acquire some self-care skills and minimal independent behaviors.

Profound. These children have an IQ of less than 20 and are totally dependent upon others throughout their lives. They are highly impaired in sensory and motor skills and have no language skills.

The profound category represents approximately 1.5 % of the MR population. The severe category represents approximately 3.5 % of the total MR population. The moderate range includes 6 % of the retarded. The largest percentage, 89 %, of retarded persons are classified in the mild range (Dickerson, 1981).

Etiology

The view of the etiology of mental retardation employed in hospitals, clinics, and other medically-oriented facilities identify the various causes of retardation (Grossman, 1977) as associated with:

1. infection
2. disease or intoxication
3. trauma or physical agent
4. disorders of metabolism
5. new growth
6. prenatal conditions
7. unknown disease but with structural reaction manifested
8. unknown disease with functional reaction manifested

The etioligy of mental retardation is complex. Some symptoms of retardation arise from dissimilar causes, while other similar causes have disparate effects. Thus, rubella in a pregnant mother, especially in the first trimester of pregnancy, may result in retardation and deafness in some infants, only deafness in others, and no ill effects in a few (Robinson & Robinson, 1970).

Infection from such diseases as rubella in or syphillis may cause retardation by attacking the central nervous system. Drugs, including alcohol and prescribed medication may seriously damage the fetus, causing retardation. A type of mental retardation receiving increasing attention is the fetal alcohol syndrome (FAS), a pattern of physical malformation observed in offspring of women who drink alcohol during pregnancy. Current estimates show that 1 to 2 children per 1,000 are born with FAS. Both prospective and retrospective studies indicate that children born to alcohol-treated mothers perform poorly on tests of cognitive ability. Since alcohol consumption is increasing among women, FAS is expected to increase also (Abel, 1980).

Meningitis and whooping cough may also cause damage to the central nervous system. Metabolic defects (Phenylketonuria, Cretinism, Galactosemia) may now be detected through diagnostic surveys while the child is in utero. Phenylketonuria (PKU) is a metabolic disorder transmitted by a recessive gene. This creates an excessive amount of phenylpyruvic acid in the urine. Approximately 1 of every 10,000 live births results in a PKU disorder (Dickerson, 1981). With detection within the first 2 years of life, PKU can be treated with dietary supplements which may prevent excessive cerebral damage.

A common type of retardation associated with new growth is hypothyroidism (cretinism), which is caused by insufficient secretion of the thyroid hormone. The physical development may be arrested creating mental retardation. A child suffering from cretinism may have unusual physical characteristics which are obvious such as a large head, round face, no forehead, flat broad nose, thick protruding tongue, short neck, or eyes set far apart (Dickerson, 1981).

Maternal malnutrition, particularly during the first trimester, may result in fewer brain cells developing in the fetus. This may produce mild retardation in the newborn child. Other abnormalities may be prompted by the carbohydrates or proteins consumed by the mother during pregnancy.

Blood type incapability may result from a mother with a RH negative blood carrying a baby with RH positive blood. During the term of the pregnancy, the mother's body will produce anti-RH antibodies destroying many of the baby's red blood cells by releasing bilirubin into the baby's blood stream. Excessive amounts of bilirubin may cause damage to the brain of the fetus. This condition can now be easily diagnosed and treated with blood transfusions upon birth (Mandelbaum, 1977).

Chromosomal abnormalities are the cause of approximately 10 % of the retardation of children who reside in institutions for the retarded (Mandelbaum, 1977). Down's syndrome (trisomy 21) is the most pervasive type of mental retardation resulting from a chromosomal aberration. The probability of its occurrence increases dramatically with the mother's age so that among expectant mothers 45 and older, the probability is 1 in 65 live births (Mikkelsen & Stene, 1970). Other trisomies of the autosomes usually lead to death of the fetus. An abnormal arrangement of the chromosomes that transmit sexual characteristics creates Klinefelter's syndrome (an extra sex chromosome, XXY, arrangement in males) affecting 1 in 450 births. Turner's syndrome, a chromosomial abnormality marked by a single X chromosome arrangement in females is recognized by the short stature, short neck, low set ears, broad nose, and mild retardation. Both Klinefelter's and Turner's syndromes cause very serious developmental delays and profound retardation. Because of the serious developmental problems associated with these syndromes, many of these children die before or at birth or at a young age. (Alexander, Ehrhart, & Money, 1966).

Microcephalus and hydrocephalus are caused by the premature closure of sutures in the skull. Microcephalus is characterized by a small head, while hydrocephalus is characterized by a very large head created by an accumulation of fluid within the brain. Since hydrocephalus develops in infancy when the skull is soft, the head may become extremely large. Hydrocephalic children may be very quiet and passive in their behavior with blindness, deafness, and seizures commonly present.

Severe injuries to the head caused by accidents or child abuse may also, as mentioned earlier, cause damage to the central nervous system resulting in retardation. Low birth weight, prematurity, and lack of oxygen during birth increase the probability of retardation of the infant.

The majority of mentally retarded children in the United States is found in the lowest socioeconomic groups (Mandelbaum, 1977). Epidemiological findings from a number of studies demonstrate high correlation between mental retardation, particularly in its milder forms, and low social, economic, and cultural status of the retarded (Mandelbaum, 1977). Factors such as the lack of proper prenatal care, mothers' and fetus' malnutrition, and a variety of correlates of premature birth (such as alcohol and drug use) that are more common among low socioeconomic status parents create many risk factors for children to be born mentally retarded (Leland & Smith, 1974). As a general rule, mild retardation is more likely to be fostered by environmental deprivation, while more serious retardation is generally genetic or organic in nature (Erickson, 1978).

Psychology disorders are sometimes associated with mental retardation. The emotional disturbance may have a damaging effect upon a child's intelligence. Psychological features such as tantrums, stereotypical movement, or aggressiveness may be caused by the same organic factors responsible for retardation. Or the psychological factors may be a result of frustration in trying to cope with and adapt to a world created for people with more sophisiticated conceptual ability. The retarded are particularly vulnerable to social stress because of deficiencies in judgment and because they learn to anticipate frustration and failure.

A study of 133 children classified as educable and trainable mentally retarded indicated that these children were significantly more likely than matched control children who were not retarded to express a number of fears. Most of the fear shown by the retarded children is realistic, learned, and relates to their difficulties coping with environmental stresses (Derevensky, 1979). They are more dependent on their families and thus disturbance in the families affects them greatly. In addition, those children with problems in impulse control often find themselves in difficulty with their parents or other caretakers. Discrepancy of developmental growth rates may be greater for the retarded than the nonretarded, leading to asymmetry of motivation and increased pressures by self and others (Robinson & Robinson, 1970). Retarded children may be inappropriately subject to demands that while appropriate for their age are inappropriate for their developmental stage of development. The inappropriate demands may create frustration and tension. Chess & Hassibi (1970) report that children with limited intellectual abilities may become anxious, restless, and engage in repetitive aimless activity when confronted with social or academic tests that they are unable to complete. It is not surprising that the possibility of a psychiatric disorder is 3 to 4 times greater among the retarded than the rest of the population (American Psychiatric Association, 1980).

Over half the children diagnosed as psychotic have tested IQ's that are well below the average score of 100. The cause and effect is not always clear. Generally, the thinking disorder seen in psychotic children creates the functional retardation. The child may demonstrate a failure to learn caused by severe anxiety. This anxiety may be provoked through childhood trauma, including the death of a parent, severe child abuse, or other early experiences. These early traumas make it difficult for the child to discriminate between internal and external signals. The lack of differentiation of self, others, and the external world may make these disturbed children function as retarded (Mengeot, 1982). If the thinking disorder is primary, the retardation may clear when the psychotic disorder is ameliorated (Robinson & Robinson, 1970). Upon early assessment, this child may be identified as an irreversible mental retardate. However, through psychiatric treatment, the retardation may be remediated to some degree. However, normal intellectual functioning is seldom restored if emotional problems are present through much of the early childhood (Mandelbaum, 1977).

Therapy with Mentally Retarded Children

Much of the clinical work with the retarded has focused on the parents and family interaction with the retarded child. Family treatment has helped parents understand and accept their children's limited behavior through education and therapy. Also, the use of groups for socialization skill building and basic living skills has helped ease the frustration many mildly retarded children feel (Proctor, 1983; Laterza, 1983; and McBroom, 1976). Our discussion will examine treatment suggestions for practitioners working with an individual emotionally disturbed retarded child.

Until the 1950's, mental retardation was seldom treated with psychotherapy. It was felt that intervention with retardates was not possible since these children lacked the motivation and verbal ability necessary for psychological change. Today, we recognize that the retarded feel personal pain as much as those that are not retarded. We know that many of the psychological problems are an emotional overlay of their frustration and can be eased with therapy.

Newcomer and Morrison (1974) reported a study in which mild to moderately retarded children were treated in individual and group play therapy. Both play therapy treatments resulted in adaptive gains as measured by a developmental screening test in comparison to nontreated controls. Morrison and Newcomer (1975) then demonstrated that the retarded children improved equally with nondirected and directed play therapy. Erickson (1978) concludes that although few studies have measured the effectiveness of play therapy with the mentally retarded, the results are no less encouraging than those studies of therapy with nonretarded children.

Several factors should be considered when conducting therapy with retarded children. First, they are subject to the same laws of behavior as other children. Behavior modification works, as does nondirective counseling. Extinction of inappropriate behavior is likely to take longer with retarded than nonretarded children (Robinson & Robinson, 1970). In the past, the mentally retarded have been viewed as fundamentally different with odd ideas and perceptions of reality. Today, therapists see them as developmentally delayed. The essential issue is to plan therapy according to the child's developmental level (Luria, 1963). Many mentally retarded children have difficulty concentrating. Their distractability may be related to their inability to filter external stimulation or to internal causes. Thus, they do not necessarily need to be worked with in an environment devoid of stimulation. They will, however, probably require extra effort and patience since their attention is limited, and they have difficulty in transferring learning from one environment to another (Robinson & Robinson, 1970).

A powerful therapeutic approach with the retarded child is modeling. A therapist can model behaviors which provide a retarded child clear, concrete examples of how to influence the environment. The use of role playing in difficult situations allows the MR child to assimilate the new knowledge (Proctor, 1983).

Medications of various sorts are often used in the treatment of retarded youngsters. Medication is helpful for controlling seizures and impulsive behavior among some retarded. However, the danger of overmedication should not be overlooked. Lipman (1970) surveyed 100 institutions for the mentally retarded and demonstrated many cases of overmedication. Approximately 37 % of the children were taking large doses of tranquilizers--probably to ease the work of the staff, not to aid the children. Modification of diet may also be helpful in some cases. As in children with phenylketonuria, a diet free of phenylalanine, although not reversing the retardation, does lead to a cessation of brain damage and to a reduction of behavioral problems. It is usually advisable for a therapist to consult with a physician prior to treating a mentally retarded child. In this way, the therapist can know something about the medication that the child is taking and what its behavioral effects should be as well as determining whether the child should or should not be on medication.

GIFTED CHILDREN

In 1972, U.S. Commissioner of Education, Sidney Marland wrote in a report submitted to the citizens of the United States that gifted children were a little acknowledged minority group and a relatively untapped natural resource. Discriminating the concept of giftedness from high I.Q. and superior academic performance, Marland (1972) identified various types of gifted children as those displaying one or more of the following: general intellectual ability, special academic aptitude, creative thinking, leadership ability, ability in the visual and performing arts, and psychomotor ability. The focus upon the special talents of gifted children has been followed by some statutory recognition of their special needs under Public Law 94-142 which mandates education for all handicapped children. At least 27 states (Karnes & Collins, 1978) now hold statutory provisions for education of children who are exceptional "by virtue of giftedness."

Nevertheless, identification of types of giftedness remains imprecise. Feldman (1979, p. 662) writes, "Giftedness is as varied as the fields in which humans produce excellence." Although it is relatively well established that a high I.Q. and/or superior academic performance do not assure giftedness, it is not clear whether a certain level of intellectual aptitude is a prerequisite for giftedness. Some operational definitions have been offered to discriminate the types of giftedness identified in the 1972 U.S. Commissioner report, but still unknown is the degree to which the varied types of giftedness draw upon similar cognitive abilities. New educational procedures for teaching the gifted are being explored but many are embryonic and others lack empirical documentation (Guilford, 1975). A yet uninvestigated area is the personal needs of gifted children. Do gifted children have special attitudes, personality traits, and emotional problems associated with their special talents?

Psychological Adjustment

The psychological adjustment of the gifted is surrounded by folklore. The idiom "genius is next to insanity" is highly accepted by the general populace. Terman's (Terman & Oden, 1959) classic study was instrumental in dispelling this myth among social scientists. Following the development of a group of gifted children over 30 years, Terman reported that as children this group tended to be taller, heavier, healthier, and to reach sexual maturity before other children. They did better in school and were advanced in reading, arithmetic, and other academic indices. As adults, Terman and his students reported that the gifted were more successful and adjusted than the general population. They were also much more likely than the general population to rate their life as "deeply satisfying."

Nevertheless, we need to recognize that gifted children are not a homogeneous group. Although the development of some gifted children is relatively uneventful, others do experience personal and social stresses because of their giftedness and are vulnerable to psychological problems and maladjustment.

Some of their vulnerability to psychological problems may be prompted by inappropriate responses of parents to their giftedness. Some parents exploit their gifted children, treating them like showpieces. Other parents may be very responsive to the child's analytic abilities, but do not take into account their physical and emotional immaturity. Still others may be angry at the child's differences and thus respond to the child as a nuisance (Chess & Hassibi, 1978). Some parents have ambivalent relationships with their gifted children. They are proud of the child, but tend to be uncomfortable with the child's differences and to denegrate them (Whitmore, 1980).

Educational Adjustment

Many gifted children are reacted to adversely by teachers and are thereby vulnerable to adjustment difficulties. What is often noted about gifted children in school settings is their atypical behavior rather than their productive or unusual products. Gifted children are generally independent in attitude, judgement, thought, and action (Roe, 1976; Torrance, 1962). They tend to be introverted, unconcerned with social norms, and often reject external constraints (Taylor & Holland, 1964; Walsh, 1975). Although they can demonstrate social presence and poise, they appear to be relatively unconcerned with societal expectations. A low level of sociability may be portrayed, and an asocial attitude may be presented (Guilford, 1968; MacKinnon, 1962; Torrance, 1975; Walsh, 1975). They seem to be more interested in reflective than concrete thinking and more preoccupied with ideas and things than with people (Guilford, 1975; Roe, 1976; Torrance, 1962). Therefore, teachers may find it difficult to become close to the gifted child. Even more distressing, the teacher may hold limited means of modifying the creative child's behavior. Because these children strive for an internal focus of control, they are often unresponsive to shaping techniques and operant disciplinary approaches. Several authors (Roe, 1976; Taylor & Holland, 1964; Torrance, 1975) have suggested that gifted children may have difficulties with their teachers because they resist the teacher's exercise of power. The gifted child may internalize aversive reactions of teachers, thereby feeling emotionally isolated and disturbed. Further, they may be ridiculed or ignored by their classmates so that they begin to retreat as social isolates or become antogonistic to their peers (Torrance, 1962; Wallach & Kogan, 1965).

Personality and Social Interaction

In addition to emotional distress spurred by the aversive reactions of a parent or teacher to the gifted child's temperament and behavior, preliminary research suggests that gifted children may be predisposed toward certain emotional problems. Some of these children tend to be perfectionistic (especially if their achievement is highly valued by their parents). They may set unrealistic goals for themselves, leading to chronic feelings of inferiority and inadequacy (Whitmore, 1980). The heightened intelligence and social awareness that is often characteristic of gifted children may at times spur emotional concern. An early study (Hitchfield, 1973) demonstrated that gifted children tend to worry more and respond more seriously to competition than their nongifted peers. These children may be hypervigilant to events and others' responses. If others are critical of their creations or behavior or if they are unsuccessful, some hypervigilant gifted children experience an exaggerated sense of isolation or rejection (Karns & Wherry, 1981; Whitmore, 1980). At times, gifted children become frustrated with their discontinuities in development and their inability to complete tasks that they can conceptualize but lack the psychomotor skills to complete (Gowan, 1960). Many gifted children lack peers with whom they can communicate. Some accept this difficulty and look for friendships with older children. The difficulty in finding friends often means that gifted children have problems in learning to socialize. The problem is often exacerbated if the child associates with older children since their lack of social skills are even more apparent. On occasion, the gifted child may attempt to dominate relationships with peers and experience much strife (Chess & Hassibi, 1978). Still others try to disguise their ability and may in time fully block the expression of their giftedness.

As a whole, the gifted are underrepresented in child guidance clinics and other mental health agencies that provide services to children (Chess & Hassibi, 1978). It is fallacious to assume that all gifted children experience an unusual degree of psychosocial stress. It is also wrong to assume that gifted children are somehow different or invulnerable to stress and won't profit from mental health intervention. If the gifted child's behavior or affect suggests that he or she is vulnerable to maladjustment because of difficulties associated with accepting and experiencing his or her giftedness, counseling is clearly appropriate. The gifted appear to be particularly good candidates for therapy because of their conceptual ability.

Therapy with Gifted Children

The gifted child is quite a challenge to the child practitioner. First of all, the therapist must be very astute in order to identify the child's giftedness. What the practitioner is likely to perceive initially is the child's nonconformity and unwillingness to cooperate. It is not possible to review here the broad issue concerning the identification of giftedness. The reader is referred to Torrance and Mourad (1978) for a review and comparison of various tests of giftedness and creativity. The sophisticated child practitioner will be alert to indirect or subtle signs of giftedness such as the child's production of unusual ideas or generation of a variety of ways of employing play objects in the play therapy room. In general, the child practitioner identifies the child's giftedness through a combined assessment of the child's divergent thinking and productive ideas when talking, playing, and/or responding to standardized tests.

Once a child practitioner identifies a child client as a highly gifted, new challenges emerge. Many of the emotional problems are a social overlay from receiving negative responses for the child's divergency. The practitioner must determine means of helping the gifted child adjust to society sufficiently so that he or she does not continue to provoke others' aversive reaction. Yet, the practitioner must guard against negating the child's constructive divergency, thereby inhibiting further his or her giftedness.

A challenge emerges also in defining appropriate therapeutic techniques with gifted child clients. Gifted children are often quite resistant to typical clinical approaches. The ineffectiveness of these approaches seems tied in the child's preference for internal control and motivation by their inspiration rather than pleasing others. Torrance (1975) writes that gifted children are less likely than other children to desire to emulate significant adults. Therefore, therapeutic procedures such as modeling and social reinforcement may be relatively less effectual with gifted children. Moreover, since motivation to identify with others is limited, transference and consequent interpretation of transference may be of limited relevance. Since these children strive for maximal self-control, they often react adversely to behavioral modification techniques. Cognitive restructuring techniques may be relatively ineffective. As mentioned previously, their high giftedness presupposes complex analytical skills. As masters of abstraction, gifted children are capable of presenting complex rationalizations that may block logical, concrete discussions about their problems. Ironically, the very divergency and autonomy of the gifted child that the practitioner wishes to nurture may stand in the way of building a therapeutic alliance!

There is a lack of empirical data about effective therapeutic techniques when working with gifted children. LeVine (1984) has identified nine strategies for conducting counseling with gifted children based upon LeVine's extensive clinical work with this population and the theoretical writings on giftedness. The principles underlying these nine strategies are: to support the child's giftedness through the therapeutic discussion and to implement the child's wisdom when selecting techniques. Therefore, the first four strategies for assisting these children involve the identification of issues of relevance to gifted children, helping these children learn what it means to be gifted, and how one can be gifted and still adapt to society. The next five strategies involve using the child's creative and bright ideas to design techniques that will capture the child's imagination, thereby maximizing the clinical alliance so that the child can successfully work through themes and issues that are identified.

1. The client needs counseling assistance to learn to identify that he or she possesses special talents. Because this child most likely has experienced criticism from those not identifying or understanding the nature of his or her giftedness, the child may have internalized very unrealistic or negative self-attributes. A beginning goal of treatment is to help the child learn to identify and to prize his or her uniqueness. During discussions and activities, it is

critical therefore for the child practitioner to point out to this child that "you are a person with many good and many unusual ideas."

2.   Once the child has learned to appreciate his or her giftedness, the practitioner helps the child understand that a degree of social marginality may be associated with the giftedness. In essence, the practitioner communicates, "Your creativity is a very special gift. As is true of most gifts, there is a certain cost. The cost of creativity is that you perceive events and objects in new ways, that most others will not understand. Because they do not understand, you will sometimes feel different and sometimes feel alone."

3.   As treatment progresses, an important theme to be discussed is the responsibility associated with the "gift" of giftedness. Many gifted children, especially those referred to therapy, have introjected such negative feelings about their unique views and products that they become very passive, refusing to produce anything and thereby defaulting upon their creativity. The reader may have noted that the second of the themes of typical relevance to gifted children that was discussed above rings familiarly of existential psychology in that the child is encouraged to analyze his or her feeling about being alone in the world. A further extrapolation from existential writings leads to this third theme to be discussed. The existentialists inform clients that because they are basically alone, they must assume responsibility for their own attitudes and actions in order to give their lives some meaning (Frankl, 1963). In working with gifted child clients, the practitioner encourages the child to view his or her creativity as a gift that should not be ignored. The therapist states in various ways, "It is not all right to always give up. You have a very special gift. It may be hard to carry that gift, but you will feel better if you use it rather than hide it. In fact, you have a responsibility to share your gift with those who are less endowed."

4.   A final theme that emerges when conducting therapy with gifted children is that they may need to learn to compromise. The issue surfaces because of their innerdirectedness and independence. The practitioner should help the client recognize that a certain degree of social marginality is quite adaptive and probably a necessary result of the child's giftedness. Yet, extreme innerdirectedness and consequent loneliness can be debilitating. The child needs to learn to identify when he or she feels so alone that anxiety ensues and overall functioning is impeded. At that point, the child must compromise, adapt to society sufficiently so that his or her overall development is not impaired.

No doubt these themes and issues will emerge at various times in various forms through treatment. The following techniques have been found most helpful for allowing the emergence of these critical issues.

5. An essential technique for working with gifted children is to guard against power struggles. This is important because creative children tend to be very independent and to value internal control (Roe, 1971). If the practitioner becomes engaged in a power struggle with the client, the child is likely to perceive the practitioner as another adult who doesn't understand and doesn't value him or her. Thus, the practitioner should support the child's present sense of autonomy and encourage further self-control.

6. An effective means for fostering the child's sense of autonomy is to allow the client to exercise maximum control over the sessions. The therapist does not surrender responsibility for the ultimate therapeutic orientation of the sessions but whenever possible does encourage the child to select topics of conversation and play material to be employed. When this principle is implemented, gifted children are likely to invent unusual ways of using play objects and novel activities in which they wish the therapist to participate.

7. The practitioner then employs the child's choice of novel activities and creative ways of using toys to emulate critical events in the child's life. The gifted child's tendency to reject concrete, rational discussion of problems has been discussed. However, through the activity of play that the child selects, life's dilemmas can be paralleled. The therapist can then stimulate the child to try out alternative behaviors for coping with the dilemma. The child is encouraged to develop his or her own answers to the existential dilemma of being creative with its inherent joy and marginality. Furthermore, this technique exploits the child's desire for increased autonomy and increased control.

8. Another helpful technique in treating gifted children is to appeal to their highly sophisticated, abstract sense of logic when discussing moral and social issues. Kohlberg (1966) writes that for most elementary age children, moral value resides in performing "good" or "right" roles and maintaining conventional order and the expectancy of others. Most children's analysis of morality is "conventional," circumscribed by their tendency to think concretely. Because of their keen analytic skills, gifted children are likely to exhibit a higher level conceptualization about morality. For example, when fourth through seventh graders were asked to fantasize about their three wishes they would most like to actualize, gifted children selected highly altruistic wishes (Karnes & Wherry, 1981). The morality of gifted children is a morality of "self-accepted principles" (Kohlberg, 1966). They recognize that moral value is not an absolute but resides in a conscious decision to adopt standards that protect both the individual and society.

The gifted child is stimulated by discussions that consider existential questions and relative truths and may be unaffected or respond adversely to discussions which focus upon the sanctions rendered by society for specific attitudes and behaviors. In treatment, gifted children may respond poorly to actions which center upon their directly modifying their behavior, and they are more incited to change by discussions in which they are prompted to analyze the relative effects of their behavior upon their personal goals and those of others.

9. Whenever possible, the practitioner employs metaphoric communication to point out self-defeating patterns and teach socially-appropriate behaviors. Because of gifted children's fine abilities at abstraction, they can easily manipulate discussions into suprarational arguments that avoid the underlying dynamic issues. The use of metaphor in therapy is well established as an effective therapeutic technique in working with a wide range of clients because metaphor allows clinicians to suggest changes at a subconscious level by circumventing typical defense that therapeutic metaphor is particularly helpful with children because it captures their imagination and attitudes while paralleling life events in a language that children understand. By virtue of their appreciation for divergency, gifted children often delight in fantasy and metaphoric communication. The therapeutic metaphors can be particularly helpful with creative children because they bypass their tendency towards rationalization while holding their attention.

In sum, the nine strategies outlined for working with children are designed to exploit the child's creative processes towards achievement of the treatment goals. Identification and discussion with the child of themes and issues typically associated with being gifted can help these children adapt to society without stiffling their special talents.

Child practitioners can also play a vital role in preventive mental health for gifted children. Working as a consultant with educators, the therapist can conduct sessions for gifted children and their families so that all better understand and appreciate the child's special talents.

CHILDREN WITH PHYSICAL LIABILITIES AND ILLNESS

When children suffer severe illnesses or catastrophic injuries, both parents and children experience traumatic grief reactions. Each may not know how to deal with the other's feelings. If the parents' and the child's concerns are consistently ignored or repressed, long-term psychological effects may ensue. A child practitioner may be vital in fostering the overall recovery of the child by helping the parent and child understand the psychological states of recovery from a traumatic illness and helping the family deal with the child's pain and/or handicap.

Coping Phases

A child generally passes through several phases in learning to cope with a chronically disabling disease or permanent physical impairment. First, the child displays reactive effects. Behavior may regress to an earlier developmental level. The child may become depressed (as exhibited by an unwillingness to talk about the physical impairment), cry without warning, show a lack of energy, and demonstrate increased dependency. Belligerence and withdrawal are a normal initial reaction to severe physical disability. The child may even misinterpret his or her illness as punishment by parents. Gradually, the child moves into a recoil phase. He or she begins to talk about the physical disability but demands increase and depression continues. Finally, the child enters a restitution phase in which he or she attempts to adjust to the impairment, to re-enter society, and master the environment. Even if a child seems to have reached a restitution phase, she or he may regress in acceptance of the disability as he or she reaches pubescence. Increasing peer rejection may lead to depression and withdrawal. The child may need to be supported through a re-enactment of the reactive and recoil phases until he or she develops a new, realistic view of how to relate to others.

Work With Parents

A child practitioner can aid parents in understanding that a child with severe, physical disability will initially experience withdrawal and regression and may react belligerently to others. The practitioner can further aid parents in learning that it is important to allow the child to express the negative feelings and attitudes, that movement from a reactive to restitution phase necessitates the child's expression of his or her frustration. Naturally, the parents want to alleviate the child's psychological and physical pain as much as possible. They may need to be taught how to allow the child to express his or her personal despair. Communication training workshops such as parent effectiveness training (Gordon, 1970) and filial therapy (Guerney, 1964) have been helpful in this regard. A practitioner can also be helpful in identifying when the child's expression of personal anguish is not promoting his or her recovery. For example, it is not conducive to positive mental health for a child to begin adopting an "invalid" identity in which the child sees all of his or her reinforcers tied to the illness. In contrast, it is a good clinical sign that the child needs assistance directly after surgery. However, if the child does not begin to express some hopefulness and desire toward mastery after basic recovery from the physical trauma, intervention with the family and child may be helpful.

The practitioner can also be of aid in alerting the parents to possible psychological consequences of certain handicaps. Literature is rapidly expanding concerning the psychological effects of particularly physical handicapping conditions. In the paragraphs that follow, we will outline a few of the behavioral and psychological effects the child practitioner will want to keep in mind and share with parents when working with hearing impaired, visually impaired, disfugured, or psychosomatic children.

Deaf Children

Many deaf children do not trust hearing persons, believing that they cannot understand their problem (Portner, 1981). Deaf children with deaf parents show better ratings on maturity, responsibility, and independence than do deaf children with hearing parents (Meadow, 1976). This may be because hearing parents have limited communication with their deaf child early in development. Because the psychosocial development of a child is closely tied to language, a deaf child has little choice but to act out what he or she is feeling or thinking (Portner, 1981). Acting out behavior in a deaf child may be inappropriately classified as impulsive behavior. For example, a number of researchers have documented motor restlessness, impulsivity, and doubt coexisting with rigidity and obstinancy as psychological concomitance of deafness among children (Lesser & Easser, 1972). Therapy with a deaf child requires far more time and specialized skill if communication must be translated with sign language. Deaf children need practitioners with signing skills and an understanding of the unique developmental dynamics of a deaf child (Portner, 1981).

Blind Children

Blind children may develop tendencies to touch others and some have short attention spans coupled with intense fear of their environment (Chess & Hassibi, 1978). If parents are aware of possible psychological and behavioral effects of certain handicaps, they will be less likely to blame the child or themselves for these unavoidable problems. For instance, visually-impaired children may break rules without meaning to. If the child is then disciplined for disobeying an order that he or she did not obey, the child will feel angry toward the parent or teacher.

Disfigured Children

Body image is closely associated with development of a positive self-image. Children may be disfigured by burns, cancer treatments, operations, amputations, and disease. For a disfigured child to gain a better self-image, he or she must have a narcissistic investment in his or her body and have positive reflections in significant others and in the community (Woods, 1975). Treatment usually includes helping the child learn that the disfigurement is limited to a body deficiency, not a personality or a social deficiency. There is mourning and then acceptance with compensatory actions, such as wigs, protheses, and plastic surgery (Woods, 1975). With the increased survival of children with cancer has come adjustment problems. One study indicates 59 % of child cancer patients have at least mild psychiatric symptoms (O'Malley, Koocher, Foster, & Slavin, 1979). Denial is the most frequent coping mechanism to moderate the emotional impact of the cancer experience. Increasing social contacts help the child's long-term adjustment (O'Malley, Koocher, Foster, & Slavin, 1979).

CHILDREN OF POVERTY

Poverty is associated with a wide range of psychosocial problems among adults. Mental illness, alcohol and drug abuse, suicide, and child abuse are all positively correlated with poverty. It is also known that there is an increase in these psychosocial problems during periods of economic recession as individuals lose their employment and consequent economic security. Psychological stress due to poverty and economic uncertainty is the most important link that has been identified in explanations of why the poor experience higher rates of psychological maladjustment.

Risk Factors

Children are not immune to the same pressures that their parents experience because of poverty and economic uncertainty. First of all, they may be the recipients of their parent's discontent. Chess and Hassibi (1978, p. 118-119) write that if parents are satisfied, they

> impart a sense of pride and satisfaction and they create family legends that are congruent with their own pride... they find heroes and retell their history in a manner that nurtures hope and optimism in their children. By the same token, parents' hopelessness, their inability to change what they do not accept, and their shame about their own past and present status within the culture adversely affects their children's outlook on life and creates the conditions for their future failure.

Furthermore, children raised in poverty are more likely subjects to certain developmental risks. The elevated risks begin before the children are born. Children who grow up in poverty are usually born of poor mothers. As we discussed in an earlier chapter on normal developmental processes, the mother's medical and nutritional history can have dramatic effects upon the child's physical and cognitive well-being. The mother's poor nutrition correlates positively with difficulties during pregnancy and prematurity, which in turn correlate with neurological difficulties of the newborn. The effects of the mother's poor nutrition may be compounded by her inability to receive and pay for good medical care.

After birth, the organic risks remain higher for poor children. They are more likely to experience malnutrition which can retard physical and intellectual growth and are less likely to receive needed medical care.

Children raised in poverty are likely to experience a number of psychosocial stresses. There is often only one parent in the home, who must work. These parents cannot afford excellent day care. The children may be left for extended times with minimal supervision. In many cases, they lack appropriate sensory and educational stimulation (Achenbach, 1974).

When the poor children attend school, their sense of vulnerability is further exacerbated. In the 1960's and early 1970's, poor children were often considered "disadvantaged" and "culturally deprived"--implying that they lack any sense of social structure and culture. Most social scientists and practitioners now recognize that these children are "culturally different" from traditional middle class norms, but not culturally deficient. Nevertheless, our school systems generally do not take into account these children's cultures. Instead, the poor children are expected to adapt swiftly to the middle class norms. Yet, these children may be unfamiliar with the materials and ideas of the typical classroom. Moreover, the children often speak a different language or special English dialect in their homes. The linguistical differences pose some difficulties in comprehending the teacher, but the inability to speak standard English is an even larger detriment as it may lead to the poor children's being evaluated negatively (Baratz & Shuy, 1969). Even if the children speak standard English, many experience prejudice and ridicule at school. They may be teased for their shabby dress. They may feel left out if they lack the money to participate in activities joined by most of their peers. Teachers also may be biased against poor children and come to: (a) expect less of them academically, (b) instill in them a sense of failure, (c) reinforce their acting out behavior, and (d) impose on them feelings of being less than adequate socially. Thus, children in poverty often must not only undergo psychologically harmful stresses at home, but must endure stress in their social sphere.

Invulnerable Children

It is important to point out that although the poor can be considered a high-risk group to develop psychological maladjustments, there is great variability in the psychological consequences of growing up in poverty. Many poor children are no more maladjusted than affluent children. In fact, some forms of childhood pathology such as autism may be more common the middle and upper class. One could posit that a great number of poor children are actually more psychologically healthy than their affluent counterparts precisely because they have not become severely maladjusted under highly stressful situations. It is important not to characterize children who grow up in poverty as less emotionally stable but instead focus upon their vulnerability and the constant stress they must endure. Garmezy (1981) has coined the term "invulnerables" to characterize youths that are raised in very aversive and poor environments who excel in personal development. According to Garmezy, these individuals complete their education, do not have an arrest record, gain meaningful employment and lead constructive, happy lives. Support for Garmezy's position can be found in a recent epidemiological survey of psychological disorders in children (Langner, Herson, Greene, Jameson, & Goff, 1970) which found higher proportions of welfare children as compared to a cross-section sample in both the "well" and "impaired" tails of the distribution. Some suggest that poor children from two parent homes and with older siblings experience the negative effects of stress less than do children from single parent homes and from homes where there are not older siblings. If we can identify the factors contributing to these "invulnerable" children's success perhaps we will be better able to assist other children in shedding the shackles of poverty.

Mental Health Services

On top of identifying and supporting the "invulnerables," mental health workers need to reach out to the many poor children who are highly vulnerable to psychological stress. In this regard, well established mental health records are quite alarming. Lower socioeconomic parents are less likely to bring their children to mental health services unless pressured by schools or law enforcement agencies (Furman, Sweat, & Crocetti, 1965). Psychotherapy is less likely to be offered to lower class children (Harrison, McDermott, Wilson, & Schrager, 1965). When counseling and psychotherapy are offered to lower class children, they are more likely to be conducted by trainees (Langner, Herson, Greene, Jameson, & Goff, 1970). Lower class children are more likely to miss counseling appointments (Speer, Fossum, Lippman, Schwartz, & Slocum, 1968). Very often, therapists and poor clients are feeling a mutual misfit and distrust of one another.

Just as therapists have described the "preferred" or "attractive" psychotherapy adult client as "Mr. or Ms. Yavis," that is young, attractive, verbal, intelligent, and successful (Shofield, 1964), we can speak of "Yavis, Junior." In other words child practitioners prefer and acknowledge that they are most successful with children from middle class backgrounds. When a lower socioeconomic emotionally disturbed child is referred for professional help, the referral is made to a middle class teacher, social worker, psychologist, or psychiatrist to whom the child is a "non-Yavis Junior." These children may receive only minimal assistance from middle class practitioners because the children lack verbal "good client" skills that make them attractive clients. Thus, the lower class emotionally disturbed child ultimately finds himself or herself hospitalized in a state mental hospital, while his or her middle class counterparts receive extensive outpatient therapy. In one study, Jennings and Davis (1977) showed that hospitalized lower class children and adolescents could be taught verbal skills that would enhance their effectiveness to communicate when being interviewed. Further, as their ability to communicate effectively increased, so too did their "attractiveness" to the interviewer.

It is also likely that the poor clients find many of the services provided to be inadequate or irrelevant to their needs. Whatever the exact reason, many lower class children experience marked psychological stress because of their poverty and are frequently not given adequate mental health care.

Achenbach (1974) stresses that even when adequate mental health services are provided to vulnerable children in poverty, the clinical sessions are clearly not adequate leverage against the organic, social, and educational stressors these children experience. In working with children in poverty the child practitioner often needs to break out of the traditional clinical role and assume an advocate position for the children, helping them receive the various medical and remediational services they need.

Prevention Services

Achenback (1974) also identifies a number of primary prevention strategies that are most important if we are to meet the needs of vulnerable poor children:

- direct provision of nutritional and medical care to low socioeconomic status pregnant women

- improved obstetrical care for this population of women

- after birth parent training programs for the poor

- provision of adequate food to poor children

- mass screening for lead poisoning and strict building code enforcement to eliminate peeling lead paint and other hazards

- routine preventive innoculations for the poor

- provision of adequate day care centers offering sensory and educational stimulation

- increased use of the media for children's education

- public school programs that are geared to mesh with preschool programs provided for the poor

- school-based educational and recreational activities after school hours and during vacations

- graduated series of mental health services offered through the educational system so that the problems are detected early and dealt with; first, by consultation between educators, parents, and mental health workers; second, by special educational planning; and lastly, by individual and group counselors who work with the child and family.

Achenback's (1974) guidelines are quite constructive. Most require tremendous social effort not yet present. On the individual basis, many practitioners experience significant barriers from society, schools, and parents when they attempt to implement these strategies. Prevention, consultation, and policy formulation for child practitioners is explained in more detail in Chapter 15.

Additional studies are necessary pertaining to techniques, strategies, and guidelines for working more effectively with children from poverty backgrounds. It is important to emphasize that the child practitioner must be every mindful of the cultural background of the child client from a poor socioeconomic status. Only when both the practitioner and the child understand one another's values is there a good probability of a successful clinical intervention.

SUMMARY

Certain biological characteristics and social or physical limitations make children vulnerable to psychological stress. In this chapter, we have reviewed some of the more common handicapping conditions (sensory impairments and illnesses), genetic traits (giftedness and mental retardation), and social conditions (poverty) that increase children's vulnerability. We have attempted to explain that knowledge about the psychosocial stresses these children incur will aid the child practitioner in several ways. First, the practitioner will be alert to subtle ways that a particular child is struggling with issues related to the social or physical condition. Secondly, the practitioner can alert parents to the issues with which their child must wrestle. By working closely with the parents of special needs children, psychological disorders prompted by the unique stresses that special needs children experience can be attenuated. Special needs children are particularly vulnerable to psychological disorders and, as such, proactive clinical intervention in their behalf is essential.

CHAPTER 14

CHILDREN WITH NEW FAMILIES

There is no greater social impact on children than their families. As we have stressed throughout this text, familial factors can cause or help resolve many of the emotional stresses children experience. In this chapter, we examine the research and dynamics of children of divorce, children in substitute care, and adopted children. Naturally, new families do not necessarily create maladjustment, but we will see that the added stress makes these children vulnerable to problems. Treatment considerations are presented for each type of new family, but it is clear that primary and secondary prevention strategies can better minimize children's vulnerability to the change of families.

CHILDREN OF DIVORCE

> I remember it was near my birthday when I was going to be 6 that Dad said at lunch he was leaving. I tried to say "No, Dad, don't do it," but I couldn't get my voice out. I was too much shocked. All the fun things we had done flashed right out of my head and all the bad things came in, like when he had to go to the hospital with his bad back, and when he got mad at me. The bad thoughts just stuck there. My life sort of changed at that moment. Like I used to be always happy and suddenly I was sad.

An 8-year-old girl. *Newsweek,* February 11, 1980

Much has been written of an editorial nature that children of divorce are vulnerable to stress. Until the 1970's, many of the empirical findings were incomplete or contradictory. In this section, a review of recent research and a background on the frequency of divorce is offered. Then, a synthesis of the complex psychological affects of divorce upon children is presented.

The Difficulties of Research About Children of Divorce

Levitin (1979) points out that many of the studies of the effects of divorce conducted during the 1950's and 1960's have major flaws.

- conceptualization of the single parent family as deviant;

- perception of single parent families as a homogeneous group, a fact that mutes differences such as ethnic and social class;

- single global variables such as single parent status with little or no attention to mediating factors such as parental adjustment, economic status, age and sex of child.

Nevertheless, the results of two classic studies (Nye, 1957 and Burchinal, 1964) have been consistently upheld by more recent investigation. Nye conducted a retrospective study of 780 adolescent boys and girls from three Washington high schools. He hypothesized that the adjustment of children is related to family functioning whether or not it is legally or physically broken. His comparison of adjustment (delinquent behavior, psychosomatic illness, relationships to parents and peers) of adolescents in broken and happy or unhappy unbroken homes revealed that children of single parent or reconstituted families were significantly better adjusted than children in unhappy (conflicted) two parent families. Burchinal (1964), in another retrospective study, compared 1,566 adolescents in selected areas of personal and social adjustment from unbroken, broken, and reconstituted families. He concluded that divorce itself was not the overwhelming influential factor; rather, family functioning was a much more important variable.

In contrast to these large scale studies, most of the clinical studies of individual children of divorce ". . . depict children as highly though often temporarily distressed" (Levitin, 1979, p. 5). Levitan (1979) maintains that these findings cannot be generalized to large populations of children of divorce but do offer poignant portraits of children for whom divorce is so traumatic and painful that they required treatment.

Intervening Variables

The sex of the child is important in identifying the psychological effects of divorce. Boys may be affected more negatively and intensely than are girls (Heatherington, 1966; Heatherington & Deur, 1971; Heatherington, Cox & Cox, 1976, 1979; Lang, Papenfuhs, & Walters, 1976; McDermott, 1970; Wallerstein & Kelly, 1975, 1976, 1980). For instance, in research examining matched pairs of children of divorce and children from intact families, Heatherington and Deur (1971) reported that boys separated from fathers before age 5 displayed more negative and less masculine self-concepts (as evidenced by playing with dolls with nurturing intent despite taunting by peers), and older boys displayed more compensatory masculine behavior (such as aggression against peers, stealing, and gang behavior) that did boys from intact families. In the same study, few significant differences between girls from divorced homes and matched girls from intact families were noted. Santrock (1976) corroborated the findings that boys from divorced families were more impulsive, less self-controlled, and less able to delay gratification.

Most researchers agree that the younger the child at the time of onset of disruption and divorce, the greater the potential for the child to be detrimentally affected (Heatherington & Deur, 1971; Lang, Papenfuhs & Walters, 1976; Santrock, 1977; Wallerstein & Kelly, 1975, 1976, 1980). Santrock (1976) states that most detrimental to a child is a divorce within the child's first two years of life. Santrock (1977) employed doll play interviews and teachers' ratings of 45 father-present boys and 45 father-absent boys and reported that early loss of a father through divorce was more highly correlated with aggressive and disobedient behaviors by the child than if the father were lost through his death.

An alternate hypothesis concerning the relationship of the child's age and the effects of divorce has been proposed. Warshak and Santrock (1980) theorize that the period of separation in the child's life determines the focus rather than the intensity of the detrimental effects. For example, children whose parents separated during the child's conceptual developmental stage where egocentrism is foremost are likely to perceive the divorce as something that the child controlled and thus blame him- or herself for the separation. Thus, the child's adjustment problems focus upon self-blame, primarily because of the limited conceptual ability of the child at that age. However, if parents separate during the child's adolescence, the child may be more likely to experience problems in his or her own love relationships.

A final intervening child variable reported to correlate with increased difficulties of adjustment following divorce is the child's previous psychological history. Generally, the divorce has more profound consequences upon the "temperamentally difficult child," those children defined by Chess and Hassibi (1978) as highly reactive to stimuli, changeable, and moody. Each child's psychological history needs to be considered when developing a prognosis of a child's adjustment to divorce (Gardner, 1977).

A number of variables about the divorcing parents also contribute to the divorced child's vulnerability to psychological stress. The sex of the custodial parent may be important in the continued development of the child. Warshak and Santrock (1980) suggest from their research comparing children in father-custody versus mother-custody homes that children adjust better if they reside with the same sex parent.

The nature of the parents' relationship following divorce can affect a child's adjustment. In about 1/3 of divorces, a turbulent relationship continues between the parents. These effects can be very destructive. If a child hears one parent frequently demeaned by the other, the child begins to view the parents ambivalently. The child may experience guilt about his or her ambivalence, and the child's ability to identify with the same-sexed parent may be hampered.

At least as important as the child's reaction to the divorce is the child's adaptation to a single parent home. Current research suggests that the traumatic effects of the divorce are vastly ameliorated if the custodial parent copes well with single parenting. If the custodial parent does not experience tremendous post-divorce depression, if that custodial parent continues to present the other parent in a positive light, and if the single parent does not sexualize or otherwise distort the relationship with the children, the children's response to the divorce is greatly eased (Chess & Hassibi, 1978).

However, some negative effects of single parenting are difficult to avoid. The single parent often must be provider and cannot be around the children as much as preferable. Until recently, almost all children remained with the mother. The degree of the father's availability is important in determining the intensity and duration of the effects of divorce (Daniel, 1977). The loss of a significant adult can prompt great mourning but can be minimized through relationships with in-laws, relatives of the custodial (or noncustodial) parent, and friends.

Often divorce leads to low socioeconomic status because of the following:

1.   loss of "economics of scale"
2.   inadequate child support and alimony payments
3.   probability of welfare dependence because of fewer work opportunities and lower wages for women than men (Espenshade, 1979).

Divorce is more prevalent among poor families (Espenshade, 1979). Thus, divorce may lead to lower socioeconomic status which, in turn, may lead to less positive child-rearing practices.

Range of Effects

Several studies shed light on the initial impact of divorce on children (McDermott, 1970; Ahrons, 1980; Bernard, 1978; Jacobson, 1979; Hess & Camara, 1979; Brown, 1983; Gardner, 1976; and Westman, Swift, & Kramer, 1970) and concluded that the short-range effect is painful and profound. A study of the short range impact of divorce on children revealed that important differences in reactions occurred among children at different developmental stages initially and one year after the separation/divorce. A five-year follow-up of 58 of the original 60 families revealed several important findings on all the age groups. Thirty-four percent of the children maintained a sense of well-being and self-confidence. Thirty-seven percent were judged to be suffering from moderately severe depression which was manifested in a variety of behaviors including drug abuse, stealing, and pronounced unhappiness. The remaining 29 % had resumed normal developmental progress, but experienced intermittent feelings of sadness about the divorce and resentment toward one or both of their parents (Wallerstein & Kelly, 1979).

Long range effects of experiencing divorce while growing up are extremely difficult to measure because of intervening variables such as parents' personal, social, and economic adjustment and personal characteristics of the child. The best research of long range effects (Nye, 1957; Burchinal, 1964; Hetherington, Cox, & Cox, 1976, and Kulka & Weingarten, 1979) seems to indicate that most children of divorce eventually adjust as well as other children and that other variables such as parental conflict are more important predictors of a child's eventual adjustment than the divorce per se. Beyond these generalizations, the limitations of the research cause much confusion. Few studies have succeeded in controlling for such confounding variables as socioeconomic status and racial background. Divorce is too often conceptualized as a static event, not a process.

A model proposed by Bohannan (1970) has helped clarify the nonstatic nature of divorce. Bohannan (1970) views divorce as comprised of six overlapping phases that vary in intensity and sequence for specific families. In the phase of "emotional divorce," spouses attend to emotional issues that are causing the disruption of the marriage and the resolution of those interpersonal conflicts. Children's feelings and adjustment may be greatly affected during this phase, although many parents believe that they are hiding their discord from the children. Younger children are given more responsibilities around the house and more decision-making power (Luepnitz, 1982). The "legal divorce" phase is the sanction-seeking phase in which the couple receive the right to remarry. Children often view the court hearing as a last chance for a fantasized reunion of their parents, and stress often ensues. The "economic divorce" is the phase in which money and property are divided. The actual as well as the perceived fairness of the distribution of the couple's assets often directly (sufficiency of financial support) and indirectly (perceptions of the child of the blame for lack of financial support) affect the child. Certainly, one of the most volatile phases is the "co-parental divorce," which lasts until one of the parents or children dies. This phase includes the potential conflict areas of custody, visitation, and the ongoing child-parent relationship. The "community divorce" phase is the evolution the divorced individual experiences with his/her friends leading to a subjective sense of less community. Lastly, the "psychic divorce" concerns the parents regaining a sense of autonomy. Often divorced parents overlook how important their movement through this phase is for the child. If a parent models insecurity or dependent behaviors and attitudes (for example, encouraging the child to become a surrogate partner, so that the child experiences stress when separating from the parent), the child may learn faulty means of achieving his or her needs. Bohannan's (1970) model aids in conceptualizing divorce as a series of overlapping phases of development that create a multiplicity of experiences and pose varied potential threats to a child's previous conceptions of family.

Detrimental Psychological Effects of Divorce Upon Children

The detrimental psychological and social effects of divorce upon children fall into three primary areas: academic and school performance; delinquency; and intrapersonal concerns.

School Performance

A popular assumption concerning children of divorce is that their academic performance is hindered by the trauma of the family disruption; yet, empirical evidence is somewhat equivocal. In their longitudinal study of 131 children whose parents divorced in the children's infancy, early childhood, and latency, Wallerstein and Kelly (1975, 1976, 1980) noted that not only did school-peer relationships deteriorate, but also half of the children declined noticeably in their academic performance. The children displayed decreased ability in concentration, and their playground behavior became more aggressive than previous to the divorce (Wallerstein & Kelly, 1975). In the one year follow-up, slightly more than 25 % of those who had suffered lowered academic performance returned to their previous education and social achievement levels. In contrast, a study investigating the effects of divorce upon the children's school behavior reported nominal detrimental effects. Acting out behaviors as well as withdrawal were more pronounced for children of divorce, but the children's school behavior improved to predivorce levels 3 to 4 months following their parent' divorces (Gonso, 1977).

Two studies comparing IQ scores of children in families with fathers and those children in which fathers are absent report that prolonged separation (especially early separation) from the father is correlated with lower IQ scores (Deutsch & Brown, 1964; Kreisburg, 1967). Edwards & Thompson (1971) examined the differences of scores on a picture intelligence test administered to 2,500 7-year-olds of divorced and intact families. No significant differences were found in their scores.

In general, the school performance of many children of divorce is impaired for a short time period following the disruption of the family unit. Well controlled studies indicate spontaneous resolution of many detrimental effects shortly (3 months to 1 year) after the onset of divorce. More research is needed to identify which children of divorce are vulnerable to school difficulties.

Delinquency

Some studies have correlated divorce and especially father absence with a propensity for children to become juvenile or child delinquents. However, lack of systematic variance of familial and psychological factors and lack of use of control groups has led to confusing conclusions (Sudia & Herzog, 1973). The Sudia and Herzog review (1973) included 400 citations before 1969 about the effects of father absence. Only 60 of these employed a control group of father-present families with similar characteristics. These studies linked father absence to child outcomes such as juvenile delinquency, mental illness, and lower intellectual and psychosocial functioning. Most of the studies neglected to distinguish (1) the cause of the father's absence; (2) the duration or degree of the father's absence; (3) the child's age when the separation occurred; (4) the differences between the effects of the father's absence and poverty; and (5) the difference between the consequences of poverty and color. Twenty-four studies supported the view that father absence leads to pathological outcomes in child behavior; twenty studies reported no significant destructive effects of father absence; and sixteen had mixed conclusions. Shinn's review (1978) included 58 studies, 75 % of which had not been included in Herzog and Sudia's (1973). Most of the studies focused on the association between father absence and cognitive development of children. Again Shinn (1978) concluded that the variable of father absence is less important than other less emphasized variables such as (1) the cause, onset, and duration of father absence; (2) the family's socioeconomic status; (3) the nature of the relationship between the child and the absent parent; and (4) parental conflict before and after divorce.

Determination of the relationship between parental divorce and child delinquency is complicated by the potential bias in police records. About one-third of the delinquency hearings result in dismissal or warning. The most common basis for dismissal is the personal conception of the police officer or judge as to "the stability of the child's family" based on whether the parent was divorced or married.

Yet, some studies do suggest that divorce and father absence can be associated with minor infringements of the law or moral codes (Santrock, 1976; Wallerstein & Kelly, 1976). Following divorced children's development over a number of years through observation and questionnaire, they reported only slight differences in acting out between children of divorce and those of intact families. Children of divorce were slightly more likely to engage in petty lying and stealing.

Interpersonal Concerns

Within the last decade, a rather large body of literature is developing about how divorce may lead to intrapersonal difficulties for children so that they are vulnerable to more profound maladjustment. Santrock (1977) reported that father-absent children are more aggressive, disobedient, and independent as rated by teachers than those children with a father present. Further, Santrock (1977) noted that father-absent children are more aggressive in their doll play and more likely to display disobedience the earlier the onset of father absence in the child's development. In another study, Santrock (1976) observed the father-absent boys were less morally advanced as evidenced by Kohlberg's scale (1968) of moral development.

A well designed study controlling for father absence identified many similarities and few differences between children with fathers and those without father in their homes. No significant differences were noted in self-concept, attitudes toward family, and in peer relationships (Thomas, 1968). However, significantly higher levels of anxiety were displayed by children without fathers present, and these children also perceived themselves as receiving less recognition for their accomplishments. As stated previously, children from one parent homes may have less opportunity for receiving attention. Increased anxiety levels have been observed in other studies conducted with children of divorce. Anxiety can be manifest in many different behaviors and psychological symptoms. Grollman (1975) in his assessment of children of divorce from his clinical experience noticed that bodily stress might be expressed as trembling, restlessness, headaches, appetite loss, stomach aches, diarrhea, fitful sleep, frequent urination, or an increase in the pulse and respiration rates.

Anger toward self or parent and issues of allegiance and loyalty are often exacerbated by custody battles. Children may feel that they are hurting a parent's feelings by expressing a preference for custody, and thus confusion and anxiety may be expressed through bodily or behavioral symptomology. As cited earlier, most symptoms diminish 1 or 2 years following divorce, but some do not. In Wallerstein and Kelly's (1975, 1976, 1980) extensive longitudinal studies, more than 3 months after divorce, some children continued to experience depression, to report low self-concept scores, and to display difficulties with their peer relationships. In a one-year follow-up (Wallerstein & Kelly, 1976), data indicated that in 25 % of the cases, the following occurred:

1. Phobic reactions spread and generalized.

2. Thievery and truancy increased.

3. Those who were isolated became more withdrawn.

Many children of divorce blame themselves for a parent leaving or for causing a divorce (Gardner, 1976; Heatherington, Cox, & Cox, 1977, 1978; Heatherington & Deur, 1971; Kelly & Berg, 1978; Wallerstein & Kelly, 1975, 1976, 1980). Consequently, they feel guilty for causing the family disruption. Frequently. the guilt is manifested somatically as well as emotionally through clinical signs of depression and grief (Grollman, 1975).

As previously described, children of divorce may be more aggressive in their play than children of intact families. Many researchers have posited that one cause of the hostility and anger might be the child's blaming a parent for the divorce that has disrupted his or her world (Daniel, 1977; Gardner, 1976; Heatherington, Cox, & Cox, 1979; Heatherington & Deur, 1971; Kelly & Berg, 1978; Wallerstein & Kelly, 1975, 1976, 1980). For example, divorced children may feel betrayed by their noncustodial parents, believing that these noncustodial parents have abandoned them. These children may seek revenge through hostile acts toward the noncustodial parents as well as the custodial parents and others (Gardner, 1976; Wallerstein & Kelly, 1975, 1976, 1980).

During the most intense conflicts of an impending divorce, the child may be left out of conversations and activities of the parents, and the child may feel alienated and lonely (Gardner, 1976). Then, following divorce, some children fear that they will be abandoned by their remaining custodial parent. They may worry intensely about the remaining custodial parent's health and fear being left alone to fend for themselves. For example, some children will fear being left alone in a car or at home even for short periods of time. In some cases, the child may run away from home to avoid the feared rejection (Gardner, 1976; Heatherington & Deur, 1971; Kelly & Berg, 1978; Wallerstein & Kelly, 1975, 1976, 1980).

Children of divorce may experience conflicts of loyalty and allegiance when asked to take sides by either parent over custody or ongoing issues of blame, finances, visitation, etc. Children may become so aligned with one parent that they reject the other and form a surrogate partnership (a fantasized relationship by the child of being the single parent's marriage partner) with the remaining parent (Gardner, 1976). Some children, expecially those of latency age, become hypermature, displaying characteristics of the absent parent to compensate for their custodial parent's loss (Gardner, 1976; Wallerstein & Kelly, 1976). Children may become distressed over loyalty and confidentiality if parents ask them information concerning the other parent and may feel like thay are tattling and breaking an allegiance or confidence (Gardner, 1976). Children of divorce may develop fantasies to defend against the personal distress they are experiencing. A common fantasy noted by researchers is that the parents will remarry and all will "live happily ever after" as a reunited family unit. Occasionally, the fantasy may be acted out in plots attempting to bring the family back together (Gardner, 1976).

Summary of the Research About the Effects of Divorce

As divorce has become increasingly prominent in our society, social scientists have begun systematic investigation of its effects upon children when young and as maturing occurs. Research consistently documents that divorce spurs behavioral disorders and psychological stress for a great number of children; however, most children from divorced families recover from the negative effects within 3 months to a year following the dissolution of the marriage. Yet, a significant minority of children from divorced homes seem particularly vulnerable to the psychosocial stresses associated with the dissolution of their intact families, and these vulnerable children may express emotional concerns about the divorce (such as feeling guilty, yearning for the reunion of the family, anger at a parent), behavior disorders (such as poor school performance, delinquency), or act out emotional concerns (promiscuous sexual behavior) into their adulthood. We do not know exactly which children are most vulnerable to divorce stress. A combination of factors about the parents (their overall adjustment, age, nature, and how well they adjust to the divorce) and variables about the child (his or her temperament, age, attachment to the parents, and to other supportive adults) interact to determine the child's sense of vulnerability. It will be helpful when we can predict which children are most vulnerable to stress from divorce so that we can provide the psychosocial support they need to prevent their experiencing significant personal problems. In the meantime, several treatment strategies have emerged that can be helpful to a broad range of children.

Clinical Intervention for Children of Divorce

One model is preventive (Holdahl & Casperson, 1977) and is aimed at teaching all children how to adjust to potential losses in their lives through death of a parent or family member, divorce, or moving away from friends. Holdahl and Casperson's (1977) model has been replicated throughout the Midwestern United States, but empirical verification is not yet available.

The remedial approaches emphasize assisting either the child and/or the family in adjusting to the divorce of the parents. Some child practitioners prefer mandatory participation of all family members, including the noncustodial parent (Goldman & Coane, 1977; Hozman & Froiland, 1976). Still other child practitioners, while not negating the importance of parental adjustment, favor treating the child either individually or in small groups (Gardner, 1976).

Some practitioners believe it is helpful to assist children of divorce in expressing their grief about the loss of the intact family. They aid family members in coping with the dissolution of the family, redefine the family, and accept new relationships (Hozman & Froiland, 1978). Another family systems approach is built upon a four-part model that emphasizes redefining the family as including all members regardless of the divorce. Boundaries of family relationships are reset. Under the family therapist's guidance, members recall the history of the marriage to gain insight into the conflicts leading to the disruption. An expression of grief is catalyzed, and finally, new supportive relationships are fostered (Goldman & Coane, 1977).

Gardner (1976, 1977) recommends working with children individually or in groups to identify and correct intrapersonal concerns, such as self-blaming, blaming a parent, and fantasies of a reunion. In addition, Gardner (1970) has written a text for children to help them understand the divorce process and to correct inappropriate perceptions.

Therapy for divorced parents has been of aid in increasing the speed of litigation and decreasing custodial fights (Margolin, 1973).

Also needed are corrective personal and social intervention programs to aid the single parent so that the ongoing environmental circumstance is conducive to the child's growth. However, much more research is needed to explicate the effects of being raised in a single parent home. This research must address the interactions of the child's sex and custodial parent's sex. Day care centers that provide a truly nurturing environment and are reasonably priced could greatly ease the load of the single parent and thus facilitate the child's and parent's adaptation. Continued opportunity for the child to relate to the noncustodial parent and other adults of the opposite sex of the custodial parent is important.

In sum, widespread supportive experiences are needed for a very large number of children who experience stress associated with divorce and single parent homes. Therapy can help family members refocus upon the beneficial aspects of divorce for both parents and children. The presence of both parents in a household is not a sufficient condition for psychological stability. In many cases, psychological equilibrium returns only after the parents separate. Until recently, this was not a popular topic when discussing child-rearing practices. Today, we recognize that in some cases a single parent is better than two parents where there is no love. Much can be done to assure a nuturing family environment for children of divorce.

SUBSTITUTE CARE (FOSTER CARE)

Foster care is the temporary (maximum from 1 to 1 1/2 years) placement of children outside their biological family with a family foster home. This is a new but temporary family for the child and therein lie many complicated issues. This drastic change is necessary when the child's basic survival is threatened. Inadequate social and emotional care is provided in the child's primary home. During the temporary placement, there is total separation from the primary family except for occasional visits from the child's family. The child experiences a change of school, peer group, sibling group, and sometimes community. The pervasiveness of change is so drastic, foster care is considered as a last resort to protect the child.

Substitute care involves a number of professional groups, because legal and physical custody must be granted to a state or temporary caretaker. Expert testimony from psychiatrists, psychologists, and case management by social workers may be necessary. Because of the complexity of the foster care system, some long term foster care placements have become permanent, so that child is not shuffled from one home to another.

Statistics

Although over 500,000 children are in out-of-home placements in the United States (Children's Defense Fund, 1978), each child has his or her own individual story of pain, neglect, illness, physical injury, or other condition which required his or her removal from home. The authors' experience with over 1,500 foster care cases has shown that children without homes are a heterogenous group. They range in age from infancy to 18 years of age. Shyne and Schroeder (1978) identified three major problems which required out-of-home placement of children: parent-related problems, child-related problems, and environmental circumstances. The parent-related problems involve parental illness, mental health condition, abuse and neglect of children, sexual abuse, and incest. Parent-related problems accounted for between 75 % and 80 % of all children placed outside their own homes. Child-related problems, the condition of the child, such as mental retardation, emotional disturbance, or delinquent behavior accounted for between 15 % and 20 % of out-of-home placements. Environmental circumstances including poverty accounted for between 3 % and 5 % of children placed (Shyne & Schroeder, 1978). The one common denominator is that the children come from stressful family situations, which make them vulnerable to additional stress.

Departments of human services are generally overloaded and understaffed. Moreover, technical constraints often prevent older children from being legally adoptable until several court hearings. As a consequence, many older children spend years in temporary foster homes before than can be and are adopted. Goldstein, Freud, & Solnit, (1979) present a powerful rationale about why older children in extended foster placements are particularly vulnerable to emotional stress. Both the child and the parents know that the placement is temporary and that the social service agency reserves the right to remove the child at any time. For the foster parents, this legal stricture is a warning against becoming deeply emotionally involved with the child. For the child, the feelings of impermanence clash with the developmental needs for emotional constancy. If on the other hand, the foster parents and child do not heed the admonitions of the social service agencies and do become deeply involved with one another, then the child is likely to experience significant trauma when taken from the foster home for placement in a permanent setting. Goldstein, et al. (1979) have coined the term "common-law adoptive parent-child relationship" to characterize extended-time foster placements in which the parents and child have bonded firmly to one another.

Foster care has become an easy course of action for social workers. "Yet, the system scars those it ensnares; it is often emotionally debilitating and humiliating. Perhaps, the saddest aspect of foster care in the United States is that it was originally designed to reunite families after providing them with temporary respite from child care--a respite that would be beneficial to both parents and children. Yet, too often the nation's foster care system fragments families and sabotages their eventual reconstruction into functioning units again" (Hubbell, 1981, p. 5). Of the 500,000 children living in foster care or group homes, 25 % remain in care for over 6 years. Most children live in foster care for at least 2 and 1/2 years. Of the children in foster homes, 47 % have lived in 2 or more foster homes (Shyne & Schroeder, 1978).

Research about the care of children outside of their own home between 1933 and 1984 demonstrates some interesting trends. The number of children in care per 1,000 has stayed fairly consistent between a low in 1960 of 3.5, to approximately 5 per 1,000 today. A shift has taken place from the use of institutions to foster family homes. In 1933, 2.5 per 1,000 children were placed in family homes, compared to 3.4 in institutions. In 1972, this trend had clearly been reversed with 3.6 per 1,000 children in family foster homes and 1.3 children in institutions (Kadushin, 1980).

Anna Freud
(Mark Peterson and Associates, with permission)

A major longitudinal study by Fanshel and Shinn (1978) of 8,600 children in New York City led to the conclusion that, as a whole, biological parents are more effective in facilitating long term adjustment of a child than are out-of-home caretakers. This study examined the impact of foster care on children. Children were rated over 5 years according to the results of psychological tests, and by parents, teachers, and social workers. Fifty-two percent of the children were rated "normal" by psychologists, while 25 % were rated "abnormal" or "suspect," after 5 years of tracking. Twelve percent of the children were always rated as "abnormal" or "suspect." At the end of the study, approximately 25 % of the children were viewed as emotionally impaired. Social workers rated children at the end of 5 years by the degree of difficulty experienced in foster care. Thirty percent of the children had no difficulty, 40 % had slight difficulty, 17 % had moderate difficulty, and 12 % were rated as showing substantial difficulty. Approximately 30 % of the children in care experienced difficulty in their lives. Teachers rated the children on overall emotional adjustment. According to their ratings, 9 % were very well adjusted, 27 % were well adjusted, 33 % were moderately adequately adjusted, and 24 % of the children were rated poor and very poorly adjusted. The last two categories were considered pathological, and again 31 % of the children experienced major adjustment problems. Although Fanshel and Shinn's (1978) study did not contain a control group, based upon careful analysis of the children over 5 years, psychologists, parents, teachers, and social workers portrayed 25 % to 33 % of the children as showing signs of emotional impairment.

The placement of minority youths in foster and substitute care is much higher than for white youths when compared by percentage of the population (Stehno, 1982). Black children comprised approximately 15 % of the total population of youths under age 18 in 1970; yet, they made up between 22 % and 32 % of the institutionalized population (Shyne & Schroeder, 1978 and Children's Defense Fund, 1978). Native American children who represent less than 1 % of the total population of youth under 18 are placed in out-of-home placements at a higher rate than any group of children. Twenty-five percent of all Native American children are placed in foster, group, and adoptive homes. An additional 25,000 Native American youths are in boarding schools which are more similar to residential than educational facilities (Stehno, 1982). Hispanic youths comprise approximately 7 % of the total population of youths under 18. Thirteen % of Hispanic children are in foster care placements, and another 6 % are in juvenile delinquency placements (Children's Defense Fund, 1978). Approximately 3/4 of the children studied in the Fanshel and Shinn study (1978) were Black or Puerto Rican.

Economics play a major role in the placement of children. With a higher percentage of minority children living at or below the poverty level, we see more of them placed in foster care where they remain for a longer period of time (Fanshel & Shinn, 1978).

When children are removed from dysfunctional families and placed in foster care, they bring with them certain defensive behaviors. Mayfield and Neil (1983) have identified four roles that children may assume upon removal from their homes.

1.   The lost child. This child is quiet and well behaved, appearing comfortable with minimal care and supervision. The lost child may be a high risk for severe depression or suicide during adolescence or adulthood because of a low sense of self-worth and an inability to create and mainain emotional attachments. The lost child may have been the victim of sexual abuse and learned the hard lesson that noninvolvement is the best course to pursue for protection from further abuse. The quiet shyness of the lost child may be a wall behind which feelings of loneliness, inadequacy, fear, and doubts of self-worth lie.

2.   The clown. Clowns hide their true feelings by joking around and being cute and charming. The clown will do anything to attract attention, is highly energetic, verbal, and appears hyperactive. The affects of abuse and trauma may appear to be minimal or nonexistent. The child in this category will probably deny any pain and quickly change the subject. The child refuses to admit even to him- or herself the fact that he or she has been abused and hides feelings of fear, insecurity, and extreme confusion.

3.   The troublemaker. This child is rambunctious and presents severe behavior problems. Troublemakers are low achievers in school, have few friends, and are often involved in petty delinquent activities. They have few close relationships, and foster parents may find caring for this type of child extremely difficult. Troublemakers may experience multiple placements, eventually ending up in residential treatment. This child may have been the scapegoat in his or her own home and may have been blamed for the family's problems. The troublemaker is a high risk child for substance abuse, using drugs to mask feelings of anger, fear, rejection, guilt, and loneliness.

4.   The achiever. This child is the foster parents' ideal child. Achievers are well behaved, pleasant, and show little reaction to being moved. The child has many friends and does average or better work in school. The achiever may appear unaffected by placement and may hide feelings of inadequacy, confusion, and anger behind independence and responsibility in a facade of maturity. These children may achieve at the cost of developing a rigid ego structure. If so, they are high risks for emotional disturbance in adulthood.

All of these children have the feeling that they are helpless and moved against their will through a series of new environments by adults.

Treatment

To help children cope with the psychological trauma of separation and reattachment, with the tension between biological parents, foster parents, and social workers, and with learning a new social system, the practitioner must address basic security issues and the precipitating factors which necessitated placement. Clearly, this is not an easy task. Mayfield and Neil (1983) use a group approach which can be applied to individual therapy to achieve their goals.

1. Attempt to build self-esteem by helping children become aware of their own individual strengths and special attributes.

2. Teach children basic coping and communication skills to enable them to reach out and establish relationships.

3. Help children assert themselves so their needs are clearly stated to the caretakers.

4. Build trust.

5. Alleviate the children's guilt by helping them realize they are not responsible for their family's dysfunctioning.

Examining the process of development of a child in substitute care is a useful tool for analyzing disruption in the child's life. The child may have difficulty developing stable, meaningful relationships with other people. He or she may lack control of destructive behaviors and fantasies. Self-esteem and the development of ego functions including adaptation through reality testing and cognition may be impaired. The foster child may lack the intense symbiotic dialogue with the parent, as his or her needs have not been met. The detachment from the mother may result in an emotionally withdrawn, apathetic child who will proclaim "love" for any adult who will pay any attention.

To an abused or special needs child, the added stress of a new environment may increase the vulnerability to maladjustment. The treatment approach needs to focus on development of self-esteem and attachment to the biological family and significant others. Other interventions should relate to the family, such as increasing the number of in-home services available to enable children to remain in their own homes while the dysfunctional family is attempting to retain homeostasis. Frazier and LeVine's (1983) Reattachment Therapy, described in the previous chapter, can be a treatment strategy for children returning to their biological families. Close contact through visits is critical to a successful reunion.

Fanshel and Shinn (1978) identified a strong correlation between the length of out-of-home placement and the visitation with biological parents. That is, the longer the child is out-of-home, the fewer the visits. Although clear difficulties are inherent in the visitation of parents with children, these visits are critical for several reasons (Kadushin, 1980).

1. Children identify with their parents, even if they have been victims of severe abuse and see foster care placement as rejection by their parents. This may create low self-esteem within the children.

2. Children may develop fantasies of the "ideal" parent if they do not occasionally see their parents. This may affect children's ego functioning in relation to reality testing.

3. Children will miss their parents and mourn their absence, resulting in at least mild depression.

4. Effective visits with the biological parents can help children adjust to the reality of separation and to remember that they are safe in their present environments.

A number of studies (Littner, 1971, Kadushin, 1980) and our experience show that visits between the biological parents and the child can be extremely disruptive to the foster family. Visits may be at inconvenient times, and the child may return from the visits and act out his or her anger and frustration. Foster parents may be threatened by the biological parents. Despite these difficulties, it is important for the case manager and the practitioner to maintain the relationship between the biological parents and the child if a return to the home is the permanent plan.

Some strides are being made for more in-home services, so few children will need to be removed. However, few alternatives to out-of-home placement exist, given the lack of homemakers, specialized day treatment, day care, public housing, and other social services. The Adoption Assistance and Child Welfare Act of 1980 (Public Law 96-272) attempts, at the policy level, to stem the placement of children in foster homes and has met limited success. Although a great amount has been written on the foster care system, reaearch on substitute care's long term and short term impact on children's emotional, social, and physical development has been somewhat limited.

ADOPTION

By the very definition of adoption, children enter a new legal family. Adoptions in the United States are evenly divided between relative and nonrelative adoptions (Kadushin, 1980). We will address primarily nonrelative adoptions.

Eighty-five percent of the children available for nonrelative adoptions are born out of wedlock. Another group of children come from abusive homes, where parental rights have been terminated. The majority of the abused children freed for adoption are older, with their own unique problems of entering a new family. A number of problems may plague adopted children. The lack of knowledge of biological parents and the adoptive parents' acceptance of their role as nonbiological parents may create special problems. The lack of knowledge about their biological parents, their roots, may prompt outbursts with teachers, parents, and other significant adults. Frisk (1964) theorized that the adoptee's genetic ego is replaced by hereditary ghost. In the case of transcultural adoptions, the cultural ghost may also complicate healthy development of an identity. Young adolescents see themselves as a link in their biological family's geneological chain. Lack of health information and a number of foster home placements may also create insecurity and emotional detachment of older children.

In their stimulating text, **Beyond the Best Interest of the Child,** Goldstein, Freud, and Solnit (1979, pp. 12, 13) write, "Blood. . .carries no weight with children who are emotionally unaware of the events leading to their birth. . . What registers in their minds are the day-to-day interchanges with adults who take care of them and who, on the strength of these, become the parent figures to whom they are attached." Given that the process of parent-child bonding, rather than the biological birth is critical to healthy development, it may seem surprising that many theorists and child practitioners view adopted children as particularly prone to stress. Therapists report adopted children are often preoccupied with fantasies about their natural parents. They may express feelings of being unwanted or different from other children. Norvell and Guy (1977) concluded that adoption status alone cannot produce a negative self-concept. Adoption status can make children vulnerable to stress. Kadushin (1980, p. 487) writes, "The adopted child faces all the general problems of development encountered by his nonadopted peers. In this sense, he is a child among other children. But, in addition, like the adopted parent, he faces some special problems that are related to the fact that he is an adopted child."

Adjustment

Perhaps our best insight on adjustment problems of adopted children comes from adoptees themselves. **The Adoption Triangle,** by Sorosky, Baran, and Pannor (1978), lists a number of letters by adoptees on their feelings and problems. "As a child I can remember how strongly my need was to know more about my birth parents. For all the love and attention I got as a child, I still knew deep inside that my uncles and aunts and cousins and grandparents were never really mine. I never really felt like I was part of the family." (Sorosky, Baran, & Pannor,1978, p.92). An adolescent states, "During my adolescence, I became very concerned with my own identity, and its relationship to my past and future. What will I look like has always been a question of great importance to me." (Sorosky, Baran, & Pannor 1978, p. 110).

Research

In a review of the adjustment patterns of adopted children, Lawton and Gross (1964) reported such inconsistency in methodology and results between studies that conclusions about adjustment among adopted children cannot be reached. Although the feelings of adopted children toward their adoption have not been systematically investigated, some studies have compared the adjustment of adopted to nonadopted children. Some of these studies speak to the success of adoptive placements and define outcomes ranging from capable and satisfactory to removed and experiencing adjustment problems.

Kadushin (1980) cites 20 major agency and nonagency adoption outcome studies from 1924 through 1980. Based upon the referral of adoptive children to mental health services 72 % of the placements were successful, 16 % of the children were labeled as having intermediate success, and 12 % had very poor adjustments and were unsuccessful. These studies address family characteristics that create stress for adopted children. There appears to be more stress if the adoptive parents are older, if the marital interaction is characterized by much strife, and if the adopted child is an only child. The acceptance of the adoption also impacts upon the effectiveness.

Adopted children are always faced with the possibility of a disruption (removal of the adopted child from the home) in their new family. Based upon his analysis of nine major studies related to failed adoptive placements, Kadushin (1980) concludes that for all adoptions, the disruption rate is 3.1 %. These studies were conducted between 1955 and 1970, a period when most placements were made for infants and not for special needs children. With the signing of Public Law 96-272, the Adoption Assistance and Child Welfare Act of 1980, states and agencies are placing more older and handicapped children in adoptive homes. These children are more likely to encounter a disruption. Spalding for Children, a highly publicized placement agency of special needs children, completed a study between 1968 and 1976 of 199 older and handicapped children. The disruption rate was 10.6 % (Unger, Dwarshuis, & Johnson, 1977). Many agencies expect disruption rates for special needs children to run approximately 12 %. A United States and Canada study of the placement success of 735 developmentally-disabled children discovered an overall disruption rate of only 8.7 %. If the child was adopted by foster parents, the disruption rate dropped to 4.4 %, and the new family adoption rate was 10.4 %. Age is an important variable for disruption rates as well. Developmentally disabled children under 7 year of age had a low, 3.3 %, disruption rate, but children 8 and over showed a very high rate, 17.7 % (Coyne & Brown, 1985).

It is estimated that only about 1 % of all children are nonrelative adoptions; however, research data indicate that 4.6 % of the children in psychiatric facilities are adoptees (Kadushin, 1980). These data are particularly interesting in light of Schechter's (1964) study which examined the tendency of adoptive parents to use pediatric clinics and concluded that adoptive parents did not frequent pediatric clinics more than biological parents. Therefore, if adoptive parents use agencies at the same level as biological parents, the 4.6 % usage of psychiatric facilities may reflect a high frequency of adjustment problems among adopted children.

Several well designed studies point to greater maladjustment of adopted than nonadopted children. Bohman (1972) systematically sampled 168 adopted children in Stockholm, Sweden. He studied the children's school records, interviewed all parents, and talked with all but five of the teachers. No difference was reported in academic performance between adopted and nonadopted boys and girls. However, 22 % of the adopted boys versus 12 % of the nonadopted boys were reported to display significant behavioral problems. A similar, nonsignificant statistical trend was noted between the adopted and nonadopted girls. Another study identified apparent differences between adopted girls' and boys' termperaments (Maurer, Cadoret, & Cain, 1980).

A study by Weiss (1984) compared the parent-child relationship of adoptive adolescents with those living with biological parents who were receiving treatment in a Philadelphia psychiatric hospital. Data were collected through a review of medical records of 140 youth between the years of 1970 and 1979. Statistical analysis demonstrated that adoptive parents were more restricted in their visits with their adopted children and that adoptive parents were more likely to have serious problems relating to the adolescents.

Telling the Child He or She Is Adopted

A parent may be secretive about the child's adoption. The child may then feel he or she is an embarrassment to the family. A classic study shows that telling the child as early as he or she is developmentally capable of understanding about the adoption minimizes this risk (Mech, 1973). Yet, some theorists believe the move to open adoptions may be detrimental to the child because the biological parent may then have an impact on the child's environment (Kraft, Palombo, Mitchell, Woods, Schmidt, & Tucker, 1985).

Parents may overestimate the child's ability to understand the adoption process and confuse the child with early discussions of adoption (Brodzinsky, Pappas, Singer, & Braff, 1981; Brodzinsky, Singer, & Braff, 1984). Brodzinsky's study used open-ended interviews with adoptive and nonadoptive children in grades 1, 3, 5, 7, 9, and 11. The children were interviewed about their knowledge of adoption. Responses were organized into "levels" of understanding the complex adoption process. Children in the first grade could usually differentiate between birth and adoption but had only a vague awareness of a third party that served as an intermediary in the process. Not until children reached the upper elementary years did a majority recognize the role an agency played in the adoption process to assure the mutual rights, needs, and welfare of children and their parents (Brodzinsky, Singer, & Braff, 1981).

In another study on the child's understanding of adoption, (Brodzinsky, Singer, & Braff, 1984) examined 200 adopted and biological children, ages 4 to 13. The results from this study indicate a clear developmental trend in the child's knowledge of adoption and its implications for families. Between the ages of 8 and 11, Brodzinsky sees a general increase in adoption knowledge, resulting for some adoptive children in a tenuous family relationship. Therefore, early telling may be important to diminish anxiety and mystique concerning adoption, but the discussion must be tailored to the child's cognitive development.

The research demonstrates the complexity of adoption and the difficulty of assessing the impact the adoption process has on a given child. Adopted boys and special needs children are subject to more adjustment problems than adoptive girls or their nonadoptive peers. In addition to this finding, the research is inconclusive on the impact of other variables such as age of parent, socioeconomic status, income, etc. on the success of the adoption. Yet, the question of importance from our perspective is success at what emotional and developmental cost to the child. Besides the fact that adopted children have a much higher representation as clients in mental health services, we have little research to guide treatment.

Treatment

The configuration of the child's presenting problem, developmental stage, previous experiences, number of placements, and the adoptive family's dynamics determine the therapeutic strategy. A case management approach can facilitate assisting the adopted child so he or she is less vulnerable to maladjustment. Enlistment of significant adults in the child's life, with an understanding of the special issues of adoption, creates an environment for the children where they feel secure. Group therapy for adoptive children, which explores at an appropriate developmental level, grief, separation, and myths regarding adoption can be very helpful.

A common issue in adoption concerns disclosure. How much information should be shared of the child's history and biological parents? Until the 1950's, this information was rarely concealed from an adopted child. Usual practice now is to conceal records with the belief that knowledge of the child's history prevents the child's adaptation to his or her present environment. Nothing in our present understanding of child development verifies this assumption. To the contrary, the knowledge of the child's past demystifies the adoption process, prevents the child from creating false fantasies about his or her parents, and lessens the adopted child's fears of being different or bad. Also, the family's ability to deal openly with the child's adoption keeps adoption from becoming a covert issue used in family interactions.

The age of the child at the time of the adoption is a key determining factor in how much to discuss the biological parents with the child. If the child was adopted as a newborn, unfortunately, the adoptive parents may know little of the biological parents. If the child is older, he or she will remember the biological parents, raising a variety of issues. Practitioners may need to deal with the child's feelings of rejection by the biological parents or of hostility toward the adoptive parents for taking them away. In both cases, the adoptive parents may be confronted intense feelings which are difficult to handle.

A nonadoptive child accepts the fact that his parents may be both loving and rejecting, but an adoptive child has two sets of parents. Adoptive children may separate these sets of parents along the lines of loving and rejecting. One set of parents assumes all the attributes of the negative parent, while the other assumes those of the positive parent. Adoptive children, of course, usually idealize the absent biological parent. On the other hand, the children understand that these are the same parents who gave them up for adoption. Thus, a dilemma in the adoptive child's development of a positive self-image emerges.

Adoptive parents may interpret a child's resistence as a test of their love. A maladaptive pattern may emerge where parent and child question their commitment to each other. The parent may compare the adopted child to nonadopted children, making the adopted child feel inferior. Parents may attribute the child's negative traits or behaviors to his or her biological parents, rather than to faulty child-rearing practices. This child becomes the "identified patient" as described in the chapter on Family Therapy. Both parents and the child in question may come to regard the child as intrinsically bad, rather than examining the problem of family interaction.

Child practitioners report that parents who have adopted a child may experience stress about the child's adoption and transmit this concern to the child. Adoptive parents may experience marital crises because of their need to have a child. This stress affects how they interact with the adopted child. Other parents are too overprotective of their adopted child, setting in motion psychologically unhealthy situations for all. On the other hand, some adoptive parents communicate verbally or nonverbally to children that, although they love them, they are different. This love-rejection relationship ultimately proves disastrous to the child and parents, especially during the early teenage years.

The onset of adolescence creates many concerns for adoptees and their families. Physical concerns become an issue. An adoptive girl's sexual development can threaten an infertile mother through seductive actions toward the father. In adoption, the incest taboo may be weakened as well. As an adoptive son's sexuality emerges, a sterile adoptive father may be threatened.

A theory on the unique identity crisis faced by an adopted teenager (Sallee & LeVine, 1985) is illustrated by the story of Narcissus. As a youth, Narcissus fell in love with his own image in a pool of water. He could never grasp the image in the pool, yet he could not leave. He learned the lesson that energy invested totally in oneself does not lead to a more enduring meaning. As we discussed in the developmental chapter, all teenagers tend to be very narcissistic. A teenager must harness dramatic physical, social, and psychological changes which will enhance his or her personal development. The changes in teenagers may preoccupy them as they spend many hours before a mirror, preening or grooming themselves. The adolescent faces many societal changes. Few meaningful contributions to society are required of today's teenagers, driving their efforts inward. Teenagers will speak for hours on the phone on rather trivial matters; however, to them, this is part of their identity. Other activities such as chores around the house pale in comparison to this powerful personal search for identity.

The psychoanalytic literature relates how children are born in almost a total narcissistic state with their existence centered on meeting their needs for comfort. As these needs are met, newborns quickly learn to reciprocate. They share coo's, smiles, and cuddles. So begins a shift from total narcissism to individualism as a social being who enjoys mutuality with the parent. Giving and taking continues through the developmental stages until the beginning of adolescence.

In young adoptive children, we may see selfishness, unreasonable demands, and other behaviors which are soundly criticized by adults. The child develops a negative self-concept which emerges during the identity crises. Even if removal from the biological mother was within the first few weeks of life, a normal attachment may fail to occur. Based upon this theory, attachment therapy, as discussed in Chapter 12, can be quite effective in working with these adoptive children.

If the process of bonding, attachment, and gradual separation is disrupted, the movement from total narcissism to the mutuality is blocked. Thus, adopted children who suffered early bonding difficulties may be particularly prone to narcissistic behavior.

Family therapy can help parents and children air their mutual worries thereby fostering bonding. Most critical is the prevention strategy of placing children in permanent adoptive homes as soon as possible. Adopted children do not necessarily experience extreme emotional problems. However, there remains a large number of adopted children who are highly vulnerable, particularly children, who in their teenage years experience troublesome identity crises, older children who have been separated from their biological parents, and children of cross-cultural adoptions. An understanding of the possible developmental interruption of bonding with the parent and the ensuing social problems will enable the therapist to work with the child, the family, and the social service system to diminish the stresses placed upon the adopted child experiencing a new family.

SUMMARY

We stressed in our earlier chapters that not all disturbed children grow up to be disturbed adults, and many disturbed adults were not overtly disturbed when young. Yet, many of the maladjusted adults who were not disturbed as youths were vulnerable children. Over and over again, clinic records of adult patients reveal a childhood of new families.

Vulnerable children are in personal and social pain, but often have enough ego strength that they are not referred to treatment. Rather than losing ego control and exhibiting encopresis, acting out, and other behaviors that would lead to clinical referral, they withdraw and fail to thrive. They are "no problem" to most until later. As an adult, the adopted or foster child may become asocial or antisocial, feeling alienated from his roots and society. As an adult, the child of divorced parents and from a single parent home may be confused about relationships with the opposite sex. If the practitioner is alert to the potential of maladjustment among children experiencing new families, the possibility of later emotional problems can be obviated.

PART FIVE
Looking Forward

PART V

LOOKING FORWARD

When we listen to our children, we realize that:

Too many are suffering tremendous personal pain.

Too many lack the personal skills to change adverse social social situations.

Too many are not receiving the mental health assistance they need.

For many, the disturbance is very profound by the time they receive assistance.

For many, amelioration of their distress will require extended intervention in the family system.

For many, intense, individual counseling will be required before they can again begin to grow toward their personal potential.

It is obvious that we best help and protect our children by, whenever possible, preventing the need for mental health intervention. Child practitioners can use their skills in many ways to help create a nourishing environment for their children. This unit reviews some of those means. If every child practitioner would consider it a part of his or her professional responsibility to participate in some preventive mental health strategy, we could indeed look forward to a world in which children have an opportunity to grow up without despair and to meet their potential. A world of such mentally healthy children is probably the only way of creating a different world ambience. For mentally healthy children once grown up would be better prepared to deal with the critical problems of our technological age. The responsibility of child practitioners is tremendous, but also great are the practitioners' potential for impact, if they are actively involved in preventive mental health intervention.

CHAPTER 15

PREVENTION, CONSULTATION, AND POLICY FORMULATION

Our review of the child practice literature has focused almost entirely on discussion of psychosocial stresses and on treatment approaches for working with children. This review is not complete without a discussion of preventive mental health strategies and policy implications for clinical practice. Clearly, efforts to prevent problems before they occur are a necessary ingredient of a systematic approach to promoting mental health. Similarly, understanding the impact of clinical decisions upon the community facilitates the long range mental health of children. Understanding the roles and functions of consultation enables the child practitioner to effectively link and mobilize community services to meet the needs of the child.

PREVENTION

Primary prevention services began in the settlement house era (late 1800's) to respond to the profound need for changing the environmental and family conditions which lead to a low quality of life. The 1915 National Conference on Social Welfare presented six papers on prevention (Bowker, 1983). By the 1930's, ideology shifted to preventing death, disabilities, and illness for mothers and infants through the U. S. Children's Bureau grant-in-aid programs (Costin, 1979). Efforts in the late 1970's to promote federal interest and funding were largely prompted by a monograph,
Primary Prevention: An Idea Whose Time Has Come (Klein & Goldston, 1977). After almost a century of effort, a clear, commonly accepted interdisciplinary model for primary prevention has yet to emerge. After we present three types of prevention, we will examine family crisis prevention.

So important is prevention of mental health-related disorders among children that the President's Commission of Mental Health (1978) indicated that "helping children must be the Nation's first priority in preventing mental disability" (p. 51). In this chapter, we will explore various ways in which child therapists can fulfill their obligation to serve as preventive mental health specialists. It is important to recognize that the area of prevention constitutes a major mental health challenge, and it is exceedingly difficult for one individual alone to be instrumental in effecting changes that result in marked reductions in childhood mental disorders. Nonetheless, it is our hope that child therapists in collaboration with one another can serve as effective advocates and change agents for children.

343

Types of Prevention

Three types of prevention have been identified by mental health professionals (Lorion & Lounsbury, 1982). We will define each type and provide several examples of how they apply to children.

Primary Prevention

Primary prevention refers to a group of approaches that share the common objectives of (1) lowering the incidence of emotional disorder (i.e., the rate at which new cases occur) and (2) promoting conditions that reinforce positive mental health. Primary prevention is concerned with populations not yet affected by individual emotional disorders, especially with groups at high risk. This approach is proactive in that it seeks to build adaptative strengths through education and reduce causes of emotional disorders through social engineering.

We can differentiate at least four distinct types of primary prevention programs (Goldston, 1978). The first type involves preventing vulnerable populations from succumbing to emotional disorders. High-risk target groups might include children having one or two schizophrenic parents, children of alcoholics and drug addicts, youngsters experiencing the death of a parent, and children with physical handicaps.

A second type of primary prevention program focuses on preventing the onset of carefully defined target disorders. Programs directed at attempting to prevent poisonings from lead-based paints, venereal diseases (e.g., syphillis), genetic diseases (e.g., Tay-Sachs, phenylketonuria), nutritional diseases (e. g., pellegra), delinquency, or addictions all illustrate this approach. In recent years, this approach has resulted in many improvements in the care of children and with a consequent decrease in a wide variety of childhood-related disorders.

A third type of prevention program seeks to promote and enhance the overall psychosocial functioning of high risk children (e.g., poor and/or minority children). Programs following this approach are oriented toward building or strengthening parents' low-probability competencies in affective behaviors, cognitive and problem-solving abilities, and social skills.

A final type of prevention intervention provides children, parents, and teachers with experiences to ease the impact of traumatic developmental milestones or unavoidable life crises. For example, a program may focus on parenting skills for teenage expectant parents, problems of separation with school entrance, strategies for lessening the impact of divorce on young children, or minimizing problems associated with working parents. This approach seeks to place these positive educational interventions at strategic points in an individual's life cycle for the explicit purpose of enhancing coping skills to successfully navigate stressful life experiences.

The President's Commission on Mental Health (1978) made primary prevention the cornerstone of its recommendations for improving the status of mental health within the United States. Further, as already noted, "helping children" was indicated as the first priority by the the Commission.

Secondary Prevention

This approach to prevention focuses on the early detection of a problem and its subsequent intervention before more intensive treatment is required. The approach may involve early and periodic development with concommitant treatment if required. The essential difference between primary and secondary prevention is that in primary prevention the focus is on the elimination of the root causes of a problem before the problem actually occurs; whereas, in secondary prevention, the goal is to reduce the problem (through treatment) before the problem worsens. For example, it is known that ingestion of lead can result in severe inflammation of the brain with resulting hemorrhage and lesions. Up to twenty years ago, lead poisoning was a severe problem among children who would become ill by chewing on furniture or windowsills covered with paint containing lead. Once the relationship was established between lead poisoning and brain damage, laws were passed (i.e., primary prevention) restricting the manufacture and use of lead-based paints. This does not mean, however, that lead poisoning has been eliminated. It is known that children, mostly in poverty areas, still can eat the toxic substance in peeling paint from walls and windowsills. Pediatricians, psychologists, and preschool educators, in their developmental assessment of young children from poverty areas, should be especially watchful of the problem of lead poisoning. Children who appear to be developmentally retarded in some aspect of their functioning may be suffering the consequences of lead ingestion. Accordingly, the screening may require a home visit, parent interview, and medical examination since the treatment (i.e., secondary prevention) for a child suffering from the initial stages of lead poisoning will differ from another child who also shows signs of retardation, which are not associated with lead poisoning.

Secondary prevention approaches seek to identify through various early screening procedures children who are demonstrating the initial signs of some physical or psychological dysfunction. Once identified, the second stage of the program is put into operation. This is the treatment phase which aims to eliminate or curtail the problem(s) resulting from the dysfunction before they become severe enough to require tertiary prevention.

Tertiary Prevention

In some respects, this type of prevention does not merit the term "prevention" at all. The focus here is on the rehabilitation through treatment of the individual once the dysfunction has reached such a magnitude that overall well being is severely threatened or where the problem has reached the point where the individual must be institutionalized. Note that the central concept here is that of "rehabilitation." It should be obvious that much of this text focuses on the tertiary aspect of working with children. Despite the interest in primary and secondary prevention (e.g., President's Commission on Mental Health, 1978), most mental health specialists still devote the majority of their time and effort to tertiary prevention. There are many reasons for this. First, despite the lip service given to primary and secondary prevention, adequate support for true preventive programs had been lacking at the federal and state governmental levels. Second, primary prevention, because of its proactive stance of eliminating the root causes of mental disorders, is extremely difficult to carry out to completion in most cases. Third, training in primary prevention techniques is sorely lacking in our graduate programs. As a consequence, few specialists can be called upon to lend their expertise to problems requiring preventive approaches.

One aspect of tertiary prevention that requires comment and which if enacted upon can result in "rehabilitation" playing a more central role in mental health concerns evaluation of treatment approaches. Throughout this book, we have discussed the various issues associated with child practice, including questions of assessment and the various treatment approaches. What we have not concentrated on is the issue of evaluation of our total approach to working with troubled children. By this, we mean that the child practitioner must apply rigorous methods to determine whether the assessment instruments and techniques are appropriate for the child being assessed. Similarly, the therapist must apply the same rigorous methods to evaluate the effectiveness of their therapeutic intervention. What should be of prime concern is whether the child is making satisfactory gains in therapy, whether the improvement is long lasting, and whether the improvement is generalizable to all facets of the child's life situation. Too often, "under the gun" of a heavy caseload, practitioners are prone to put aside questions of evaluation of treatment. When evaluation of tertiary prevention is undertaken, this type of prevention becomes at least as important as the other approaches to prevention discussed above.

Family Crisis Prevention

Throughout this text, we have made reference to the critical role the family unit plays in childhood problems. Family crisis prevention can reduce stress that vulnerable children may feel. Primary prevention programs, to be most effective, relate to the family as a system and maximize relevant family program involvement.

Broad prevention programs prevent multiple dysfunctional behaviors and can be applied to the general population as well as to targeted populations. The intervention timing in generic programs is generally "long before" the prevented dysfunction is known to occur. Early research in generic prevention points to two ideal times to intervene in the family cycle. The preparent stage (example: high school parenting classes) and the stage when families have children 0-5 years old (Sallee, D., 1982).

The existence of a dysfunctional member in the family is a stressor that may catalyze other family members to develop compensatory dysfunctional behavior. When an alcoholic, highly emotionally disturbed, child abuser, or criminal is a family member, overall family functioning is highly disturbed. The primary intervention would best occur as soon after the dysfunction emerges as possible.

Life passages such as childhood, puberty, menopause, old age, parenthood, and death are stressors which can trigger dysfunctional behavior. Other stressors such as divorce, unemployment, and poverty can be contributing factors (Sallee, D., 1982). In these cases, primary prevention intervention for individual family members or the entire family can be quite helpful.

A year-long consultation concerning prevention conducted with professionals from education, criminal justice, child care, medicine, mental health, and private child and family practitioners led to the development of policies and implementation strategies in New Mexico for family crisis prevention (Sallee & Downes, 1982). A summary of the recommendations follows:

1. Educational Services

    ■   Policies should promote family life education activities with suggested focus for curriculum and skill training.

    ■   A strong public information emphasis is endorsed, as well as a system of electronic information and referral services networking communities across the state.

2. Early Screening and Intervention Services

    ■   public health services

    ■   school-based programs

    ■   Medicaid-financed medical care

    ■   employees assistance program

    ■   protective services

- mental health services

- law enforcement services

3. Support Services to Families

- Comprehensive attention should be given to day care services as a vehicle for family crisis prevention.

- The economic stability of families is seen as a fundamental means of preventing family crises.

- Policies supporting the professionalism of the service providers to families should be promoted through training and certification.

- The role of the homemaker services is a critical means of preventing family crisis.

4. Funding

- A family-oriented philosophy should be promoted in the purchase of services through the state funding mechanisms.

- Policies must address more efficient coordination of state services to families, as well as a financial mechanism for funding such services.

- Adequate funding is needed to attract and support a high level of professional care.

The consultation demonstrated that child practitioners can play vital roles in improving policy which affects their clients. Implementing the policies is a long and ongoing process.

Overviewing Prevention

Professionals in the field of child therapy have been only nominally effective in designing preventive mental health programs for children. As we suggested in the previous chapters, many vulnerable children remain undetected. Often, preventive mental health measures for children are aimed at a secondary level of prevention such as removing them from overcrowded classrooms or understaffed, in-patient clinics. Ideally, goals in preventive mental health for children should be twofold. First, we must strive to identify the contingencies that foster healthy development in children and families. Second, we should ensure that these conditions are maximally present in all homes, schools, and community environments that constitute the child's primary domain. In short, the child practitioner should be an advocate for children and play the role of an "inspirator" in assisting the community to build upon existing resources to best foster the mental health of children.

THE PRACTITIONER AS CONSULTANT

One of the primary ways in which the child practitioner can effectively serve the community as a prevention specialist is through consultation with community organizations. Fullmer and Bernard (1972), in their well reputed text on consultation by child practitioners, state that social service agencies are often very innovative in their approaches to children's mental health. However, they contend that short-term governmental policies and funding practices do not allow for the blossoming of many of these innovative programs. For example, in the early 1970's, the federal government funded a number of model programs to prevent child abuse. Today, very few of these programs exist. The reasons for the lack of viability of such programs are varied. Fullmer and Bernard (1972) propose that a basic difficulty is that not enough of the community affected by these programs is involved in their planning and implementation. The major role of the consultant as Fullmer and Bernard see it is to foster and guide interaction of involved parties so that innovative programs are prompted and pursued on a long-term basis if they prove effective.

The child therapist is a likely consultant for working with various groups involved in preventive mental health programs for children because of her or his knowledge about child development and skill in facilitating communication (Morales & Sheafor, 1983). The role of the child consultant differs from that of the child therapist. As consultant, the child specialist relies first and foremost upon communication skills. The consultant may provide some answers and asks critical questions. Primarily, the consultant attempts to uncover and process the wisdom of the group. The primary functions of the child consultant as summarized by Fullmer and Bernard (1972) are:

1. Provide in-service education functions for teachers, parents and other mental health professionals.

2. Stimulate self-help organizations, that is, teach new approaches for relating to children to teachers, parents and other professionals so that they continue preventive mental health measures.

3. Bring together persons of diverse roles and functions to engage in common tasks.

4. Improve communication and enhance information flow among significant persons in the milieu.

5. Extend the services of experts to the assigned task.

In successfully carrying out the dual roles of consultant on child related problems and advocate for children, numerous skills are required besides those of being a good therapist. These skills fall into the following categories: consultant competencies, education and training competencies, and organizer competencies. Each of these categories is discussed below.

Consultant Competencies

The consultant must have an understanding of and skill in the consultative process so that he or she is perceived as a "friendly helper" who is nonthreatening, nonjudgmental, and willing to listen. In some respects, the required skills are the same as those deemed essential in a good therapist. However, there are some differences that necessitate discussion. Insight into the knowledge and skills needed to function effectively as a consultant can be gleaned from a review of the literature which suggests the importance of the following consultant competencies (Rapoport, 1977; Caplan, 1970; Mannino, MacLennan & Shore, 1975; Williams, 1971; and Morales & Sheafor, 1983).

1. A thorough theoretical and practical understanding of the behavioral sciences.

2. Knowledge and use of authority for change in organizations.

3. Evaluation skills for both individuals and programs.

4. Ability to form relationships with other professionals based upon trust and knowledge.

5. Ability to plan and implement change with teams and community groups.

6. Ability to identify resources.

7. Possess strong problem-solving skills.ng, and other

8. Be honest, competent, sure of values, mature, and have a strong ego.

From the list of required skills, it is clear that the consultant must simultaneously use both technical and interpersonal skills. Consultants must have excellent diagnostic, conceptual, and problem-solving abilities. They must be actively goal-directed: defining areas for consultation, suggesting ideas and alternatives to clients, referring clients to appropriate resources, and specifying desired outcomes. They must be knowledgeable about specific programs and how similar programs have resolved problems in the past. They must possess good communication skills, both orally and in writing, and must be able to both calmly assess difficult situations and "think on their feet." Moreover, consultants must develop the capacity to assess and influence an organization's readiness for consultation. Organization readiness refers to the organization's perceptions of the existence of a problem, its recognition of the need for consultation, and the clarity of its expectations for the consultant. Finally, and not surprisingly, consultation requires that all of the above be done in a tactful, friendly, yet professional manner, generating trust, remaining flexible and tolerant of ambiguity, showing a good sense of timing, and being able to handle both frustration and criticism.

Education and Training Competencies

In the role of child advocate the therapist must know how to plan and design training programs and be able to utilize a variety of educational and training techniques, such as role-playing, simulations, and problem-solving exercises. They must be able to use the media--radio, television, and newspapers. Knowledge of multiple information dissemination strategies (such as pamphlets, leaflets, posters, bumper stickers, public service announcements, mailings, speakers, workshops, colloquia, and retreats) is essential, as is knowledge of evaluation techniques for assessing the effectiveness of various educational or training programs.

As an educator the therapist must be able to tailor different programs to specific populations. What may be effective with parents groups may be inappropriate for teachers and vice versa. Similarly, a program designed for radio presentation may be ineffective when done on television. If all of this were not enough the therapist/ educator must learn to overcome resistances to change within the targeted group.

Another function of the therapist/educator in many situations is the need to identify and train natural helpers who can participate in the education and change process. Sometimes these helpers may be other professionals, but more often they are concerned parents. For example, parents of several autistic children in a community may seek the assistance of a therapist in their efforts to obtain therapeutic and educational programs for their children from school officials or related social service agency in the community. Other natural helpers may include community leaders (e.g., local elected officials, clergy, media personalities, etc.), businessmen, or any other individual recognized by members of the community as knowledgeable of the dynamics of the community and capable of moving people to action.

In sum, the therapist/educator must be able to set clear objectives for educational efforts, to develop instructional materials, and to disseminate information that addresses identified needs. The person must also possess the energy and capacity to work with a diverse group of individuals on behalf of children.

Organizer Competencies

The therapist functions as an organizer when in the task of instituting a prevention program for children he or she attempts to develop networks and coalitions to address an identifiable problem, such as child abuse) (Maguire, 1984). Two specific skills required of the organizer can be identified: linking/outreach and group facilitation skills.

Linking/outreach skills are required when organizers move into the community. Organizers must have the ability to establish trust and a close working relationship with an ever-expanding network of individuals and groups brought together to achieve a common goal. Building trust in turn implies acting in a consistent and reliable manner with these frequently diverse constituencies. Organizers must also possess the ability to identify appropriate resources and to make them available to different client or consumer groups. To accomplish this, organizers must be able to access a range of resources (e.g., experts and sources of funds) as well as be knowledgeable about how to put such resources in the hands of appropriate client groups. Finally, effective organizers must have good political skills which enable them to build coalitions and to employ strategies designed to shift the balance of power in the community.

It is essential to recognize that the key in organizing is skill at group facilitation. Facilitation skills enable the organizer to keep a group functioning effectively, achieving a balance between accomplishing group tasks and maintaining healthy interpersonal relationships among group members. Problem-solving skills are also required as the organizer assists the group(s) in creatively and effectively moving through the stages of problem identification, proposal and review of alternative solutions, selection of a plan of action, implementation of the plan, and evaluation of the overall problem-solving effort. The organizer must assist the group in moving through the problem-solving steps while at the same time maintaining open communication among members and seeking advice from the outside where necessary. Finally, the organizer must use both group facilitation and problem-solving skills in promoting the emergence of leadership within the group, so that future group activities will draw more heavily on the capacities of group members.

Overviewing Consultation Role

We have discussed the complexity involved in the consultative role. The therapist who intends to advocate for children's right must function in multiple roles. The skills required of the therapist in each of these roles almost demand that the person be capable of "walking on water." The consultant must possess both technical and interpersonal competencies. In the role of consultant practical experience is as essential as formal training. Nevertheless, without individuals willing to become engaged in the consultative role, many prevention programs for children would never have become instituted. This is especially true of many primary and secondary prevention programs set up for the well-being of children.

Viewing the Therapist as Consultant

Let us now look more specifically at how a child therapist/consultant works in a preventive mental health capacity with two different groups of individuals who are extremely influential in the development of a child. Obviously, we are speaking of parents and educators.

<u>Consultation with parents</u>

The child consultant may work with parents individually or in groups. The exact structure of the consultation should be based on the goals defined by the involved parties. Regardless of the defined tasks, the child consultant will hold several broad goals. First the consultant will attempt to aid the parents in gaining an objective view of their relationships with their children. Thus, the consultant helps the parents set realistic goals and appreciate their children's progress. Secondly, the consultant wants to help the parents understand their own motives in dealing with children. If the relationship between parent and child is highly dysfunctional or has potentially destructive elements, the consultant helps parents identify these patterns and begin to establish a more appropriate interaction pattern (Freedman, Kaplan & Sadock, 1976; Smirnoff, 1968). Thirdly, the consultant wants to facilitate the parents' empathy for the child. Once the parents can empathize with the child's stresses and conflicts, they are better able to identify appropriate childrearing procedures. In order to sharpen parents' empathy, the consultant will provide information about child development. At times, it may be necessary for parents to deal with their own conflicts and repressions so that they will feel comfortable in identifying their children's stresses (Chess, et al, 1978). In order to accomplish these goals, the consultant must take the parents concerns seriously. The consultant's intense interest, as indicated by reflection and summarization of the parents' feelings and concerns, offers reassurance. The consultant will not surface the parents' possible role in the childrens' stresses too suddenly. If the parents feel they are being blamed, they are likely to become defensive. In this rigid state, the parents' abilities to be empathic with the child's dilemma is limited (Smirnoff, 1971). The consultant should expect some stereotyping about her- or himself or transference from some parents. Some parents react to the consultant as a "bad parent," feeling that the consultant can do nothing but destroy hopes. Others respond as if the consultant is an omnipotent parent who can resolve any conflict (Freedman, Kaplan & Sadock, 1976). The consultant will want to guard against providing excess advice as it may place the parent in a dependent position and reinforce the feeling that he or she is an inadequate parent.

In the role of consultant, the professional provides information and advice and serves as a general resource person on issues pertaining to children. This role is different from that of therapist and the two must be kept distinct. In consultation with parent groups, many of the same problems and resistances may occur that are seen in family therapy, but the consultant must strive to maintain an educative/preventive rather than a therapist role.

Parents will seek the aid of a child consultant for a variety of reasons. Sometimes therapy is a more appropriate intervention than preventive mental health consultation. Thus, the child consultant needs to consider which parents can be helped by the preventive mental health strategies and make referrals to therapy when that course of action seems more warranted than consultation. Sometimes, parents describe their children as experiencing "normal growing up problems" but to the consultant the problem may sound more serious (e.g., excessive stress reaction, learning disability, or even psychotic-like symptomology); in these cases, the consultant should recommend that the child be seen by a therapist (Chess, et al, 1978). Generally, if the parents' personal problems do not seem to interfere with their ability to empathize with the child, preventive mental health consultation can be helpful. If the parents lack motivation to change their responses, if they are very narcissistic, or their pathology interlocks with the child, family therapy and/or individual psychotherapy may be needed (Ack, Beal & Ware, 1975).

Parent groups can be conducted in a variety of ways. They may be open-ended discussion groups in which parents are encouraged to ask one another questions about childrearing techniques. The consultant may semistructure these discussion groups by having parents write down and then discuss their approaches to specific dilemmas. Another approach is parent education programs which focus upon discussion of a text or specific parenting material. Commonly employed procedures include the STEP Kit (Systematic Training for Effective Parenting) by Dinkmeyer & McKay (1976), humanistic approaches of Ginott (1965) and communication techniques of Gordon (1970). A number of consultants are teaching parents in groups to conduct counseling with their children (Ack, Beal & Ware, 1975). For example, parents may watch the therapist-consultant conduct play therapy sessions with a child. Parents then attempt the play therapy approaches at home. Later parent group sessions are employed to discuss the effectiveness of the home play approach (Keat, 1974). In other programs, parents are instructed in behavior management techniques and then are encouraged to carry out these techniques in their own childrearing practices (e.g., Gordon, 1970).

Programs which encourage parents to be change agents of their own offspring's behavior are not new. Perhaps the classic case is that of Little Hans who was treated by his father following the directions for therapy received from Sigmund Freud (Freud, 1955). Perhaps the two factors contributing to the growing interest to provide parents with the skills to change children's behavior stem from the large shortage that exists in each of the helping professions and from the increasing demand for child and family intervention. Interest in child consultation ranges from single parent groups to special interest groups such as parents of hyperactive, autistic, or retarded children. Increased interest by parents in parenting skills and knowledge of child development will support that goal of primary prevention discussed earlier in the chapter.

Although there has not been extensive study of the effectiveness of consultation with parents, preliminary results are very promising. Brown (1976) compared families in directive guidance groups to a waiting list control and reported significant changes in parents' attitudes toward the child and in the family interaction. Donofrio (1976) has shown that many parents can be helped to change destructive childhood behaviors in just 2 one-hour sessions. In a two year follow-up study of 66 cases, Donofrio found that 57 of the parents reported that their child had shown sustained improvement over the two year time period, while 9 cases were not improved. In another study, Lang (1975) reported on group consultation with mothers of high academic risk first graders. Although the consultation did not affect academic achievement scores, there was an increase in the mothers' positive attitudes towards their children.

Donofrio (1976) points out that parents spend so much time with their children that they are the natural and most potent source for primary and secondary intervention. Clearly, consultation with parents is an important activity for all child therapists. An important task for the future will be to find ways to maximize the consultant role with parents.

Consulting with Educators

A primary role for the child practitioner is to consult with teachers. Yet, little has been written about this important professional activity. Of even greater concern is the fact that child therapists not employed by schools typically have little contact with school personnel. Berkowitz (1968). reviewed the records of 4 mental health clinics serving children to ascertain the number of contacts with schools. He reported that at one clinic with a mean length of treatment of 20.8 months for 18 chilren, only 4 school contacts had been made. In the remaining clinics, 3.2 was the highest number of contacts per child. Thus, although teachers spend a large amount of time with children and can have enormous effects upon their psychosocial development, little is written about the means by which child therapists can assist educators in their work with children. Outside of the assistance of school counselors and school social workers, little preventive mental health support for children is offered to educators.

Until recently, most mental health consultation with teachers was of a rather dogmatic style. The practitioner would listen to the teacher's concerns, then provide information about the child's I.Q., personality and/or family life and finally offer recommendations for dealing with the child in the classroom. It was felt that the consultant should not take an active role in assisting the teacher in understanding his or her personal concerns regarding the child. Rather, the consultant's relationship was circumscribed to a present or future time orientation and focused only on the children's adjustment in the classroom setting. Yet, teaching can be as emotionally and personally stressful as parenting. Teachers need avenues of support in order to maintain their effectiveness. We now recognize that child specialists can offer social and emotional support to teachers in a variety of ways.

One of the primary functions of the school consultant is that of providing support to educators. The teacher needs empathy and support for dealing with difficult children. By using effective communication skills, the consultant can help the teacher clarify his or her teaching objectives so that he or she feels more confident in responding to problem children. It is easy for a consultant to become defensive if a teacher presents a very difficult case for assistance and the consultant feels that he or she lacks an answer to the dilemma. It is important for the consultant to recognize that the teacher possesses many skills and answers. Often, support and understanding may be all that are requested and needed.

The child consultant can also assist the teacher in working with special children (e.g., handicapped, gifted, hyperactive, etc.). The consultant can conduct a systematic study of the child's behavior in the classroom, playground and lunchroom so that appropriate reinforcers can be identified. Then, the consultant can work with the teacher to set up an effective management procedure. Often, the teacher is well versed in behavior management principles, but within the confines of the classroom may not be able to systematically observe a given child to identify problem behaviors and arrange for reinforcement contingencies for the shaping of new target behaviors. The consultant, as a "free agent" can provide valuable individual assistance.

The child consultant may chair or participate in staff conferences about specific children. In these conferences, it is often the child consultant's responsibility to recommend or bring in other professionals that may be of assistance. It is important that the consultant follow-up on the results of these case conferences to assure that recommendations have been completed and that the consequences are desirable.

The consultant may also offer in-service training for school personnel. The consultant can educate teachers about new principles in child management and innovative materials for affective education in the areas of coping with divorce, death of a parent or other loved one, sexuality, adjusting to a handicap, and so on. It may also be necessary for the consultant to assist the school counselor in gaining the skills necessary to work with teachers on a wider basis.

Finally, the child consultant can conduct groups with teachers to help them maximize their interperonal skills and deal with their feelings of stress. Some teacher groups focus upon the teacher in classroom management. In these groups, problems are identified. Teachers express their feelings about the problems and the ideas about the causes of behavioral problems. They brainstorm possible solutions and develop techniques for measuring gain. Later meetings are used for assessing results and brainstorming modifications to the procedures. Some teacher groups focus upon the teachers' self-development and enhancement because they are based on the premise that if teachers are well adjusted, then they are better able to manage in the classroom. Clearly, ways must be sought to facilitate long term stress reduction in teachers who find their jobs especially stressful. This is particularly true of teachers who work with severely emotionally disturbed or handicapped children, inner city school teachers, and teachers who are employed by poor school districts who do not have access to many of the educational resources available in wealthier school districts.

Overviewing Consultation

The child therapist possesses the skills to be of immense help to both parents and educators. The role of consultant is distinct from that of therapist. As a consultant, the practitioner lends his or her expertise to parents and teachers and attempts to facilitate their involvement with children through information on child development, behavioral management, and supportive problem solving. The ultimate goal of consultation is the promotion of positive mental health among children, parents, teachers, and any other individual whose interests bring them into contact with children.

FORENSIC CHILD PSYCHOLOGY AND SOCIAL WORK

Forensic psychology and social work involve the interfacing of applied psychology with the judiciary system. Theoretical questions such as what constitutes insanity and specific court actions such as whether an individual should be committed belong to this field. Thus, forensic work is concerned with legal ways of protecting an individual's right to emotional well-being. In recent years, the legal rights of children have become extremely important and demand discussion.

In 1948, the Ohio Supreme Court (Haley vs. Ohio 332, US 5961) ruled that the rights guaranteed to adults are also applicable to children. However, the ruling has provoked some critical questions. Since children are developmentally different from adults, in what ways must the laws be modified to protect their rights? When do parents rights conflict with the rights of children; and if they do, whose rights should be honored? Also what rights are unique to children? We are only at the beginning stages of answering these questions (Shore, 1979). The child therapist interested in preventive mental health will want to be familiar with the questions and tentative answers so that he or she can, when necessary, appeal to the judiciary system for children's betterment.

Some basic definitions of children's unique rights have emerged in the field of child therapy. In 1970, the Joint Commission on the Mental Health of Children presented these rights as essential:

1. To be wanted

2. To be born healthy

3. To live in a healthy environment

4. To obtain satisfaction of basic needs

5. To receive continuous loving care

6. To acquire intellectual and emotional skills necessary to achieve individual aspirations

7. To cope effectively in our society

8. To receive care and treatment through facilities that are appropriate to children's needs

The commission's eight rights constitute a sublime list that we wish for all children but enacting these rights is a monumental task. Enacting these rights would require an enormous thrust for children's preventive mental health. We have already discussed several ways of intervening for children's improved mental health. Let us add some legalistic ways of aiding children to ensure their rights to a healthy and productive life.

Precedent has been established for guaranteeing due process to children. According to the Gault decision (387, US 1 1967), children and adolescents cannot be held for crimes (regardless of parent's testimony) without a due process hearing. Recently, the courts have upheld a child's right to privacy. One example of how this has been applied concerns the child's employment in research. Until the 1970's, parents could volunteer their institutionalized children for medical and behavioral studies. Now, these children must be asked if they wish to participate. If they cannot understand the request, an unbiased committee representing the child's best interests reviews the pros and cons of the research to be conducted.

Some precedent concerning the disposition of child custody cases has also been established so that the child's needs are best protected. Most states have adopted the doctrine of "best interest of the child" which holds that the basis for a legal decision of a court custody case is based upon:

- the nature of the child's relationship with each parent

- the capacity and willingness of each parent to care for the child

- the presence of a stable environment and length of time of the child in that environment

- the likelihood that the home will serve as a family unit

- the nature of the child's adjustment at school and community

- the moral fitness of each parent

- the physical and mental fitness of each parent

- the child's preference (Chess & Hassibi, 1978).

Special guidelines have been set for dealing with legal offenses abuse. Children under 16 can be legally declared "persons in need of supervision." The children who are out of control by parents and authorities may be sanctioned by the courts for behaviors not considered criminal offenses if committed by adults (truancy, runaway, glue-sniffing, and promiscuity are all considered legal offenses for minors, although they do not constitute adult illegal acts). A legal record of prosecutions under the doctrine of "persons in need of supervision" is not maintained if the child and parent participate in a social remediation program.

Special juvenile courts now handle the disposition of criminal acts by youths. These juvenile courts have been highly criticized for supporting ambiguous definitions of delinquency and for setting arbitrary penalties. Typically, a maximum of 15 minutes is spent on each case. In efforts to reach the "whole child," judges' decisions are often a curious mixture of punishment, parenting and psychotherapy. A new penal code for youths is being established which concentrates on the criminal behavior and recommends specific penalties for particular acts. The new code promises to correct the arbitrary nature of the present juvenile court system and places more responsibility upon the community to provide social remediation for acting out youths (Erickson, 1978).

The emerging precedence in juvenile courts suggests the need for child consultants who specialize in forensic child psychology. This child specialist can play several crucial roles. He or she can serve as an expert witness in child custody cases or institutionalization of children. The child therapist/expert witness needs to be familiar with judicial rights of children as well as psychological assessment procedures and child development. The child consultant who is an expert in forensic psychology can also serve as a child advocate. Children cannot initiate legal action on their own behalf. The child advocate insists that program and services are based upon sound child developmental knowledge. In the future, the child advocate may be involved in all cases of class action litigation (e.g., foster care, school segregation, overrepresentation of minority children in classes for the retarded, etc.) and legislative advocacy involving children. In some situations, the judiciary can be an important arm for implementing preventive mental health strategies for children. Its effectiveness depends in part upon wise input from and wise use by informed child clinicians.

CLINICAL PRACTICE CREATES POLICY

Child practitioners are involved in policy in many ways. The everyday practice decisions made by child practitioners create and evaluate policy (Schorr, 1985). Policy is defined as the set of regulations, laws, procedures, and implicit rules which guide how a practitioner functions outside of the intrapsychic realm. Any action a practitioner or child wants to take that is subject to external control reflects policy. The child practitioner can exert some choice over the external arena that will in turn influence him or her. For example, the type of child referred to a practitioner is dictated by location of the office, type of licensure, cases taken before, professional training, or use of appointments.

A practitioner's involvement in policy is viewed in three ways by Schorr (1985). The nature of professional practice is the first. The length of time in practice, theoretical base, or education and training provide a focus of the practice for most practitioners. Their view of the nature of practice with children shapes policy. For example, the adoption placement of minority children with white parents rarely took place before the mid-1960's. With the lower Anglo birth rate of unwanted babies because of effective contraceptives, Anglo families wanting to adopt turned to interracial adoptions. This sudden change in practice has raised serious policy questions, resulting in new laws such as the Indian Child Welfare Act, which requires tribal permission for placement with a non-Indian family.

Schorr's second point is how the agency practice forms policy. The agency objectives, location, attitudes of staff and board, fee structure, choice of therapists, and intake procedures are policy-based decisions made in every agency and by many private practitioners. The client's perspective of the control the practitioner and agency have over her or him is not only a treatment constraint but also a policy and value choice. For example, until recehtly, minority and poor clients were often placed with short-term intervention programs, while Anglo and middle-to-upper class clients were more likely to be referred for long-term intervention (LeVine & Padilla, 1980). Societal change will be reflected in the cases that come to the practitioners. The increased use of drugs by children or the increase of violent child abuse cases are indications of significant and changing social problems. Practitioners need to be sensitive to patterns of social change and assess their impact upon the family and the child. In that way, the practitioner can help formulate effective policy rather than reinforce existing social problems such as prejudice and family violence.

Clinicians are engaged in policy formation and issues whenever they practice. We must be sensitive and better trained to understand and act on policy. From political involvement to testimony before legislative bodies, to the location of our offices, we are making policy decisions. The choices we make affect more than the children we work with. The choices we make affect families, society, and future children.

THE FUTURE

In Chapter 2, overview of the history of children in society, we asked ourselves the question, "How far have we progressed since the days when children had little importance in society?" As you read through the text, you may have felt that the answer to this question was bleak. We have discussed the high incidence of childhood emotional problems and the confusion about etiology of childhood maladjustment. In contrast to the high incidence reports and confusion in some research, we also discussed a variety of therapeutic intervention strategies for working with children that are demonstrating increasing promise. We have also reviewed a wealth of information about vulnerable children that aids practitioners in being alert to who needs help, so that we are more attuned to listening to our children. Hopefully, you are as encouraged as we are about the advancements that have been made in listening to and working with children. Our final question in this text is, "With our increased understanding of child developmental processes and the application of intervention strategies for troubled children, how far can we go in assisting children to reach their full potential?" Obviously, we would like to eradicate crises in childhood, and we would like to create environments that maximize children's physical, personal, and social development.

We believe that the President's Commission on Mental Health (1978) which stated that "helping children must be the Nation's first priority in preventing mental disability" (p. 51) is an important step in the right direction. Also important was the designation of 1979 as the International Year of the Child since concern for children was elevated above our own national interest and placed within an international scope for study and debate. The outcome of these two events hopefully will have a full impact.

Both Freud and Watson proposed that experiences during early childhood exerted a powerful constraint on the topography of adult behavior. Further, before Freud, few if anyone credited children with sexual and aggressive emotions and conflicts. Similarly, before Watson, hereditary factors such as "degeneracy," seemed the obvious cause of delinquency, insanity, and mental retardation. Stimulated by these theorists and the work of other developmental theorists, we now know a great deal about the genetic and environmental contributions to intelligence and abnormal behavior; new investigations have revealed much about the cognitive, linguistic, and social development of children; and research has shown us the importance of parent-infant bonding, to cite just a few of our important research findings with children. In short, we have accumulated a vast storehouse of information about children since the turn of the century.

Coupled with advances in our knowledge of child development, therapists have provided us with many new techniques for working with children and families. We are now at the crossroads where we must use our knowledge about children and work diligently and constructively to create primary prevention programs for children. The

President's Commission on Mental Health (1978) acknowledged that good care during pregnancy and childbirth can prevent some conditions that lead to later mental disability and can detect others early enough for effective treatment. Also noted was the importance of detecting and correcting at the earliest stages problems of physical, emotional, and cognitive development which can lead to emotional maladjustment and learning difficulties. Our work leads us to support these areas of concern identified by consultants to the President's Commission.

Child preventive mental health programs will be the challenge of the future--a challenge for the following reasons:

1.   There are yet few experts in the area of prevention.

2.   Preventive programs are long term ventures that often require years before they can be evaluated to determine their efficacy, and most practitioners do not have the luxury of time to wait to see if their preventive strategies have been effective.

3.   Prevention programs are costly, and all indications point to fewer federal and state dollars for social service programs of any type.

4.   The establishment of primary prevention programs usually takes place within a sociopolitical context of some type, and most therapists are not expert in the political process.

A start in the direction of prevention and policy formation has been noted. Our task now is to continue the struggle for children's rights. Advocacy for children is essential. To listen deeply to our children and respond powerfully, our role for the future must be more than just that of a traditional practitioner who sits and talks with a child client behind a closed door. The practitioner of the future will consider meaningful contact with the child as well as significant others, agencies, and legislative bodies that affect their child clients an integral part of her or his role.

References

Abel, E. L. (1980). Fetal alcohol syndrome: Behavior teratology. *Psychological Bulletin, 87,* 29-50.

Abramowitz, C. V. (1976). The effectiveness of group psychotherapy with children. *Archives of General Psychiatry, 33,* 320-330.

Achenbach, T. (1974). *Developmental Psychopathology.* New York: Ronald Press.

Ack, M., Beale, E., & Ware, L. (1975). Parent guidance: Psychotherapy of the young child via the parent. *Bulletin of the Menninger Clinic, 39,* 436-447.

Ackerman, N. W. (1966a). Family psychotherapy today: Some areas of controversy. *Comprehensive Psychiatry, 7,* 375-378.

Ackerman, N. W. (1966b). *Treating the troubled family.* New York: Basic Books.

Ackerman, N. W. (1971). Prejudicial scapegoating and neutralizing forces in the family group. In J. G. Howells (Ed.), *Theory and practice of family psychiatry.* New York: Brunner/Mazel.

Adler, A. (1927). *Understanding human nature.* New York: Greenberg.

Adler, A. (1958). *What life should mean to you.* New York: Capricorn.

Ahrons, C. (1980). Redefining the divorce family: A conceptual framework. *Social Work, 25* (6), 437-441.

Ainsworth, M. D. S. (1973). The development of infant-mother attachment. In B. Caldwell & H. Riccuiti (Eds.), *Review of child development research* (Vol. 3, pp. 1-94). Chicago: University of Chicago Press.

Alexander, D., Ehrhardt, A. A., & Money, J. (1966). Defective figure drawing, geometric and human, in Turner's syndrome. *Journal of Nervous and Mental Disease, 142,* 161-167.

Alexander, F. G., & Selesnick, S. T. (1966). *The history of psychiatry: An evaluation of psychiatric thought and practice from prehistoric times to the present.* New York: Harper and Row.

Allen, F. H. (1942). *Psychotherapy with children.* New York: W. W. Norton.

Allen, F. H. (1963). *Positive aspects of child psychiatry: As developed in the selective writings of Dr. Frederick H. Allen.* New York: W. W. Norton.

Alpern, G. D., & Boll, T. J. (1972). *Developmental profile.* Indianapolis: Psychological Development.

American Association on Mental Deficiency. (1973). Rights of the mentally handicapped. *Mental Retardation, 11* (5), 56.

American Humane Association. (1985). *Highlights of official child neglect and abuse reporting for 1983.* Denver: Author.

American Psychiatric Association. (1980). *Diagnostic and statistical manual of mental disorders.* Washington, DC: Author.

Anastasi, A. (1976). *Psychological testing.* New York: Macmillan.

Anderson, S. C., & Lauderdale, M. L. (1982). Characteristics of abusive parents: A look at self-esteem. *Child Abuse and Neglect, 6,* 285-293.

Anonymous. (1972). Differentiation of self in one's family. In J. Framo (Ed.), *Family interaction.* New York: Springer.

Anthony, E. J. (1959). A group of murderous mothers. *Acta Psychotherapeutica, 7* (Supplement), 1-6.

Anthony, E. J. (1970). The behavior disorders of childhood. In P. H. Mussen (Ed.), *Carmichael's manual of child psychology* (Vol. II). New York: Wiley.

Aries, P. (1962). *Centuries of childhood: A social history of family life.* New York: Alfred A. Knopf.

Austin, D. M., & Caragonne, P. (1981). *A comparative analysis of twenty two settings using case management components.* Austin: University of Texas at Austin School of Social Work.

Axline, V. (1969). *Play therapy* (Rev. ed.). Cambridge: Houghton Mifflin.

Azima, F. (1976). Group psychotherapy for latency-age children. *Canadian Psychiatric Association Journal, 21,* 210-211.

Azrin, N. H., & Foxx, R. M. (1971). A rapid method of toilet training the institutionalized retarded. *Journal of Applied Behavior Analysis, 4,* 89-99.

Bandler, R., Grinder, R., & Satir, V. (1976). *Changing with families.* Palo Alto, CA: Science and Behavior Books.

Bandura, A. (1969). *Principles of Behavior Modification.* New York: Holt, Rinehart & Winston.

Bandura, A. (1977). *Social learning theory.* Englewood Cliffs, NJ: Prentice Hall.

Baratz, J. C., & Shuy, R. W. (Eds.). (1969). *Teaching Black children to read.* Washington, DC: Center for Applied Linguistics.

Barkley, R. A. (1971). Stimulant drugs in the classroom. *School Psychology Digest, 88,* 412-425.

Barkley, R. A. (1977). A review of stimulant drug research with hyperactive children. *Journal of Child Psychology and Psychiatry, 18,* 137-165.

Barrett, D. (1976). The effects of play therapy on the social and psychological adjustment of five- to nine-year-old children. *Dissertation Abstracts International, 36,* 5032A-5033A. (University Microfilms No. 76-4394)

Bateson, G. (1972). *Steps to an ecology of mind.* New York: Ballantine.

Bateson, G., Jackson, D. D., Haley, J., & Weakland, J. H. (1956). Toward a theory of schizophrenia. *Behavioral Science, 1,* 251-264.

Bayley, N. (1969). *Bayley Scales of Infant Development manual.* New York: Psychological Corporation.

Belkin, G. S. (1980). *Contemporary psychotherapies.* Chicago: Rand McNally.

Bell, J. E. (1964). The family group therapist: An agent of change. *International Journal of Group Psychotherapy, 14,* 72-83.

Bellak, L., & Bellak, S. S. (1971). *Children's Apperception Test.* Larchmont, NY: C. P. S.

Bem, S. L. (1974). The measurement of psychological androgeny. *Journal of Consulting and Clinical Psychology, 42,* 155-162.

Bem, S. L. (1975). Sex-role adaptability: One consequence of psychological androgyny. *Journal of Personality and Social Psychology, 31,* 634-643.

Bender, B. (1976). Self-chosen victims: Scapegoating behavior sequential to battering. *Child Welfare, 55,* 417-422.

Bender, L. (1938). *A visual motor gestalt test and its clinical use.* New York: American Orthopsychiatric Association.

Bender, L. (1947). Childhood schizophrenia: Clinical study of one hundred schizophrenic children. *American Journal of Orthopsychiatry, 17,* 40-56.

Bender, L. (1955). Twenty years of clinical research on schizophrenic children with special reference to those under six years of age. In G. Caplan (Ed.), *Emotional problems of early childhood.* New York: Basic Books.

Bender, L. (1962). *A visual-motor gestalt test and its clinical use.* New York: American Orthopsychiatric Association.

Bender, L. (1974). Aggression in children. In S. Frazier (Ed.), *Aggression.* Baltimore: William & Wilkins.

Berkowitz, H. (1968). A preliminary assessment of the extent of interaction between child psychiatric clinics and public schools. *Psychology in the Schools, 5,* 291-295.

Bernard, J. M. (1978). Divorce and young children: Relationships in transition. *Elementary School Guidance Counseling, 12* (3), 188-197.

Bessell, H., & Palomares, U. (1973). *Methods in human development.* La Mesa, CA: Human Development Training Institute.

Bettelheim, B. (1967). *The empty fortress: Infantile autism and the birth of the self.* New York: The Free Press.

Blackham, G. A., & Silberman, A. (1971). *Modification of child behavior.* Belmont, CA: Wadsworth.

Bloom, L. (1973). One word at a time: The use of a single word utterance before syntax. *Janua Linguarum, Series Minor,* 154.

Bloom, M. (1984). *Configurations of human behavior: Life span development in social environments.* New York: Macmillan.

Bloom, M. (1985). *Life span development: Basis for prevention and interventive helping* (2nd ed.). New York: Macmillan.

Boehm, A. E. (1971). *Boehm Test of Basic Concepts.* New York: Psychological Corporation.

Bohannan, P. (1970). *Divorce and after.* Garden City, NJ: Anchor Books.

Bohman, M. (1972). *Adopted children and their families - A follow up study of adopted children, their background environment and adjustment.* Stockholm: Proprius.

Bostow, D. E., & Barley J. B. (1969). Modification of severe disruptive and aggressive behavior using brief time-out and reinforcement procedures. *Journal of Applied Behavior Analyses, 2,* 31-37.

Bott, E. (1971). *Family & social network.* New York: The Free Press.

Bowen, M. (1960). A family concept of schizophrenia. In D. Jackson (Ed.), *The etiology of schizphrenia.* New York: Basic Books.

Bowen, M. (1966). The use of family theory in clinical practice. *Comprehensive Psychiatry, 7,* 345-374.

Bowker, J. P. (Ed.). (1983). Overview: Education for primary prevention in social work. *Education for Primary Prevention in Social Work* (pp.1-7). New York: Council on Social Work Education.

Bowlby, J. (1951). Maternal care and mental health. *World Health Organization Monograph 2.* Geneva: World Health Organization.

Bowlby, J. (1969). *Attachment and loss: Attachment* (Vol. 1). New York: Basic Books.

Braine, M.D.S. (1976). Children's first word combinations. *Monographs of the Society for Research in Child Development, 41* (1).

Brase, D., & Loh, H. (1975). Possible role of 5-hydroxytryptamine in minimal brain dysfunction. *Life Sciences, 16,* 1005-1015.

Brodzinsky, D., Pappas, C., Singer, L., & Braff, A. (1981). Childrens' conception of adoption: A preliminary investigation. *Journal of Pediatric Psychology, 6,* 177-189.

Brodzinsky, D., Singer, L., & Braff, A. (1984). Children's understanding of adoption. *Child Development, 55,* 869-878.

Brown, D. (1976). Directive parental counselling: An appraisal to its effect on extra-conditioning variables. *Dissertation Abstracts International, 36,* 4680B. (Microfiche available from National Library of Canada and Ottawa)

Brown, J. V., & Bakeman, R. (1977, March). *Antecedents of emotional involvement in mothers of premature and full-term infants.* Paper presented at the meeting of The Society for Research in Child Development, New Orleans.

Brown, K. (1983). *The effects of divorce on children.* Unpublished paper.

Brown, R. (1973). *A first language.* Cambridge, MA: Harvard University Press.

Bruner, J. S. (1964). The course of cognitive growth. *American Psychologist, 19,* 1-15.

Buck, J. N. (1950). *House-Tree-Person Test.* Beverly Hills, CA: Western Psychological Services.

Burchinal, L. A. (1964). Characteristics of adolescents from unbroken, broken and reconsituted families. *Journal of Marriage and the Family, 26* (1), 44-51.

Burgemeister, B. B., Blum, L. H., & Lorge, I. (1972). *Columbia Mental Maturity Scale* (3rd ed.). New York: Harcourt Brace Jovanovich.

Burks, H. F. (1969). *Burks' Behavior Rating Scale.* El Monte, CA: Arden Press.

Buros, O. K. (Ed.). (1972). *Seventh mental measurements yearbook.* Highland Park, NJ: Gryphon Press.

Campbell, M., & Small, A. M. (1978). Chemotherapy. In B. B. Wolman, A. O. Ross, & J. Egan (Eds.), *Handbook of treatment of mental disorders in childhood and adolescence.* Englewood Cliffs, NJ: Prentice Hall.

Caplan, G. (1970). *The theory and practice of mental health consultation.* New York: Basic Books.

Carkhuff, R. R., & Berenson, B. G. (1977). *Beyond counseling and therapy* (2nd Ed.). New York: Holt, Rinehart, & Winston.

Caron, S. (1980, Dec.). *The case of the ill-tempered artist.* Unpublished case notes, Las Cruces, NM.

Cattell, P. (1940). *The measurement of intelligence of infants and young children.* New York: Psychological Corporation.

Chambers, M. J. (1980, Nov.). The murder of Robbie Wayne age six. *Reader's Digest,* pp. 216-251.

Chase, N. F. (1975). *A child is being beaten.* New York: Holt, Rinehart & Winston.

Chess, S., & Hassibi, M. (1970). Behavior deviation in mentally retarded children. *Journal of the American Academy of Child Psychiatry, 9,* 282-297.

Chess, S., & Hassibi, M. (1978). *Principles and practice of child psychology.* New York: Plenum Press.

Child Abuse Prevention and Treatment Act of 1974, SS 42 U.S.C. SS 5101.

Child Abuse Prevention and Treatment Amendments of 1981. (Report 97-66). Washington DC: U.S. House of Representatives.

Child sexual abuse: Incest, assault and sexual exploitation. (1981). Washington DC: National Center on Child Abuse and Neglect. (DHHS Publication No. (OHDS) 81-30166)

Children's Defense Fund. (1978). *Children Without Homes.* Washington, DC: Author.

Chuda, R., & Sankar, D. (1976). Demographic studies in child psychiatry II -- General data from second study. *Research communications in psychology, psychiatry and behavior, 3,* 478-483.

Cohen, A. H. (1979a). Effective treatment of child abuse and neglect. *Social Work, 24* (6), 513-519.

Cohen, A. H. (1979b). An evaluation of three demonstration child abuse and neglect treatment programs. *Journal of American Academy of Child Psychiatry, 18,* 283-291.

Cohen, L. B. (1979). Our developing knowledge of infant perception and cognition. *American Psychologist, 34,* 894-899.

Cohen, S. M., Allan, M. G., Pollin, W., & Hrubec, Z. (1972). Relationship of schizo-affective psychosis to manic depressive psychosis and schizophrenia. *Archives of General Psychiatry, 26* (6), 539-545.

Cohen, T. (1983). The incestuous family revisted. *Social Casework, 63* (3), 154-161.

Colletta, N. D. (1979). The impact of divorce: Father absence or poverty? *Journal of Divorce, 3* (1), 27-35.

Committee on the Family Group for the Advancement of Psychiatry. (1970). *Treatment of families in conflict: The clinical study of family process.* New York: Jason Aronson.

Compton, B., & Galaway, B. (1984). *Social Work Processes* (3rd ed.). Homewood IL: Dorsey Press.

Conners, C. K., & Rothschild, G. H. (1968). Drugs and learning in children. In J. Hellmuth (Ed.), *Learning disorders* (Vol. III). Seattle: Special Child Publications.

Connolly, A. J., Nachtman, W., & Pritchett, E. M. (1973). *Key Math Diagnostic Arithmetic Test.* Circle Pines, MN: American Guidance Service.

Conte, J. R. (1984). Progress in treating the sexual abuse of children. *Social Work, 29* (3), 258-263.

Coopersmith, S. (1967). *The antecedents of self-esteem.* San Francisco: W. H. Freeman.

Costin, L. B. (1979). *Child welfare: Policies and practice.* New York: McGraw-Hill.

Coyne, A., & Brown, M. E. (1985). Developmentally disabled children can be adopted. *Child Welfare LXIV* (6), 607-616.

Crabtree, M. (1963). *Houston Test for Language Development.* Houston: Houston Test.

Daniel, R. M. (1977). Father-child intimacy in divorced families (Doctoral dissertation, California School of Professional Psychology). *Dissertation Abstracts International, 38* (6-B), 2854.

Davidson, W. S., & Seidman, E. (1974). Studies of behavior modification and juvenile delinquency: A review, methodological critique, and social perspective. *Psychological Bulletin, 81,* 998-1011.

Department of Health, Education and Welfare, Office of Child Development. *Report of the conference on the use of stimulant drugs in the treatment of behaviorially disturbed young school children.* Washington, DC: Author.

Derevensky, J. L. (1979). Children's fears: A developmental comparison of normal and exceptional children. *Journal of Genetic Psychology, 135,* 11-21.

Deutsch, M., & Brown, B. (1964). Social influences in Negro and white intelligence differences. *Journal of Social Issues, 20* (2), 24-35.

Dickerson, M. U. (1981). *Social work practice with the mentally retarded.* New York: The Free Press.

Dimick, K., & Huff. V. (1970). *Child counseling.* Dubuque, IA: W. C. Brown.

Dinkmeyer, D., & Caldwell, E. (1970). *Developmental counseling and guidance.* New York: McGraw-Hill.

Dinkmeyer, D., & McKay, G. (1976). *Systematic training for effective parenting.* Circle Pines, MN: American Guidance Services.

Doll, E. (1965). *The Vineland Social Maturity Scale: Manual of directions.* Minneapolis: American Guidance Service.

Donofrio, A. (1976). Parent education vs child psychotherapy. *Psychology in the Schools, 13,* 175-180.

Douglas, J. W. B., & Mulligan, D. C. (1961). Emotional adjustment and educational achievement - the preliminary results of a longitudinal study of a national sample of children. *Proceedings of the Royal Society of Medicine, 54,* 885-891.

Dreikurs, R., & Soltz, V. (1964). *Children: The challenge.* New York: Hawthorne.

Drillien, C. M. (1970). Complications of pregnancy and delivery. In J. Wortis (Ed.), *Mental retardation: An annual review* (Vol. 1). New York: Grune & Stratton.

Dunn, L. M. (1965). *Expanded manual for the Peabody Picture Vocabulary Test.* Minneapolis: American Guidance Service.

Durost, W. N., Bixler, H. H., Writestone, J. W., Prescott, G. A., & Balow, I. (1971). *Metropolitan Achievement Test.* New York: Harcourt Brace Jovanovich.

Durrell, D. D. (1955). *Durrell analysis of reading difficulty.* New York: Harcourt Brace Jovanovich.

Duvall, E. M. (1971). *Family Development* (4th ed.). Philadelphia: J.B. Lippincott.

Edwards, H., & Thompson, B. (1971). Who are the fatherless? *New Society, 17* (436), 192-193.

Eimas, P. D. (1974). Auditory and lingiustic processing of cues for place of articulation by infants. *Perception and Psychophysics, 16,* 513-521.

Eimas, P. D. (1975). Auditory and phonetic coding of the cues for speech: *Perception and Psychophysics, 18,* 341-347.

Elkind, D. (1974). *Children and adolescents: Interpretive essays on Jean Piaget.* New York: Oxford University Press.

Ellis, A. (1962). *Reason and emotion in psychotherapy.* New York: Lyle Stuart.

Ellison, R., & LeVine, E. (1982). *Counseling children of divorce.* Unpublished manuscript.

Elwell, M. E. (1979). Sexually assaulted children and their families. *Social Casework, 60* (4), 227-235.

Erickson, M. T. (1978). *Child psychopathology: Assessment, etiology and treatment.* Englewood Cliffs, NJ: Prentice Hall.

Erikson, E. H. (1963). *Childhood and society* (2nd ed.). New York: W. W. Norton.

Ervin-Tripp, S. M. (1973). Imitation and structural change in children's language. In C. A. Ferguson & D. I. Slobin (Eds.), *Studies of child language development.* New York: Holt, Rinehart & Winston.

Espenshade, T.J. (1979). The economic consequences of divorce. *Journal of Marriage and the Family, 41* (3), 615-625.

Evaluation of child abuse & neglect: Demonstration projects 1974-1977. (1977, Dec.). Vol. 6: Child client impact: Final report (PB 178-448). Washington, DC: U.S. Department of Commerce.

Evans, I. M., & Nelson, R. O. (1977). Assessment of child behavior problems. In A. R. Ciminero, A. R. Calhoun, K. S. Calhoun, & H. E. Adams (Eds.), *Handbook of behavioral assessment* (pp. 603-681). New York: Wiley.

Ewing, C. (1976). Family crisis intervention and traditional child guidance: A comparison of outcomes and factors related to success in treatment. *Dissertation Abstracts International, 36,* 4686B. (University Microfilms No. 76-5933)

Fanshel, D., & Shinn, E. B. (1978). *Children in foster care: A longitudinal investigation.* New York: Columbia University Press.

Feigelson, C. I. (1974). Play in child analysis. *Psychoanalytic Study of the Child, 29,* 21-26.

Feldman, D. (1979). Toward a nonelitist conception of giftedness. *Phi Delta Kappan, 60,* 660-663.

Finkelhor, D. (1979). *Sexually victimized children.* New York: The Free Press.

Finkelhor, D. (1984). Child sexual abuse: New theory and research. New York: The Free Press.

Fisher, J., & Gochros, H. L. (1975). *Planned behavior change: Behavior modification in social work.* New York: The Free Press.

Framo, J. L. (1979). Family theory and therapy. *American Psychologist, 34,* 988-992.

Frankel, S. (1977). The management aspect of psychotherapy with aggressive children. *Child Psychiatry and Human Development, 7,* 169-185.

Frankenburg, W. K., & Dodds, J. B. (1970). *Denver Developmental Screening Test.* Denver: University of Colorado Medical Center.

Frankl, S. (1963). *Man's search for meaning.* New York: Washington Square Press.

Frazier, D., & LeVine, E. (1983). Reattachment therapy: Intervention with the very young physically abused child. *Psychotherapy: Theory, Research and Practice, 20* (10), 90-100.

Freedman, A. M., Kaplan, H., & Sadock, B. (1976). *Modern synopsis of comprehensive textbook of psychiatry II.* Baltimore: Williams & Wilkins.

Freud, A. (1928). Introduction to the technique of child analysis. *Nervous and Mental Disease Monograph No. 48.* New York.

Freud, A. (1965). *Normality and pathology in childhood: Assessment of development.* New York: International Universities Press.

Freud, S. (1953). Three essays on the theory of sexuality. *The standard edition of the complete psychological works of Sigmund Freud* (Vol. 7). London: Hogarth Press.

Freud, S. (1955). *Analysis of a phobia of a five-year-old boy.* London: Hogarth Press.

Frey, J. III, Heckel, R. V., Salzberg, H. C., & Wackwitz, J. (1976). Demographic variables as predictors of outcome in psychotherapy with children. *Journal of Clinical Psychology, 32,* 713-721.

Friedman, E. C., & Barclay, A. (1963). The discriminative validity of certain psychological tests as indices of brain damage in the mentally retarded. *Mental Retardation, 1,* 291-293.

Friedrich, W. N., & Borinskin, J. A. (1976). The role of the child in abuse: A review of the literature. *American Journal of Orthoropsychiatry, 46* (4), 580-590.

Frisk, M. (1964). Identity problems and confused conceptions of the genetic ego in adopted children during adolscence. *Acta Paedo Psychiatrics, 31,* 6-12.

Frostig, M., Lefever, D. W., & Whittlesey, J. R. B. (1964). *The Marianne Frostig Developmental Test of Visual Perception.* Palo Alto, CA: Consulting Psychologists Press.

Fuller, J. (1977). Duo therapy case studies: Process and techniques. *Social Casework, 58,* 84-91.

Fullmer, D. W., & Bernard, H. W. (1972). *The school counselor-consultant.* Boston: Houghton Mifflin.

Furgeson, J. (1981, Feb.). *The case of the unsure, angry, eight-year-old.* Unpublished case notes, New Mexico State University, Las Cruces.

Furman, S., Sweat, L., & Corcetti, G. (1965). Social class factors in the flow of children to outpatient psychiatric facilities. *American Journal of Public Health, 55,* 385-392.

Gagnon J. (1965). Female child victims of sex offenses. *Sociological Problems, 13,* 176-192.

Gambrill, E. D. (1981). A behavioral perspective of families. In E. R. Tolson & W. J. Reid (Eds.), *Models of family treatment.* New York: Columbia University Press.

Gannon, W. J. (1972). *The effects of the gestault oriented group approach on the interpersonal contact attitudes of selected high school students.* Unpublished doctoral dissertation, Case Western Reserve University, Ann Arbor. (University microfilms No. 72-26)

Gardner, R. A. (1970). *The boys and girls book about divorce.* New York: Science House.

Gardner, R. A. (1971). *Therapeutic communication with children: The mutual story-telling technique.* New York: Science House.

Gardner, R. A. (1975). *Psychotherapeutic approaches to the resistant child.* New York: Jason Aronson.

Gardner, R. A. (1976). *Psychotherapy with children of divorce.* New York: Jason Aronson.

Gardner, R. A. (1977). *Parents book about divorce.* New York: Doubleday.

Gardner, R. A. (1979). *The objective diagnosis of minimal brain dysfunction.* Cresskill, NJ: Creative Therapeutics.

Garmezy, N. (1981). Children under stress: Perspectives on antecedents and correlates of vulnerability and resistance to psychopathology. In R. A. Zucken & A. I. Rabin (Eds.), *Further explorations in personality.* New York: Wiley.

Gates, A. I., & Russell, D. H. (1962). *Diagnostic and Remedial Spelling Manual.* New York: Bureau of Publications, Teachers College, Columbia University.

In re Gault, 387 U.S. 1428 (1967).

Gelles, R. G., & Straus, M. A. (1985, Nov. 11). Child abuse shows sharp decline. *Las Cruces Sun News* (AP).

Germain, C. B., & Gitterman, A. (1980). *The life model of social work practice.* New York: Columbia University Press.

Giaretto, H. (1976). Humanistic treatment of father-daughter incest. In R. E. Helfer & C. H. Kempe (Eds.), *Child abuse and neglect: The family and the community.* Cambridge, MA: Ballinger.

Gil, D. G. (1970). *Violence against children: Physical child abuse in the U.S.* Cambridge, MA: Harvard Press.

Ginott, H. G. (1961). *Group psychotherapy with children: The theory and practice of play therapy.* New York: McGraw-Hill.

Ginott, H. G. (1965). *Between parent and child: New solutions to old problems.* New York: Macmillan.

Glasser, W. (1965). *Reality therapy: A new approach to psychiatry.* New York: Harper and Row.

Glucksberg, S., Krauss, R., & Higgins, E. T. (1975). The development of referential communication skills. In F. D. Horowitz (Ed.), *Review of child development research* (Vol. 4), 305-347. Chicago: University of Chicago Press.

Glueck, S., & Glueck, E. T. (1950). *Unraveling juvenile delinquency.* New York: Commonwealth Fund.

Glueck, S., & Glueck, E. T. (1952). *Delinquents in the making.* New York: Harper.

Goldfarb, W. (1961). *Childhood schizophrenia.* Cambridge, MA: Harvard University Press.

Goldfarb, W. (1970). Childhood psychosis. In P. H. Mussen (Ed.), *Carmichael's manual of child psychology* (3rd ed., Vol. 2). New York: Wiley.

Goldman, J., & Coane, J. (1977). Family therapy after the divorce: Developing a strategy. *Family Process, 16* (3), 357-362.

Goldstein, J., Freud, A., & Solnit, A. (1979). *Beyond the best interests of the child.* London: The Free Press.

Goldstein, K. M., Caputo, D. V., & Taub, H. B. (1976). The effects of parental and perinatal complications on development at one year of age. *Child Development, 47,* 613-621.

Goldston, S. E. (1978). A national perspective. In D. G. Forgays (Ed.), *Primary prevention of psychopathology series, Vol. 2: Environmental influences* (pp. 25-36). New Hampshire: University of New England Press.

Gongola, P. A. (1977). Social relationships after marital separation: A study of women with children (Doctoral dissertation, Case Western Reserve University). *Dissertation Abstracts International, 30* (9-A), 5742.

Gonso, J. L. (1977). The effects of divorce on children (Doctoral dissertation, Indiana University). *Dissertation Abstracts International, 38* (11-B), 5568.

Goodenough, F. L. (1926). *Measurement of intelligence by drawings.* Yonkers on Hudson, NY: World Book.

Goodenough, F., & Harris, D. (1963). *Goodenough-Harris Drawing Test.* New York: Harcourt Brace Jovanovich.

Goodman, J. D., & Sours, J. A. (1967). *The child mental status examination.* New York: Basic Books.

Gordon, T. (1970). *Parent effectiveness training.* New York: Wydene.

Gottesman, I. I., & Shields, J. (1972). *Schizophrenia and genetics.* New York: Academic Press.

Gough, H. G. (1969). *California Psychological Inventory.* Palo Alto, CA: Consulting Psychologists Press.

Gowan, J. C. (1960). The organization of guidance for the able. *Personnel and Guidance Journal, 4,* 275-279.

Graham, F. G., Ernhart, C. B., Craft, M., & Berman, P. W. (1963). Brain injury in the preschool child: Some developmental considerations. *Psychological Monographs, 77* (Whole 10 & 11).

Graham, F. G., Ernhart, C. B., Thurston D., & Craft M. (1961). Development three years after perinatal anoxia and other potentially damaging new born experience. *Psychological Monographs, 76* (Whole 522).

Gray, W. S., & Robinson, H. M. (Eds.). (1967). *Gray Oral Reading Test.* Indianapolis: Bobbs-Merrill.

Green, A. H. (1978). Self-destructive behavior in battered children. *American Journal of Psychiatry, 135,* 579-582.

Gregg, G. S., & Elmer, E. (1969). Infant injuries: Accident or abuse. *Pediatrics, 44,* 434-439.

Grollman, E. A. (1975). *Talking about divorce: A dialogue between parent and child.* Boston: Beacon Press.

Grossman, H. (Ed.). (1977). *Revised manual on terminology and classification in mental retardation.* Washington, DC: American Association on Mental Deficiency.

Guerney, B., Jr. (1964). Filial therapy: Description and rationale. *Journal of Consulting Psychology, 28,* 304-310.

Guerney, L. F. (1979). Play therapy with learning diasabled children. *Journal of Clinical Child Psychology, 8,* 242-244.

Guilford, J. P. (1968). *Intelligence, creativity, and their educational implications.* San Diego: Robert R. Knapp.

Guilford, J. P. (1975). Creativity: A quarter century of progress. In I. A. Taylor & J. W. Getzels (Eds.), *Perspectives in creativity.* Chicago: Aldine.

Haley, J. (1963). *Strategies of psychotherapy.* New York: Grune & Stratton.

Haley v. Ohio, 332 U.S. 5961 (1948).

Hall, C. S., & Lindzey, G. (1970). *Theories of Personality* (2nd ed.). New York: Wiley.

Hall, R. V., Panyon, M., Rabon, D., & Broden, M. (1972). The effective use of punishment to modify behavior in the classroom. In K. D. O'Leary & S. O'Leary (Eds.), *Classroom management: The successful use of behavior modification.* Elensford, NY: Pergamon Press.

Halpern, F. (1953). *A clinical approach to the children's Rorschach.* New York: Grune & Stratton.

Hammill, D. D., & Larsen, S. C. (1974). The effectiveness of psycholinguistic training. *Exceptional Children, 41,* 5-14.

Hansen, J., Niland, T., & Zani, L. (1969). Model reinforcement in group counseling with elementary school children. *Personnel and Guidance Journal, 47,* 741-744.

Hardcastle, D. (1977). A mother-child, multiple-family counseling program: Procedures and results. *Family Process, 16,* 67-74.

Harlow, H. (1958). The nature of love. *American Psychologist, 13,* 673-685.

Harrell, R. F., Woodyard, E., & Gates, A. I. (1955). *The effects of mother's diets on the intelligence of offspring.* New York: Teachers College.

Harris, D. B. (1963). *Children's drawings as measures of intellectual maturity.* New York: Harcourt, Brace & World.

Harris, T. A. (1969). *I'm O.K. - You're O.K.* New York: Harper and Row.

Harrison, S., McDermott, J., Wilson, P., & Schrager, J. (1965). Social class and mental illness in children. *Archives of General Psychiatry, 13,* 411-417.

Harry, J., & DeVall, W. B. (1978). *The social organization of Gay males.* New York: Praeger.

Hartman, A. (1978). Diagramatic assessment of family relationships. *Social Casework, 59* (8), 465-476.

Hartman, A. (1979). The extended family as a resource for change. In C. B. Germain (Ed.), *Social work practice: People and environments.* New York: Columbia University Press.

Hartman, A. (1981). Bowen Family Systems: Theory & practice. In E. R. Tolson & W. J. Reid (Eds.), *Models of family treatment.* New York: Columbia University Press.

Harvald, B., & Hauge, M. (1965). Hereditary factors elucidated by twin studies. In J. V. Neel, M. S. Shaw, & W. J. Schull (Eds.), *Genetics and the epidemiology of chronic diseases.* Washington, DC: U.S. Department of Health, Education and Welfare.

Haworth, M. (1964). *Child psychotherapy: Practice and theory*. New York: Basic Books.

Heath, A. (1981, Feb.). *Never insult the cook before you eat.* Unpublished case study, Family Research Institute, Purdue University, West Lafayette, IN.

Heatherington, E. M. (1966). Effects of paternal absence on sex-typed behavior in Negro and white preadolescent males. *Journal of Personality and Social Psychology, 4* (1), 87-91.

Heatherington, E. M., Cox, M., & Cox, R. (1976). Divorced fathers. *The Family Coordinator, 24,* 416-428.

Heatherington, E. M., Cox, M., & Cox, R. (1979). Family interaction in the social emotional and cognitive development of children following divorce. In V. Vaughn & T. B. Brazelton (Eds.), *The family: Setting priorities.* New York: Science and Medicine.

Heatherington, E. M., & Deur, J. (1971). The effects of father absence on child development. *Young Children, 26,* 233-248.

Heatherington, E. M., Stouwie, R. J., & Ridberg, E. H. (1971). Patterns of family interaction and child-rearing attitudes related to three dimensions of juvenile delinquency. *Journal of Abnormal Psychology, 78,* 160-176.

Heber, R. (1959, Sept.). A manual on terminology and classification in mental retardation. *American Journal of Mental Deficiencies, 64* (Monograph Supplement).

Herzog, E., & Sudia, C. E. (1973). Children of fatherless families. In B. M. Caldwell & H. N. Ricciuti (Eds.), *Review of child development research* (Vol. III). Chicago: University of Chicago Press.

Hess, R. D., & Camara, K. A. (1979). Post-divorce family relationships as mediating factors in the consequences of divorce for children. *Journal of Social Issues, 35* (4), 79-96.

Hewett, F. M., & Forness, S. R. (1977). *Education of exceptional learners* (2nd ed.). Boston: Allyn and Bacon.

Hill, D. (1952). EEG in episodic psychiatric and psychopathic behavior. *Electroencephalography and Clinical Neurophysiology, 4,* 419.

Hill, R. (1949). *Families under stress.* New York: Harper.

Hitchfield, E. M. (1973). *In search of promise.* London: Longman Group.

Holdahl, S., & Casperson, P. (1977). Children of family change: Who's helping them now? *Family Coordinator, 26* (4), 473-477.

Hoorwitz, A. N. (1983). Guidelines for treating father-daughter incest. *Social Casework, 63* (11), 515-524.

Howells, J. G. (1971). *Theory and practice of family psychiatry.* New York: Brunner/Mazel.

Howells, J. G. (1975). *World history of psychiatry.* New York: Brunner/Mazel.

Hozman, T. L., & Froiland, D. J. (1976). Families in divorce: A proposed model for counseling children. *The Family Coordinator, 25* (3), 271-276.

Hubbell, R. (1981). *Foster care and families: Conflicting values and policies.* Philadelphia: Temple University Press.

Hug-Hellmuth, H. (1962). Aus dem seelenhen des kindes. In L. Kanner (Ed.), *Child psychiatry* (3rd ed.). Springfield, IL: Charles C. Thomas. (Original work published: Leipzig, Deuticke, 1913)

Hunt, J. McV. (1975). Reflections on a decade of early education. *The Journal of Abnormal Child Psychology, 3,* 275-330.

Hunter, R. S., Kilstrom, N., Kraybill, E. N., & Loda, F. (1978). Antecedents of child abuse and neglect in premature infants: A prospective study in a newborn intensive care unit. *Pediatrics, 61* (4), 629-635.

Hurlock, E. B. (1942). *Child development.* New York: McGraw-Hill.

Hutchinson, J. R., & Nelson, K. E. (1985, June). How public agencies can provide family-centered services. *Social Casework, 66.6,* 367-371.

Inhelder, B., & Piaget, J. (1958). *The growth of logical thinking from childhood to adolescence.* New York: Basic Books.

Jackson, D. D. (1959). Schizophrenic symtoms and family interaction. *Archives of General Psychiatry, 1,* 618-621.

Jacobson, D. S. (1979). The impact of marital separation/divorce on children: Parent-child separation and child adjustment. *Journal of Divorce, 1* (4), 314-360.

Janzen, C., & Harris, O. (1980). *Family treatment in social work practice.* Itasca, IL: F. E. Peacock.

Jastak, J. F., Jastak, S. R., & Bijou, S. W. (1965). *The Wide Range Achievement Test manual of instructions.* Wilmington, DE: Guidance Associates.

Jennings, R., & Davis, C. (1977). Attraction-enhancing client behaviors: A structured learning approach for "Non-Yavis, Jr.". *Journal of Consulting and Clinical Psychology, 45,* 135-144.

Jensen, A. R. (1969). How much can we boost IQ and scholastic achievement? *Harvard Educational Review, 39,* 1-123.

Johnson, P. J., (1985). Case Management. In A. Fink, J. H. Pfouts, & A. W. Doblestein (Eds.), *The field of social work* (8th ed.). Beverly Hills, CA: Sage.

Joint Commission on Mental Health of Children. (1970). *Crisis in child mental health: Challenge for the seventies.* New York: Harper and Row.

Jones, M. C. (1926). *Development of early behavior patterns in young children.* Berkeley, CA: Author.

Justice, B., & Justice R. (1976). *The Abusing Family.* New York: Human Science Press.

Kabcenell, R. (1974). On countertransference. *Psychoanalytic Study of the Child, 29,* 27-33.

Kaczmarek, M., & LeVine, E. (1980). Expansion training: A counseling stance for the withdrawn rigid child. *Elementary School Guidance and Counseling, 15,* 31-47.

Kadushin, A. (1980). *Child welfare services* (3rd ed.). New York: Macmillan.

Kallmann, F. (1953). *Heredity in health and mental disorder.* New York: Norton.

Kamerman, S. B. (1985). Young, poor, and a mother alone: Problems and possible solutions. In H. McAdoo & J. Pardham (Eds.), *Service to young families* (pp. 1-38). Washington, DC: American Public Welfare Association.

Kanner, L. (1962a). *Child psychiatry* (3rd. ed.). Springfield, IL: Charles C. Thomas.

Kanner, L. (1962b). Emotionally disturbed children: A historical review. *Child Development, 33,* 97-102.

Kanner, L. (1973). *Childhood psychosis: Initial studies and new insights.* New York: Wiley.

Kaplan, E., & Kaplan, G. (1971). The prelinguistic child. In J. Elliot (Ed.), *Human development and cognitive processes* (pp. 359-381). New York: Holt, Rinehart and Winston.

Karnes, F. A., & Collins, E. C. (1978). State definitions of gifted and talented: A report and analysis. *Journal for the Education of the Gifted, 1,* 44-62.

Karnes, F. A., & Wherry, N. (1981). Wishes of fourth and seventh grade students. *Psychology in the Schools, 2,* 238-242.

Kazdin, A. E. (1977). *The token economy: A review and evaluation.* New York: Plenum Press.

Keat, D. II. (1974). *Fundamentals of child counseling.* Boston: Houghton Mifflin.

Keat, D. II. (1979). *Multimodal therapy with children.* New York: Pergamon Press.

Kelly, R., & Berg, B. (1978). Measuring children's reactions to divorce. *Journal of Clinical Psychology, 34,* 215-221.

Kempe, C. H., & Helfer, R. E. (1980). *The battered child.* Chicago: University of Chicago Press.

Kempe, R., & Kempe, C. H. (1976). Assessing family pathology. In R. E. Helfer & C. H. Kempe (Eds.), *Child abuse and neglect: The family and the community.* Cambridge, MA: Ballinger.

Kempe, R., & Kempe, C. H. (1978). *Child abuse.* Cambridge, MA: Harvard University Press.

Kennell, J. H., Jerauld, R., Wolfe, H., Chesler, D., McAlpine, W., Kreger, N. C., Steffa, M., & Klaus, M. H. (1974). Maternal behavior one year after early and extended post-partum contact. *Developmental Medicine and Child Neurology, 16,* 172-179.

Kenny, B. F., & Ross, J. M. (1985). *Mind in therapy.* New York: Basic Books.

Kent, J. T. (1976). A follow up study of abused children. *Journal of Pediatric Psychology, 1,* 25-31.

Kinard, M. E. (1980). Emotional development in physically abused children. *American Journal of Orthopsychiatry, 50* (4), 686-696.

Kirk, S. A., McCarthy, J. J., & Kirk, W. D. (1968). *Illinois Test of Psycholinguistic Abilities* (Rev. ed.). Urbana, IL: University of Illinois Press.

Kissel, S. (1974). Mothers and therapists evaluate long-term and short-term therapy. *Journal of Clinical Psychology, 30,* 296-299.

Klein, D. C., & Goldston S. E. (Eds.). (1977). *Primary prevention: An idea whose time has come.* Washington, DC: U.S. Government Printing Office.

Klein, M. (1937). *The psychoanalysis of children* (2nd ed.). London: Hogarth Press.

Klein, M. (1960). *The psychoanalysis of children.* New York: Grove Press.

Klein, M., & Stern L. (1971). Low birth weight and battered child syndrome. *American Journal of Diseases of Children, 122,* 15-18.

Knights, R. M., & Hinton, G. G. (1969). The effects of methylphenidate (Ritalin) on the motor skills and behavior of children with learning problems. *The Journal of Nervous and Mental Disease, 148,* 643-653.

Knopf, I. J. (1979). *Childhood psychopathology: A developmental approach.* Englewood Cliffs, NJ: Prentice Hall.

Kohlberg, L. (1966). A cognitive developmental analysis of children's sex-role concepts and attitudes. In E. Maccoby (Ed.), *The development of sex differences.* Stanford, CA: Stanford University Press.

Kohlberg, L. (1968). The child as a moral philosopher. *Psychology Today, 2,* 25-30.

Kohlberg, L. (1969). *Stages in the development of moral thought and action.* New York: Holt, Rinehart and Winston.

Koppitz, E. M. (1964). *The Bender Gestalt Test for Young Children.* New York: Grune and Stratton.

Koppitz, E. M. (1968). *Psychological evaluation of children's human figure drawings.* New York: Grune and Stratton.

Kraft, A. D., Palombo, J., Mitchell D. L., Woods, P. K., Schmidt, A. W., & Tucker, N. G. (1985). Some theoretical considerations on confidential adoptions. Part III: The adopted child. *Child and Adolescent Social Work, 2* (3), 139-153.

Kreisberg, M. (1967). Rearing children for educational achievement in fatherless families. *Journal of Marriage and the Family, 29,* 288-301.

Kulka, R. A., & Weingarten, H. (1979). The long term effects of parental divorce in childhood on adult adjustment. *Journal of Social Issues, 35* (4), 50-78.

Ladd, E. T. (1973). Pills for classroom peace? In A. Davis (Ed.), *Issues in abnormal child psychology.* Monterey, CA: Brooks/Cole.

Lang, D. M., Papenfuhs, R., & Walters, J. (1976). Delinquent females perceptions of their fathers. *The Family Coordinator, 25* (4), 475-481.

Lang, F. (1975). Effects of maternal group counseling on the academic achievement of high risk first grade children. *Dissertation Abstracts International, 36,* 1309A. (University Microfilms No. 75-20, 925)

Langner, T., Herson, J., Greene, E., Jameson, J., & Goff, J. (1970). Children of the city: Affluence, poverty, and mental health. In V. L. Allen (Ed.), *Psychological factors in poverty.* Chicago: Markham.

Lansky, L. M. (1967). The family structure also affects the model: Sex-role attitudes in parents of preschool children. *Merrill-Palmer Quarterly, 13,* 139-150.

Lapouse, R., & Monk, M. (1959). Fears and worries in a representative sample of children. *American Journal of Orthopsychiatry, 29,* 803-818.

Laterza, P. (1983). An eclectic approach to group work with the mentally retarded. In F. J. Turner (Ed.), *Differential diagnosis and treatment in social work* (3rd ed., pp. 520-529). New York: The Free Press.

Lawton, J. J., & Gross, S. F. (1964). Review of psychiatric literature on adopted children. *Archives of General Psychiatry, 11,* 635-644.

Lazarus, A. (1966). Behavior rehearsal vs. non-directive therapy vs. advice in effecting behavior change. *Behavior Research and Therapy, 4,* 209-210.

Lazarus, A. (1976). *Multimodal behavioral therapy.* New York: Springer.

Lazarus, A., Davison, G. C., & Polefka, D. A. (1965). Classical and operant factors in the treatment of a school phobia. *Journal of Abnormal Psychology, 70,* 225-229.

Ledwidge, B. (1978). Cognitive behavior modification: A step in the wrong direction? *Psychological Bulletin, 70,* 225-220.

Leifer, A. D., Leiderman, P. H., Barnett, C. R., & Williams J. A. (1972). Effects of mother-infant separation on maternal behavior. *Child Development, 43,* 1203-1218.

Leiter, R. G. (1959). Part I of the manual for the 1948 revision of the Leiter International Performance Scale: Evidence of the reliability and validity of the Leiter Tests. *Psychological Service Center Journal, 11,* 1-72.

Leland, H., & Smith, D. (1974). *Mental retardation: Present and future perspectives.* Worthington, OH: Charles A. Jones.

Lenneberg, E. H. (1967). *Biological foundations of language.* New York: Wiley.

Lerner, J. W. (1971). *Children with learning disabilities: Theories, diagnosis and teaching strategies.* Boston: Houghton Mifflin.

LeRoy, J., & Derdeyn, A. (1976). Drawings as a therapeutic medium: The treatment of separation anxiety in a 4-year-old boy. *Child Psychiatry and Human Development, 6,* 155-169.

Lesser, S. R., & Easser, B. R. (1972). Personality differences in the perceptually handicapped. *American Academy of Child Psychiatry, 11*, 458-466.

Lester, B. M., Kotelchuck, M., Spelke, E., Sellers, M. J., & Klein, R. E. (1974). Separation protest in Guatemalan infants: Cross-cultural and cognitive findings. *Developmental Psychology, 10*, 79-85.

Lester, E. P. (1975). Language behavior and child psychotherapy. *Canadian Psychiatric Association Journal, 20*, 175-181.

LeVine, E. (1980). Indirect suggestions through personalized fairy tales for the treatment of childhood insomnia. *American Journal of Clinical Hypnosis, 23*, 57-63.

LeVine, E. (1984). The challenge of the creative child: Implementing their divergency in the service of therapy. *Psychotherapy: Theory, Research & Practice, 21*, 31-39.

LeVine, E., & Padilla, A. (1980). *Crossing cultures in therapy: Pluralistic counseling for the Hispanic.* Monterey, CA: Brooks/Cole.

LeVine, W. (1985). *Personal communication.* Wichita: University of Kansas Medical School.

Levitin, T. E. (1979). Children of Divorce. *Journal of Social Issues, 35* (4), 1-25.

Lewis, H. (1954). *Deprived children.* London: Oxford University Press.

Lewis, J. M., Beavers, W. R., Gossett, J. T., & Phillips, V. A. (1976). *No single thread: Psychological health in family systems.* New York: Brunner/Mazel.

Lincoln, A. L. (1955). *Lincoln Diagnostic Spelling Tests.* Indianapolis: Bobbs-Merrill.

Lipman, R. S. (1970). The use of psychopharmacological agents in residential facilities for the retarded. In F. J. Menolascino (Ed.), *Psychiatric approaches to mental retardation.* New York: Basic Books.

Littner, N. (1971). The importance of the national parents to the child in placement. *Preliminary Conference Report of the First Conference of Foster Parents.* Washington DC: U.S. Department of Health, Education and Welfare. (Dept. of H.E.W., Publication No. 72-5)

Lorion, R. P., & Lounsbury, J. W. (1982). Conceptual and methodological considerations in evaluating prevention interventions. In W. R. Trash & G. Stahler (Eds.), *Innovative approaches to mental health evaluation.* New York: Academic Press.

Lovaas, O. I., & Bucher, B. D. (Eds.). (1974). *Perspectives in behavior modification with deviant children.* Englewood Cliffs, NJ: Prentice Hall.

Lovaas, O. I., Koegel, R., & Schreibman, L. (1979). Stimulus overselectivity in autism: A review of research. *Psychological Bulletin, 86*, 1236-1254.

Lovaas, O. I., Koegel, R., Simmons, J. Q., & Stevens-Long, J. (1973). Some generalization and follow-up measures on autistic children in behavior therapy. *Journal of Applied Behavior Analysis, 6*, 131-166.

Luepnitz, D. A. (1982). *Child custody: A study of families after divorce.* Lexington, MA: D. C. Heath.

Luria, A. R. (1961). *The role of speech in the regulation of normal and abnormal behavior.* New York: J. B. Lippencott.

Luria, A. R. (1963). *The mentally retarded child.* New York: Pergamon Press.

Lutey, C. (1977). *Individual intelligence testing: A manual and sourcebook.* Greeley, Colorado: Author.

Maccoby, E. (1980). *Social Development.* New York: Harcourt, Brace and Jovanovich.

MacFarlane, J. W., Allen, L., & Honzik, M. P. (1954). *A developmental study of the behavior problems of normal children.* Berkeley: University of California.

MacGregor, R. (1962). Multiple impact psychotherapy with families. *Family Process, 1*, 15-29.

MacGregor, R., Ritchie, A. M., Serrano, A. C., & Schuster, F. P. (1964). *Multiple impact therapy with families.* New York: McGraw-Hill.

Machover, K. (1949). *Personality projection in the drawing of the human figure.* Springfield, IL: Charles C. Thomas.

Machover, K. (1953). Human figure drawings of children. *Journal of Projective Techniques, 17*, 85-91.

MacKinnon, D. W. (1962). The nature and nurture of creative talent. *American Psychologist, 17*, 484-495.

Maguire, L. (1984). Networking for self-help: An empirically based guideline. In F. M. Cox, J. L. Erlich, J. Rothman, & J. E. Tropman (Eds.), *Tactics and techniques of community practice* (pp. 198-208). Itasca, IL: F. E. Peacock.

Mahler, M. (1968). *On human symbiosis and the vicisstitudes of individuation: Infantile psychosis.* New York: International Universities Press.

Mahler, M., Pine, F., & Bergman, A. (1975). *The psychological birth of the human infant: Symbiosis and individuation.* New York: Basic Books.

Mahoney, M. (1974). *Cognition and behavior modification.* Cambridge, MA: Ballinger.

Mandelbaum, A. (1977). Mental health and retardation. In J. B. Turner (Ed.), *Encyclopedia of social work* (17th Issue, Vol. 2). Washington, DC: National Association of Social Workers.

Mannino, F. V., MacLennan, B. W., & Shore, M. F. (1975). (Eds.). *The practice of mental health consultation.* Adelphi, MD: National Institute of Mental Health.

Margolin, F. (1973). An approach to resolution of visitation disputes post-divorce: Short-term counseling. *Dissertation Abstracts International, 34*, 1754B. (University Microfilms No. 73-22, 680)

Marland, S. P. (1972). *Education of the gifted and talented: A report submitted to the citizens of the United States by the Commissioner of Education.* Washington, DC: U.S. Department of Education.

Marshall, R. J. (1976). "Joining techniques" in the treatment of resistant children and adolescents: A learning theory rationale. *American Journal of Psychotherapy, 30*, 73-84.

Martin, H. P. (Ed.). (1976). *The abused child: A multidisciplinary approach to developmental issues and treatment.* Cambridge, MA: Ballinger.

Martin, H. P. (1980). The consequences of being abused and neglected: How the child fares. In C. H. Kempe & R. E. Helfer (Eds.), *The battered child.* Chicago: University of Chicago Press.

Maudsley, H. (1880). *The pathology of the mind.* New York: Appleton.

Maurer, R., Cadoret R. J., & Cain, C. (1980). Cluster analysis of childhood temperament data on adoptees. *American Journal of Orthopsychiatry, 50* (3), 522-534.

Mayfield, J., & Neil J. B. (1983). Group treatment for children in substitute care. *Social Casework, 64* (10), 579-584.

Mayhall, P. D., & Eastlack-Norgard, K. (1983). *Child abuse and neglect: Sharing responsibility.* New York: Wiley.

McBroom, E. (1976). Socialization through small groups. In R. W. Roberts & H. Northern (Eds.), *Theories of social work with groups* (pp. 272-299). New York: Columbia University.

McConville, B. J. (1976). Opening moves and sequential strategies in child psychotherapy. *Canadian Psychiatric Association Journal, 21*, 295-301.

McCoy, S. A. (1976). Clinical judgements of normal childhood behavior. *Journal of Consulting and Clinical Psychology, 44*, 710-714.

McDermott, J. F. (1970). Divorce and its psychiatric sequelae in children. *Archives of General Psychiatry, 23*, 421-427.

McDowell, R. (1976). Parent counseling: The state of the art. *Journal of Learning Disabilities. 9*, 614-619.

McKay, H., Sinisterra, L., McKay, A., Gomez H., & Lloreda, P. (1978). Improving cognitive ability in chronically deprived children. *Science* (200), 270-278.

Mead, G. H. (1934). *Mind, self and society.* Chicago: University of Chicago Press.

Meadow, K. (1976). Personality and social development of deaf persons. *Journal of Rehabilitation of the Deaf, 9*, 1-12.

Mech, E. V. (1973). Adoption: A policy perspective. In B. Caldwell & H. Riccuitti (Eds.), *Review of child development research* (Vol.3, pp. 467-508). Chicago: University of Chicago Press.

Meichenbaum, D. (1977). *Cognitive-behavior modification: An integrative approach.* New York: Plenum Press.

Meier, M. (1974). Some challenges for clinical neuropsychology. In R. Reitan & L. Davison (Eds.), *Clinical neuropsychology: Current status and application.* New York: John Wiley.

Meiselman, K. C. (1978). *Incest: A psychological study of causes and effect with treatment recommendation.* San Francisco: Jossey Bass.

Mellsop, G. W. (1972). Psychiatric patients seen as children and adults: Childhood predictors of adult illness. *Journal of Child Psychology & Psychiatry, 13*, 91-101.

Mengeot, S. W. (1982). The impact of cumulative trauma in infancy: Some treatment techniques. *Clinical Social Work Journal, 10* (4), 265-274.

Mikkelsen, M., & Stene, J. (1970). Genetic counselling in Down's syndrome. *Human Heredity, 20*, 457-464.

Milazzo-Sayre, L. (1978a). *Changes in the age and sex composition of first admissions to state and county mental hospitals, United States 1962-1975.* (Mental Health Statistical Note No. 145.). U.S. Department of Health, Education and Welfare: National Institute of Mental Health, Survey and Reports Branch.

Milazzo-Sayre, L. (1978b). *Changes in the age, sex, and diagnostic composition of additions to state and county mental hospitals, United States 1969-1975.* (Mental Health Statistical Note No. 148). U.S. Department of Health, Education and Welfare: National Institute of Mental Health, Survey and Reports Branch.

Milazzo-Sayre, L. (1978c). *Changes in the age, sex, and diagnostic composition of the resident population of state and county mental hospitals, United States 1965-1975.* (Mental Health Statistical Note No. 146). U.S. Department of Health, Education and Welfare: National Institute of Mental Health, Survey and Reports Branch.

Miller, W., & Ervin, S. (1970). *The development of grammar in child language, in cognitive development in children* (pp. 309-334). Chicago: University of Chicago Press.

Minskoff, E. (1975). Research on psycholinguistic training: Critique and guidelines. *Exceptional Children, 42*, 136-147.

Minton, C., Kagan, J., & Levine, J. A. (1971). Maternal control and obedience in the two-year-old. *Child Development, 42*, 1873-1894.

Minuchin, S. (1974). *Families and family therapy.* Cambridge, MA: Harvard University Press.

Minuchin, S., & Fishman, H. C. (1981). *Family therapy techniques.* Cambridge, MA: Harvard University Press.

Minuchin, S., Montalvo, B., Guerney, B. G. Jr., Rosman, B. L., & Schurmer, F. (1967). *Families of the slums.* New York: Basic Books.

Mischel, W. (1968). *Personality and assessment.* New York: Wiley.

Morales, A., & Sheafor, B. W. (1983). *Social work: A profession of many faces* (3rd Ed.). Newton, MA: Allyn and Bacon.

Morrison, T. L., & Newcomer, B. L. (1975). Effects of directive vs. nondirective play therapy with institutionalized mentally retarded children. *American Journal of Mental Deficiency, 79,* 666-669.

Moustakes, C. (1959). *Psychotherapy with children: The living relationship.* New York: Ballantine.

Moustakes, C. (1973a). *Children in play therapy.* New York: Jason Aronson.

Moustakes, C. (1973b). The dying self within the living self. In C. Moustakes (Ed.), *The child's discovery of himself* (pp. 9-29). New York: Jason Aronson.

Moustakes, C. (1975). *Who will listen?* New York: Ballantine.

Mowrer, O. H., & Mowrer, W. M. (1938). Enuresis: A method for its study and treatment. *American Journal of Orthopsychiatry, 8,* 436-459.

Murray, H. A. (1943). *Thematic Apperception Test manual.* Boston, MA: Harvard College.

Myklebust, H. (1965). *Picture Story Language Test: The development and disorders of written language* (Vol. 1). New York: Grune and Stratton.

Nagi, S. (1977). *Child maltreatment in the United States: A challenge to social institutions.* New York: Columbia University Press.

Narabayashi, H. (1972). Stereotaxic amagdelectomy. In B. E. Eleftheriou (Ed.), *The neurobiology of the amydala.* New York: Plenum Press.

National Institute of Mental Health, Survey and Reports Branch, Division of Biometry and Epidemiology. (1979). *NIMH on children, adolescents and young adults (i.e., age groups under 25 years of age) under care in various types of mental health treatment facilities/services.* Unpublished NIMH material.

Nay, W. R. (1979). Parents as real life reinforcers: The enhancement of parent training effects across conditions other than training. In A. P. Goldstein & F. H. Kanfer (Eds.), *Maximising treatment gains' transfer enhancement in psychotherapy.* New York: Academic Press.

Newcomer, B. L., & Morrison, T. L. (1974). Play therapy with institutionalized mentally retarded children. *American Journal of Mental Deficiency, 78,* 727-733.

Nichols, M. P. (1984). *Family therapy concepts and methods.* New York: Gardner.

Nihira, K., Foster, R., Shellhaas, M., & Leland, H. (1974). *Adaptive Behavior Scale.* Washington, DC: American Association on Mental Deficiency.

Norvell, M., & Guy, R. (1977). A comparison of self-concept in adopted and non-adopted adolescents. *Adolecence, 12* (47).

Nye, F. J. (1957). Child adjustment in broken and in unhappy un-broken homes. *Marriage and Family Living, 19,* 356-361.

Oaklander, V. (1978). *Windows to our children: A gestalt therapy approach to children and adolescents.* Moab, UT: Real People Press.

Oates, R. K., Davis, A. A., Ryan, M. G., & Stewart, L. F. (1978). Factors associated with child abuse. *Abstracts: Second International Congress on Child Abuse & Neglect.* London: Pergamon Press.

O'Brien, S. (1983). *Child Pornography.* Dubuque, IA: Kendall/Hunt.

O'Malley, J. E., Koocher, G., Foster, D., & Slavin L. (1979). Psychiatric sequelae of surviving childhood cancer. *American Journal of Orthropsychiatry, 49* (4), 608-616.

O'Neal P., & Robins, L. N. (1959). Childhood patterns predictive of adult schizophrenia: A thirty year follow-up study. *American Journal of Psychiatry, 115,* 385-391.

Ornstein, A. (1976). Making contact with the inner world of the child. *Comprehensive Psychiatry, 17,* 3-36.

O'Rourke, J. (1963). Field laboratory: The decision making behavior of family groups in two experimental conditions. *Sociometry, 26,* 422-534.

Palmer, J. 0. (1970). *The psychological assessment of children.* New York: Wiley.

Pasamanick, B., & Knobloch, H. (1966). Retrospective studies on the epidemiology of reproductive causality: Old and new. *Merrill Palmer Quarterly, 12,* 7-29.

Passons, W. (1975). *Gestalt approaches in counseling.* New York: Holt, Rinehart and Winston.

Patterson, G. R. (1971). *Families.* Champaign, IL: Research Press.

Perlman, H. H. (1957). *Social casework: A problem solving process.* Chicago: University of Chicago Press.

Perls, F. (1969). *Gestalt therapy verbatim.* Lafayette, CA: Real People Press.

Piaget, J. (1951). *The child's conception of the world.* New York: Humanities Press. (Originally published in French in 1926)

Piaget, J. (1976). *The grasp of consciousness: Action and concept in the young child.* Cambridge, MA: Harvard University Press. (Originally published in French in 1974)

Piers, E. V., & Harris, D. B. (1969). *The Piers-Harris Children's Self Concept Scale (The way I feel about myself).* Nashville: Counselor Recordings & Tests.

Pinkston, E. M., Levitt, J. L, Green, G. R., Linsk, N. L., & Rzepnicki, T. L. (1982). *Effective social work practice.* San Francisco: Jossey Bass.

Portner, D. (1981). Clinical aspects of social group work with the deaf. *Social Work with Groups* (Vol. 4), 123-133.

Presidents Commission on Mental Health. (1978). *Task Panel Reports* (Volume II-IV). Washington, DC: U.S. Government Printing Office.

Pritchard, M., & Graham, P. (1966). An investigation of a group of patients who have attended both the child and adult departments of the same psychiatric hospital. *British Journal of Psychiatry, 112,* 603-612.

Proctor, E. K., (1983). New Directions for work with parents of retarded children. In F. J. Turner (Ed.), *Differential diagnosis and treatment in social work* (3rd. ed., pp. 511-519). New York: The Free Press.

Quinn, B., & Goldberg, S. (1977, March). *Feeding and fussing: Parent-infant interaction as a function of neonatal medical status.* Paper presented at a meeting of the Society for Research on Child Development, New Orleans.

Quinn, P. O., & Rapoport, J. L. (1975). One year followup of hyperactive boys treated with imipramine or methylphenidate. *American Journal of Psychiatry, 32,* 241-245.

Radbill, S. X. (1980). Children in a world of violence: A history of child abuse. In C. H. Kempe & R. E. Helfer (Eds.), *The battered child.* Chicago: University of Chicago.

Rapoport, J. L., Mikkelsen, E. J., & Zavadil, A. (1980). Childhood enuresis II: Psychopathology tricyclic concentration in plasma, and antineuretic effect. *Archives of General Psychiatry, 37,* 1146-1152.

Rapoport, L. (1977). Consultation in social work. In J. B. Turner (Ed.), *Encyclopedia of social work* (pp. 193-196). Washington, DC: National Association of Social Workers.

Redl, F., (1972). The concept of "therapeutic milieu". In J. K. Whittaker & A. E. Trieschman (Eds.), *Children away from home. A source book of residential treatment.* Chicago, IL: Atherton.

Regier, D. A., Goldberg, I. D., & Taube, C. A. (1978). The de facto U.S. Mental Health Services System. *Archives of General Psychiatry, 35,* 685-693.

Reiss, D. (1980). Pathways to assessing the family: Some choice points and a sample route. *The Family: Proceedings of the 1979 Annual Meeting of the American College of Psychiatrists.* New York: Brunner/Mazel.

Reitan, R. (1964). *Manual for administering and scoring the Reitan-Indiana Neuropsychological Battery for Children (Aged 5 through 8).* Indianapolis: University of Indiana Medical Center.

Reitan, R., & Davison, L. (Eds.). (1974). *Clinical neuropsychology: Current status and application.* New York: Wiley.

Renaud, H., & Estess, F. (1961). Life history interviews with one hundred normal American males: "Pathogenicity" of childhood. *American Journal of Orthopsychiatry, 31,* 786-802.

Resnick, P. (1969). Child murder by parents: A psychiatric review of filicide. *American Journal of Psychiatry, 126,* 325-334.

Ribble, M. (1945). Anxiety in infants and its disorganizing effects. In N. Lewis (Ed.), *Trends in child psychiatry.* New York: International Universities Press.

Richmond, M. E. (1917). *Social Diagnosis.* New York: Russell Sage Foundation.

Robinson, H. B., & Robinson, N. M. (1970). Mental retardation. In P. H. Mussen (Ed.), *Carmichael's manual of child psychology* (Vol. II). New York: Wiley.

Roe, A. (1976). Psychological approaches to creativity in science. In A. Rothenberg & C. R. Hausman (Eds.), *The creativity questions.* Durham, NC: Duke University Press.

Rogers, C. (1951). *Client-centered therapy.* Boston: Houghton Mifflin.

Roll, S., Lockwood, J., & Roll, E. J. (1980). *P.A.S.I.: Parent attachment structured interview.* Albuquerque, NM: Authors.

Rosenzweig, S. (1950). Levels of behavior in psychodiagnosis with special reference to the Picture Frustration Study. *American Journal of Orthopsychiatry, 20,* 63-72.

Ross, H. L., & Sawhill, I. V. (1975). *Time of transition.* Washington, DC: The Urban Institute.

Rotter, J. B., Rafferty, J. E., & Schachtitz, E. (1965). Validation of the Rotter Incomplete Sentence Test for College Screening. In B. I. Murstein (Ed.), *Handbook of projective techniques.* New York: Basic Books.

Routh, D.K. (1979, Fall). Activity, attention, and aggression in learning disabled children. *Journal of Clinical Child Psychology,* 183-186.

Russell, D. (1983). Incidence and prevalence of intrafamilial and extrafamilial sexual abuse of female children. *Child Abuse and Neglect, 7,* 133-146.

Sabatini, S. (1976). An investigation of play group counseling. *Dissertation Abstracts International, 36,* 7875A. (University Microfilms No. 76-13, 496)

Safer, D. J., Allen, R., & Barr, E. (1972). Depression of growth in hyperactive children on stimulant drugs. *New England Journal of Medicine, 287,* 217-232.

Sallee, A. L., & Downes, B. (1982). *A report to the Governor on family crisis prevention: Policy recommendations and implimentation strategies.* Santa Fe, NM: Governor's Office.

Sallee, A. L., & LeVine, E. (1985, August 9). *Identity crisis of adopted children at adolescence.* Paper presented at the meeting of the North American Council on Adoptable Children, Albuquerque, NM.

Sallee, D. K. (1982, June 22). *Family crisis prevention: An explanation.* Keynote address to Governor's Forum on Family Crisis Prevention, Albuquerque, NM.

Sanford, L. T. (1980). *The silent children.* Garden City, NY: Anchor Doubleday Press.

Santrock, J. (1976). Father absence, perceived maternal behavior, and moral development in boys. *Child Development, 46* (3), 753-757.

Santrock, J. (1977). Effects of father absence on sex-typed behaviors in male children: Reason for absence and age of onset of absence. *Journal of Genetic Psychology, 130,* 3-10.

Sapir, E. (1921). *Language.* New York: Harcourt Brace. (reprinted in 1958)

Satir, V. (1967). *Conjoint family therapy* (Rev. ed.). Palo Alto, CA: Science and Behavior Books.

Satir, V. (1972). *People making.* Palo Alto, CA: Science and Behavior Books.

Sattler, J. M. (1974). *Assessment of children's intelligence.* Philadelphia: Saunders.

Schaffer, H. R., & Emerson, P. E. (1964). The development of social attachment in infancy. *Monographs of the Society for Research in Child Development, 29* (94).

Schechter, M. (1964, Feb.). Emotional problems of the adoptee. *General Achives of Psychiatry, 10.*

Schneider, C., Hoffmeister, J., & Helfer, R. (1976). A predictive screening questionnaire for potential problems in mother-child interaction. In R. Helfer & C. Kempe (Eds.), *Child abuse and neglect: The family and the community.* Cambridge, MA: Ballinger.

Schorr, A. L. (1985). Professional practice as policy. *Social Service Review, 59* (2), 178-196.

Schwartz, A., & Goldiamond, I. (1975). *Social casework: A behavioral approach.* New York: Columbia University Press.

Selye, H. (1950). *The physiology and pathology of exposure to stress.* Montreal: Acta.

Shepherd, M., Oppenheim, A. N., & Mitchell, S. (1966). Childhood behavior disorders and the child guidance clinic: An epidemiological study. *Journal of Psychology and Psychiatry, 7,* 39-52.

Sheridan, M. S., & Kline, K. (1978). Psychosomatic illness in children. *Social Casework, 59* (4), 227-232.

Sherman, S. N. (1981). A social work frame for family therapy. In E. R. Tolson & W. J. Reid (Eds.), *Models of family treatment* (pp. 7-32). New York: Columbia University Press.

Shinn, M. (1978). Father absence and children's cognitive development. *Psychological Bulletin, 85* (2), 295-324.

Shofield, W. (1964). *Psychotherapy: The purchase of friendship.* Englewood Cliffs, NJ: Prentice Hall.

Shore, M. F. (1979). Legislation, advocacy, and the rights of children and youth. *American Psychologist, 34,* 1017-1019.

Shostrom. E. H. (1967). *Man, the manipulator; The inner journey from manipulation to actualization.* Nashville: Abingdon Press.

Shulman, L. (1979). *The skills of helping: Individuals and groups.* Itasca, IL: F. E. Peacock.

Shyne, A. W., & Schroeder, A. (1978). *National study of social services to children and their families.* Rockville, MD: Westat.

Skinner, B. F. (1938). *The bahavior of organisms.* New York: Appleton Century Crofts.

Slossum, R. L. (1963). *Slossum Intelligence Test.* East Aurora, NY: Slossum Education.

Smalley, R. E. (1971). Social casework: The functional approach. In R. Morris (Ed.), *Encyclopedia of social work.* New York: National Association of Social Workers.

Smirnoff, V. (1971). *The scope of child analysis.* New York: International Universities Press.

Smith, D., Jr. (1976). Effects of modeling/role playing counseling technique on second-grade socially withdrawn children. *Dissertation Abstracts International, 36,* 4140B-4141B. (University Microfilms No. 76-4416)

Snapper, K. J. (1976). The American legacy. In H. E. Grotberg (Ed.), *200 years of children* (pp. 13-38). Washington, DC: U.S. Department of Health, Education and Welfare, Office of Human Development. (DWEW Publication No. OHD 77-30103)

Snow, C. (1972). Mothers' speech to children learning language. *Child Development, 43,* 549-565.

Solomon, M. A. (1973). A developmental, conceptual premise for family therapy. *Family Process, 12,* 179-188.

Sorosky, A. D., Baran, A., & Pannor R. (1978). *The adoption triangle: The effects of the sealed record on adoptees, birth parents and adoptive parents.* Garden City, NY: Anchor Books.

Specht, H. (1981). Professionalism: Weighed and found wanting? An opinion by Harry Specht. *Public Welfare, 39* (3), 8-9.

Speck, R. V. (1967). Psychotherapy of the social network of a schizophrenic family. *Family Process, 6,* 208-214.

Speer, D., Fossom, M., Lippman, H., Schwartz, R., & Slocum, B. (1968). A comparison of middle- and lower-class families in treatment at a child guidance clinic. *American Journal of Orthopsychiatry, 38,* 814-822.

Spence, J. T., & Helmreich, R. L. (1978). *Masculinity and femininity: Their psychological dimensions, correlates and antecedents.* Austin: University of Texas Press.

Spiegel, J. P. (1981). An ecological model with an emphasis on ethnic families. In S. R. Tolson & J. R. Williams (Eds.), *Models of family treatment.* New York: Columbia University Press.

Spock B. (1960). *Baby and child care.* New York: Affiliated Publishers.

Sprague, R. L. (1977). Psychopharmacotherapy with children. In M. McMillan & S. Henao (Eds.), *Child Psychiatry: Treatment and research.* New York: Bruner/Mazel.

Starr, R. H. (1979). Child Abuse. *American Psychologist, 34,* 872-878.

Stehno, S. M. (1982). Differential treatment of minority children in service systems. *Social Work, 27* (1), 39-45.

Stein, M. (1976). Therapeutic initiatives with inaccessible preschoolers. *American Academy of Child Psychiatry, 15,* 385-394.

Stone, L. J., & Church, J. (1973). *Childhood and adolescence.* New York: Random House.

Straus, M. A., Gelles, R. J., & Steimetz, S. K. (1979). *Behind closed doors: Violence in the American family.* Garden City, NY: Doubleday.

Straus, M. A., & Tallman, I. (1971). SIMFAM: A technique for observational measurement and experimental study of families. In J. Aldous (Ed.), *Family problem solving.* Hinsdale, IL: Dryden Press.

Sudia, C. E., & Herzog, E. (1973). Children in fatherless families. In C. Anderson (Ed.), *Review of child development research* (Vol. 3, pp. 233-282). Chicago: University of Chicago Press.

Taylor, C. W., & Holland, J. (1964). Predictors of creative performance. In C. W. Taylor (Ed.), *Creativity: Progress and potential.* New York: McGraw-Hill.

Terman, C. M., & Oden, M. (1959). *Genetic studies of genius* (Vols. 1-5). Stanford, CA: Stanford University Press.

Terman, L. M., & Merrill, M. A. (1973). *Stanford-Binet Intelligence Scale: Manual for the third revision, form L-M.* Boston: Houghton Mifflin.

Thomas, A. (1968). Children with absent fathers. *Journal of Marriage and the Family, 30* (1), 89-96.

Thomas, A., Birch, H. G., Chess, S., & Hertzig, M. E. (1960). A longitudinal study of primary reaction patterns in children. *Comprehensive Psychiatry, 1,* 103.

Thomas, E. J. (1967). *The socio-behavioral approach and application to social work.* New York: Council on Social Work Education.

Thomas, E. J. (1977). Social casework and social groupwork: The behavioral modification approach. In J. B. Turner (Ed.), *Encyclopedia of social work.* Washington DC: National Association of Social Workers.

Thompson, S. K. (1975). Gender labels and early sex roles development. *Child Development, 46,* 339-347.

Thorndike, E. L. (1898). Animal intelligence: An experimental study of the associative process in animals. *Psychological Review* (Monograph Supplement), (Whole 80).

Thornman, G. (1967). Helping Troubled Families. In C. B. Truax & R. R. Carkhuff (Eds.), *Toward effective counseling and psychotherapy: Training and practice.* Chicago: Aldine.

Thornman, G. (1982). *Helping troubled families: A social work perspective.* New York: Aldine.

Tiegs, E. W., & Clark, W. W. (1970). *California Achievement Test.* Hightown, NJ: CTB/McGraw-Hill.

Tolor, A., & Schulberg, H. (1963). *An evaluation of the Bender-Gestalt Test.* Springfield, IL: Thomas.

Tooley, K. M. (1977). The young child as victim of sibling attack. *Social Casework, 58* (1), 25-28.

Torrance, E. P. (1962). *Guiding creative talent.* Englewood Cliffs, NJ: Prentice Hall.

Torrance, E. P. (1975). Creativity research in education: Still alive. In I. A. Taylor & J. W. Getzels (Eds.), *Perspectives in creativity.* Chicago: Aldine.

Torrance, E. P., & Mourad, S. (1978). Some creativity and style of learning and thinking correlates of Guglielmino's Self-Directed Learning Readiness Scale. *Psychological Reports, 43,* 1167-1171.

Trehub, S. E. (1973). Infants' sensitibity to vowel and tonal contrasts. *Developmental Psychology, 9,* 91-96.

Trehub, S. E., & Rabinovitch, M. S. (1972). Auditory-linguistic sensitivity in early infancy. *Developmental Psychology, 6,* 74-77.

Trevarthen, C. (1977). Descriptive analyses of infant communicative behavior. In H. R. Schaffer (Ed.), *Studies in mother infant interaction.* London: Academic Press.

Truax, C. B., & Carkhuff, R. R. (1967). *Toward effective counseling and psychotherapy: Training and practice.* Chicago: Aldine.

Unger, C., Dwarshuis, G., & Johnson, E. (1977). *Choas, madness and unpredictability.* Chelsea, MI: Spaulding for Children.

Urie R. G. (1975). Effects of preparing children for psychotherapy. *Dissertation Abstracts International, 36,* 924B-925B. (University Microfilms No. 75-17, 691)

U.S. Bureau of the Census. (1978). *Special studies* (Series p-23, No. 75). Washington, DC: U.S. Government Printing Office.

U.S. Bureau of the Census. (1979a). *Characteristics of the population below the poverty level.* (Series p-20, No. 119). Washington, DC: U.S. Government Printing Office.

U.S. Bureau of the Census. (1979b). *Current population reports.* (Series p-20, No. 338). Washington, DC: U.S. Government Printing Office.

U.S. Bureau of the Census. (1979c). *Population Profile of the United States: 1978.* (Series p-20, No. 336). Washington, DC: U.S. Government Printing Office.

U.S. Bureau of the Census. (1983). Marital status and living arrangements: March, 1982. *Current population reports* (Series p-20, No.380). Washington, DC: U.S. Government Printing Office.

U.S. Bureau of the Census. (1984). *Statistical abstracts of the United States 1985* (105 ed.). Washington, DC: U.S. Government Printing Office.

U.S. Department of Health and Human Services. (1980). *The status of children.* Washington, DC: Office of Human Services. (DHHS Publication No. (OHDS) 80-302740)

U.S. Department of Health and Human Services. (1981). *Study finding: Natural study of the incidence and severity of child abuse and neglect.* Washington, DC: U.S. Government Printing Office. (DHHS Publication No. (OHDS) 81-30325)

U.S. National Center for Health Statistics. (1978). In J. A. Weed (Ed.), *Trends in divorce: Implications for family health.* Hyattsville, MD: Author.

Visher, E. B., & Visher, J. S. (1979). *Stepfamilies: A Guide to working with steparents and stepchildren.* New York: Brunner/Mazel.

Vygotsky, L. S. (1962). *Thought and language.* Cambridge, MA: MIT Press.

Wallach, M. A., & Kogan, N. (1965). *Modes of thinking in young children.* New York: Holt, Rinehart and Winston.

Wallerstein, J. S., & Kelly, J. B. (1975). The effects of parental divorce: Experiences of the preschool child. *Journal of the American Academy of Child Psychiatry, 14* (4), 600-616.

Wallerstein, J. S., & Kelly, J. B. (1976). The effects of parental divorce: Experiences of the child in later latency. *American Journal of Orthopsychiatry, 46* (2), 256-269.

Wallerstein, J. S., & Kelly, J. B. (1979). Children of divorce: A review. *Social Work, 24* (6), 468-475.

Wallerstein, J. S., & Kelly, J. B. (1980). California's children of divorce. *Psychology Today, 13* (8), 66-76.

Walsh, G. S. (1975). *Creativity and intelligence: A personality approach.* Chapel Hill, NC: Institute for Research on Social Sciences, University of North Carolina at Chapel Hill.

Warshak, R. A., & Santrock, J. W. (1980). Children of divorce: Impact of custody disposition on social development. In E. J. Callahan & K. A. McCluskey (Eds.), *Life developmental psychology: Non-normative life events.* New York: Academic Press.

Wechsler, D. (1944). *The Measurement of adult intelligence.* Baltimore: Williams & Wilkins.